Yale Studies in English
Richard S. Sylvester, Editor
Volume 172

Scene and Symbol from George Eliot to James Joyce

Studies in Changing Fictional Mode

Peter K. Garrett

Yale University Press
New Haven and London
1969

Published with assistance from the foundation
established in memory of Philip Hamilton
McMillan of the Class of 1894, Yale College.

Library of Congress catalog card number: 69–15443

Designed by Marvin Howard Simmons,
set in Baskerville type,
and printed in the United States of America by
The Carl Purington Rollins Printing-Office
of the Yale University Press, New Haven, Connecticut.
Distributed in Great Britain, Europe, Asia, and
Africa by Yale University Press Ltd., London; in
Canada by McGill University Press, Montreal;
and in Latin America by Centro Interamericano
de Libros Académicos, Mexico City.

Acknowledgment is hereby made to the Viking Press
for quotations from the following:
Sons and Lovers by D. H. Lawrence, copyright 1913
by Thomas Seltzer, Inc., All rights reserved.
The Rainbow by D. H. Lawrence, copyright 1915 by
David Herbert Lawrence, renewed 1943 by Frieda
Lawrence.
Women in Love by D. H. Lawrence,
copyright 1920, 1922 by David Herbert Lawrence,
renewed 1948, 1950 by Frieda Lawrence.
All passages are reprinted by permission of
The Viking Press, Inc.

To Nina

Acknowledgments

The initial version of this book was written as my doctoral dissertation at Yale University. I am much indebted to my director, Martin Price, who both suggested the original conception and guided its development. To Charles Feidelson Jr. I am also greatly indebted, especially in my view of Henry James' fictional mode. Laurence Holland kindly read the manuscript at a later stage and made a number of valuable suggestions. I am grateful to the English Department and the Committee on Research of Princeton University for assistance in preparing the manuscript.

I should also like to acknowledge the following permissions to quote from copyrighted works.

From the Riverside editions of George Eliot's *The Mill on the Floss* and *Middlemarch*. Reprinted by permission of Gordon S. Haight.

From Francis Steegmuller's translation of Flaubert's *Madame Bovary*. Reprinted by permission of Random House, Inc.

From *The Works of Joseph Conrad*. Reprinted by permission of J. M. Dent and Sons Ltd. and the Trustees of the Joseph Conrad Estate.

From D. H. Lawrence, *Sons and Lovers, The Rainbow,* and *Women in Love*. Reprinted by permission of Laurence Pollinger Ltd. and the Estate of the late Mrs. Frieda Lawrence.

From James Joyce, *Dubliners* and *A Portrait of the Artist as a Young Man*. Reprinted by permission of The Viking Press, Inc., Jonathan Cape Ltd., and The Executors of the James Joyce Estate.

From James Joyce, *Stephen Hero*. Reprinted by permission of the Society of Authors as the literary representatives of the Estate of the late James Joyce, Jonathan Cape Ltd., and the Executors of the James Joyce Estate.

From James Joyce, *Ulysses*. Reprinted by permission of Random House, Inc., and The Bodley Head Ltd.

Contents

Introduction

Radical changes take place in the English novel in the fifty years between the publication of *Middlemarch* (1871–72) and *Ulysses* (1922), greater than those of either the preceding or subsequent half-centuries. Some of the aspects of this transition with which I shall be concerned may be illustrated by contrasting passages from novels written at the beginning and end of this period. The first is taken, not from *Middlemarch*, but from George Eliot's last novel, *Daniel Deronda* (1876). Sir Hugo Mallinger is showing his stables at the Abbey to some guests, including Grandcourt, Gwendolen, and Deronda.

> They walked on the gravel across a green court, where the snow still lay in islets on the grass, and in masses on the boughs of the great cedar and the crenelated coping of the stone walls, and then into a larger court, where there was another cedar, to find the beautiful choir long ago turned into stables, in the first instance perhaps after an impromptu fashion by troopers, who had a pious satisfaction in insulting the priests of Baal and the images of Ashtoreth, the queen of heaven. The exterior—its west end, save for the stable door, walled in with brick and covered with ivy—was much defaced, maimed of finial and gargoyle, the friable limestone broken and fretted, and lending its soft grey to a powdery dark lichen; the long windows, too, were filled in with brick as far as the springing of the arches, the broad clerestory win-

dows with wire or ventilating blinds. With the low wintry afternoon sun upon it, sending shadows from the cedar boughs, and lighting up the touches of snow remaining on every ledge, it had still a scarcely disturbed aspect of antique solemnity, which gave the scene in the interior rather a startling effect; though, ecclesiastical or reverential indignation apart, the eyes could hardly help dwelling with pleasure on its piquant picturesqueness. Each finely-arched chapel was turned into a stall, where in the dusty glazing of the windows there still gleamed patches of crimson, orange, blue, and palest violet; for the rest, the choir had been gutted, the floor levelled, paved, and drained according to the most approved fashion, and a line of loose-boxes erected in the middle: a soft light fell from the upper windows on sleek brown or grey flanks and haunches; on mild equine faces looking out with active nostrils over the varnished brown boarding on the hay hanging from racks where the saints once looked down from the altar-pieces, and on the pale-golden straw scattered or in heaps; on a little white-and-liver-coloured spaniel making his bed on the back of an elderly hackney, and on four ancient angels, still showing signs of devotion like mutilated martyrs—while over all, the grand pointed roof, untouched by reforming wash, showed its lines and colours mysteriously through veiling shadow and cobweb, and a hoof now and then striking against the boards seemed to fill the vault with thunder, while outside there was the answering bay of the bloodhounds.[1]

---

1. *Daniel Deronda*, Harper Torchbooks edition (New York, 1961), p. 314. Subsequent references are incorporated in the text.

in spite of 'the fact that these spars are properly called "yards," because he wanted to make an allusion to the crucifixion.[5] The double sense of the word is later confirmed within the novel in Stephen's parody of the Creed, where Christ is "nailed like bat to barndoor, starved on crosstree" (197). In the light of this religious meaning, we recognize the significance of the ship being a "three-master."

It thus takes its place as part of a pattern of religious allusions, especially those to the relation between the persons of the Trinity (with which Stephen is intermittently concerned in both chapters), used as one expression for the central theme of paternity. In the context of the novel's general intellectual ambiance, the image also makes ironic reference to the state of a world which has lost religious meaning, especially symbolic religious meaning. As a homeward-bound ship, it furthermore announces the entrance of Odysseus-Bloom, who is introduced immediately after it.

A comparison of these two passages reveals the greater degree and importance of symbolism in Joyce's fictional mode. It is characteristic of George Eliot's realism that her stable scene relates much of its meaning directly to the characters present in it. Joyce's ship is, of course, also related to his character, Stephen, but it remains much more independent of the human action which has preceded it. George Eliot's manner of presenting her choir-stable does not, moreover, insist on its symbolic implications. A reader might take it simply as a piece of picturesque description and proceed to the dramatic action of the scene without damage to the continuity of his reading, but if he failed to

5. *James Joyce and the Making of Ulysses* (Bloomington, Ind., 1960), p. 56.

recognize Joyce's ship as symbolic he would have no other way to account for it and would be left with a blank, a puzzle. Because of both the ship's immediate symbolic quality and its connections with multiple symbolic patterns, we might wish to contrast it with George Eliot's choir-stable as an object whose actuality is completely sacrificed to its function as symbol, opposed to the symbol which also has particularized actuality, whose numerous realistic details are not given the multiple symbolic meanings of "three-master" and "crosstrees." To a large extent such a contrast is valid but must be qualified, for Joyce's ship has, in the novel as a whole, its own curious kind of actuality. We later learn that it is "the threemasted schooner *Rosevean* from Bridgewater with bricks" (249, and again 625), and that it has brought home to his family an actual sailor, W. B. Murphy (624–25).[6] The contrast between these passages reveals a profound change of mode, a transition from the realistic to the symbolistic novel, but it also reveals the resistance of actual novels to convenient historical classification. The presence of symbolic elements in George Eliot's realism and of realistic elements in Joyce's symbolism indicates that all fictional modes are mixed, that modal changes are shifts of proportion and relation. The developments we shall be examining include an increasingly powerful impulse toward a fully autonomous symbolic mode which completely dominates the actuality of the given, but this impulse is only one factor in a complex movement and is always conditioned by others.

6. It is also in fact more truly historical than George Eliot's choir-stable; the schooner *Rosevean* did bring a cargo of bricks from Bridgewater to Dublin on June 16, 1904—a fact established by the researches of Robert M. Adams, in *Surface and Symbol: The Consistency of James Joyce's Ulysses* (New York, 1962), pp. 229–30.

The use I have made of these passages also suggests a method for examining shifts in fictional mode. Both present minor moments of revelation, concentrations of meaning. In the midst of the dynamic forward movement of narrative, they provide moments of arrest, an effect George Eliot achieves simply by pausing to elaborate the description, while Joyce uses the more sophisticated, and obtrusive, devices of structural isolation and stylistic emphasis. I believe it is possible to select such moments of stasis, of revelation, from several different novels written during the period with which we are concerned, and by analyzing them and their relations to their contexts, and by comparing them with each other, to arrive at a description of the changes in fictional mode.

At this point I should make it clear that I shall be considering fictional mode not as representational but as constitutive, regarding a novel as a complex structure which is, in its totality, constitutive of meaning rather than as an imitation of life. I do not claim exclusive validity for this view. It need only be regarded as one among several possible approaches, one which emphasizes poiesis rather than mimesis. Nor shall I offer a general theoretical defense of my position, although I do believe it to be philosophically more defensible than a strictly mimetic view.[7] Since my purposes in this study are not those of theoretical but of practical criticism, the validity of my methods need be judged only on the pragmatic basis of the results they can yield. If the approach I have adopted can result in a greater understanding of the changing way the novelists

7. Such an argument could be derived from the aesthetic theory of Eliseo Vivas, in which art is presented as an independent mode of constitutive symbolic activity. See especially the long essay which lends its title to *The Artistic Transaction and Essays on Theory of Literature* (Columbus, Ohio, 1963), pp. 3–93.

under consideration have created fictional meaning, it will have been sufficiently justified.

I have specified that the totality of the novel is involved in its constitution of meaning, because I would not have that meaning misconceived as a paraphrasable thematic content which can be abstracted from form. All of a novel's elements, from its basic verbal units to its composite units of character and event, ordered as the novel presents them, combine to produce its meaning. Criticism can describe that process and product, but it can never provide a substitute for them. Nevertheless, a novel's meaning is not uniformly diffused throughout all its elements. Certain words, characters, and events are more important than others; certain points in its structure, moments in its evolving processes, create concentrations of meaning. The passages from *Daniel Deronda* and *Ulysses* with which I began are minor examples of such moments, but these and other novels also move toward major concentrations of meaning, crucial moments of recognition and revelation. Once we consider fictional mode as constitutive of meaning, such moments, if properly analyzed in themselves and in relation to their context, can provide epitomes of a novel's mode. Such analysis can reveal both the way in which each novel and novelist creates meaning and the kind of meaning peculiar to each novelist.[8]

8. These moments of concentrated meaning need not be symbolic, although for historical reasons both my examples involve symbolism. Jane Austen's novels, for example, repeatedly move toward moments of recognition which are unaccompanied by symbolic presentation. The possibility of selecting these moments and making of them a basis for discussing her meaning has been demonstrated by C. S. Lewis, in "A Note on Jane Austen," *Essays in Criticism, 4* (1954), 359–71. The basic principle of such an "entelechial" mode of critical thought has been formulated by Kenneth Burke: "look for *moments* at which, in your opinion, the work comes to *fruition*" and work out-

Because the development with which we are concerned is that of an increasingly symbolic mode, we can obtain a consistent perspective on it by determining the function and degree of symbolism in a succession of novelists. Because meaning becomes concentrated in crucial moments, or scenes, such a perspective can be fruitfully applied to scenes which epitomize the mode of the novels in which they appear. What follows is therefore a study of symbolism and scenic method considered primarily in terms of each other. In this way we can develop a cross section of changing mode in the novel, one which may be expected to have both the virtues and the limitations of the cross section. On the one hand, it has the virtue of proceeding at a consistent angle of attack, thus making valid comparison possible. On the other, it is never able to display the object of study in all its dimensions; it can reveal only a few selected aspects of a complex development.

Obviously, my basic terms require further elucidation, especially the problematic conception of symbolism, which has occupied a central place in much modern philosophy and literary theory, which have in turn extensive roots in the intellectual and literary history of the past two centuries. Because my concerns are practical rather than theoretical, I have not attempted to place my studies of individual novels and novelists within a conceptual framework which would relate them to these developments. "Symbolism" here means not a theoretical outlook but the use of symbols, which, as they appear in the novel, I take to be images, objects, events, or complexes of these which are both literal and suggestive of further, usually more

---

ward from them. See "Fact, Inference, and Proof in the Analysis of Literary Symbolism," in *Terms for Order,* ed. Stanley Edgar Hyman (Bloomington, Ind., 1964), p. 167.

abstract, meaning. Such meaning may range from the most explicit to the most ambiguous and indefinite. I shall consider a symbol's associations as primarily grounded not just in universal human experience (which would define the symbol as archetype), or in particular historical conventions, but in the context created by the individual work. A symbol's meaning will be considered primarily as the function of its place in the structure of internal relations between the component elements of a novel.

This minimal definition covers a broad range of possible applications, including several types of literary signification, such as allegory, from which symbolism has often been distinguished. This inclusiveness is deliberate. Such distinctions will be employed when they can further the analysis of an author's fictional mode, but I shall use them simply to indicate diverging tendencies of symbolization (the concept of allegory, for example, seems particularly helpful in describing one tendency in Lawrence's symbolism). This procedure seems preferable to establishing a set of preliminary definitions; the resultant categories, no matter how elaborate, can never succeed in capturing the complexity and individuality of particular novels and novelists.

Similarly, my subordination of archetypal and conventional symbolism cannot be carried to the extreme of categorical exclusion. The roles of the former in Lawrence and of the latter in Joyce will require us to consider them as well, but in the novel such extrinsically grounded symbolism is generally of subordinate importance. My earlier example from *Ulysses* will also serve to illustrate this point. The significance of the three-masted ship is clearly based on conventional Christian symbolism. This, however, is only a point of departure and is of minor importance compared with the additional meaning created by Joyce's intrinsic context. The importance of religion and religious symbolism to the apostate Stephen and their indifference to the secular Bloom and, beyond these contexts, the central paradigm of the paternal relation, of which the relation of the Christian Father and Son becomes one instance, all contribute far more to the ship's significance than does its extrinsic reference. The archetypal or conventional basis of fictional symbolism is rarely as important as the intrinsic context which the novel itself creates.

My second major term is less difficult to define. The conception of "scene" is part of the critical legacy of Henry James, but James' preoccupation with the analogy of the drama led him to define it too narrowly to be useful for general critical purposes. As in the case of many of James' terms, its sense seems to shift as it is used in different contexts, but in general "scene" refers to a structural unit composed primarily of dialogue and fully presenting a brief, continuous, and unified segment of the novel's action. The term is usually opposed to "picture," a passage centered in a character's consciousness which may also present a single unit of action or may summarize a longer period of time than could be represented in a playlike dramatic scene. It seems more useful to expand the meaning of "scene" to include those instances of "picture" which present "a single and particular hour," rather than an "extended, general view."[9] Whether these units are presented mainly in dialogue or as reflected in an individual consciousness is an important but nevertheless secondary distinction. James himself seems to recognize the difficulty of maintaining his distinction, admitting

9. These phrases are Percy Lubbock's, who also extends the term "scene" to include such moments even when not dramatically rendered in dialogue. See *The Craft of Fiction* (New York, 1957), p. 69.

11

that "to report at all clearly and completely of what 'passes' on a given occasion is inevitably to become more or less scenic," and finding "beautiful exceedingly . . . those occasions or parts of an occasion when the boundary line between picture and scene bears a little the weight of the double pressure."[10]

This enlarged view of scene provides us with a conception of a functionally defined component form in which moments of recognition and revelation of meaning may occur. Analysis of scenic method in different novelists, of the use and composition of scenes and their relation to narrative context, will provide a framework for the examination of these crucial moments as indices of fictional mode, just as my view of symbolism provides a conception of an important, though not exclusive, way in which meaning becomes concentrated. Scene and symbol are thus not my subject, but instruments for examining changing modes in the constitution of meaning. Developments in the novel from George Eliot to Joyce will be considered under the aspect of increasing symbolism and in terms of scenic method. It should be realized, however, that, since the meaning of an individual symbol or scene depends on its place in the context of the novel's internal relationships, it may at times be necessary to devote more attention to this context than to the individual element in question itself. The changes which take place in fictional mode will appear in the changing nature of such contexts and in the way they are related to individual scenes or symbols.

The novelists I have chosen for these considerations are all major figures of the period, each of whom develops a

10. *The Art of the Novel*, ed. Richard P. Blackmur (New York, 1934), pp. 325 and 300.

unique fictional mode. In the perspective established by my adopted terms, George Eliot, James, and Joyce appear as particularly significant, because each in his own way creates novels which move insistently toward moments of revelation. Conrad and Lawrence exemplify different symbolic modes which create their own kinds of revelatory focal points, even though they do not occupy such dominant structural positions. I have included brief considerations of Dickens and Meredith in my discussion of George Eliot so that her fictional mode may be seen in comparison with that of other Victorian novelists as well as with later ones. The short examination of Flaubert's *Madame Bovary* provides an example of alternatives to English modes as well as influences on them. Together, I believe these novelists form a group sufficiently representative to make the following studies a valid cross section of a period of extensive change.

GEORGE ELIOT: The Primacy of the Real

George Eliot's novels employ scenic presentation for a variety of narrative purposes. Our concern with symbolism and other ways of concentrating meaning will necessarily direct attention toward scenes of heightened significance, but this procedure carries a greater risk of distortion when applied to George Eliot than to any of the later novelists with whom we shall be dealing. We must recognize that many of her most characteristic scenes do not display a notable concentration of meaning. An important element of her realism is its concern with, indeed its insistence on, the normal, and several scenes in each of her novels,[1] such as those at the Hall Farm in *Adam Bede,* or the childhood scenes of *The Mill on the Floss,* are largely devoted to rendering normality, creating a sense of "the flow of real and ordinary life."[2] We must remember that the drama of

1. Page references are to the following editions of George Eliot's works and are embodied in the text: *Adam Bede,* Rinehart edition (New York, 1964); *The Mill on the Floss,* Riverside edition, ed. Gordon S. Haight (Boston, 1961); *Silas Marner,* Rinehart edition (New York, 1962); *Felix Holt, The Radical,* Everyman's Library edition (London, 1964); *Middlemarch,* Riverside edition, ed. Gordon S. Haight (Boston, 1956); *Daniel Deronda,* Harper Torchbooks edition (New York, 1961). Since there is no generally available standard edition, I have used these current reprintings. Professor Haight's editions of *The Mill on the Floss* and *Middlemarch* are furthermore probably the best texts ever printed. I have also noted chapter and, where necessary, book numbers to facilitate reference to other editions.

2. Barbara Hardy, *The Novels of George Eliot: A Study in Form* (London, 1963), p. 186. See also Mrs. Hardy's discussion of such

crisis and tragedy is always played out against this background of normality.

Even the moments of greater intensity are often com-
paratively subdued in George Eliot's novels. An interesting evidence of this is to be found in her notes for *Middlemarch*, where we see her planning the scenes in which
Dorothea's crisis of jealousy and despair was to be dramatized. Originally she imagined Dorothea's discovery of
Will and Rosamond together as leading to a "Scene between her & Will—anger, jealousy, reproach, ending in
Dorothea's passionate avowal [i.e. of her love], & declaration that she will never marry him."[3] Typically for George
Eliot this melodramatic confrontation is later suppressed;
we have instead Dorothea's terse, controlled delivery of her
message, her day-long suppression of her feelings, leading
at last to her solitary outburst, self-confrontation ("Oh, I
did love him!"—lxxx, 576), and entry into what is for
George Eliot a far more significant sort of crisis, that which
takes place within the individual character's moral nature.

Such crises are usually presented in scenic form; the
slowing of pace and increase of visualization which occur
in George Eliot's scenes expand and intensify the significance of crucial moments in the characters' development. These moments are generally crises of perception

---

scenes "standing outside crisis and symbolic vividness" as characteristic
in general of what she calls "the expansive novel," a form created not
only by George Eliot but also by Dickens and Tolstoy, in *The Appropriate Form: An Essay on the Novel* (London, 1964), p. 16.

3. *Quarry For Middlemarch,* ed. Anna T. Kitchel (Berkeley and
Los Angeles, 1950), pp. 56–57. Published as a supplement to *Nineteenth-Century Fiction, 4* (1950). The elucidation of Dorothea's
"avowal" as one of her love for Will is based on the later note for
the scene (p. 58): "Scene of anger & jealousy between Will &
Dorothea, ending in her avowal of love & resolve not to marry him."

and decision. All too often the characters' decisions proceed from faulty perceptions, inadequate knowledge of themselves and of others. Such choices may be deliberate, however misguided, as in the case of Dorothea's marriage to Casaubon in *Middlemarch,* but decisions for George Eliot's characters are seldom fully deliberate. Their fates are more often determined by many minor, almost unconscious choices, definitively exemplified in the slow attrition of Lydgate's character. Such gradual processes do not lend themselves to dramatization, but George Eliot does present scenes where, even with the failure, or in some cases avoidance of consciousness, crucial decisions are in effect made.

A striking example is the scene which presents Lydgate's engagement to Rosamond. The "decision" is unpremeditated, never consciously deliberated, yet George Eliot is highly successful in rendering dramatically the psychological movements in each character: Lydgate covering his embarrassment by speaking "almost formally," Rosamond unable to conceal her distress, and its effect on him: "That moment of naturalness was the crystallizing feather-touch: it shook flirtation into love" (xxxi, 222). The drama of such a scene is very different from that of the stage; we are given only one line of direct speech. As W. J. Harvey has noted, "The scene is conveyed to us mainly by description and comment, yet at the same time it does achieve a peculiar kind of concreteness and immediacy." He rightly attributes this quality to "the sharply visualized nature of the passage, the way in which emotions are expressed by physical postures or gestures."[4] Here such a strategy also involves a heavy reliance on the narrator's point of view,

4. *The Art of George Eliot* (London, 1961), p. 59. See his extended discussion of the scene and its connections with other elements in the novel, pp. 57–62.

necessary because of the inadequacy of the characters' own consciousness of what is happening.

Similar to this scene, but far more intense, are the two successive scenes in Chapters 26 and 27 of *Daniel Deronda* where Gwendolen must decide first what to write to Grandcourt, and then whether to accept him. Here the complex psychological factors urging Gwendolen toward and away from Grandcourt are conveyed with a greater use of dialogue and fuller presentation of the character's point of view. The conflict of Gwendolen's emotions makes her incapable of decision; she can only move in response to the promptings of her interlocutors, first her mother and then Grandcourt. In the first scene the inability to decide results itself in a kind of decision. She forces herself to act quickly in order to avoid further thought: "To act in a hurry was to have a reason for keeping away from an absolute decision, and to leave open as many issues as possible" (219). The second interview eliminates these possibilities one by one in her answers to Grandcourt's advancing questions, until only one possibility remains.

> "You accept my devotion?" said Grandcourt, holding his hat by his side and looking straight into her eyes, without other movement. Their eyes meeting in that way seemed to allow any length of pause; but wait as long as she would, how could she contradict herself? What had she detained him for? He had shut out any explanation.
>
> "Yes," came as gravely from Gwendolen's lips as if she had been answering her name in a court of justice. (225).

Commitment is finally reached through the avoidance of decision. Again there is the insistent visualization, focusing our awareness on the crucial moment in which the character makes his fate, an awareness briefly shared by Gwendolen here: "There was an instant in which she was conscious of being at the turning of the ways" (224).

Scenes such as these, where crucial choices result from deficient perception, give primary emphasis to the act of decision itself. In other cases, where the characters achieve more adequate levels of awareness, the presentation concentrates upon the act of perception, from which decisions then naturally follow. The problem of perception is always at bottom a moral problem in George Eliot, and several of her most important scenes are crises of moral perception in which the characters achieve a dramatic advance in awareness. Such moments mark the moral growth of characters in nearly all of George Eliot's novels, and we will have occasion to consider several of them in the course of this discussion. Here we may note as one example the scene in Chapter 42 of *Adam Bede* on the morning of Hetty's trial, where Adam, whose fault has been his rigid moralism and lack of fellow feeling, experiences, in his "deep, unspeakable suffering" a kind of "baptism, a regeneration, the initiation into a new state." In his sense of "new awe and new pity" he becomes capable of fellow feeling with all human suffering: " 'O God,' Adam groaned, as he leaned on the table, and looked blankly at the face of his watch, 'and men have suffered like this before . . . and poor helpless young things have suffered like her' " (436). Again there is the insistent visualization of the character's physical presence in order to help render the growth of moral awareness as a scene in a human drama.

These crises of decision and perception are not the only occasions on which George Eliot employs scenic presentation, but they are moments for which the method is particularly important; they are therefore passages which we should examine for symbolic and other means of concentrating significance. But before we can make an accurate analysis of the degree of scenic symbolism in George Eliot's art we must consider the other elements in her narrative method which create a context for scenes in order to understand the way they are given significance.

George Eliot's general narrative mode depends primarily on the convention of the omniscient, commenting narrator. The various functions performed by her narrator, by the author's voice within the work, have been described at length by both Barbara Hardy and W. J. Harvey;[5] my concern here is only with its relation to scene. The narrator's comments and analysis provide a supporting, illuminating context for scenes, reducing their responsibility for conveying meaning directly. As an example we may take the first scene in *Middlemarch*, the division of the jewels. Here, with very little explicating interruption by the narrator, we see dramatized various elements in the characters of Dorothea and Celia, with emphasis on certain of Dorothea's qualities, especially her sensuous nature, of which she herself is not, or is imperfectly, aware. But we are not wholly dependent on the dialogue and description to perceive these elements. The scene occupies only the second half of the chapter; the first half has been devoted to an authorial exposition of the situation and characters of the two sisters. We are given, in the form of abstract analysis, information which will assist our understanding of later developments. Thus,

5. See *The Novels of George Eliot*, Chapter 8, "The Author's Voice: Intimate, Prophetic, and Dramatic," pp. 155–84, and *The Art of George Eliot*, Chapter 3, "The Omniscient Author Convention," pp. 64–89.

we are told that "Dorothea, with all her eagerness to know the truths of life, retained very childlike ideas about marriage" (i, 7), preparing us for her response to Casaubon. The narrator's knowing irony reveals sensuous qualities in Dorothea which conflict with her doctrinaire asceticism and indicates as well the way she rationalizes the two: "Riding was an indulgence which she allowed herself in spite of conscientious qualms; she felt that she enjoyed it in a pagan sensuous way, and always looked forward to renouncing it" (7). In the scene, Dorothea, after disclaiming any interest in such worldly vanities as jewels, is attracted by a gleam of sunlight to the previously unnoticed emeralds.

> "How very beautiful these gems are!" said Dorothea, under a new current of feeling, as sudden as the gleam. "It is strange how deeply colours seem to penetrate one, like scent. I suppose that is the reason why gems are used as spiritual emblems in the Revelation of St. John. They look like fragments of heaven." (10)

The preceding analysis has given us the necessary terms for perceiving her rationalization and self-deception. The scene is established within a conceptual context.

The author's voice does not, however, remain outside the scene. In the passage we have been discussing, the relation of Dorothea's sensuous and religious feelings is also suggested by the narrator's brief analytic commentary:

> "They are lovely," said Dorothea, slipping the ring and bracelet on her finely-turned finger and wrist, and holding them towards the window on a level with her eyes. All the while her thought was trying to justify her delight in the colours by merging them in her mystic religious joy. (10)

The last sentence may be seen as a brief, unobtrusive appearance (or intrusion, if we can use the word without prejudice) of the contextual material in the scene. Only in retrospect do we recognize that the narrative has moved a degree toward omniscience, presenting Dorothea from the vantage point of a greater awareness of her motives than she herself enjoys. For the reader prepared by the contextual example of Dorothea's attitude toward riding, the comment comes as a reinforcement of his ironic view of her talk of "spiritual emblems."

Analysis, outside or within scenes, is George Eliot's main mode of characterization. It may appear in large blocks, as in Chapter 15 of *Middlemarch,* which is entirely devoted to making "the new settler Lydgate better known to any one interested in him than he could possibly be even to those who had seen the most of him since his arrival in Middlemarch" (105). Indeed, by the end of the chapter we know him far better than he knows himself, thanks to George Eliot's omniscience. Analysis is not, however, limited to static presentation. It is capable of brief, penetrating notations within scenes, such as the comment on Dorothea's rationalization in the passage quoted above, and often carries the burden of the scene itself. In the scene of Lydgate's engagement the crucial movement from flirtation to love is presented in analysis as Lydgate, picking up Rosamond's chain-work, sees that she is weeping.

> Remember that the ambitious man who was looking at those Forget-me-nots under the water was very warm-hearted and rash. He did not know where the chain went; an idea had thrilled through the recesses within him which had a miraculous effect in raising the power of passionate love lying buried

there in no sealed sepulchre, but under the lightest, easily pierced mould. (xxxi, 222)

Here, more openly than in our first example, George Eliot refers the reader to the established context of analysis for a full understanding of Lydgate's behavior. The function of tone in this comment is complex: at the same time that it urges sympathetic understanding of Lydgate's motivation it prevents identification with him by associating the reader with the narrator's superior point of view. The allusion which the imagery makes to the Resurrection is not a local irrelevance. As W. J. Harvey suggests, it makes an implicit contrast between Lydgate and Casaubon, whose capacity for love *is* buried in a "sealed sepulchre" and who is repeatedly associated with images of deathly enclosure.[6] This is another, less obvious way in which the comment refers us to the narrative context. It is important to note again how this use of analysis differentiates George Eliot's scenes from those closer to the drama, depending more on dialogue and description of behavior. Mr. Harvey is concerned to defend her method, maintaining that "superbly handled, as it generally is by her, analysis is a literary mode in no way inferior to full dramatic representation."[7] For our purposes the question of the two modes' respective merits is not so important as the recognition of their difference, a point which George Eliot's defenders have sometimes attempted to obscure.[8]

We may locate analysis, and other functions of the author's commenting voice, on a scale of increasing abstraction. At the most concrete level is dialogue and ex-

6. *The Art of George Eliot*, pp. 61–62.

7. Ibid., p. 76.

8. See, for example, F. R. Leavis, *The Great Tradition* (Garden City, N.Y., 1954), p. 125.

ternal description, from which we move to an internal
view of the characters. There is no necessary reason why
this last should be any more abstract than externals, but
in George Eliot it usually tends that way. Her usual stylistic device for presenting her characters' minds is free indirect discourse, which, because it consists of the narrator
indirectly voicing the character's thoughts, blends easily
into analysis, where we clearly occupy a level of awareness
above the character's. From analysis we may move to
further levels of generalization, to comments which do
not only apply to the particular scene before us.

This movement of increasing generalization may be
observed within a single paragraph in Chapter 7 of
Middlemarch. The scene begins with an external view of a
brief interchange between the newly engaged Casaubon
and Dorothea, who, eager for the enlightenment she ex-
pcts from his wisdom, asks whether, "to be more useful,"
she shouldn't learn some Latin and Greek so as to be able
to read to him "as Milton's daughters did to their father."
Casaubon finally grants that "it might be a great advantage if [she] were able to copy the Greek character, and to
that end it were well to begin with a little reading." The
narrator then moves to an internal view of Dorothea, presenting her mental response and the state of mind which
lies behind it.

> Dorothea seized this as a precious permission. She
> would not have asked Mr. Casaubon at once to teach
> her the languages, dreading of all things to be tire-
> some instead of helpful; but it was not entirely out of
> devotion to her future husband that she wished to
> know Latin and Greek. Those provinces of masculine
> knowledge seemed to her a standing-ground from
> which all truth could be seen more truly. As it was,

she constantly doubted her own conclusions, because she felt her own ignorance: how could she be confident that one-roomed cottages were not for the glory of God, when men who knew the classics appeared to conciliate indifference to the cottages with zeal for the glory? Perhaps even Hebrew might be necessary—at least the alphabet and a few roots—in order to arrive at the core of things, and judge soundly of the social duties of the Christian. (47)

From description of response the narrator moves to a brief analytical noting of motivation ("it was not entirely out of devotion to her future husband . . . "), and then into a progressively interiorized rendering of her attitude. From noting how things "seemed to her" we move to their unmediated semblance in the concluding sentences of free indirect discourse, where the irony is all implicit in the naïveté of her attitudes ("Perhaps even Hebrew might be necessary"). From this point, where the internal view of this particular mental state has been fully established, the passage continues in a series of ascending generalizations. First, in analytical summary of Dorothea's attitude, the narrator's own voice clearly reappears as the tone adds pity to the irony: "And she had not reached that point of renunciation at which she would have been satisfied with having a wise husband: she wished, poor child, to be wise herself." The narrator then begins to withdraw from the character, designating her more formally, and making a generalization in a comment which is now abstracted from the particular circumstances: "Miss Brooke was certainly very naïve with all her alleged cleverness." We have been brought to an explicit statement of the obvious conclusion. But this judgment is not sufficiently balanced for George Eliot; it must be placed in perspective by further generalization, a perspective which is reached in a summary review of the contrast between the two sisters: "Celia, whose mind had never been thought too powerful, saw the emptiness of other people's pretensions much more readily." The irony here suggests that Celia's greater safety depends on insulation in her narrow range of imagination. These implications are then made explicit in a final moral generalization which moves to a level of abstraction above the particular individuals who have been considered, applying the conclusions to the general human state: "To have in general but little feeling, seems to be the only security against feeling too much on any particular occasion." We have moved a great distance from the particular situation of a few lines before. The closing apothegm might, if taken out of context, have qualified for inclusion in the *Wise, Witty, and Tender Sayings,* but it is important to note how this level of abstraction is reached through a process of rendering, analysis, and progressive generalization, moving outward from the scene to its conceptual context.

Because these are all functions of George Eliot's narrator, because the author's voice can so easily penetrate a scene and link it to the context, her scenes are firmly embedded in their context. The narrative as a whole exhibits a high degree of textural continuity, an effect which, as we shall see, stands in sharp contrast to the discontinuity of Lawrence and Joyce, where scenes are much more isolated and hence independent.

The dependence of George Eliot's scenes on context appears much more clearly when we turn from elements of characterization to those of theme. The generalizations of the narrator provide formulations of theme, establishing terms in which the significance of individual scenes may be recognized. For example, in the scene in *The Mill*

on the Floss where Maggie is struggling to leave Stephen
(Book VI, Chapter 14), he argues that "the feeling which
draws us towards each other is too strong to be overcome:
that natural law surmounts every other; we can't help
what it clashes with." Maggie replies that "if we judged
in that way, there would be a warrant for all treachery
and cruelty—we should justify breaking the most sacred
ties that can ever be formed on earth. If the past is not to
bind us, where can duty lie? We should have no law but
the inclination of the moment" (417). The strength of this
speech is not merely that of one argument against another.
It is supported by a context of thematic statements which
George Eliot has established earlier in the novel. There
is, for example, the passage which closes Book I, Chapter 5:

> We could never have loved the earth so well if we
> had had no childhood in it . . . What novelty is worth
> that sweet monotony where everything is known, and
> *loved* because it is known? . . . Our delight in the sun-
> shine on the deep-bladed grass to-day, might be no
> more than the faint perception of wearied souls, if it
> were not for the sunshine and the grass in the far-off
> years which still live in us, and transform our percep-
> tion into love." (37–38)

Or again, there is the passage at the end of Book II, Chapter 1, which presents these childhood experiences as the
basis not only of feeling but of value. Where might not the
striving for sheer novelty lead us "if our affections had not
a trick of twining round those old inferior things [of childhood experience]—if the loves and sanctities of our life
had no deep immovable roots in memory?" (135). In such
comments we are given a view of experience made meaningful by our ties with the feelings of the past, of duty,
therefore, not as socially or divinely imposed, but as some-

thing created by this investment of loyalties in past experience. Thus when Maggie exclaims, "If the past is not to bind us, where can duty lie?" the context prepared for the scene enables us to recognize that she has voiced one of the fundamental truths of the world in which she lives. She has, in this respect at least, risen to the level of awareness represented by "George Eliot" and created in the reader. This is one way of describing the crisis of increasing perception noted earlier as one of the crucial occasions for scenes. The character's advance of awareness takes place within the scene, but our full recognition of its significance depends on the prepared contextual terms.

These thematic terms are generally clear and unambiguous, qualities reflected in the large extent of agreement on their nature among George Eliot's critics.[9] We can easily recognize a basic moral theme such as that of egoism and its transcendence, not only because it is repeated and elaborated in each of the novels, but because we are provided with general formulations of it. Thus, there is the well-known passage in *Middlemarch:* "We are all of us born in moral stupidity, taking the world as an udder to feed our supreme selves; Dorothea had early begun to emerge from that stupidity . . ." (xxi, 156). These terms generate the novels' organizing moral categories; they classify, in this case, characters into those who, like Dorothea, emerge from the moral stupidity of egoism and those

9. It is, of course, still possible for a critic to make a complete misreading. See, for example, W. R. Steinhoff, "Intention and Fulfillment in the Ending of *The Mill on the Floss*," in *The Image of the Work*, by B. H. Lehman and others (Berkeley, Calif., 1955), pp. 231–51, where Maggie's affirmation of duty to the past is seen as the choice of "spiritual death," and, despite George Eliot's clear thematic statements, it is maintained that she "does not in the least imply that old loyalties should rule action" (p. 248).

like Casaubon who never do (or like Rosamond, who emerges briefly once and then relapses forever); they organize the characters' stories into those of emergence or the failure to emerge. Unlike most modern novelists, George Eliot provides us with clear directions for reading.

Of course her realism creates a tension between these general categories and the individual characters. In *The Mill on the Floss* the reader is admonished that "moral judgments must remain false and hollow, unless they are checked and enlightened by a perpetual reference to the special circumstances that mark the individual lot" (VII, iii, 435). In *Middlemarch* this becomes a general structural principle; the complex system of parallels and contrasts between the characters derives its general outlines from the basic moral categories but is also capable of qualifying them by unexpected juxtapositions. Thus we see, in Chapter 74, so limited a character as Harriet Bulstrode, who has hardly appeared before, achieving her own moment of moral growth in forgiving and accepting her unlovable husband in a more complete abnegation of self than Dorothea ever achieves in her marriage with Casaubon. Realistic fidelity to human complexity prevents oversimplification. Characters who are initiated into a new moral state are not thereby elevated to a higher sphere, relieved of the pressure of normal conditions. Dorothea does undergo such a development, but "the effect of her being on those around her" still remains "incalculably diffusive" ("Finale," 613). As Barbara Hardy observes, "The moral pattern of *Middlemarch* is blurred by its human truth."[10]

Nevertheless the pattern remains. It is more insistently present in the other novels than in *Middlemarch,* the apex of George Eliot's realism, but even there the general moral

10. *The Novels of George Eliot*, p. 101.

categories remain valid. The treatment of Bulstrode is indicative. George Eliot repeatedly insists on our recognition of his psychological complexity, refusing to make him merely a stock religious hypocrite. Nevertheless, the understanding and even sympathy developed for this character do not remove the burden of moral judgment. The general organizing terms of George Eliot's world are too firm ever to let us believe that to understand all is really to forgive all. Judgment is controlled, meaning made clear through the clear conceptual framework established for George Eliot's novels.

By examining the relationship between this framework, which provides the basic terms for meaning, and some of the specific elements which serve to focus that meaning, we can now begin to analyze George Eliot's symbolism. One element in her novels which has lately received a great deal of attention is their extensive imagery. Since images which are repeated and woven into patterns may move toward symbolism, this is a promising area of investigation. In general, George Eliot's imagery (and symbolism) tend to gravitate toward the conceptual, under the influence of the strong conceptual framework available to inform them.[11] Imagery therefore tends to be more a part of the context than of the scene, performing the same function as, and most often located in, the comments of the narrator. Evidence supporting this thesis

11. This is the view implied in Mark Schorer's observation on George Eliot's metaphors, contrasting them with those of Jane Austen and Emily Brontë: "Their significance lies, then, not so much in the choice of area (as, 'commerce,' or 'natural elements' and 'animals') as in the choice of function, and one tests them not by their field, their context, but by their conceptual portent." "Fiction and the 'Analogical Matrix,'" in *Critiques and Essays on Modern Fiction, 1920–1951*, ed. John W. Aldridge (New York, 1952), p. 91.

may be deduced from Barbara Hardy's discussion of the "ironical image," so called because of its function of "gradually creating a private ironical understanding between the author and the reader."[12] Mrs. Hardy finds an increasing use of such imagery in the later novels, replacing, to an extent, the direct comments of the narrator. This replacement, although it does indicate an increasing obliquity in George Eliot's method, reveals by the very fact of substitution the contextual nature of the imagery.[13]

Because such ironical imagery is often associated with individual characters' consciousnesses, it may seem strange to assign it to context, but we must remember the style in which consciousness is usually presented. Owing to the ease with which George Eliot's free indirect discourse moves into analysis, the location of these images is often ambiguous; they are shared by character and author. For example, there are the water images which express Dorothea's early overestimation of Casaubon. When she exclaims to herself, "And his feelings too, his whole experience—what a lake compared with my little pool!" (iii, 18), the image is obviously located in her mind. But the presentation of a character's mind in direct self-address is rare for George Eliot. Instead, we find much more often passages like the following: "Dorothea by this time had looked deep into the ungauged reservoir of Mr. Casaubon's mind, seeing reflected there in vague labyrinthine extension every quality she herself brought" (17). Is the image Dorothea's or

12. *The Novels of George Eliot*, p. 218. See the entire chapter, pp. 215–32.

13. This increasing obliquity might be seen as a tendency toward a more symbolic mode, but the continuing reliance on direct means of conveying significance prevents such elements from playing as important a role as they do in later novelists.

George Eliot's? Dorothea, as we know from the previously quoted passage, tends to think of Casaubon as a large body of water, so "the ungauged reservoir" may well be attributable to her. But the observation that what she sees there is not a quality of the perceived but of the perceiver is one of which she is definitely not capable; it is part of George Eliot's analysis. The image is thus suspended between the two, and its bearing, its "conceptual portent," is a part of the context in which we view Dorothea's delusion. It is a very different method from that of the later Henry James, where the characters' consciousnesses directly convert the world of their perceptions into images and symbols. George Eliot's imagery is, by contrast, much more outside character and outside scene, though, as we have seen in the case of other contextual elements, it is capable of penetrating them.

This movement of penetration is one from context to scene, from general to individual, and the direction of this movement seems to typify a fundamental quality of George Eliot's imagination. "We feel in her, always," wrote James, "that she proceeds from the abstract to the concrete; that her figures and situations are evolved, as the phrase is, from her moral consciousness, and are only indirectly the products of observation."[14] We can recognize the penetration of this insight without agreeing with James and others of George Eliot's detractors that her novels are therefore only "moralized fables" rather than "pictures of life." Beginning in the abstract need not prevent an imaginative movement from ending with a thorough immersion in the concrete particular. This is, I

14. "The Life of George Eliot," in *Discussions of George Eliot,* ed. Richard Stang (Boston, 1960), p. 8. Compare James' own very different method of development from a concrete "germ," described in several of his Prefaces.

believe, what happens in all of George Eliot's successful creations, but the inherent imaginative direction must be recognized, since it produces some of her most distinctive qualities. Her defenders, asserting the concreteness of George Eliot's "pictures," often cite her artistic credo stated in the famous letter to Frederic Harrison: "I think aesthetic teaching is the highest of all teaching because it deals with life in its highest complexity. But if it ceases to be purely aesthetic—if it lapses anywhere from the picture to the diagram—it becomes the most offensive of all teaching."[15] Less often noted is the sentence immediately preceding this, in which she describes the process by which she arrives at this "aesthetic," particularized, realistic creation as "the severe effort of trying to make certain ideas thoroughly incarnate, as if they had revealed themselves to me first in the flesh and not in the spirit." In the same letter she describes *The Spanish Gypsy*, to which she was now returning, as being "in that stage of Creation or 'Werden,' in which the idea of the characters predominates over the incarnation." George Eliot was well aware of the direction in which her imagination habitually moved.[16]

The movement from abstract to concrete is most obvious where incomplete. In characterization we can clearly see such a failure in figures like Mordecai in *Daniel Deronda*, who is almost wholly a vehicle and enunciator of significances, embodied in a very scant human reality. A less extreme case is Will Ladislaw in *Middlemarch*, who fails to show in his behavior qualities which would adequately support the values he is supposed to represent. These

15. *The George Eliot Letters*, ed. Gordon S. Haight (New Haven, Conn., 1954–55), IV, 300.

16. These passages, and their implications regarding George Eliot's aesthetic, have recently been noted by Darrel Mansell, Jr., in "Ruskin and George Eliot's 'Realism,'" *Criticism*, 7 (1965), 203–16.

may be viewed as instances of idealization, resulting, as W. J. Harvey has noted, "from George Eliot's failure to make her vision thoroughly incarnate."[17] But this imaginative movement is not only observable in such failures, especially failures at solving the perennial difficult problem of creating convincing embodiments of an artist's positive values; it is also to be found in her most successful creations of character. Early in her career George Eliot wrote to her publisher: "my stories always grow out of my psychological conception of the dramatis personae,"[18] and we have already seen the close relation of her psychological and moral analyses. Even in such a character as Lydgate, surely one of the greatest triumphs of her realism, we can see the development from abstract to concrete. His character proceeds from a fundamental psychological-moral conception, one which remains, in conceptual terms, within the finished novel. It is expounded primarily in Chapter 15, with its well-known passage on Lydgate's "spots of commonness" (111). We are given the more abstract formulation as well as its concrete development.

George Eliot's imagery is the vehicle of her fundamental organizing concepts. It is, as we have seen, primarily located in or closely associated with the context of the narrator's commentary, but it is also capable of penetrating the characters' thought and speech and of being reflected in the material world they inhabit. In the last case, the convergence of figurative imagery and literal details is possible because George Eliot's vehicles are often natural objects which may find their counterparts in actuality. It would be misleading, however, to say, as Mr. Harvey

17. *The Art of George Eliot*, p. 178. See his discussion of these and other problems of idealization, pp. 177–98.
18. *Letters*, II, 299.

does, that her imagery is derived from the material world,[19] for this would imply a movement from the concrete to the abstract. A train of imagery may merge with natural fact, as in the music and stream imagery of *The Mill on the Floss* or the horse imagery of *Daniel Deronda,* but this is not necessary. We also find water imagery in *Silas Marner:* "The fountains of human love and of faith in a divine love had not yet been unlocked, and his soul was still the shrunken rivulet" (x, 106), and an extensive pattern of water imagery in *Middlemarch,* of which some instances have been cited, but these make no contact with actuality, with the pond in which Dunstan Cass is drowned or with the stream at Lowick. They are not, however, any the less effective for this; their function is to bear a conceptual portent, not to illuminate the natural world and transmute it to symbol.

There are, of course, cases where George Eliot's concepts confer an organization on segments of actuality, but it is precisely in such cases that we see most clearly the predominance of concept. An example is the use of the spatial metaphor in *Middlemarch,* which organizes elements of figurative as well as literal imagery. Its conceptual structure is derived from two of George Eliot's basic moral categories: egoism is associated with contraction and confinement, its opposite with expansion and extension. Thus, in terms of the water imagery, we find the opposition: "Having once embarked on your marital voyage, it is impossible not to be aware that you make no way and that the sea is not within sight—that, in fact, you are exploring an enclosed basin" (xx, 145). The water images associated with Casaubon contract from the "ungauged reservoir" and "lake" which Dorothea anticipates to a

19. *The Art of George Eliot,* p. 226.

"shallow rill," "swampy ground," and finally to a mist.[20] Similarly, the enclosure of his egoism is, as I have noted, linked with images of the labyrinth and tomb, which connect with the subjects of his researches, as in "the extremely narrow accommodation which was to be had in the dwellings of the ancient Egyptians" (iii, 24). Just as Dorothea's anticipation of a marital voyage on the open sea yields to her sense of an enclosed basin, so "the large vistas and wide fresh air which she had dreamed of finding in her husband's mind were replaced by anterooms and winding passages which seemed to lead nowhither" (xx, 145). The two passages occur within the same paragraph; the shifting of vehicles reveals the more important underlying spatial metaphor, and behind it the concepts it represents.

The metaphor is extended to the material world in the house at Lowick, with its contrasting views. Casaubon is associated with the south and east, where his library is located. The grounds here "looked rather melancholy even under the brightest morning"; they are "more confined," with their "large clumps of trees, chiefly of somber yews, [which] had risen high, not ten yards from the windows." On the southwest, where Dorothea has her boudoir with its bow window, in contrast to the rest of the "small windowed" house, there is "an avenue of limes," where the view "swept uninterruptedly along a slope of greensward till the limes ended in a level of corn and pastures" (ix, 54). Casaubon's moody, ingrown egoism prefers the Yew-Tree Walk, with its gloom and confinement, where the irregularly planted clumps of trees prevent any extensive outward view, and it is here that Dorothea must come to

20. These and other images in the series are traced by Barbara Hardy, *The Novels of George Eliot*, pp. 218–21. She also discusses the images of the "dark or narrow place" (pp. 221–23), but does not consider them as part of a larger spatial metaphor.

pledge herself to the completion of his futile works. The outward-leading avenue of limes presents at least a potential for a movement away from self, a potential which is at last fully realized in that setting in the scene at the end of Chapter 80, where Dorothea decides to return to Rosamond. This moment, to which I shall return later, is an excellent example of George Eliot's method of creating a symbolic scene, based on the conceptual organization of figurative and literal imagery.

This organization is not limited to the opposition of Dorothea and Casaubon; the spatial metaphor is repeatedly used to express the theme of egoism. Thus we find it in the form of explicit equation in this analysis of Lydgate's "sense that there was a grand existence in thought and effective action lying around him, while his self was being narrowed into the miserable isolation of egoistic fears, and vulgar anxieties for events that might allay such fears" (lxiv, 473). It is also present in the suggested metaphorical overtones of the contrast between Dorothea's "voice of deep-souled womanhood," whose depth suggests perhaps the space for reverberation in her "grand woman's frame" (lxxx, 576), juxtaposed in the same paragraph with Rosamond's "silvery neutral" voice (lviii, 433), whose high fluting tones seem to be extruded through her graceful long neck. The basic opposition of expansiveness and constriction organizes even these characterizing details.

The consistent conceptual organization of George Eliot's imagery is emphasized by comparison with Meredith, who often sacrifices consistency for the sake of local effect. Barbara Hardy has performed an extended analysis of this quality in *The Adventures of Harry Richmond*, finding that "Meredith's imagery moves out of its apparently fixed pattern in many places and for many reasons. There is no single centre in scene and action from which a trail of thematic imagery emerges. There are several sources, and the imagery from each crosses and overlaps and confuses classification."[21] I would like to consider this kind of shifting imagery in one series of passages from *The Egoist,*[22] where we can observe the effect of Meredith's "casual and wayward richness" on the novel's thematic organization. Here imagery is organized by an underlying myth, that of Andromeda, which presents Clara as the enchained maiden offered for sacrifice, Willoughby as the monster, and Vernon as the rescuing Perseus. It is first made explicit when Clara, longing for release from her engagement, thinks admiringly of Willoughby's first fiancée, Constantia Durham, who left him for a soldier. She considers her predecessor's rescuer in terms of her father's classical studies: "His name was Harry Oxford. Papa would call him her Perseus" (x, 84). Having implicitly imaged herself as Andromeda, Clara fills in the remaining terms. Thus when Willoughby approaches her:

> The gulf of a caress hove in view like an enormous billow hollowing under the curled ridge.
> She stooped to a buttercup; the monster swept by. (xiii, 106)

Likewise, she images her plight as being "between sea and rock" (xv, 124), and thinks with regret that Vernon does not seem quite up to the role of Perseus: "Mr. Whitford meant well; he was conscientious, very conscientious. But he was not the hero descending from heaven bright-sworded to smite a woman's fetters off her limbs and

21. *The Appropriate Form,* p. 92. See "The Structure of Imagery: George Meredith's *Harry Richmond,*" pp. 83–104.

22. Page references are to the Riverside edition, ed. Lionel Stevenson (Boston, 1958). Chapter numbers have also been noted to facilitate reference to other editions.

deliver her from the yawning mouth-abyss" (xvi, 125). The analogy is kept alive with subsequent references to Willoughby as the "monster" (xxxix, 323, and xlii, 357). Thus it comes as a shock when Meredith unmistakably invokes the myth in a rather different context: "The Rev. Doctor smothered a yawn. The repression of it caused a second one, a real monster, to come, big as our old friend of the sea advancing on the chained-up Beauty" (xxxii, 268). However we judge this shift, it presents a clear and striking example of the subordination of a pattern of thematic imagery to local effect. In George Eliot imagery is the servant of concept; here we see an image take on an independent life of its own.

These images provide other illuminating contrasts with George Eliot. The use of myth contrasts with her predominantly natural imagery; it is a part of Meredith's greater artificiality and stylization and accords with such phrases as "The gulf of a caress hove in view." For George Eliot "art is the nearest thing to life," with the implication that the nearer the better, because "it is a mode of amplifying experience and extending our contact with our fellow-men beyond the bounds of our personal lot,"[23] that is, a movement away from our own egoism. Thus any element of style which calls attention to itself, to art as artifice, impairs realism and distracts attention from the human actuality which is, on moral grounds, the primary concern. Meredith's "Prelude" to *The Egoist* establishes his opposition to such a view in a statement whose highly mannered style is a program in itself, declaring "that the realistic method of a conscientious transcription of all the visible, and a repetition of all the audible, is mainly

23. "The Natural History of German Life," in *The Essays of George Eliot,* ed. Thomas Pinney (New York, 1963), p. 271.

accountable for our present branfulness, and for that pro-
longation of the vasty and the noisy, out of which, as from
an undrained fen, steams the malady of sameness, our
modern malady" (5–6). I have objected to the description
of George Eliot's imagery as *derived from* the natural
world, but her choice of natural vehicles remains significant. Her natural imagery represents the movement of
concepts into close proximity to the natural world as their
portent is brought to bear upon it. The use of natural and
commonplace objects is part of the general strategy of
style which does not call attention to itself but directs
it toward the central human drama, maintaining the
primacy of the real.

The elaboration of imagistic structures, such as the
spatial metaphor in *Middlemarch,* is not George Eliot's
only way of creating symbolic significance. Several scenes
in her novels also present symbolic objects which are not
parts of larger patterns. Generally, these are made symbolic
by association with actions whose moral significance is
clear; natural and domestic objects are thus given conceptual import for the symbolic enactment of moral qualities. A familiar example is George Eliot's use of two of
her standard properties, the mirror and the window, associated with the self-absorption of egoism and the outward orientation of its opposite. The two are immediately
juxtaposed in Chapter 15 of *Adam Bede,* "The Two Bed-
Chambers" (150–63), where we first see Hetty performing
her ritual of self-worship as she parades in her cheap finery
before the mirror and then turn to the adjacent room
where Dinah sits before her window and thinks first of
the natural scene, then of other individuals, then of God,
turning finally to particular concern and sympathy for
Hetty, which is given direct expression in her attempt to
communicate with her. The significance of the contrasting

actions is clear, and made clearer by George Eliot's comments and analyses, but it is also placed in a context established by commentary which has already formulated the contrast: "it made a strange contrast to see [Hetty's] sparkling self-engrossed loveliness looked at by Dinah's calm pitying face, with its open glance which told that her heart lived in no cherished secrets of its own, but in feelings which it longed to share with all the world" (xiv, 142). Our understanding the significance of this double scene does not depend on interpretation of the symbols, but it is enhanced by them. They act as reinforcements of significance and present an opportunity for it to be dramatized as well as presented through comment and analysis.

Once these objects have been given a stable conceptual significance it remains available to be drawn on whenever required. Thus they recur in the later novels. In *Daniel Deronda* we find Gwendolen, in her naïve egoistic self-delight, kissing her image in the mirror (ii, 10), and in *Felix Holt,* where Esther Lyon is struggling to overcome her egoism, she draws the blind and looks out of her window: "She wanted the largeness of the world to help her thought" (xlix, 430).

In these cases, as in *Adam Bede,* the symbolism of mirror and window is only an auxiliary method of creating significance. This subordinate function seems to typify the role of symbolism in the realistic novel, or at least in George Eliot's realism. Barbara Hardy, defending George Eliot's artistry, asserts that her "composition is usually as complex and as subtle as the composition of Henry James or Proust or Joyce, but it is very much less conspicuous because of the engrossing realistic interest of her human and social delineation."[24] Such an emphasis can be mis-

24. *The Novels of George Eliot,* p. 5.

leading if it obscures the differences between traditional
and modern novelistic practice. Even assuming an equal
complexity of pattern, of imagery and symbolism (and it
is a dubious assumption), the fact remains that these elements are inherently less important in George Eliot's
novels. Their relative inconspicuousness is functional.
Like the suppression of melodrama noted in the composition of *Middlemarch* and the avoidance of stylistic artifice
noted in the comparison with Meredith, it proceeds from
the necessity to focus attention on the "human and social
delineation." Mrs. Hardy gives us a more satisfactory formulation of the role of symbolism and other quasi-symbolic details of pattern in George Eliot in describing them
as "reinforcements of value rather than totally responsible
vehicles."[25] This subordination of symbolism is required
by the fundamental moral purpose underlying George
Eliot's realism, a purpose which is also served by her use
of the omniscient narrator and her conceptual framework.
The essentially clear and authoritative terms in which
meaning is framed and the open channel which the narrator's commentary provides for directly conveying this
meaning reduce the importance of the indirect, suggestive
techniques of symbolism, again directing the primary
emphasis toward the realistic human and social drama.

The importance of this general subordination of symbolism in George Eliot's fictional mode may be seen by
examining some of the rare occasions on which symbolism
assumes a more prominent role. A striking example of
movement from a realistic to a symbolic level occurs in
the development of the river imagery in the last two books

25. *The Appropriate Form*, p. 199. Whether symbolism in the novel
can ever become a *totally* responsible vehicle of meaning is a problem
we shall have to consider in examining later novelists.

of *The Mill on the Floss* which leads to Maggie's and Stephen's drifting away together and to the final flood. There are from the beginning references which anticipate the final catastrophe and which keep the actuality of the Floss before us, but it is largely in the last books that the imagery is given definite conceptual associations, as the stream becomes an image for feeling. It is first so used in describing a moment between Maggie and Philip: "It was one of those dangerous moments when speech is at once sincere and deceptive—when feeling, rising high above its average depth, leaves flood-marks which are never reached again" (V, iv, 294). This imagery is primarily used to define Maggie's relationship with Stephen. Thus, listening to him sing, she is "borne along by a wave too strong for her" (VI, vii, 366). As the relationship nears its crisis the image becomes more and more closely associated with the forces of passion which bear Maggie before them. Wishing she could yield to Stephen's arguments, she feels, "If it were *not* wrong—if she were once convinced of that, and need no longer beat and struggle against this current, soft and yet as strong as the summer stream!" (VI, xi, 393).

The use of water imagery for feelings is not unique to *The Mill on the Floss;* it seems to be as much a part of George Eliot's basic imaginative vocabulary as the mirror and the window. The example from *Silas Marner* of "the fountains of human love" has already been cited, and the equation is also present in *Adam Bede:* "human feeling is like the mighty rivers that bless the earth" (xvii, 181). It is probably the implicit rationale for the use of water imagery in *Middlemarch,* and may help to explain why Daniel Deronda is borne toward his crucial encounters with both Mirah and Mordecai upon the river. But in none of these cases is there such an elaborate preparation for the investment of a literal object with conceptual significance so that, in Book VI, Chapter 13, Maggie is both literally and figuratively "Borne Along by the Tide" past the point of no return. The scene has become symbolic, so that both levels are present in passages such as that where Maggie yearns to believe "that the tide was doing it all—that she might glide along with the swift, silent stream, and not struggle any more" (408). It is a symbolism which requires a delicate balance of the two levels; the overassertion of symbol will distort realistic probablity, but if symbolic meaning is not fully present in the actual it remains on the usual contextual, auxiliary level.

Such a balance is rare in George Eliot's novels, which normally function in a more realistic mode, and when attained, as it is here, it is in danger of toppling over into a situation where symbol is asserted at the expense of realism. This is what happens in the last chapter of *The Mill on the Floss*. The river has not been restricted to association with Maggie's passion; George Eliot's commentary has analyzed the stream of feeling into some of its moral components: "the stream of vanity was soon swept along and mingled imperceptibly with that wider current" (VI, ix, 382). Such contextual preparation still allows some moments of double reference in the final chapter like those in "Borne Along by the Tide": "there was no choice of courses, no room for hesitation, and she floated into the curent" (VII, v, 454). But, as the passage presses forward to the catastrophe, realism is increasingly subordinated to symbol. The very use of the extraordinary event of the flood contrasts with the normal use of the river in the earlier chapter; as we near the end this heightening of events drives toward a complex of largely symbolic resolutions. F. R. Leavis has claimed that the "flooded river has no symbolic or metaphorical value," [26] but it would

26. *The Great Tradition*, p. 62.

seem, rather, that it has too much. Maggie's reconciliation with the past in the shape of Tom is essentially symbolic, more asserted as gesture than realized, and the fate which overtakes them is likewise shaped by symbolic motives, its physical causes representing the combination of more intangible internal (moral and psychological) and external (social) factors which have led to destruction. The stream has already been equated with Maggie's fatal passion, and balancing this, the actual agents of destruction represent the outward causes of tragedy, her hostile social environment. This explains why the boat should be overwhelmed by "machinery," a symbol of impersonal, deterministic forces rather than any natural object, with "wooden" added in the proof of the first edition in an attempt to lend plausibility and explain how the machinery comes to be floating on the stream.[27] Nothing could explain why it moves at a faster rate than the boat when both are in the same current (since Tom is rowing, he would actually pull away from it). This is obviously a purely symbolic contrivance, also revealed in the telling rare appearance of the pathetic fallacy: "the huge mass was hurrying on in hideous triumph" (456). Clearly, the ending of *The Mill on the Floss* involves a shift in mode; this is one way of accounting for the general dissatisfaction with it.

A similar shift in mode occurs in *Daniel Deronda,* in the parts dealing with Mordecai and with Deronda's growing sense of his mission, which are similarly unsatisfactory. A clear example is the crucial meeting of Deronda and Mordecai at Blackfriars Bridge in Chapter 40. As in the case of the river in *The Mill on the Floss,* literal fact is given a prepared symbolic meaning, but instead of spe-

27. See Professor Haight's note, p. 456, and *Letters*, III, 279, where the insertion is requested.

cific psychological associations we find vague and visionary
ones. In Mordecai's prophetic reveries he thinks of the
disciple who is to come to realize his dreams: "he habitually thought of the Being answering to his need as one
distantly approaching or turning his back toward him,
darkly painted against a golden sky" (xxxviii, 356), a
scene associated with Blackfriars Bridge at sunset, as the
Messianic figure becomes associated with Deronda. In
the scene of their meeting reality is made to fulfill vision;
all these images are made actual. The visionary quality
of the scene is stressed. Mordecai feels "that his inward
prophecy was fulfilled. . . . The prefigured friend had
come from the golden background, and had signalled to
him: this actually was: the rest was to be" (370–71). The
scene presents, not a confrontation of realistically rendered individuals, but "a meeting-place for the spiritual
messengers" (371). It is a scene of "moral fantasy,"[28] an
attempt to lend conviction to the birth of a vocation which
can only be expressed symbolically because it has no realistic counterpart. As in the end of *The Mill on the Floss*,
when the narrative moves onto a primarily symbolic level
the resultant shift of mode does not carry George Eliot
toward modern symbolism but into fantasy and romance.
Such a shift is fatal to her realism.

We can learn more about George Eliot's realism and the
consistency of fictional mode which it requires by comparing her novels with those of Dickens, where shifts of
mode occur continually and without damage. Here not
only do we find different characters operating on very
different levels of conventionality, but also see them meet
and interact without any effect of incongruity. Thus, in

28. Barbara Hardy, *The Novels of George Eliot*, p. 128. See her discussion of the way the images of river, bridge, sunset, and wide sky
are given symbolic significance, pp. 128–29.

Bleak House, Esther Summerson, who is presented in a realistic and subdued manner, can wander through a gallery of Dickensian grotesques such as Krook, Miss Flite, and the Smallweeds with so little artistic friction that they seem to inhabit the same world. Or again, in Chapter 10 of *Little Dorrit,* we move with Arthur Clennam from the satiric fantasy world of the Circumlocution Office to encounter, on its very threshold, the far more realistically conceived Daniel Doyce. In theory, it is an abrupt transition from one mode to another, sharply different one, and yet in practice there is no sense of a shift. Dickens is not under the realist's obligation to remain within a single mode, and he manipulates a number of them with an ease which does not reappear in the English novel until Joyce. It is easier to describe this multiplicity of modes than to provide an adequate general explanation for its success.[29] A brief consideration of some aspects of Dickens' fictional method may, however, indicate a partial explanation and at the same time shed further light on George Eliot's different ways of creating meaning.

A major difference may be seen in their methods of characterization and uses of scenic presentation. Characterization in Dickens does not involve George Eliot's psychological and moral analysis; he therefore makes greater use of scenes and confines his narrator chiefly to dealing with externals. George Eliot, especially in the later novels,

29. Explanation of the immediate causes for success in the two examples I have cited can be given in terms of technical analysis, though this provides little basis for generalization. In *Bleak House,* Esther, as self-effacing narrator, calls little attention to herself, directing it rather toward the more vivid figures she encounters. We are thus unlikely to notice the discrepancy in modes of characterization. In the scene from *Little Dorrit,* Dickens has interposed the incensed Mr. Meagles to create a distraction and smooth the transition before Doyce is actually introduced.

brushes past externals to reach her characters' inner natures, while Dickens' strategy often seems to be, as J. Hillis Miller says, to seek the truth behind the surface "by giving an exhaustive inventory of the surface itself."[30] Analysis is unnecessary for most of Dickens' characters; they reveal themselves thoroughly in speech. Thus, in *Bleak House,* on the first appearance of Mr. Chadband:

> "My friends," says Mr. Chandband, "Peace be on this house! On the master thereof, on the mistress thereof, on the young maidens, and on the young men! My friends, why do I wish for peace? What is peace? Is it war? No. Is it strife? No. Is it lovely, and gentle, and pleasant, and serene, and joyful? O yes! Therefore, my friends, I wish for peace upon you and upon yours."[31]

His character is apparent; the narrator's comments can be devoted to descriptions which intensify the satiric effect but which, unlike George Eliot's commentary, are not crucial to our understanding. Characterization is thus more dramatic, located more fully within the scene.[32]

The quality of this drama is furthermore much closer to that of the stage. Dickens' tendency toward theatricality has often been observed since Ruskin remarked that "he

---

30. *Charles Dickens: The World of His Novels* (Cambridge, Mass., 1959), p. xvi.

31. *Bleak House,* Riverside edition, ed. Morton Dauwen Zabel (Boston, 1956), Chapter 19, p. 200. Subsequent references are to this edition and are incorporated in the text. Chapter numbers have also been given to facilitate reference to other editions.

32. For some of Dickens' theoretical statements on the dramatic presentation of character and avoidance of analytical "dissection," see Richard Stang, *The Theory of the Novel in England, 1850–1870* (London, 1959), pp. 99–103.

chooses to speak in a circle of stage fire."[33] While this impulse frequently leads to the sort of melodrama which George Eliot consistently avoids, it also contributes, as we shall see, to Dickens' characteristic type of symbolism. This aspect of Dickens' scenic technique is an element in his general creation of character in speech and action and thus through the externalization of psychology, a psychology which can be just as profound as George Eliot's even though not rendered in analysis. Dickens' greatest psychological penetration is, however, into the abnormal, while George Eliot is, as we have noted, far more concerned with normal experience, with the depths of suffering and possibilities for growth which may be hidden there.

Dickens' externalization of psychology is in itself a somewhat symbolic method, since outward behavior is made to represent inner qualities, but the tendency is carried much further. It involves not only the characters' speech and appearance but also their physical surroundings, to which a great deal of their inner lives is often transposed. Repeatedly we find rooms and houses which, presented in vivid and detailed descriptions, characterize their inhabitants, such as Vholes' office, Mrs. Clennam's house, Satis House, or Boffin's Bower. We have seen a similar figurative technique in George Eliot's use of the house at Lowick, but there the symbolism does not proceed so much from the direct projection of psychological characteristics as from the application of general moral

33. John Ruskin, "A Note on *Hard Times*," in *The Dickens Critics*, ed. George H. Ford and Lauriat Lane, Jr. (Ithaca, N.Y., 1961), p. 47. Concerning Dickens' use of contemporary theatrical conventions, see William Axton, "*Dombey and Son:* From Stereotype to Archetype," *ELH, 31* (1964), 301–17, and Kathleen Tillotson, *Novels of the Eighteen-Forties* (Oxford, 1961), pp. 175–85.

categories. Such devices are furthermore less important in George Eliot because of the greater burden of meaning carried by authorial commentary. The projection of internal states upon environment is a variant of the pathetic fallacy, an effect more immediately recognizable in scenes where the natural world mirrors the human. In Chapter 2 of *Bleak House,* for example, we first see Chesney Wold from a point of view close to Lady Dedlock's. A long paragraph elaborates the description of continual rain, the grounds flooded, everything saturated. The dreary scene clearly functions as an introduction to the character's state of boredom and despair: "it rains in Lincolnshire . . . because it rains in the heart of Lady Dedlock."[34]

Such projection is not the only source of Dickens' symbolism; he also creates symbols which embody thematic meaning apart from individual characters. We may distinguish such symbolism both from George Eliot's and from that of modern novelists, however, by emphasizing its *emblematic* quality, its greater simplicity and more limited range. Instead of simply describing Dickens as a symbolist, it is thus more accurate to stress, in John Killham's words, that "pathetic fallacy and emblematic writing are his stock-in-trade."[35] Emblematic symbolism often results from the externalization of psychology, producing repeated conceits, such as Wemmick's post-office mouth, or gestures, such as Miss Wade's repressing hand on the bosom, which represent a character's essential trait. Thematic symbols like the fog in *Bleak House* or the dust

34. Robert Liddel, *A Treatise on the Novel* (London, 1965), p. 115.
35. *"Pickwick:* Dickens and the Art of Fiction," in *Dickens and the Twentieth Century,* ed. John Gross and Gabriel Pearson (London, 1962), p. 39. The primary concern of this essay is to differentiate Dickens' fictional mode from that of modern symbolists like Kafka and Joyce with whom he has often been associated.

heaps in *Our Mutual Friend* are also emblematic. Like the emblems associated with characters, they are simple, limited analogues whose significance proceeds from direct resemblance. As Mr. Killham points out, they do not control and unify theme and action in the way often claimed for them: the fog does not permeate all of *Bleak House* but is limited almost entirely to the first chapter, where it functions only as "an emblem for the 'old miasmal mist' of Chancery"; the dust heaps do reappear several times, but only intermittently exercise their symbolic function as analogues for filthy lucre.

A Dickensian emblem can, however, become a pervasive and central element, as does the prison in *Little Dorrit*. This image becomes the basis for a general organizing metaphor which operates in a manner analogous to that of George Eliot's fundamental moral categories. The metaphor of imprisonment is seen with increasing clarity to apply to the characters' spiritual states as it is extended to more and more of them. We see that, just as surely as Edward Dorrit is imprisoned in the Marshalsea, so are Mrs. Clennam in her Calvinism, Merdle in his fraud, or Miss Wade in her neurosis, that society itself is a prison. Such a principle of organization is much less conceptual, more imagistic, than those of George Eliot; the category of egoism is capable of many metaphorical embodiments, while the meaning of imprisonment is almost inseparable from its image. A greater separation of image and meaning is characteristic of George Eliot's illustrative symbolism, created by the movement from abstract to concrete. In Dickens we see the potentiality, extensively developed in the prison metaphor of *Little Dorrit,* for a more integral, central symbolism. This symbolism is still emblematic in that it applies the simple, clear, and direct equation of imprisonment to all the various forms of restriction and repression which the novel displays, but it is no longer, like the other examples I have cited, merely a local or inconsistent embodiment of meaning. Instead, it performs a central, unifying function more important than any performed by George Eliot's symbolism.

George Eliot also occasionally employs an emblematic symbolism which, though far less obtrusive, is comparable with that of Dickens. One example is her use of the metaphor of physical for moral vision. Thus Dorothea is noted in the early chapters of *Middlemarch* as being "rather short-sighted" (iii, 22), obviously the state in which she blunders into her marriage. The same emblem is developed more elaborately in *Silas Marner,* where Silas, in his phase of isolation and withdrawal is also short-sighted, but, when we see him at the opening of Part Two after he has been reintegrated into the human community, "his large brown eyes seem to have gathered a longer vision, as is the way with eyes that have been short-sighted in early life, and they have a less vague, a more answering gaze" (xvi, 170). The inclusion of the naturalistic explanation along with the emblematic significance is typical of the general unobtrusive use of natural images and symbols already observed.

Such a simple, local equation of literal detail with moral significance does not, however, typify George Eliot's symbolism. It might seem that her symbolism of mirrors and windows is equally emblematic. Taken in isolation, they would indeed appear no different from the emblem of eyesight in *Silas Marner,* but viewed in context they create a greater concentration of meaning. Through them the underlying conceptual framework, the source of significance, can be focused in the complex of a dramatized scene, creating a greater depth and range of implication. I shall attempt to demonstrate the complexity and concentration of which George Eliot's symbolic images and scenes are capable in the concluding section of this discussion, but I should like first to complete the comparison with Dickens by considering a way in which their differences of mode are reflected in their total narrative forms.

In George Eliot's later novels figurative imagery is elaborated into complex patterns which also include elements of actuality. There is less of this structuring of imagery in Dickens' novels, but a comparable organization is observable in the deployment of his characters, who thus in effect become a kind of imagery. The great majority of Dickens' characters are, as has often been noted, static, and those few who do change are rarely convincing, as may be seen in comparing Richard Carstone with Lydgate as studies in deterioration. These unchanging figures, with their few but vividly rendered characteristics which are presented each time they appear, lead an existence detached from time; the plot does not so much trace their development in time as relate them to each other in a spatial pattern like that of imagery. Thus Dickens' novels present a version of what Joseph Frank has called spatial form.[36] W. J. Harvey considers the theoretical problem of spatial form and its opposite, which we may as well call temporal form, arguing that their opposition is "more apparent than real." He views them as contrasting "acts of mind, modes of perception and apprehension" in the reader, provoked by different aspects of structure, and finds both in George Eliot.[37] It is necessary to recognize the liabilities inherent in applying spatial metaphors to literature, but it is also necessary to recognize that these

36. See "Spatial Form in Modern Literature," in *The Widening Gyre: Crisis and Mastery in Modern Literature* (New Brunswick, N.J., 1963), pp. 3–62.

37. *The Art of George Eliot*, pp. 95–108.

are not only critical but artistic metaphors. The weakness of reducing the spatial and temporal aspects of fictional form to the level of the reader's apprehension is that it dissociates them from the novel's presentation of space and time. Spatiality in Dickens' novels is, however, not only a quality of the characters' formal interrelations but of the world in which they move.

Thus, in *Bleak House,* the famous atmospheric overture shifts rapidly from one place to another:

> Fog everywhere. Fog up the river, where it flows among green aits and meadows; fog down the river, where it rolls defiled among the tiers of shipping . . . Fog on the Essex marshes, fog on the Kentish heights. . . . out on the yards . . . Greenwich . . . on the bridges . . . divers places in the streets . . . the spongy fields . . . the shops . . .

until we arrive "at the very heart of the fog," the Court of Chancery (1). The fog connects these separated points in space, anticipating the spatial connections to be elaborated by the plot. Thus, in Chapter 16, the narrator directs our attention to connections of places as well as persons as the plot begins to thicken:

> What connexion can there be, between the place in Lincolnshire, the house in town, the Mercury in powder, and the whereabout of Jo the outlaw with the broom, who had that distant ray of light upon him when he swept the churchyard-step? What connexion can there have been between many people in the innumerable histories of this world, who, from opposite sides of great gulfs, have, nevertheless been very curiously brought together! (167)

Although the plot proceeds in time, it works largely to reveal the pattern of connections which has existed from the beginning, whether the secret links between Lady Dedlock, Captain Hawdon, and Esther, or the entanglement of so many of the characters in the case of Jarndyce and Jarndyce. Even connections established in the course of the action, such as those between Jo and Esther or Lady Dedlock, between Tom-all-Alone's and Bleak House or Chesney Wold, are only particular dramatizations of the state of total interconnection in which all the characters and places exist through their membership in an organic, though diseased, society.

Little Dorrit exhibits an even greater domination of spatial relation over temporal development. As John Wain says, "It is his most stationary novel; its impact is even less dependent on 'plot' than is customary throughout Dickens' work; its development is by means of outward radiation, rather than linear progression." Or again, adopting another spatial metaphor, he finds that the novel is "an intricate labyrinth, designed so that the reader, on whatever path he sets out, will always be brought back to the point where one or other of the two principal metaphors [the prison and the family] is confronting him."[38] Whether we are concerned with a pattern of characters or metaphors, spatial qualities predominate over temporal in Dickens. This may help to explain the affinities which recent criticism has felt between his novels and modern symbolism.[39] Despite such differences of mode as those I have tried to indicate by my emphasis on the emblematic quality of his symbolism, we must also recognize that Dickens' spatial form provides a matrix which can accom-

38. *"Little Dorrit,"* in *Dickens and the Twentieth Century,* p. 175.
39. Thus Lionel Trilling: "There is scarcely a cherished modern text that does not instruct us in [reading Dickens]—we cannot read Kafka or Lawrence or Faulkner without learning a little better how to read Dickens." "The Dickens of Our Day," in *A Gathering of Fugitives* (Boston, 1956), p. 42.

modate his multiple modes and in which fictional elements, freed from the restrictions of temporal circumstance, can move more easily toward symbolic configurations.

George Eliot's novels also present patterns which may be read spatially, primarily those which establish her characteristic parallels and contrasts between characters, but her mode is nevertheless predominantly temporal, because, above all, she presents character as deeply immersed in time. Thus change is almost as common in George Eliot's characters as it is rare in Dickens', whether it is the growth of a Dorothea or the deterioration of a Lydgate. It is impossible to imagine such characters, as we often do Dickens', in a kind of imaginative eternity, detached from a particular scene or even from the context of the novel in which they appear, because her major figures are always in process. For George Eliot, as Mr. Farebrother says, "character is not cut in marble—it is not something solid and unalterable. It is something living and changing" *(Middlemarch,* lxxii, 538). The predominance of temporal over spatial aspects in George Eliot is another facet of her general subordination of symbolic to realistic elements.

George Eliot's realistic temporal form may be observed in one aspect of her scenic technique, the creation of parallel scenes which refer to each other and thus emphasize progression in the changes between them. It is true that parallel scenes, like those of "The Two Bed-Chambers" in *Adam Bede* may juxtapose simultaneous contrasting actions, but more often they link different moments in a span of time. Thus, again in *Adam Bede,* there are the two meetings in the grove, the first, in Chapter 27, when Adam discovers Arthur with Hetty and fights him, the second, in Chapter 68, when, after the tragedy, the two men meet again and are finally reconciled. The parallel is stressed by the later chapter's title, "Another Meeting in the Woods," and there are numerous references which, against the backdrop of the same place and the same time of day, emphasize the changes which have taken place in both characters. The parallel scenes provide a formal index to the effects of time.

In *Daniel Deronda* this parallelism controls a series of several scenes which show Gwendolen before her mirror. The first, when she actually kisses her image, has been mentioned (ii, 10); this early scene becomes a point of reference for indicating the changes which take place in Gwendolen. Thus, when her family's financial downfall has darkened her prospects, "the self-delight with which she had kissed her image in the glass had faded before the sense of futility" (xxi, 169). As she is forced to assess the resources which may be used in her present situation, she examines her image again, not with delight but with an attempt at cool appraisal, thinking " 'I *am* beautiful'— not exultingly, but with grave decision" (xxiii, 187). Later, after her marriage to Grandcourt, she "no longer felt inclined to kiss her fortunate image in the glass; she looked at it with wonder that she could be so miserable" (xxxv, 317), and shortly thereafter we see her "looking at herself in a mirror—not in admiration, but in a sad kind of companionship" (323). Finally, further reduced by the misery of her marriage and the effort of dissembling it, she paces her large drawing room "like an imprisoned dumb creature, not recognizing herself in the glass panels" (xlviii, 443). This series of parallel scenes (which includes others not cited here) traces the change in Gwendolen and then ceases, as her self-concern, whether in delight or misery, finally yields to the sense of a larger world beyond her which Deronda brings.

In *Middlemarch,* Dorothea's development is also presented in the temporal form of parallel scenes, but in a series far richer and more suggestive than those we have examined in *Adam Bede* and *Daniel Deronda,* a series which culminates in one of George Eliot's finest symbolic scenes. By tracing the development of this series and by examining several aspects of its thematic context, we can arrive at a final epitome of her fictional mode. The series is initiated by the scenic image which crystallizes Dorothea's sense of the "stupendous fragmentariness" of Rome joined with the beginning of her disillusionment with Casaubon. The importance of the moment is stressed by the omniscient, foreseeing comment that it is to become a permanent part of her experience:

> Forms both pale and glowing took possession of her young sense, and fixed themselves in her memory even when she was not thinking of them, preparing strange associations which remained through her after-years. Our moods are apt to bring with them images which succeed each other like the magic-lantern pictures of a doze; and in certain states of dull forlornness Dorothea all her life continued to see the vastness of St Peter's, the huge bronze canopy, the excited intention of the attitudes and garments of the prophets and evangelists in the mosaics above, and the red drapery which was being hung for Christmas spreading itself everywhere like a disease of the retina. (xx, 144)

The final image is probably the most forceful in George Eliot, but it has more than simply local significance and thus exemplifies the relation of scene and context. The image of "a disease of the retina" not only bears a powerful emotive charge but also a conceptual portent, for it is a part of the pervasive theme of vision in this novel. As Barbara Hardy says, "*Middlemarch* is, amongst other things, a novel about distorted vision."[40] She is particularly concerned with the metaphor of the mirror, which includes the well-known image of the pier glass, expounded at the opening of Chapter 27 as a central emblem of vision distorted by egoism, but this is only a part of the pattern. It includes all the different ways in which the characters, through their different kinds of egoism, distort reality and enter the nearly universal "fellowship of illusion" (xxxiv, 237). In this scene the image of the diseased retina suggests the egoistic distortion of Dorothea's perceptions, both those which, influenced by her naïve conceptions and hopes, have led to her marriage, and those which are now colored by the misery of her disappointment. The complexity which George Eliot's context can create in a scene is shown by this image, which at once conveys the intensity of Dorothea's affective state and reminds us that it is nevertheless a state of egoism.

The theme of perception has another side, one which relates it to the image George Eliot presents of herself and hence relates it to her whole theory of art. The paragraph of generalizing commentary which immediately follows the description of St. Peter's makes a gesture of qualifying the intensity with which Dorothea's feelings have been rendered. George Eliot admits that there is not "anything very exceptional" here, and thus she can hardly suppose that "the situation will be regarded as tragic," for "we do not expect people to be deeply moved by what is not unusual." But her irony then becomes sharper:

> That element of tragedy which lies in the very fact of frequency, has not yet wrought itself into the

40. *The Novels of George Eliot*, p. 223.

coarse emotions of mankind; and perhaps our frames
could hardly bear much of it. If we had a keen vision
and feeling of all ordinary human life, it would be
like hearing the grass grow and the squirrel's heart
beat, and we should die of that roar which lies on
the other side of silence. As it is, the quickest of us
walk about well wadded with stupidity. (xx, 144)

It is, of course, just such a "keen vision and feeling of
all ordinary human life" which George Eliot's realism
seeks to communicate, to make us realize the possibility
of tragedy there and thus, in the resultant extension of
sympathy, to pierce our own wadding of egoistic stupidity.
The passage recalls moments from the early works, such
as the opening of Chapter 5 of *Amos Barton,* where the
reader is exhorted to learn to see the possibility of tragedy
beneath the surface of undistinguished lives, or from the
essays, where it is asserted that "the greatest benefit we
owe to the artist . . . is the extension of our sympathies."[41]
George Eliot's expression of her theory is subtler and more
oblique in the later novels, but the theory is not altered.

Perception as the enterprise of author and reader as
well as characters is implicit in George Eliot's commentary
on Lydgate: "He went home and read far into the smallest
hour, bringing a much more testing vision of details and
relations into this pathological study than he had ever
thought it necessary to apply to the complexities of love
and marriage" (xvi, 122). His failure to apply his intelligence outside his medical work is, of course, the cause
of his downfall, but the implication is that George Eliot,
on the other hand, does bring a "testing vision of details
and relations" to all of human experience. The passage
continues with sustained double reference, describing

41. "The Natural History of German Life," in *Essays,* p. 270.

George Eliot's attitude toward her art in the same terms used for Lydgate's toward his science: he feels himself "amply informed" on the subjects of love and marriage by literary stereotype and gossip,

> whereas Fever had obscure conditions, and gave him that delightful labour of the imagination which is not mere arbitrariness, but the exercise of disciplined power—combining and constructing with the clearest eye for probabilities and the fullest obedience to knowledge; and then, in yet more energetic alliance with impartial Nature, standing aloof to invent tests by which to try its own work.

The commentary then elaborates the conception of the realistic imagination as opposed to the arbitrary or fanciful, which can only exaggerate reality, producing "reports of very poor talk going on in distant orbs; or portraits of Lucifer coming down on his bad errands as a large ugly man with bat's wings and spurts of phosphorescence; or exaggerations of wantonness that seem to reflect life in a diseased dream." The passage is closely reminiscent of one in Chapter 17 of *Adam Bede,* George Eliot's most famous declaration of artistic principles: "Falsehood is so easy, truth so difficult. The pencil is conscious of a delightful facility in drawing a griffin—the longer the claws, and the larger the wings, the better; but that marvellous facility which we mistook for genius is apt to forsake us when we want to draw a real unexaggerated lion" (180). In *Middlemarch* the notion of realism as the reproduction of surfaces is corrected by that of penetration. The object, for Lydgate in a physiological sense, for George Eliot in social, moral, and psychological senses, is "to pierce the obscurity of those minute processes which prepare human misery and joy, those invisible thoroughfares which are the first lurking-places of anguish, mania, and crime, that delicate poise and transition which determine the growth of happy or unhappy consciousness" (xvi, 122).

The metaphor of scientific penetration should be supplemented by that of scientific connection, as found in *The Mill on the Floss:* "In natural science, I have understood, there is nothing petty to the mind that has a large vision of relations, and to which every single object suggests a vast sum of conditions. It is surely the same with the observation of human life" (IV, i, 239). The association of realism with science, usually made by naturalists like Zola, is here given the ethical emphasis characteristic of George Eliot's melioristic realism.[42] The relations, or connections between her characters, are not only causal, as the plot involves them in each other's lives, but also formal, in the parallels between the situations of characters who have little or no contact with each other.[43] Such connections are important objects for the author's and reader's joint enterprise of perception, which, as we have seen, forms a part of the context for the series of scenes which proceeds from Dorothea's experience in St. Peter's.

The scene in Chapter 34, where Dorothea and a few others watch Peter Featherstone's funeral from an upper window is, in the manner characteristic of George Eliot's temporal form, explicitly linked with the earlier moment. This scene "always came back to her at the touch of certain sensitive points in memory, just as the vision of St Peter's at Rome was inwoven with moods of despondency"

42. Bernard J. Paris has recently dealt at length with the role played by George Eliot's conception of science in relation to her realism and moral concerns. See *Experiments in Life: George Eliot's Quest for Values* (Detroit, 1965).

43. For George Eliot's conception of artistic form as an organic structure of interrelations, see "Notes on Form in Art (1868)," in *Essays*, pp. 431–36.

(238). Like Rome in her earlier experience, the funeral is "something alien and ill-understood" to Dorothea; its significance lies in the contrast of her response with those of the other spectators. "The country gentry of old time lived in a rarefied social air: dotted apart on their stations up the mountain they looked down with imperfect discrimination on the belts of thicker life below. And Dorothea was not at ease in the perspective and chilliness of that height." She has thus begun to resist the distorted vision her position enforces. Celia refuses to look any longer at a spectacle of such "melancholy things and ugly people," and to Mrs. Cadwallader the people they watch are "as curious as any buffaloes or bison," but Dorothea refuses to assent to this aloof attitude: "I am fond of knowing something about the people I live among. . . . It seems to me we know nothing of our neighbours, unless they are cottagers. One is constantly wondering what sort of lives other people lead, and how they take things." We can perhaps see here the effect of Dorothea's relations with Casaubon, creating an increasing awareness that he, like every other individual, has "an equivalent centre of self, whence the lights and shadows must always fall with a certain difference" (xxi, 157). Such recognition, and the concern it entails, is the ethical core of the task of perception; its artistic consequences are reflected in George Eliot's realistic rendering of a multiplicity of consciousnesses.[44] Al-

44. For a theoretical discussion of this aspect of the realistic novel as a parmount value, see Iris Murdoch, "The Sublime and the Beautiful Revisited," *Yale Review, 49* (1960), 247–71. Miss Murdoch maintains on epistemological and ethical grounds that the most important thing which the novel can reveal "is that other people exist" (p. 267). J. Hillis Miller, in *Poets of Reality: Six Twentieth-Century Writers* (Cambridge, Mass., 1965), places a similar emphasis on this feature of realism: "The objectivity of nineteenth-century fiction . . .

though Dorothea's concern cannot lead to action at this point, its expression marks her development toward clearer vision.

The development is completed in Chapter 80, when, as at Featherstone's funeral, Dorothea looks out from an upper window in the scene where, overcoming her anguish of jealousy and despair, she resolves to return to Rosamond. After a long struggle with her own feelings, she is able to subordinate them to her sense of the reality of those three other individuals, Will, Rosamond, and Lydgate. She asks herself, "What should I do—how should I act now, this very day, if I could clutch my own pain, and compel it to silence, and think of those three?" (577). The growth of sympathy and perception implicit here is then given symbolic form:

> It had taken long for her to come to that question, and there was light piercing into the room. She opened the curtains, and looked out towards the bit of road that lay in view, with fields beyond, outside the entrance-gates. On the road there was a man with a bundle on his back and a woman carrying her baby; in the field she could see figures moving—perhaps the shepherd with his dog. Far off in the bending sky was the pearly light; and she felt the largeness of the world and the manifold wakings of men to labour and endurance. She was a part of that involuntary, palpitating life, and could neither look out on it

is guaranteed not so much by the presence of independent material objects as by the presence of more than one consciousness. The realism of fiction is a realism of intersubjectivity" (p. 137). One could contrast Joyce, where realism does involve "the presence of independent material objects" at the same time that the range of consciousnesses is reduced.

from her luxurious shelter as a mere spectator, nor hide her eyes in selfish complaining. (578)

The large, receding perspective provides an appropriate setting for the recognition of the otherness of these figures and of their membership in the human community. The scene has been moved toward symbolism under the pressure of the crucial significance this moment bears in the novel and the impetus of diverse contextual elements. The window carries the recurrent symbolic value given it throughout George Eliot's works, and this particular setting has been given thematic significance by the integration of the house at Lowick into the novel's spatial metaphor. The scene is further illuminated by its position as the culmination of a series (one which involves other scenes besides those I have considered, such as those presenting Dorothea in her boudoir in Chapters 28, 37, and 54), a series which firmly establishes its connection with the theme of perception and its implications for author, reader, and characters. Thus the creation of symbolism is the result of an enormously rich and complex context as it is brought to bear upon the scene.

Yet even so the symbolism does not become the totally responsible vehicle of significance. The transcendence of egoism which is enacted symbolically is also presented in the narrator's commentary and rendering of Dorothea's thought, also embodying the spatial metaphor and theme of perception:

It was not in Dorothea's nature, for longer than the duration of a paroxysm, to sit in the narrow cell of her calamity, in the besotted misery of a consciousness that only sees another's lot as an accident of its own.

65

> She began now to live through that yesterday
> morning deliberately again, forcing herself to dwell
> on every detail and its possible meaning. Was she
> alone in that scene? Was it her event only? (577)

Symbolism thus remains a reinforcement, though a highly
powerful one, as it always does in the successful achievement of George Eliot's realism. Scenes remain primarily
the arena of a realistic human, not a symbolic, drama.

A Parenthesis on *MADAME BOVARY:*
New Directions and Indirections

In George Eliot's realism, symbol and the quasi-symbolic devices of imagery and metaphor generally remain auxiliary elements. They are capable of giving sharp focus to the significance of character and event and of relating the different characters and events of parallel plot lines in a pattern of larger significance, but they are rarely the primary agents of this process. Instead they appear as subordinate components of the general context established by George Eliot's narrator, a narrator of whose presence and characteristics we are made so fully aware that one critic of *Middlemarch* has been led to claim that "George Eliot is present as the only fully realized individual in her book."[1] In the half-century which saw the evolution of the English novel from *Middlemarch* to *Ulysses,* one of the most often noted developments is the disappearance of such a narrator. The subsequent critical rationalization of this process has led both to an exaggeration of its extent and to a hardening of its procedures, oversimplified, into prescriptive dogma,[2] but the basic fact of the personal, commenting narrator's progressive withdrawal remains, and is of fundamental importance.

1. Quentin Anderson, "George Eliot in *Middlemarch,*" in *From Dickens to Hardy,* ed. Boris Ford (Baltimore, 1958), p. 287.

2. For an account of this critical development as well as a detailed and energetic rebuttal of its excesses, see Wayne C. Booth, *The Rhetoric of Fiction* (Chicago, 1961).

Our understanding of developments in the novel after George Eliot can be greatly assisted by a brief consideration of Gustave Flaubert's *Madame Bovary*, where so many of them are prefigured. In this novel, published in 1856, when George Eliot was just beginning to turn to fiction, Flaubert had already largely abandoned the convention of the commenting narrator, which was to remain central in all her work. Flaubert's famous policy of impersonality ("No lyricism, no comments, the author's personality absent"[3]) is elaborated in many well-known pronouncements in his correspondence; our concern is to examine its practical implications regarding symbolism. Without authorial commentary to convey significance directly, Flaubert must turn to more indirect methods. Instead of explicit statements he develops various techniques of suggestion; *Madame Bovary* is, as Baudelaire observed, an "essentially suggestive book."[4]

One of the most characteristic of these techniques is that of juxtaposition. Flaubert creates several scenes in which the ironic implications arising from immediately contrasted elements act as a substitute for direct commentary. The most famous example is the brilliant scene of the *Comices Agricoles* (II, viii)[5] with its progressively tighter interplay of three levels of action as Emma and Rodolphe's romantic clichés are juxtaposed and merged with the rhetoric of the officials and the sounds of the

3. *The Selected Letters of Gustave Flaubert*, tr. and ed. Francis Steegmuller (New York, 1957), p. 127.

4. Charles Baudelaire, *"Madame Bovary,"* in *Flaubert: A Collection of Critical Essays*, ed. Raymond Giraud (Englewood Cliffs, N.J., 1964), p. 95.

5. Page references are to the translation by Francis Steegmuller (New York, Random House, 1957). I have also noted part and chapter numbers for the scenes to which I refer.

crowd and livestock. But this is only the most spectacular
instance of the technique. It is also used in the long scene
in the inn where Emma and Leon first meet (II, ii). Their
discussion of stock romantic settings, seascapes, sunsets,
and the mountains, is interwoven with Homais' pretentious scientific discourse on the advantages of the locality;
the two equally banal and self-congratulatory conversa-
tions cancel each other in the light of Flaubert's ironic
juxtaposition. Again, there is the scene in the cathedral at
Rouen (III, i), which juxtaposes Leon's impatient desire
with the verger's guidebook descant. Flaubert produces
not only comedy of cross-purposes but ironic implications
when Emma, about to enter her second squalid adultery,
is brought before the tomb of the royal mistress Diane de
Poitiers, or when the couple, about to enter the cab, their
mobile boudoir, are exhorted to observe "the Resurrection, the Last Judgment, Paradise, King David, and the
souls of the damned in the flames of Hell" (277–78). Such
scenes place far more weight on dialogue than George
Eliot's; her interspersed commentary is replaced by ironic
juxtaposition.

Another kind of oblique commentary is produced by
Flaubert's use of full-fledged symbols. As in George Eliot's
later novels, these may emerge from repeated images, of
which a well-known example is that of the butterflies,
black in the ashes of Emma's wedding bouquet, whose
destruction marks a stage in the deterioration of her marriage, and white in the fragments of the repudiating letter
to Leon, whose destruction marks her final acceptance of
adultery, the butterflies themselves perhaps suggesting
her aimless romantic aspirations. In George Eliot such a
parallel between scenes would be noted and perhaps
glossed by authorial commentary; Flaubert provides only
the symbolic suggestions of the repeated image. An object

may become symbolic, as does the plaster statue of the priest in the garden at Tostes, which reappears at intervals, scaling away under the effect of the weather as Emma deteriorates in her boredom, and finally smashed during the move to Yonville, prefiguring her destruction. Simple realistic incidents thus become symbolic through association. A more obtrusive creation of symbol is the blind beggar, whose song joins the erotic with his physical corruption. He is maneuvered into position so as to reappear while Emma lies on her deathbed, setting a capstone of horror on her death and symbolically emphasizing the corruption to which her own "dreams of love" have led. Such symbolism, like dialogue in the scenes, plays a more important part than it does in George Eliot, since it appears without any explicating commentary, but it does not in itself represent any fundamental innovation in the novel. More striking than this overt symbolism is Flaubert's ability to develop suggestions from descriptions which do not fully convert their objects to symbols, the techniques whereby he moves his narrative onto a level between the exclusively literal meaning of surface realism and one where the real is subordinated to the control of symbolic motives.

In the world of *Madame Bovary* every object is capable of being made to yield suggestions of meaning, like Charles' grotesque schoolboy cap, which "suggests unplumbed depths, like an idiot's face" (4). The depths are, of course, only reflected in the object; they are actually located in the human mind which creates it or perceives it in a certain light, as Charles' cap and, later, Emma's wedding cake, which contains a similar mélange of styles, reflect the pretentious tastelessness of the bourgeois society which creates and admires them. These are presented in bravura set pieces, but Flaubert can also make quite ordinary objects yield glimpses of the depths under the pressure of his style. A striking and sustained example is the treatment of Les Bertaux, the Rouault farm. We see it from the viewpoint of Charles, for whom it is, without his ever becoming very fully conscious of it, a new realm of sensuous richness. The reader, remembering Charles' emotional deprivation under the domination first of his mother and then of the widow he marries, senses in the first description of the farmyard in Chapter 2 of Part I that this is to be a new development. But we are not dependent only on the general context of preceding narrative to recognize the contrast; Flaubert employs his characteristic technique of immediate juxtaposition to emphasize it. As Charles, half asleep, rides through the half-light toward Les Bertaux, his mind blends fragments of past and present, his life as student and husband, in a composite image of his experience up to this point. At the same time, the landscape through which he passes symbolically suggests the quality of this experience: the rutted road and leafless trees, the flat countryside, a "vast gray surface that merged at the horizon into the dull tone of the sky," combine to image his drab past. As he enters the farmyard, it opens before him and the reader as a promise of new delight:

It was a prosperous-looking farm. Through the open upper-halves of the stable doors great plough-horses could be seen placidly feeding from new racks. Next to the out-buildings stood a big manure pile, and in among the chickens and turkeys pecking at its steaming surface were five or six peacocks—favorite show pieces of *cauchois* farmyards. The sheepfold was long, the barn lofty, its walls as smooth as your hand. In the shed were two large carts and four ploughs complete

71

> with whips, horse collars and full trappings, the blue
> wool pads gray under the fine dust that sifted down
> from the lofts. The farmyard sloped upwards, planted
> with symmetrically spaced trees, and from near the
> pond came the merry sound of a flock of geese. (16)

It is a realistic description; the details are not in themselves symbolic, but in context their cumulative effect of
prosperity and sensuous life creates symbolic suggestions.
These are developed in Charles' observations of Emma.
He finds himself noting the whiteness of her fingernails,
her dark eyes, and the way her hair waves slightly over her
temples, "a detail that the country doctor now observed
for the first time in his life" (18). Les Bertaux acquires for
Charles, unconsciously, the meaning it has already been
given symbolically for the reader, and he finds himself
returning again and again. "He enjoyed the moment of
arrival, the feel of the gate as it yielded against his
shoulder" (19), savoring his sensations and emotions without attempting to comprehend them. The growing unconscious sexual feelings between Charles and Emma
are beautifully suggested in this well-known description:

> She always accompanied him to the foot of the steps
> outside the door. If his horse hadn't been brought
> around she would wait there with him. At such
> moments they had already said good-bye, and stood
> there silent; the breeze eddied around her, swirling
> the stray wisps of hair at her neck, or sending her
> apron strings flying like streamers around her waist.
> Once she was standing there on a day of thaw, when
> the bark of the trees in the farmyard was oozing sap
> and the snow was melting on the roofs. She went
> inside for her parasol, and opened it. The parasol was
> of rosy iridescent silk, and the sun pouring through it

painted the white skin of her face with flickering patches of light. Beneath it she smiled at the spring-like warmth: and drops of water could be heard falling one by one on the taut moiré. (20)

The superficial reader might see here only a lovely description (one whose beauty is increased by the delicate rhythms and patterned vowel sounds of the original), bearing no organic relation to the narrative as a whole.[6] But in fact it is as suffused with sexuality as Emma's face is with the rosy light. The characters' silence, the tautness of the silk, the drops measuring time in a moment of suspension, all contribute to an image of sexual tension of which only the author and his reader, not the characters, are aware.

The scenic presentation of emotional states in the characters which their own inadequate consciousnesses are incapable of reflecting and which the narrator usually declines to convey directly requires such techniques of indirection. To meet this necessity Flaubert uses his powers of description to create analogues in the external world for the internal states of his characters. The use of such analogues or objective correlatives was not in itself an innovation; we have seen comparable effects created by both Dickens and George Eliot. Flaubert's method differs in two respects. First, because he avoids the more direct means of narrative analysis and commentary, these analogues play a more prominent role, functioning as more important vehicles of meaning than they do in George Eliot. Second, because they are not made so obviously and insistently correlative as those created by Dickens' use of pathetic fallacy and emblematic writing, they remain far more oblique and hence closer to modern

6. Such is the reaction of Martin Turnell. See *The Novel in France* (New York, 1958), p. 316.

73

symbolism. In scenes such as the one presented above, the creation of an objective correlative does not involve establishing detailed correspondences but rather depends on the suggestive power of style and the articulation of the entire passage as an integral verbal construct. Such scenes, vibrating between realism and symbolism, clearly point forward to the Joycean epiphany.

More directly relevant to novelists of the period, especially George Eliot and James, is Flaubert's management of point of view. His techniques of indirection, in which the implications of ostensibly neutral descriptions move toward symbolism as they fill the vacuum left by the commenting narrator's withdrawal, serve to communicate with the reader behind the characters' backs. The denial of clear perception to his characters is closely akin to Flaubert's sharper ironic effects and is a part of his consistent maintenance of a point of view superior to theirs. The selection and ordering of the material makes it appear to comment on itself, rendered in a slightly distanced, finely wrought style which constitutes, as Erich Auerbach has observed, a point of view in itself, the only locus of intelligence in a world filled by human stupidity.[7]

George Eliot also creates ironic communication, often, in the later novels, by the indirect means of imagery as well as by direct comment. But her irony is always balanced by pity, and her characters, unlike those of Flaubert, are sometimes capable of developing to a level of perception equal, in essentials, with that of author and reader. Such moments occur in Maggie's declaration of loyalty to the past and in Dorothea's affirmation of responsibility to others. Not only moral perception but a kind of awareness

7. *Mimesis: The Representation of Reality in Western Literature* (Garden City, N.Y., 1957), p. 432. See his stylistic analysis of Flaubert's techniques of revelation in a single paragraph, pp. 426–34.

of symbolic significance seems open to these characters; Dorothea, ordering her ritual change of dress before seeing Rosamond, seems almost as conscious as the reader that she is acting on a symbolic level. This kind of awareness is rare in George Eliot, but it reveals the greater possibilities open to consciousness in the world of her novels, possibilities which Henry James was to extend much further.

HENRY JAMES: The Creations of Consciousness

The work of Henry James occupies a central position in the transition from traditional to modern fictional modes. Beginning in a mode quite close to that of George Eliot's realism, he develops increasingly symbolic techniques of presentation. Not only does James' career present a prominent example of changing mode, but his high degree of artistic consciousness, reflected in his novels as well as in his criticism, offers valuable indications of the crucial factors involved in this change. Thus his own critical comments help to indicate his relationship to the two novelists we have already examined.

Flaubert's denial of perception to his characters was the aspect of his method to which James most objected. It is not clear how fully he appreciated Flaubert's ability to arrange and stylize the external world into a set of objective correlatives for his characters' inward states; it was the sheer externality of the method that struck him most. "M. Flaubert's theory as a novelist, briefly expressed," he wrote in an early essay, "is to begin on the outside. Human life, we may imagine him saying, is before all things a spectacle, an occupation and entertainment for the eyes."[1] To James the visual rendering of externals could never assume such great importance; his method was to begin from the inside. When he looked within Flaubert's charac-

1. "Charles de Bernard and Gustave Flaubert" (1876), in *French Poets and Novelists* (New York, 1964), p. 201.

ters, he felt the inadequacy of their consciousnesses for any comprehension of their experience, any reflection of it for the reader. Emma Bovary as a "vessel of experience," was "really too small an affair." She and Frédéric Moreau, the hero of *L'Education Sentimentale,* are hopelessly inadequate "as special conduits of the life [Flaubert] proposed to depict," and his choice of "such limited reflectors and registers" seems explicable only "by a defect of his mind."[2]

The desire for central characters who can act as more capacious vessels of experience, more highly polished reflectors, aligns James with George Eliot, whose protagonists, unlike those of Flaubert, often progress to a level of awareness where they can grasp at least a part of the meaning of their experience. In the Preface to *The Princess Casamassima,* which, of all the Prefaces, is the one most fully concerned with the reflecting central consciousness, James clearly relates this concern to the work of George Eliot. He admires her efforts to center interest in the minds of her major characters and records the effect, comparable to his own: "Their emotions, their stirred intelligence, their moral consciousness, become thus . . . our own very adventure."[3] But James also had his quarrel with George Eliot: her novels failed to become works of art intensely organized and "done" in that manner for which Flaubert provided a striking example. This objection was most often stated in terms of form; George Eliot's novels seemed to him insufficiently unified. He judged *Middlemarch* as "a treasure-house of detail, but . . . an indifferent whole."[4]

2. "Gustave Flaubert" (1902), in *Selected Literary Criticism,* ed. Morris Shapira (New York, 1965), p. 222.

3. "Preface to *The Princess Casamassima,*" in *The Art of the Novel,* ed. Richard P. Blackmur (New York, 1934), p. 70.

4. "George Eliot's *Middlemarch*" (1873), in *The Future of the Novel,* ed. Leon Edel (New York, 1956), p. 81.

Madame Bovary, despite its less attractive subject matter, displayed "a final unsurpassable form," which forced him to conclude that "the work is a classic because the thing, such as it is, is ideally *done,* and because it shows that in such doing eternal beauty may dwell."[5]

Recent criticism has effectively shown how James' limited conception of form, with its demand for a single center of composition, prevented his perceiving the different sort of unity achieved in George Eliot's novels, with their structure of multiple, interrelated centers.[6] But James' emphasis on the more conspicuous kind of form created by Flaubert indicates not only a difference between his own and George Eliot's conceptions of unity but a more fundamental difference in their methods of creating meaning. In Flaubert, form, creating such effects as ironic juxtaposition, becomes an indirect vehicle of meaning, replacing the more direct comments and generalizations of the omniscient narrator. James reveals a desire for a more indirect, more suggestive method than George Eliot's when, quite early in his career, he criticizes the explicitness of the ending of *Adam Bede.* Instead of showing the marriage of Adam and Dinah, he would prefer simply the suggestion of its possibility:

> The assurance of this possibility is what I should have desired the author to place the sympathetic reader at a standpoint to deduce for himself. In every novel the work is divided between the writer and the reader; but the writer makes the reader very much as he makes his characters. When he makes him ill, that

5. "Gustave Flaubert," in *Selected Literary Criticism,* p. 221.

6. See, for example, the examination of James' criticism of George Eliot in the first chapter of W. J. Harvey, *The Art of George Eliot* (London, 1961), especially pp. 17–32.

is, makes him indifferent, he does no work; the writer
does all. When he makes him well, that is, makes him
interested, then the reader does quite half the labor.
In making such a deduction as I have just indicated,
the reader would be doing but his share of the task;
the grand point is to get him to make it. I hold that
there is a way. It is perhaps a secret; but until it is
found out, I think that the art of story-telling cannot
be said to have approached perfection.[7]

This looks forward to the more open endings of James'
novels, but more generally it shows him already groping
toward a method in which indirect presentation would
force a more active role on the reader in the creation of
meaning.

This sketch of the theoretic relationship between James
and his two predecessors, indicating his affinities and
quarrels with each, suggests the lines along which his own
practice develops. Like Flaubert, he seeks an indirect, suggestive method of presentation; but unlike him, and more
like George Eliot, he achieves this indirect presentation
through reflection in the consciousnesses of his characters.
Despite the increasing divergence between James' fiction
and George Eliot's, his novels, like hers, repeatedly center
on the growth of individual consciousnesses. What he
wrote of *The Ambassadors* could be applied to many of the
major works of both novelists: "the business of my tale and
the march of my action, not to say the precious moral of
everything, is just my demonstration of this process of
vision."[8]

The ways in which James shares, modifies, and departs

7. "The Novels of George Eliot" (1866), in *A Century of George
Eliot Criticism*, ed. Gordon S. Haight (Boston, 1965), p. 48.
8. "Preface to *The Ambassadors*," in *The Art of the Novel*, p. 308.

from George Eliot's practice can be observed in *The Portrait of a Lady*. Its indebtedness to *Daniel Deronda* has been sufficiently discussed by F. R. Leavis, and its connections with *Middlemarch* are no less close; Isabel surely owes as much to Dorothea as to Gwendolen. The similarities of method are often as striking as those of subject, especially in James' use of the omniscient narrator. The narrator frequently steps forward, admitting not only his presence, but his role in organizing and presenting the narrative: " 'Tell me what they do in America,' pursued Madame Merle, who, it must be observed, parenthetically, did not deliver herself all at once of these reflections, which are presented in a cluster for the convenience of the reader."[9] He also refers at several points to the fact of his omniscience. Caspar Goodwood is first presented from Isabel's point of view, "but," the narrator remarks, "the reader has a right to a nearer and clearer view,"[10] and he proceeds with an exposition of Caspar's background. Similarly, he later informs us that "the reader already knows more about [Ralph] than Isabel was ever to know" (II, 247), where his omniscience provides not only a superior viewpoint but also foreknowledge. At times this drawing

9. *The Portrait of a Lady* (London, 1881), I, 255. Since I am taking this novel as an example of James' early practice, I refer to the first, unrevised edition. Certain of James' later revisions are indicated where relevant. Subsequent references are to this edition, except where noted, and are incorporated in the text.

References to other James novels are, unless otherwise noted, to the New York Edition: *The Novels and Tales of Henry James* (26 vols. New York, Charles Scribner's Sons, 1907–17). Page and, where appropriate, volume numbers are incorporated in the text.

10. This is actually the revised form of the phrase (New York Edition, I, 163), which originally read "but the reader has a right to a description less metaphysical" (I, 147). In this case, the revision makes the narrator's function and presence even clearer.

of attention to the narrator can become as superfluous a mannerism as it does in George Eliot's earliest and most awkward uses of the convention: when Henrietta writes Caspar a note, we are told that "It is our privilege to look over her shoulder, and if we exercise it we may read the brief query" (III, 72).

More important than these indications of the operative convention is the use James makes of it for extended exposition and analysis of character. In Chapter 6 the progress of the narrative is suspended for several pages while the narrator provides a detailed analysis of Isabel's character, just as George Eliot does with Lydgate in Chapter 15 of *Middlemarch*. In both cases, we are given information to fill in the character's background and a probing, judicious evaluation of strengths and weaknesses which prepares us for subsequent developments. James stresses Isabel's imaginative, "theoretical" outlook and suggests the way it involves both a valuable sensitivity and a liability to error: "The girl had a certain nobleness of imagination which rendered her a good many services and played her a great many tricks" (I, 62). At the same time that he humorously exhibits her weaknesses, he also takes the stance of the protective author who would not have his heroine judged too harshly. The long concluding sentence attempts to balance all these elements in a final summation:

> Altogether, with her meagre knowledge, her inflated ideals, her confidence at once innocent and dogmatic, her temper at once exacting and indulgent, her mixture of curiosity and fastidiousness, of vivacity and indifference, her determination to see, to try, to know; her combination of the delicate, desultory, flame-like spirit and the eager and personal young girl; she

> would be an easy victim of scientific criticism, if she
> were not intended to awaken on the reader's part an
> impulse more tender and more purely expectant. (63)

Despite James' similarity and, indeed, indebtedness to George Eliot in his use of the omniscient narrator, there remain important differences. His narrator is never the full, personal presence which "George Eliot" becomes; no one would claim that James is the most fully realized individual in *his* book. This more restrained use of the convention also affects the function of the narrator as a source for a context in whose terms meaning may appear. James' narrator never rises to the levels of generalization reached by George Eliot's. He may provide us with analysis and limited evaluation of character, but there is nothing like the passage at the close of Chapter 21 of *Middlemarch,* which generalizes on the universality of egoism and locates Dorothea as emerging from "that stupidity." Such general, philosophic passages establish, as I have shown, a stable conceptual framework in whose terms the meaning of George Eliot's novels may be formulated. James provides no such framework. Its absence is reflected in the criticism devoted not just to *The Portrait of a Lady* but to all James' works; there is no general agreement on the terms in which they should be read.[11]

The greater difficulty of interpreting James' fiction is not caused by gratuitous elusiveness, a willful avoidance of the explicit, but by the greater complexity of his meaning. This complexity becomes, of course, more apparent in the later novels, but its origins may be noted in the

11. In a general historical perspective, this difference reflects a cultural change. The stable conceptual terms of value which still served George Eliot no longer bear sufficient authority for James.

early work. The reader of *The Portrait of a Lady* is not left without a context of elements providing a basis for interpretation, but none of them bears the authority of George Eliot's moral and philosophical generalizations. One such element is the novel's imagery, more conspicuous because more elaborate and sustained than George Eliot's. There is, for example, the recurrent architectural imagery, often noted by commentators, which performs numerous variations on the traditional analogy of self and house. I have already discussed its use in Dickens and George Eliot, but here it is developed far more extensively and consistently. Dickens vividly animates surroundings with the psychic qualities of their inhabitants, but the results tend to be local, emblematic configurations rather than parts of an extended symbolic structure. George Eliot presents the house at Lowick as a symbolic setting for the moral qualities of Casaubon and Dorothea, but again it is an isolated case, not reinforced by the development of comparable significance in other houses or by architectural imagery in the narrator's figures (just as the narrator's figurative water imagery for moral states finds no literal counterpart). In James this thematic imagery is woven through both figurative and literal levels, in the narrator's comments and in the characters' thoughts and speech. Thus Ralph characterizes Henrietta as "too personal. . . . She walks in without knocking at the door," and Isabel agrees: "She thinks one's door should stand ajar" (I, 117).

Conversely, literal structures characterize their inhabitants. Osmond's house in Florence suggests his duplicity long before it appears in his actions: its "imposing front" has a "somewhat incommunicative character."

> It was the mask of the house; it was not its face.
> It had heavy lids, but no eyes; the house in reality

> looked another way—looked off behind. . . . The
> windows of the ground-floor, as you saw them from
> the piazza, were, in their noble proportions, ex-
> tremely architectural; but their function seemed to
> be less to offer communication with the world than
> to defy the world to look in. (II, 27–28)

The description makes a sustained double reference, so detailed and precise that it tends toward the emblematic. Looser and more suggestive is the way Isabel's whole career is presented in terms of a succession of houses. Her home in Albany, and especially her favorite room there, create an image of imaginative self-enclosure; the bolted outside door, its sidelights filled with green paper, allows her as a child to imagine "a strange, unseen place on the other side." She has "no wish to look out" and even when she is grown up has "never assured herself that the vulgar street lay beyond" (I, 27–28). From this confinement she moves suddenly to the large, expansive world of Garden-court, with its great ancient trees and "wide carpet of turf" stretching off toward the distant river. The contrast of setting suggests the expansion of consciousness which Isabel will experience in Europe, just as the weathered old house itself, with "a name and a history" presents an image of the rich, historical reality she is to encounter there. These images must be remembered if we are fully to appreciate the disastrous reversal given to this movement of expansion when Isabel at last finds herself not moving in realms of space and light, but trapped in the darkly named Palazzo Roccanero. "She could live it over again, the incredulous terror with which she had taken the measure of her dwelling. Between those four walls she had lived ever since; they were to surround her for the rest of her life. It was the house of darkness, the house of dumbness, the

house of suffocation" (III, 37). Here literal and metaphorical levels have joined, focusing all the sequences of
architectural imagery at a climactic moment.

So extensive is the organization of this imagery that it is
capable of touching even the most incidental details with
suggestions of significance. It seems ominously appropriate, for example, that Isabel sees Madame Merle again for
the first time after learning of her inheritance, appearing
for the first time to that worldly woman as someone who
can be used, under the sign on the Touchetts' house in
Winchester Square: "This noble freehold mansion to be
sold" (II, 1). Such a degree of organization creates a system of signifying devices which is not only more complex
but more self-contained and self-referential than George
Eliot's structures of imagery. The same basic spatial metaphor of confinement and expansion runs through both
authors' imagery, but in James it is not so readily trans-
latable into fixed conceptual terms; we cannot make such
equations as that of confinement with egoism. Value and
disvalue, the opposition between development and restriction of the self, are sufficiently apparent, but they are
not very easily abstracted from the images in which they
are embodied. One reason for this is that George Eliot's
architectural imagery is only one embodiment of the
larger spatial metaphor, itself controlled in turn by her
conceptual framework. In James, however, the architectural imagery is a larger system than the spatial metaphor
and includes other thematic problems, such as the relation
between a character's facade and inner nature. The result
is a complex cluster of intersecting analogies rather than
an illustrative embodiment of a single general category.

The problematic nature of James' thematic context appears more clearly when concrete images become associated with more abstract elements. At one point the

series of architectural images becomes the basis for a
philosophical debate which provides conceptual terms for
the novel's themes.[12] Madame Merle asks Isabel whether
her ideal suitor has a "castle in the Apennines" or "an
ugly brick house on Fortieth Street."

> "I don't care anything about his house," said Isabel.
> "That's very crude of you. When you have lived as
> long as I, you will see that every human being has his
> shell, and that you must take the shell into account.
> By the shell I mean the whole envelope of circum-
> stances. There is no such thing as an isolated man or
> woman; we are each of us made up of a cluster of
> appurtenances. What do you call one's self? Where
> does it begin? Where does it end? It overflows into
> everything that belongs to us—and then it flows
> back again."

Isabel takes the opposite position in this "very metaphysical" discussion:

> "I don't agree with you," she said. "I think just the
> other way. I don't know whether I succeed in express-
> ing myself, but I know that nothing else expresses me.
> Nothing that belongs to me is any measure of me; on
> the contrary, it's a limit, a barrier, and a perfectly
> arbitrary one." (I, 259–60)

This debate introduces terms which are directly relevant
to the novel's subsequent action. The question of the relation of externals and the self (which points toward the
traditional problems of both appearance and reality and
free will and determinism), set in the context of choosing

12. The thematic relevance of this debate has been discussed by
Frederick C. Crews, in *The Tragedy of Manners: Moral Drama in the
Later Novels of Henry James* (New Haven, Conn., 1957), pp. 13–18.

a suitor, bears closely on Isabel's subsequent career. She believes that Osmond is what he seems and that she is a free agent in choosing him but discovers that his appearance was false and that, in effect, "Madame Merle had married her" (III, 151).

The novel does not enable us to identify either side of the debate as correct. The introduction of these generalizations by the characters themselves rather than by the omniscient narrator diminishes their authority. Isabel is forced to reconsider the relation of circumstances to the self. She *must* begin to consider her husband's "house" when she at last recognizes it as "the house of darkness, the house of dumbness, the house of suffocation." Events show the power of externals to exert greater influence on the self than Isabel had admitted, but they do not establish their "true" relation. The questions of what to call one's self, whether or not it "overflows into everything . . . and then . . . flows back again," whether appearance and reality interpenetrate or are opposed, whether free will or determinism controls events, remain unanswered. The contextual terms generated by the characters' debate are clearly relevant, but their effect is more to introduce a problem than to present a thesis.

The introduction of contextual elements in the form of debate dramatizes the tension which often exists between James' thematic terms. Another such set of terms, especially noteworthy because of the important role they play in the later novels, are those usually categorized as "moral" and "aesthetic," designating rival orders of value or modes of experience. Their importance is attested by the frequency with which critics have found them necessary for interpreting *The Portrait of a Lady,* and their problematic nature is reflected in the lack of critical agreement on the relation between them. Moral terms are clearly involved,

for example, in Isabel's several decisions and in the exploitation of her by Osmond and Madame Merle. The
realm of the aesthetic is explicitly involved in the novel's
extensive art imagery, in the way the characters view each
other as works of art, and in their direct aesthetic experiences. What is the relation between these two areas? According to W. J. Harvey, it is one of substitution: "Aesthetic value becomes a metaphor for moral value,"[13]
while Dorothea Krook is equally certain that the aesthetic
is subordinated to the moral: James' "truth . . . is in the
first instance moral and only secondarily and derivatively
aesthetic."[14] Dorothy Van Ghent attributes to James a
conviction of "the profound identity of the aesthetic and
the moral,"[15] but (since there can be no harm in introducing one more variation) I would suggest that this
phrase is more descriptive of James' goal than his assumption. Mr. Harvey complains that "the traffic between the
two areas is often equivocal and ambiguous";[16] I believe
that, rather than indicating a weakness in the novel, this
describes an aspect of its meaning, a meaning which arises
from the tensions established between its terms rather
than from any stable ordering of them. Again, we are confronted more with a problem than a thesis. I shall not
attempt to support these suggestions by presenting an
interpretation of *The Portrait of a Lady;* the problems
indicated here can be considered more profitably in the
later novels, where they receive fuller development, especially in *The Golden Bowl.* My present concern is only
to introduce another, and crucial, instance of the greater

13. *Character and the Novel* (London, 1965), p. 46.

14. *The Ordeal of Consciousness in Henry James* (Cambridge, 1962), p. 59.

15. "On *The Portrait of a Lady*," in *The English Novel: Form and Function* (New York, 1961), p. 217.

16. *Character and the Novel,* p. 50.

complexity of the context from which James' meaning emerges. In such elements we can see the origins of the famous Jamesian ambiguity and irony and thus can note, even in this early work, which is in many ways much closer to George Eliot's novels than to his own later works, the beginning of James' divergence from her practice.

The contrast which appears in contextual elements of the two novelists is also reflected in their different creative processes. George Eliot proceeds from the general concept to its particular embodiment; James' imagination characteristically moves in the opposite direction. Beginning with a "germ," a suggestive fragment of concrete experience, he develops its implications into narrative form. The process is described in several of the Prefaces, most fully in that to *The Spoils of Poynton,* and its record is preserved in the notebooks, where we can see James "ciphering out" the ramifications of each initial germ. Remembering this basic opposition, we can understand James' uneasiness in sensing that George Eliot "proceeds from the abstract to the concrete." The most general levels of his novels' meaning tend not to reflect stable, a priori concepts, but to be the furthest extension of his germ's suggestion, bearing the reflexive quality we have already seen in *The Portrait's* imagery, and therefore potentially more problematic and ambiguous. He feels in George Eliot's sensibility the predominance of "her moral consciousness" and "the absence of free aesthetic life";[17] I have already briefly noted the way in which the interaction of these two areas complicates James' meaning in *The Portrait of a Lady.* This review of Cross' biography, written only five years later, reflects his awareness of the

17. "The Life of George Eliot," in *Discussions of George Eliot,* ed. Richard Stang (Boston, 1960), p. 8.

factors which have begun to differentiate his practice from
George Eliot's.

To consider as contextual such elements of *The Portrait
of a Lady* as the narrator, imagery, and general terms introduced by the characters is to impose a somewhat artificial, though useful, analytic scheme upon factors involved
in the creation of meaning. Meaning actually emerges
from this context in specific scenes; it becomes concentrated primarily through the agency of the central consciousness, the factor whose crucial importance I have
already noted in my opening examination of James'
theory. Isabel Archer is one of those characters in whom
James always found "the leading interest of any human
hazard," possessed of "a consciousness . . . subject to fine
intensification and wide enlargement."[18] She exemplifies
the expansion of consciousness experienced by several of
James' central characters, passionate pilgrims to Europe
who encounter the greater richness of its aesthetic and historical reality as well as the greater complexity and possible treachery of its moral reality. This expansion, symbolized by her movement from the enclosure of the house in
Albany to the amplitude of Gardencourt, involves not only
a quantitative increase of experience but an increasing
awareness of new modes. "Hitherto her visions of a completed life had concerned themselves largely with moral
images" (I, 130),[19] but her encounters with Madame

18. "Preface to *The Princess Casamassima*," in *The Art of the
Novel*, p. 67.

19. James' revision of this phrase reveals the particular aspect
under which "life" appears: Isabel's "visions of a completed life" become "visions of a completed consciousness" (New York Edition, I,
143). James frequently replaces such terms as "feelings" or "thoughts"
with "consciousness," a reflection of his fuller awareness of the precise
nature of his subject.

Merle, and later with Osmond, reveal new possibilities. Madame Merle introduces her to aesthetic appreciation, whether in an attitude of connoisseurship toward other persons or in`the savoring of simple sensations like the smells of "English rain" or a wool coat (I, 244). Osmond helps introduce her to the aesthetic and historical qualities of Italy, with which he is always associated. Isabel's first experience of Rome is presented as a continuous expansion of consciousness. This, for example, is her response to St. Peter's:

> The first time she passed beneath the huge leathern curtain that strains and bangs at the entrance—the first time she found herself beneath the far-arching dome and saw the light drizzle down through the air thickened with incense and with the reflections of marble and gilt, of mosaic and bronze, her conception of greatness received an extension. After this it never lacked space to soar. (II, 114)

It presents a striking contrast to Dorothea Brooke's experience on the same spot. The Jamesian consciousness is engaged in problems of aesthetic as well as moral perception in its process of growth and enrichment.

Yet even in this process of expansion Isabel is moving toward a disastrous failure of perception, leading to her acceptance of Osmond and the subsequent frustration of all expansive efforts. The problem of perception, generating the theme usually categorized as Illusion and Reality, is traditional in the novel, but James departs from the traditional scheme. In George Eliot, as in Jane Austen and many others, it is a problem of discovery, of recognizing what is there, morally and factually, a goal to be achieved by the removal of obstacles to clear perception. The "sensibility" of Marianne Dashwood or the "prejudice" of

Elizabeth Bennet, like the egoism of George Eliot's heroes and heroines, are such obstacles, which must be overcome. In Isabel, the crucial factor, repeatedly indicated by James' commentary, is her imagination, but it does not only appear under the negative aspect of obstacles; it has the dual quality already noted: "The girl had a certain nobleness of imagination which rendered her a good many services and played her a great many tricks" (I, 62). Isabel's favorite room in the house in Albany suggests not only enclosure but deliberate insulation; she ignores the "vulgar" reality beyond in order to indulge her imagination. James likewise suggests that in her "repressed ecstasy of contemplation" in Rome she may be similarly out of touch with reality, "seeing often in the things she looked at a great deal more than was there, and yet not seeing many of the items enumerated in 'Murray'" (II, 105). A set of revisions which bears significantly on this aspect of Isabel's character introduces into the novel's conceptual context the term "romantic," applied to her attitudes and also used by her as a term of value.[20] James defined the term, as opposed to "real," in his Preface to *The American:*

> The real represents to my perception the things we cannot possibly *not* know, sooner or later, in one way or another. . . . The romantic stands, on the other hand, for the things that, with all the facilities in the world, all the wealth and all the courage and all the wit and all the adventure, we never *can* directly know; the things that can reach us only through the beautiful circuit and subterfuge of our thought and our desire.[21]

20. These revisions are cited by F. O. Matthiessen in *Henry James: The Major Phase* (New York, 1963), pp. 154–55.

21. "Preface to *The American*," in *The Art of the Novel*, pp. 31–32.

This romanticism, rather than acting simply as a liability, bears the dual aspect of which I have spoken. It is surely the subterfuge of Isabel's romantic, theoretical thought and desire, in conjunction with the subterfuge of others, which leads to her mistake. She later realizes that, during Osmond's courtship of her, "she had imagined a world of things that had no substance" (III, 34). But it is also only by the indirection of subjective response, the circuities of consciousness, that the bare facts of the real can acquire meaning and value. We, and James, may no longer wish to describe this positive aspect with the loaded term "romantic," but we must recognize that it involves the same qualities of imagination, which may exercise either a deceptive or valuably creative function.

For the result of Isabel's tragic experience is not merely the loss of romantic illusions and a recognition of harsh reality. We see instead a growth of consciousness, a new sensitivity of imagination in her state of suffering, reflected in the change in her response to Rome:

> She had long before this taken old Rome into her confidence, for in a world of ruins the ruin of her happiness seemed a less unnatural catastrophe. She rested her weariness upon things that had crumbled for centuries and yet still were upright; she dropped her secret sadness into the silence of lonely places, where its very modern quality detached itself and grew objective, so that as she sat in a sun-warmed angle on a winter's day, or stood in a mouldy church to which no one came, she could almost smile at it and think of its smallness. Small it was, in the large Roman record, and her haunting sense of the continuity of the human lot easily carried her from the less to the greater. She had become deeply, tenderly

acquainted with Rome; it interfused and moderated her passion. But she had grown to think of it chiefly as the place where people had suffered. This was what came to her in the starved churches, where the marble columns, transferred from pagan ruins, seemed to offer her a companionship in endurance, and the musty incense to be a compound of long-unanswered prayers. (III, 152)

Here James presents, in a kind of prose poem which again involves the pervasive architectural imagery, the greater depth of meaning which Isabel is capable of feeling and, in that act of consciousness, creating for herself and for the reader. The meaning she creates is not a great deal more "objective" than were her earlier romantic fantasies, but it is more valid. Although it could be viewed simply as a projection of her own sadness on her surroundings, an example of pathetic fallacy, it also reaches out to one genuine meaning to be found in history. Her creation is a discovery as well. Furthermore, its effect is not the indulgence of her personal feelings but rather the opposite. The passage, indeed, presents the way in which James' heroine succeeds in transcending her egoism, and the phrase about "the continuity of the human lot" strikes a note quite close to George Eliot's in indicating the considerations which lead away from egoistic self-absorption. But besides her recognition of continuity with others, Isabel's experience also includes creative, imaginative qualities which play no part in the meaning revealed to Dorothea. Her vision seems to offer, on its own modest scale, a tentative reconciliation of the romantic and the real.[22]

22. It should furthermore be noted that this imaginative capacity is not only expressed in a generalized sense of "the continuity of the

The potential creativity of the imaginative Jamesian consciousness is from the first an important factor in his fictional mode, but only in the later novels does it receive full dramatic presentation and assume a central thematic function. In the earlier novels, such as *The Portrait of a Lady,* the crucial moments in which meaning is crystallized tend to take the form of more traditional recognition scenes. Dorothy Van Ghent notes that, "in adopting as his compositional center the growth of a consciousness, James was able to use the bafflements and illusions of ignorance for his 'complications,' as he was able to use, more consistently than any other novelist, 'recognitions' for his crises."[23] In *The Portrait of a Lady* the plot turns on the series of recognitions in which Isabel becomes fully aware of the position in which her marriage has placed her and perceives as well the hidden forces which have manipulated her. Her growing awareness of the true relationship between Osmond and Madame Merle begins, like the growth of a Jamesian novel, with a small germ, the chance discovery of the pair together in a situation suggesting a closer relationship than they have allowed to appear. Osmond is seated, Madame Merle standing, each silent but looking at the other; the brief vision "made an image,

---

human lot." We also find it when, even as the Countess Gemini reveals how Isabel has been deceived and exploited by Madame Merle and Osmond, she is able to feel imaginative sympathy for the woman who has had to resign any claim to her child: "Ah, poor creature!" —"Poor woman!" she says of Madame Merle (III, 185–86). James also emphasizes the positive value of this capacity by contrasting Isabel with Mrs. Touchett, whose habitual denial of her feelings has left her unable to respond adequately to her son's death, deprived of any sense of pain or remorse, which are described as "enrichments of consciousness" in the New York Edition, II, 407.

23. *The English Novel,* pp. 215–16.

lasting only a moment, like a sudden flicker of light. Their relative position, their absorbed mutual gaze, struck her as something detected" (III, 10). The minute germ of suggestion, planted here in her consciousness, eventually flowers in shattering recognition.

The memory of this moment returns to Isabel at the beginning and end of her long meditative vigil, the novel's central recognition scene (III, 29–45). One index to its functional importance is the number of passages from these pages I have already cited, recognitions which present crucial formulations concerning Isabel, Osmond, and their marriage. These observations do not depend on the analysis of the omniscient narrator; they are produced by the character's consciousness. "Her mind, assailed by visions, [is] in a state of extraordinary activity" (44), achieving a great advance in understanding her situation. At the close of his Preface James singles out this scene as exemplifying the possibility of "an 'exciting' inward life":

> Reduced to its essence, it is but the vigil of searching criticism; but it throws the action further forward than twenty "incidents" might have done. It was designed to have all the vivacity of incident and all the economy of picture. She sits up, by her dying fire, far into the night, under the spell of recognitions on which she finds the last sharpness suddenly wait. It is a representation of her motionlessly seeing, and an attempt withal to make the mere still lucidity of her act as "interesting" as the surprise of a caravan or the identification of a pirate. It represents, for that matter, one of the identifications dear to the novelist, and even indispensible to him; but it all goes on without her being approached by another person and without her leaving her chair. It is obviously the best thing

in the book, but it is only a supreme illustration of the general plan.[24]

James' general plan is to center his narrative in the growth of his heroine's consciousness, and this is the scene in which that consciousness makes its most dramatic advance. Such capacity for growth enables James' central characters to penetrate and master, ultimately to confer meaning upon, their experience. "Their being finely aware . . . *makes* absolutely the intensity of their adventure, gives the maximum of sense to what befalls them."[25] It is thus primarily through the consciousness of his characters that James achieves, in his later novels, the fusion of scene and symbol.

"The very bulk of [James'] *oeuvre*," as F. R. Leavis remarks, "leads to a centering of attention upon development, rather than upon the achieved thing as such."[26] Because I wish to concentrate on the achievements of the later novels, on the culmination rather than the process of James' evolution, I must only note briefly what are for our concerns the most important developments in the long middle period, especially in the years which follow the disastrous venture at writing for the stage.

The influence of dramatic technique, as has often been noted, resulted in the increasing use of dramatic scenes and a corresponding decline in the narrator's role. The change of method is apparent in *The Spoils of Poynton,*

24. "Preface to *The Portrait of a Lady*," in *The Art of the Novel*, p. 57.

25. "Preface to *The Princess Casamassima*," in *The Art of the Novel*, p. 62.

26. *The Great Tradition* (Garden City, N.Y., 1954), p. 159.

which, in a swift succession of scenes, achieves "the completeness of the drama-quality" James desired.[27] The expository function of the narrator is now largely subsumed by scenic presentation, but like *The Portrait of a Lady*, *The Spoils of Poynton* is centered, as a stage drama cannot be, in the consciousness of its heroine, Fleda Vetch. *The Awkward Age* carries the use of dramatic techniques to a further extreme, presenting all its action in dialogue and description, almost never "going behind" into the characters' minds. One result of this strategy is the loss of scenes which provide an internal view of consciousness in pursuit and recognition of meaning, but as partial compensation James develops another type of scene, one which plays an important part in the later novels. Here the characters' pursuit of meaning is reflected in their efforts to divine each other's attitudes and intentions, creating scenes of probing dialogue, filled with questions and evasions or admissions, elliptical and allusive, where more is always meant than said. Such are the scenes which James singled out in his Preface as exemplifying "the conduct of so much fine meaning, so many flares of the exhibitory torch through the labyrinth of mere immediate appearances, mere familiar allusions."[28] Such techniques allow the presentation not only of narrative content, but of the fundamental concern with its meaning in dramatic scenes.

The same period (1896–1901) which contains this experiment in an extreme objectivity of presentation also includes works which plunge into an equal extreme of subjectivity, *The Turn of the Screw* and *The Sacred Fount*. Both are first-person narratives, so that, instead of being

27. *The Notebooks of Henry James*, ed. F. O. Matthiessen and Kenneth B. Murdock (New York, 1961), p. 198.
28. "Preface to *The Awkward Age*," in *The Art of the Novel*, p. 117.

only centered in the consciousnesses of their protagonists, they are totally immersed in them. As a result, the reader has no adequate means of verifying or disproving the account he is given. In *The Turn of the Screw,* as a large body of critical controversy has shown, it is possible either to accept the validity of the governess' account, the reality of the apparitions and the children's corruption, or to consider them delusions, the products of her diseased imagination. The novel is so constructed as to present "two meanings, both equally self-consistent and self-complete";[29] this is the irreducible ambiguity of *The Turn of the Screw.*

The Sacred Fount conducts a more elaborate and explicit exploration of the problem of the adequacy of consciousness for penetrating and interpreting its experience. Here the objects of consciousness are not apparitions, derived from the minor genre of the ghost story, but the relations between characters, which, though in their way made equally fantastic here, are also the focus of James' other novels. The narrator, a writer, presents himself as dedicated to the " 'exciting' inward life" whose possibility James demonstrated in *The Portrait of a Lady.* For him "reflection [is] the real intensity,"[30] and he is capable of feeling "an undiluted bliss in the intensity of consciousness" he achieves (177). Proceeding by "a high application of intelligence" (66) to the presumed psychological and

29. Dorothea Krook, *The Ordeal of Consciousness,* p. 388. Dr. Krook's appendix on the problem, pp. 370–89, reviews several of the major contributions to the controversy in arriving at this conclusion, a conclusion whose implications, however, do not seem to be fully recognized in her chapter on *The Turn of the Screw.*

30. *The Sacred Fount,* ed. Leon Edel (New York, 1953), p. 190. Since the novel is not included in the New York Edition, all references are to this reprint of the first American edition (1901) and are subsequently incorporated in the text.

erotic relations of his fellow weekend guests, he constructs an elaborate theoretical structure, "a perfect palace
of thought" (311), from limited observations and unlimited inferences and hypotheses. Again, as in *The Turn
of the Screw*, the narrator's version of events can neither be
proved nor disproved; James creates a structure of radical
ambiguity. The scene in Chapter 4 where several characters offer comments on an obscure painting (55–59) presents a paradigm of the novel's conflicting possible interpretations. Is the painting of a man holding a mask to be
called "The Mask of Death" or "The Mask of Life"? Is
the man taking the mask off or putting it on? Which of the
guests does he resemble? The conflict of multiple possible
meanings is never resolved. Just so, in the novel's final
scene, the narrator's perfect palace of thought receives a
crushing attack from Grace Brissenden, who has previously aided in its construction. Now she repudiates all
his theories, offers alternative explanations for the facts
which they have seemed to fit, and tells him he is crazy.
Many readers have accepted her argument, but, as Laurence Holland points out, "the novel is not so constructed
as to demonstrate in retrospect that the Narrator's specula-
tions were wrong."[31] Instead it provides possible support
for both structures. The ability of the narrator's consciousness, or any other, to create a valid interpretation of
this world is left uncertain.

James' concern seems to have shifted from the possibility of "an 'exciting' inward life," the "fine intensification and wide enlargement" of consciousness, to the problem of whether that inward life can achieve a valid relation with reality, the danger of its isolation in solipsistic

31. *The Expense of Vision: Essays on the Craft of Henry James*
(Princeton, N.J., 1964), p. 209.

confinement. Such an epistemological problem would threaten James' primary basis for the creation of meaning. The shift, however, is only one of emphasis; we have already seen such a danger in the negative aspect of the imaginative consciousness in *The Portrait of a Lady*. Here it moves into the foreground and receives exhaustive development, intensifying the difficulty of making sense to a point of crisis for the interpretative imagination. In the three great novels which immediately follow *The Sacred Fount* this threat is again confronted, but with results which finally carry the Jamesian consciousness beyond the point of hopeless ambiguity.

These three late works, *The Ambassadors, The Wings of the Dove,* and *The Golden Bowl,* show a continuing development in many ways, but they also have enough in common, particularly from a technical standpoint, to constitute a unified phase, consistently exemplifying James' later method. I shall therefore examine some of their common elements before considering these novels individually. In all the elements which create a context for meaning, we find marked changes from James' early method. There is, however, more continuity than has often been recognized. This is especially true in the case of James' narrator, who, although often supposed to have entirely disappeared, continues to play a significant role. In each of these novels the narrator reveals his presence in the first person or performs his traditional function of implicating the reader, as when, in *The Ambassadors,* he refers several times to Strether as "our friend" (e.g. I, 28, 89, and 172; II, 82) and at least once as "our hero" (I, 127), or when after presenting a scene as reflected in a character's consciousness, he steps back to comment on how it appears "to us" (e.g. *The Wings of the Dove,* II, 139 and 255; *The*

Golden Bowl, I, 167 and 326). Such phrases are not, as one critic has claimed, mere "lapses and shifts" from an impersonal narrative mode, careless "intrusions" into which James slips because "he was still so close to the conventions of nineteenth-century fiction that he could never quite eschew their besetting manners and methods."[32] These phrases are, in fact, not accidental but functional. James, working out of the traditions of nineteenth-century fiction, transformed their conventions into a unique narrative mode in which the narrator still plays a part, though a very different and far less obvious one than in George Eliot or in James' early novels.

The narrator's presence is seldom brought to our attention, although it is perhaps implicit in the highly idiosyncratic style. He usually remains quite close to the characters' point of view, and indeed the consciousnesses of the characters sometimes merge indistinguishably into the narrator's.[33] An evidence of this close relation is the difficulty which several students of James' imagery have encountered in attempting to determine whether certain images are located in a character's consciousness or the

32. John E. Tilford, Jr., "James the Old Intruder," *Modern Fiction Studies, 4* (1958), 157–64.

33. Passages in which this occurs are cited and analyzed by Leo Bersani, "The Narrator as Center in *The Wings of the Dove," Modern Fiction Studies, 6* (1960), 131–44. His interpretation of the situation, indicated in his title, seems to me to overemphasize the narrator's importance, thereby reducing the characters to allegorical representations of "possible moral choices internal to [the narrator's] own mind." A more accurate description is that given by Laurence Holland *(The Expense of Vision,* p. 286): "The narrative convention of *The Wings of the Dove* is founded on neither the author's voice alone nor on the center of consciousness alone but on the intimate connection between them."

narrator's.[34] The narrator performs almost none of the
traditional functions of providing commentary and analysis. His omniscience is usually only implicit in his access
to the characters' minds, although it sometimes provides
us with parenthetical revelations of past or future, as
when, in *The Ambassadors,* he remarks that "it may even
now frankly be mentioned that [Strether] in the sequel
never *was* to tell" Maria Gostrey the name of the "vulgar"
little article manufactured in Woollett (I, 61). Such passages indicate that the whole narrative, both as completed
pattern and as evolving process, is contained within the
narrator's consciousness. The narrator functions as a further level of consciousness, lying beyond and encompass-
ing those of the characters, rendering them accessible and
intelligible to the reader. Such is the narrator's function
described by Ian Watt in his explication of the opening
paragraph of *The Ambassadors.* He finds "a very idiosyncratic kind of multiple Impressionism: idiosyncratic because [of] the dual presence of Strether's consciousness
and that of the narrator, who translates what he sees there
into more general terms."[35] Unlike the first-person nar-
rators of *The Turn of the Screw* and *The Sacred Fount,*
this narrator is, in his limited function, entirely "reliable";
he acts as an overlying consciousness, capable of providing
a range of awareness beyond that of the characters.[36]

34. See, for example, Austin Warren, "Henry James: Symbolic
Imagery in the Later Novels," in *Rage for Order* (Ann Arbor, Mich.,
1959), p. 149.

35. Ian Watt, "The First Paragraph of *The Ambassadors:* An Explication," *Essays in Criticism, 10* (1960), 260.

36. Wayne C. Booth, who is concerned with the problem of the
unreliable narrator, has devoted several pages to this element in
James' works. See *The Rhetoric of Fiction* (Chicago, 1961), especially
pp. 311–16 and 339–64.

Our recognition of the narrator's continuing presence and refined function in the later novels should not obscure the general trend of his declining importance. The famous maneuver "exit author," though often exaggerated and oversimplified in critical accounts, is indeed a progressive tendency in the course of James' career and in the course of the entire period with which we are concerned.[37] It corresponds, most immediately, with the increasing importance of dramatic presentation, the conveying of meaning within scenes and, in James' case, within and through the characters' consciousnesses. In this regard, the closeness of the relation between character and narrator is important, because the character as central consciousness is in effect assuming a part of the narrator's (or "author's") function, and, as we shall see, their shifting relations are a part of the drama in which the protagonist moves toward mastery of meaning.

The narrator's role may decline in the later novels, but that of other contextual elements, those which can be presented within scenes and through the characters as well as by the narrator, increases. This is especially true of James' imagery, which even in *The Portrait of a Lady* was developed more consistently than George Eliot's. In the later novels the imagery becomes far denser, more elaborate

37. The phrase is the title of the second chapter of Joseph Warren Beach, *The Twentieth Century Novel: Studies in Technique* (New York, 1932), pp. 14–24, which begins by proclaiming that "In a bird's-eye view of the English novel from Fielding to Ford, the one thing that will impress you more than any other is the disappearance of the author." Like the disappearance of the stable conceptual terms which provided a basis for George Eliot's meaning, the declining importance of the authoritative narrator reflects a general cultural change. In a time when received values carry less authority than formerly, the novel is less able to draw on external sources of meaningfulness; more of its meaning must be created internally.

and exotic. It flows through the characters' meditations, is reinforced by correspondences in the material world, and, to a far greater extent, is introduced in speech. The characters continually create images for themselves and their situations with an imaginative energy which sometimes approaches violence. Here, for example, is the Prince attempting to convey to Maggie Verver the difference between his "form" and that of her father: "I'm like a chicken, at best, chopped up and smothered in sauce; cooked down as a *crème de volaille,* with half the parts left out. Your father's the natural fowl running about the *bassecour.* His feathers, his movements, his sounds—those are the parts that, with me, are left out" *(The Golden Bowl,* I, 8).

Characters eagerly collaborate, expanding images and exploring their implications, helping to elaborate them into what sometimes become key metaphors. Such are the dove images in *The Wings of the Dove,* whose title, a factor lying outside the characters' consciousnesses, indicates their central importance. They are introduced and developed, however, by the characters themselves, beginning when Kate tells Milly, "you're a dove," and Milly, pondering its significance, accepts the designation: *"That* was what was the matter with her. She was a dove" (I, 283). Its implications emerge in the contrasting meanings the image acquires for Kate and for Densher. Watching Milly in her old lace and priceless pearls, Kate observes to him that "She's a dove . . . and one somehow doesn't think of doves as bejewelled. Yet they suit her down to the ground." Densher agrees: "Milly was indeed a dove; this was the figure, though it most applied to her spirit," but he realizes that what Kate sees is "that element of her wealth in her which was a power . . . and which was dovelike only so far as one remembered that doves have wings and wondrous

flights, have them as well as tender tints and soft sounds"
(II, 218).

The two senses are ironically juxtaposed in the interchange between Densher and Aunt Maud after they have
just learned of Milly's death, she using the image in
clichés about flights to heaven, while he, through it, is
made more aware of his guilt, his loss, and the growing influence of Milly's spirituality over him.

> "Our dear dove then, as Kate calls her, has folded
> her wonderful wings."
> "Yes—folded them."
> It rather racked him, but he tried to receive it as she
> intended, and she evidently took his formal assent for
> self-control. "Unless it's more true," she accordingly
> added, "that she has but spread them the wider."
> He again but formally assented, though, strangely
> enough, the words fitted a figure deep in his own
> imagination. "Rather, yes—spread them the wider."
> (II, 356)

The image is given its final extension in the last scene, as
Kate and Densher realize that, because of Milly, they will
never be again as they were, and the divergence of the two
senses, the two kinds of power, now necessitate their own
divergence. Kate says:

> "I used to call her in my stupidity—for want of
> anything better—a dove. Well she stretched out her
> wings, and it was to *that* they reached. They cover
> us."
> "They cover us," Densher said. (II, 404)

These images do not stand alone, of course. They are reinforced by others which involve the novel's material set-

ting and incorporate the dove's flight in a whole meta-phorical system of heights and depths, from the scene where Milly looks down from an Alpine precipice "on the kingdoms of the earth," choosing among them or perhaps wanting them all, before her descent on London (I, 124), to the point where she stays on the upper levels of her Venetian palace and longs "not to go down—never, never to go down!" (II, 147). But these elaborations of the central metaphor are also established by the characters, in the first case through Susan Stringham's interpretation, and in the second through Milly.

The creation of images by the characters in speech or meditation is an important part of their efforts to discover and create meaning. To image a situation is to move toward mastery of it, to make it more firmly possessed by consciousness, a truth comically reflected in the relations of the Assinghams in *The Golden Bowl*. Fanny sees her husband, the retired Colonel, in his habitual use of extravagant barrack-room language, as playing with toy soldiers, indulging in a "military game." He is "less fortunate," because, "in spite of his wealth of expression, he had not yet found the image that described *her* favorite game" (I, 64). Images may become pivotal points in the evolution of consciousness when a character achieves "an emblematic perception, a symbolized intuition—in form an original image, sometimes comic, sometimes horrendous, often grotesque."[38] The problem, to which I have already referred, of determining whether a given image proceeds from the character's consciousness or from the narrator is therefore quite important; the locus of the image will indicate responsibility for the creation of meaning. In my discussion of *The Golden Bowl*, I shall show how this situa-

38. Warren, "Symbolic Imagery," pp. 148–49.

tion is exploited by James as a functional element in the development of his central consciousness. For Austin Warren, and others after him, these "emblematic perceptions" constitute one of James' primary "modes of knowing," or, in the terms I have been using, one of his primary vehicles of meaning.[39] It seems more accurate, however, to place imagery, even that of the later novels, in the category of context. In itself James' imagery remains an auxiliary element, only one component in a complex of factors which are joined and focused through consciousness in crucial symbolic scenes. As Barbara Hardy says, "the bulk of James's generalization is done . . . by scenes rather than metaphors."[40]

The characters of the late novels introduce not only images but other thematically significant words which somewhat correspond in function to the conceptual terms of George Eliot or the early novels. We saw in *The Portrait of a Lady* how the introduction of such terms by the characters in the form of debate rendered them more problematic than those used by George Eliot's narrator. Here the thematic vocabulary is much farther removed from George Eliot's stable moral and philosophical concepts and even more intermingled with the dramatic action; it now largely consists of a thoroughly idiosyncratic repetition by the characters of vague portentous epithets: "wonderful," "terrible," "magnificent," "extraordinary,"

39. See "Symbolic Imagery," p. 145. Jean Kimble, in "The Abyss and the Wings of the Dove: The Image as Revelation," *Nineteenth-Century Fiction, 10* (1956), 281–300, exemplifies the apparent assumption that, as her title implies, the image alone can convey meaning.

40. *The Appropriate Form: An Essay on the Novel* (London, 1964), p. 25. It is necessary to recognize, however, that my analytical segregation of elements into the categories of context and dramatic action, while still useful, becomes increasingly arbitrary for the later novels, where all elements interpenetrate to a high degree.

"prodigious," "sublime," and so forth. On the level of social reality this simply reflects the cliquish repetition of cant phrases ("wonderful" appears more than forty times in *The Ambasadors*[41]) which tends to rob them of all meaning; but, as they are controlled by James' structure, their vagueness becomes loaded with multiple suggestions of meaning, creating rich effects of ambiguity and irony. As in the case of James' metaphors, multiple meanings may reflect conflicting orders of value. In *The Wings of the Dove* Kate and Densher describe Milly several times as "stupendous"; in the last scene its meanings for them diverge as do those of the dove. For Kâte the amount of Milly's bequest is "stupendous," while to Densher the word suggests the spiritual qualities reflected in her final act (II, 403).

A more explicit concern with the ambiguous meaning of such words emerges in the play on "good" in *The Ambassadors*. Strether, equipped at the outset with only the simplistic moral conceptions of Woollett, uses the word in a purely moral sense: the question of whether Chad is "good" depends on whether he is involved with a mistress. He is thus confused when Chad declares "I'm not so bad now." To Strether this can imply only one thing: "Do you mean," he asks, "that there isn't any woman with you now?" To Chad, however, it clearly has a different bearing. "What has that to do with it?" (I, 157). Whatever his moral status, Chad seems to Strether markedly improved in his manner, a challenge to his expectations which disturbs "not only his moral, but also, as it were, his aesthetic sense" (I, 149). Chad and his friend little Bilham play on "good" in a way which prevents Strether from knowing

<hr />

41. See Mary K. Michael, "Henry James's Use of the Word 'Wonderful' in *The Ambassadors*," *Modern Language Notes*, 75 (1960), 114–17.

whether the word is being given a moral or aesthetic sense. Bilham agrees on Chad's improvement, but adds, "I'm not sure . . . that I didn't like him about as well in his other state. . . . I'm not sure he was really meant by nature to be quite so good" (I, 177). Strether wants to be assured that this refers to Chad's "morals," but it may just as well refer to his aesthetic improvement. The questionable nature of Chad's "goodness" in either moral or aesthetic terms is suggested when Maria Gostrey warns Strether that "He's not so good as you think!" (I, 171). The complex of possible meanings Strether encounters in this word dramatizes and provides a context for the complication which his moral preconceptions undergo, until at the end he is urging Chad to continue a relationship which he now knows to be, by his original definition, "bad."

The ambiguity with which extravagant epithets are endowed may result in their complete transvaluation, exemplified by an ironic climax in *The Golden Bowl,* where the Prince and Charlotte agree that they must join to protect Maggie and Adam:

> With which, as for the full assurance and the pledge it involved, their hands instinctively found their hands. "It's all too wonderful."
>
> Firmly and gravely she kept his hand. "It's too beautiful."
>
> And so for a minute they stood together, as strongly held and as closely confronted as any hour of their easier past even had seen them. They were silent at first, only facing and faced, only grasping and grasped, only meeting and met. "It's sacred," he said at last.
>
> "It's sacred," she breathed back to him. They vowed it, gave it out and took it in, drawn, by their intensity, more closely together. Then, of a sudden, through this

tightened circle, as at the issue of a narrow strait into the sea beyond, everything broke up, broke down, gave way, melted and mingled. Their lips sought their lips, their pressure their response and their response their pressure; with a violence that had sighed itself the next moment to the longest and deepest of still-nesses they passionately sealed their pledge. (I, 312)

They thus commit themselves to adultery in a litany of in-verted values. The way in which James' later novels dramatically expand the connotations of conventional terms, in effect creating their own language, is an indica-tion of the extent to which they have become reflexive verbal structures. Their self-referential quality may seem to create a meaning which is limited by being self-con-tained, but the very openness of James' ambiguity allows him to capture a wide range of conflicting values and to bring their conflict into sharp focus.

One further example of the operation of contextual terms in the later novels is required to show how they can not only contain polarities of meaning but generate whole spectra of significance, where each use of the word at one point in the broad span of meaning it creates invokes the whole range as context. This is true of the cluster of words centering on "safe" in *The Golden Bowl,* used by nearly every character at one time or another. It moves along a scale which extends from the vulgar sense in which Char-lotte tells the Prince they're *"safe"* in their liaison (I, 343) all the way to its final suggestions of salvation, being "saved," especially as the goal of Maggie's efforts. This final aura of suggestion touches many references to her, from Charlotte's comfortable statement that Maggie "saves one such trouble" (I, 101), to Fanny's prediction that she will "have to save" her father (I, 386). What Maggie most

111

wants to save is her marriage, and to do so, she must, as Fanny says, "carry the whole weight" of the others (I, 381). Settling for something less than such an absolute conception of saving, the Assinghams agree merely "that Charlotte and the Prince must be saved—so far as consistently speaking of them as still safe might save them" (I, 378). The acceptance of appearances or the remaking of reality are thus involved in the permutations of this single word, in which James has compacted such a range of meaning, maintaining a tightly controlled significance beneath the seeming looseness of usage. Like imagery, however, such thematic vocabulary remains a part of these novels' context, helping to illuminate the meaning of their dramatic action.

The scenic method by which that dramatic action is presented also shows considerable change in the later novels. A much more important part is played by the type of scene which has already been briefly noted in my discussion of *The Awkward Age,* that primarily composed of dialogue. Such scenes make the fullest use of the techniques which James mastered in writing for the stage; as in a play, exposition is now accomplished in dialogue. The opening scenes of *The Ambassadors,* for example, quickly provide Strether with his confidante, Maria Gostrey, to whom he can explain his background and purpose, thus presenting them to the reader without the narrator's assistance. But even where the function of dialogue is ostensibly exposition, the question "What are the facts?" quickly gives place, as Joseph Warren Beach has observed, to the more important question, "What do they mean?"[42] The pursuit

42. *The Method of Henry James* (Philadelphia, 1954), p. 78. The entire chapter on "Dialogue," pp. 72–86, is relevant, as is Austin Warren's discussion of "close conversation" as a dialectical mode of knowledge, in "Symbolic Imagery," pp. 145–47.

of meaning can be seen in Strether's efforts to understand what Chad, Bilham, or Maria mean by "good," a part of his continuing attempt to discover the nature of Chad's relation with Madame de Vionnet and in what way it is "a virtuous attachment." Such efforts may be incidental in scenes which forward the narrative progression; they become central in those where Strether and Maria dissect a preceding incident in the search for its meaning, its implications about the position and motives of the others, and where Strether, with her help, attempts to understand his own constantly shifting position.

Such dialectical inquiry into meaning is developed even more elaborately in the scenes which feature the Assinghams in *The Golden Bowl*. Fanny too acts as a confidante, first for the Prince and Charlotte and later for Maggie, but she also appears alone, with her husband as foil, in scenes where she attempts to analyze the most recent developments and predict the next. This function is especially prominent in Book Third, where the relationship of the Prince and Charlotte develops and moves toward consummation in a sequence of scenes: the Ambassador's reception, the afternoon when the two find themselves alone at tea, and finally the weekend at Matcham, which alternate with those devoted to the Assinghams' analyses. In the same passage where James locates his leading interest "in a consciousness . . . subject to fine intensification and wide enlargement," he also acknowledges the need for fools, a need which the Assinghams fill admirably. Their frequent absurdity should not, however, be allowed to obscure their valuable exegetical contributions. They provide revealing commentary on the relationship of the Prince and Charlotte and, even more important, set the stage for the countermovement of the second volume, in which the focus shifts to Maggie. Fanny is ludicrous in her

solemnity when she announces that Maggie's "sense will
have to open . . . to what's called Evil—with a very big E"
(I, 384–85), but she is nevertheless correct, as she also is in
perceiving that Maggie will now have to "carry the whole
weight" (I, 381). Though far less authoritative than those
of an omniscient narrator, such comments do contribute
to the novel's emerging meaning.

The use of dialogue as dialectic, whether between an-
tagonists or confederates, permits the presentation of the
conscious concern with meaning in that form of scene
James called "drama," but precisely because it is the concern of consciousness, the problem of meaning is developed
more fully in scenes which are centered in a character's
mind, those he classified as "picture."[43] Scenes presented
in dialogue, moreover, are often only islands of objective
drama in a sea of consciousness. The long scene in *The
Wings of the Dove* where Milly and Densher are first
brought together, for example, is presented only as reflected in Densher's consciousness for the first ten pages
(II, 72–82), after which the actual dialogue begins. Those
pages do convey the progress of the conversation, but they
are much more occupied with Densher's response to it, his
interpretations of Milly's meaning and his attempts to
understand his own position. He is not so much concerned
with the things she says as with "what such things meant
in the light of what he knew" (II, 78). Even when dialogue
assumes a greater role it continues to alternate with the
responses of Densher's consciousness, his increasing awareness of being committed to a false position, leaving him at
the end with "the sense of having rounded his corner" and
"with his consciousness charged to the brim" (II, 90). Thus

43. Regarding the aspects of James' theory specifically concerned
with scenic method, see my Introduction, pp. 11–12.

the events of the narrative are always located in a continuum of consciousness, and its most crucial moments, its scenes of recognition and symbolic perception, will tend to be those closer to "picture," products of vision, where consciousness occupies the foreground.

In *The Ambassadors* this prominent position is held by Lambert Strether, whose experience constitutes the definitive version of the expansion of consciousness which we have already observed in the development of Isabel Archer. More than that of any other Jamesian protagonist, his career is literally as well as figuratively a "process of vision."[44] He notes the predominance in his Parisian acquaintances of the "visual sense" (I, 206), but his own also becomes highly developed. Through it we receive his experience of Europe as a series of striking visual impressions, such as those of the pink-shaded candles at his dinner with Maria Gostrey or of little Bilham casually smoking a cigarette on the balcony of Chad's apartment. But through the operation of Strether's imaginative consciousness these impressions do not merely remain on the visual level; they expand into the meaning he sees in them. Maria, in her low-cut dress and broad red velvet band around her throat, becomes mentally opposed to Mrs. Newsome, in her black silk and ruff. The forbidding lady of Woollett appears "rather imperfectly romantic" by contrast (I, 51). Similarly, and more explicitly, the figure on the balcony becomes another representative of Europe and summons up the opposing image of Strether's incorrigibly American friend:

> It came to pass before he moved that Waymarsh, and Waymarsh alone, Waymarsh not only undiluted but

44. "Preface to *The Ambassadors*," in *The Art of the Novel*, p. 308.

positively strengthened, struck him as the present alternative to the young man in the balcony. When he
did move it was fairly to escape that alternative.
Taking his way over the street at last and passing
through the *porte-cochère* was like consciously leaving
Waymarsh out. (I, 98–99)

"When the mind is imaginative," James wrote in "The
Art of Fiction," "it takes to itself the faintest hints of life, it
converts the very pulses of the air into revelations."
Strether typifies this ability of the imaginative Jamesian
consciousness to convert impressions into symbols, and
Europe forces him to develop his "power to guess the
unseen from the seen, to trace the implication of things."[45]

His visual sense reveals the greater aesthetic richness of
Europe to Strether, its style and charm, but he is troubled
about the relation of these values to others. After commenting on the extensive visual sense of his new friends,
he adds, " 'There are moments when it strikes one that
you haven't any other.' 'Any moral,' little Bilham explained" (I, 206). As we have noted, Strether arrives with
only the overly simple moral sense of Woollett; his European experiences act "to carry on and complicate . . . his
vision" (I, 50). Such complications are primarily caused by
his encounter with Paris, which becomes, as James noted
in his Preface, the "symbol for more things than had been
dreamt of in the philosophy of Woollett."[46] Paris is dazzling, but its reality is elusive:

It hung before him . . . the vast bright Babylon, like
some huge iridescent object, a jewel brilliant and
hard, in which parts were not to be discriminated nor

45. "The Art of Fiction," in *The Future of the Novel*, pp. 12–13.
46. "Preface to *The Ambassadors*," in *The Art of the Novel*, p. 316.

differences comfortably marked. It twinkled and trembled and melted together, and what seemed all surface one moment seemed all depth the next. (I, 89)

Miss Barrace explains to Strether that "in the light of Paris one sees what things resemble," but he wants to know whether it also shows them "for what they really are" (I, 207). The reality with which he is particularly concerned is that of Chad's relationship with Madame de Vionnet. He had expected it to be morally "bad" but has found this by no means apparent, while its aesthetically improving effect on Chad impresses him deeply.

Strether's problems of perception arise from the same dual quality of the imagination which we have seen in Isabel Archer. On the one hand its sympathetic response enables him to perceive new values, to appreciate qualities of life in Paris which his own past has not included. This is the first and most obvious sense in which he experiences an expansion of consciousness. But on the other hand, his imaginative nature also generates a powerful romanticism which for a long time prevents his full recognition of the nature of that life. In part the long delay of recognition results from unconscious self-deception, the avoidance of a conflict between moral and aesthetic values. When he is finally made to realize that Chad and Madame de Vionnet are indeed lovers, Strether wonders what on earth he has been supposing. "He recognized at last that he had really been trying all along to suppose nothing" (II, 266). But the delay is also spontaneously produced by the same qualities of imagination which make his European experience meaningful both to himself and to the reader. At the dinner with Maria, Strether finds himself subject to "uncontrolled perceptions" (I, 50), just as, looking for the first time at the house where Chad lives, he is made to recognize "that wherever one paused in Paris the imagination reacted before one could stop it." In spite of all his prepared disapproval he finds that the aesthetic appeal of the house with its stone of "a cold fair grey, warmed and polished a little by life," its proportions characterized "by measure and balance, the fine relation of part to part and space to space" (I, 96–97) suggests, even before he has seen Chad, that, as F. O. Matthiessen says, "the life which goes on behind those windows and that balcony must also be characterized by tact and taste."[47]

Similarly, his romantic tendency to identify the good with the beautiful also colors Strether's response to his encounter with Madame de Vionnet in Notre Dame (II, 6–10). He first sees her, without recognizing her, as a figure praying at a shrine and is immediately reminded, "since it was the way of nine-tenths of his current impressions to act as recalls of something imagined—of some fine firm concentrated heroine of an old story." He has just bought a seventy-volume set of Victor Hugo, out of whose romantic ambiance she suddenly appears like a figure from *Notre Dame de Paris,* becoming "romantic for him far beyond what she could have guessed." He thus allows his association with a romanticized Catholicism to convince him that "unassailably innocent was a relation that could make one of the parties to it so carry herself. If it wasn't innocent why did she haunt the churches?—into which, given the woman he could believe he made out, she would never have come to flaunt an insolence of guilt." As Strether himself is forced to admit, he has "rather too much" imagination (II, 244), but in spite of all the delusions into which this quality leads him, his position is

47. "James and the Plastic Arts," in *Discussions of Henry James,* ed. Naomi Lebowitz (Boston, 1962), p. 25.

superior to that of a Sarah Pocock, whose total immunity to imaginative appeal effectively prevents both confusion and growth.

The novel progresses as a sequence of scenes such as those I have been noting, the continuity and interrelations between them established through Strether's consciousness. His lunch with Madame de Vionnet, for example, which follows their meeting in Notre Dame, forms a parallel to the earlier dinner with Maria. In George Eliot the significance of such parallel scenes is explicated by the narrator, but here it is Strether who is aware of the formal correspondence as an index of development: "He was to feel many things on this occasion, and one of the first of them was that he had travelled far since that evening in London, before the theatre, when his dinner with Maria Gostrey, between the pink-shaded candles, had struck him as requiring so many explanations" (II, 13). Two scenes in particular present crucial moments in Strether's mental travels. The first takes place in Gloriani's garden and contains the incident which was the germ of the novel, Strether's passionate exhortation to little Bilham to "Live all you can" (I, 217). It brings to a crisis his growing sense of Paris and its aesthetic life as opportunities now lost to him. The setting affects him strongly: "the place itself was a great impression," and its details are presented impressionistically, as an "assault of images" which, again, do not remain merely visual but become weighted with a vague but intense meaningfulness, giving him a "sense of names in the air, of ghosts at the windows, of signs and tokens, a whole range of expression, all about him too thick for prompt discrimination" (I, 195–96). It is his sense of this meaning which he expresses in the outburst to little Bilham: "This place and these impressions," he explains, "have had their abundant message for me" (217). The scene is one of those in which "the boundary line between picture and scene bears a little the weight of the double pressure,"[48] combining passages which present Strether's impressions and his response to them with passages of dialogue which express his concern with their meaning, playing on "good" and "wonderful," probing the relation of the visual and moral senses.

His crisis of appreciation and regret coincides with the introduction of Madame de Vionnet and her daughter Jeanne. From this point on, the process of his vision is concerned less with the whole world of Paris than with the nature of the particular relationship in which Chad is involved. Immediately after his speech to little Bilham he becomes aware, looking at the sculptor Gloriani, of "something in the great world covertly tigerish, which came to him across the lawn and in the charming air, as a waft from the jungle." He can for a moment feel admiration and envy for the amoral power of this "glossy male tiger, magnificently marked," but such reactions are only "absurdities of the stirred sense, fruits of suggestion ripening on the instant" (219), which must fade the next because of their inevitable conflict with his moral sense. He is thus prepared to turn from the suspect appeal of the great world to the alternative with which he is immediately presented as Chad brings the young Jeanne de Vionnet toward him. For Strether, "it was the click of a spring—he saw the truth"—or rather he seizes on an interpretation which is both morally and aesthetically acceptable. In his vision the girl in white becomes a romanticized figure of innocence, "bright gentle shy happy wonderful" (220). This must be the "virtuous attachment," since to believe

48. "Preface to *The Wings of the Dove*," in *The Art of the Novel*, p. 300.

so resolves the ambiguity of the phrase. The latter part of
the scene thus sets Strether on the course he will follow
through the central section of the novel, trying "to suppose nothing" unacceptable, while he becomes more and
more committed to Madame de Vionnet's cause and
alienated from Woollett.

The second crucial scene is the one which at last brings
recognition and reversal, the famous afternoon Strether
spends alone in the country. It carries to its highest point
the development of his visual and aesthetic sense, now not
just as imaginative appreciation but in terms of a work of
art, the landscape by Lambinet, which he had seen years
before in a Tremont Street gallery in Boston and had been
unable to afford. It thus represents all his past deprivation,
and now, as he seeks and finds or recreates it in the French
countryside, his consciousness achieves its recompense.

> The oblong gilt frame disposed its enclosing lines; the
> poplars and willows, the reeds and river—a river of
> which he didn't know, and didn't want to know, the
> name—fell into a composition, full of felicity, within
> them; the sky was silver and turquoise and varnish;
> the village on the left was white and the church on the
> right was grey; it was all there, in short—it was what
> he wanted: it was Tremont Street, it was France, it
> was Lambinet. (II, 247)

As he proceeds to the village and the inn, "not once over-
stepp[ing] the oblong gilt frame," his aesthetic vision becomes intensified and stylized; the village is perceived
impressionistically as "a thing of whiteness, blueness and
crookedness, set in coppery green" (252).

The setting is conceived not only as a picture but also
in terms of James' other basic metaphor for representational method, the drama: "For this had been all day at

bottom the spell of the picture—that it was essentially more than anything else a scene and a stage" (253). In either perspective, Strether is not merely a passive spectator. His consciousness plays an active, creative part; "one had to make one's account with what one lighted on" (254). At the inn, "the picture and the play seemed supremely to melt together," fusing as they move toward a culmination which will force Strether to revise his account radically. He gazes out at the river from the garden of the inn; "the view [has] an emptiness" which requires something more to complete the composition, and

> what he saw was exactly the right thing—a boat advancing round the bend and containing a man who held the paddles and a lady, at the stern, with a pink parasol. It was suddenly as if these figures, or something like them, had been wanted in the picture, had been wanted more or less all day, and had now drifted into sight, with the slow current, on purpose to fill up the measure. (256)

The fulfillment of the aesthetic, however, leads directly to the violent reentry of the moral, the shattering of the gilt frame in "a sharp fantastic crisis," for the couple are of course Chad and Madame de Vionnet, and their appearance finally forces on Strether the recognition that they are indeed lovers. Both sides maintain the pretense of innocence, but Strether becomes increasingly aware of the *"lie* in the charming affair." The metaphor of drama now, significantly, carries unpleasant connotations of falsity. Madame de Vionnet's manner is seen as a faltering "performance," and the whole air of "fiction and fable" no longer has the sense of aesthetic creation but simply of a lie (262–63). Strether, and the reader, have been abruptly shifted from the aesthetic to the moral perspective, and "the quantity of make-believe . . . disagree[s] with his spiritual stomach" (265).

This brilliant recognition scene, with its dramatic opposition of aèsthetic creation and moral discovery, brings to a crisis the conflict of values in Strether's consciousness, a conflict which he can never fully resolve. His sympathetic imagination leads, in his last interview with Madame de Vionnet, to an understanding of the fear and suffering her passion inflicts, and thus to a greater appreciation of what she has done for Chad. He can urge Chad to stay, but he cannot stay himself. The fullness of his expanded consciousness will not let him sacrifice one realm of value to another, but there is still no way to reconcile them. His only possible action is one of renunciation, his only gain, like Isabel Archer's, his enrichments of consciousness. He will have, as Maria says, his "wonderful impressions" (II, 326), "a handful of gold-pieces for imagination and memory."[49]

The Wings of the Dove creates a more pervasive and intense symbolism, a quality reflected in its title, which subsumes the novel under a single symbolic image. (The tendency is continued in *The Golden Bowl* and *The Ivory Tower,* whose titles are taken from symbolic objects.) This increased degree of symbolism is also present in the novel's scenes of recognition and perception, where the central consciousness now makes fuller interpretations of significance, creating more intense concentrations of meaning.

I have already touched on some of these scenes. There is the tableau which presents Milly poised on an Alpine

49. James' "Project for *The Ambassadors*," in *The Notebooks,* p. 406.

precipice in a situation which becomes symbolic through Susan Stringham's interpretations. For a moment she fears that the girl is about to leap but decides that she is "much more in a state of uplifted and unlimited possession . . . looking down on the kingdoms of the earth. . . . Was she choosing among them or did she want them all?" (I, 124). Pondering the significance of what she has seen, Susan becomes convinced that "the future wasn't to exist for her princess in the form of any sharp or simple release from the human predicament. It wouldn't be for her a question of a flying leap and thereby a quick escape. It would be a question of taking full in the face the whole assault of life" (125). The meaning she finds in the scene is conditioned by the terms in which Susan places it: Biblical ("looking down on the kingdoms of the earth") and romantic ("her princess"). These ideal interpretations are controlled by others, such as those of Merton Densher, to whom for a large part of the novel Milly is simply a typical "American girl." But the scene still establishes one important perspective and provides valuable prefiguration, as does another scene we have noted, the party Milly gives in her Venetian palace, where Densher and Kate reveal their contrasting interpretations of the sense in which Milly is a dove (II, 218).

Milly does not only appear as interpreted by others. She is intensely conscious of herself and of the possible meaning of her experiences. At Aunt Maud's dinner party she is seated next to Lord Mark, who assures her with pleasant exaggeration, "You'll see everything. You *can,* you know—everything you dream of." To her troubled consciousness he is "inexpressive but intensely significant" and seems to meet "as no one else could have" the question that possesses her: "Should she have it, whatever she did have . . . for long? 'Ah so possibly not,' her neighbour

appeared to reply: 'therefore, don't you see? *I'm* the way' "
(I, 158–59). She is aware, however, that this meaning is
the creation of her speculative interpretation, not his intention, that in this respect his nature is the diametric
opposite of her own. "You're familiar with everything,"
she tells him, "but conscious really of nothing. What I
mean is that you've no imagination" (162). Milly, familiar
with nothing but conscious of everything and, like all
Jamesian consciousnesses, highly imaginative, continues
for a while with Lord Mark as her foil, the representative
of a world which can present meaning but never realize it.

This is his function when he acts as her guide at Matcham, "the great historic house" which appears to Milly
"as the centre of an almost extravagantly grand Watteau-
composition." Its "largeness of style" becomes "the great
containing vessel" for the moment which serves her, "then
and afterwards, as a high-water mark of the imagination"
(I, 208–10). Here Lord Mark presents the Bronzino, the
portrait which is "so much like" her. It is Milly's consciousness, however, which gives the picture meaning by
interpreting the way in which it is like her. She is moved
to tears as she senses that the pictured woman is "a very
great personage—only unaccompanied by a joy. And she
was dead, dead, dead. Milly recognized her exactly in
words that had nothing to do with her. 'I shall never be
better than this' " (I, 221). She refers to the whole episode
as the climax of her London "success," beyond which she
senses her approaching death. In her later interpretations,
it is these moments "that had exactly made the high-water-
mark of her security, the moments during which her tears
themselves, those she had been ashamed of, were the sign
of her consciously rounding her protective promontory,
quitting the blue gulf of comparative ignorance and reaching her view of the troubled sea" (II, 144).

She is launched upon this troubled sea of fuller awareness by her interview with Sir Luke Strett, who refuses to
confirm her fears that she is seriously ill but urges her to
"see all [she] can," and "to live" (I, 245–46). Milly realizes,
however, that "one wasn't treated so . . . unless it had come
up . . . that one might die" and knows she has left behind
"the small old sense of safety" (248). Her eyes thus opened,
she sets out immediately to see all she can, immersing
herself in the "grey immensity" of the London streets. The
persons and objects in the scene before her take on meaning in terms of her personal situation.

> She had come out, she presently saw, at the Regent's
> Park, round which on two or three occasions with
> Kate Croy her public chariot had solemnly rolled.
> But she went into it further now; this was the real
> thing; the real thing was to be quite away from the
> pompous roads, well within the centre and on the
> stretches of shabby grass. Here were benches and
> smutty sheep; here were idle lads at games of ball,
> with their cries mild in the thick air; here were
> wanderers anxious and tired like herself; here doubt-
> less were hundreds of others just in the same box. This
> box, their great common anxiety, what was it, in this
> grim breathing-space, but the practical question of
> life? They could live if they would; that is, like her-
> self, they had been told so: she saw them all about her,
> on seats, digesting the information, recognizing it
> again as something in a slightly different shape fa-
> miliar enough, the blessed old truth that they would
> live if they could. All she thus shared with them made
> her wish to sit in their company; which she so far did
> that she looked for a bench that was empty, eschewing
> a still emptier chair that she saw hard by and for

which she would have paid, with superiority, a fee.
(250)

In her state of recognition Milly consciously moves on a
symbolic level; going into the park, sitting on a bench, she
acts out the movement away from her "old sense of safety"
enjoyed in her "public chariot." It is a recognition of her
bond with these others in their common mortality, their
common confinement in "the human predicament." The
analogy she creates between their poverty and her immi-
nent death illuminates both. Her creation of meaning
proceeds by giving a new, double sense to conventional
phrases: "she went into it further now," "in the same box,"
"breathing-space," creating a new unity of signficance
which contains an insight into both her situation and that
of the others and makes the two inseparable, members of
an extended metaphor in which each is seen in terms of the
other.

From one point of view James' method here might be
described, in Barbara Hardy's words, as an "extremely
sophisticated use of pathetic fallacy," sophisticated because
the effect of the character's conscious creation of meaning
is to "admit the fallacy and the residual facts beyond it."[50]
But I believe this view creates a distortion, that it analyzes
the Jamesian symbolic scene into an opposition of external and internal reality not actually present there. Instead, the presentation of the scene through a central
consciousness creates a situation in which, "to some extent, the distinction between external and internal dis-
appears: all that matters is the world as possessed and
defined by the central figure."[51] The disappearance of the

50. *The Appropriate Form*, p. 24.

51. Richard Ellmann and Charles Feidelson, Jr., Introduction to
selections on "Self-Consciousness," in *The Modern Tradition: Backgrounds of Modern Literature* (New York, 1965), p. 686.

distinction is not, however, just the result of technique, the control of point of view. It is achieved here because Milly's recognition is a true one, "the real thing." Her imaginative creation is at the same time a discovery of a truth beyond herself. Like that of Isabel Archer among the Roman ruins, it is validated by the context of the novel and by general human experience. The unity of subject and object is therefore not breached by the introduction of epistemological problems or undercutting suggestions of romanticism, self-deception, or self-indulgence. This may be seen more clearly by contrasting this scene with a later one which in some ways forms a parallel to it and in which Mrs. Hardy appears to find no difference.

In Book Ninth Merton Densher is suddenly confronted with his own troubled sea, one which is given a more literal counterpart as the weather of Venice turns to storm on the day when he is first turned away from the Palazzo Leporelli. His shock and fear convert the setting into a symbolically appropriate environment:

> It was a Venice all of evil that had broken out . . . a Venice of cold lashing rain from a low black sky, of wicked wind raging through narrow passes, of general arrest and interruption, with the people engaged in all the water-life huddled, stranded and wageless, bored and cynical, under archways and bridges. (II, 259)

Like Milly in the earlier scene, he wanders through the city, finally arriving at the Piazza San Marco; as in her case, the people and objects he encounters seem to represent his personal situation.

> Here, in the high arcade, half Venice was crowded close, while, on the Molo, at the limit of the expanse,

the old columns of the Saint Theodore and of the Lion were the frame of a door wide open to the storm. It was odd for him, as he moved, that it should have made such a difference—if the difference wasn't only that the palace had for the first time failed of a welcome. There was more, but it came from that; that gave the harsh note and broke the spell. The wet and the cold were now to reckon with, and it was to Densher precisely as if he had seen the obliteration, at a stroke, of the margin on a faith in which they were all living. The margin had been his name for it—for the thing that, though it had held out, could bear no shock. The shock, in some form, had come, and he wondered about it while, threading his way among loungers as vague as himself, he dropped his eyes sightlessly on the rubbish in shops. There were stretches of the gallery paved with squares of red marble, greasy now with the salt spray; and the whole place, in its huge elegance, the grace of its conception and the beauty of its detail, was more than ever like a great drawing-room, the drawing-room of Europe, profaned and bewildered by some reverse of fortune. (260–61)

The disastrous reversal is explained to him when a moment later he recognizes Lord Mark in a café: "The weather had changed, the rain was ugly, the wind wicked, the sea impossible, *because* of Lord Mark. It was because of him, *a fortiori,* that the palace was closed" (263).

Here, unlike the scene in Regent's Park, the presentation invites us to consider Densher's role in terms of fallacy. His projection of emotion onto the setting allows him to avoid turning his attention inward on his guilt for the deception in which he has participated and from

whose exposure he is now suffering. There is a fine concentration of irony in his recognition of Lord Mark, at
once a flash of clairvoyance in which he truly sees the immediate cause of what has happened and the evasion of
any acknowledgement of his own responsibility. When
Densher tells himself that "the weather had changed . . .
because of Lord Mark," the extravagance of the fallacy
indicates his failure to achieve true moral recognition.
The scene is thus very different from the earlier one in
which Milly's conversion of her surroundings into symbols of her condition facilitates rather than impedes her
self-recognition. The large metaphor she creates enables
her to face rather than avoid her predicament, as she sees
herself as "a poor girl—with her rent to pay for example
—staring before her in a great city. Milly had her rent to
pay, her rent for the future; everything else but how to
meet it fell away from her in pieces, in tatters. . . . Well,
she must go home, like the poor girl, and see" (I, 254).

The novel's greater degree of symbolism also appears
in the way its language is charged with a more intense concentration of meaning, a quality which is particularly
prominent in the cluster of key words and images centering on the notion of "acting." As in the case of the clichés
and dead metaphors which are given new meaning in the
recognition Milly experiences in Regent's Park, symbolization proceeds here by exploiting the latent ambiguities
of a pun. To "act" can mean simply to engage in action
but also to engage in pretense or deception, playacting,
acting as if, or acting out a role. I have already noted the
conflict of moral and aesthetic values which is focused in
the theatrical metaphor in the recognition scene of *The
Ambassadors*. Now the complex of meanings is expanded
to include not only a number of theatrical images but the
extensively repeated words, "act," "acting," and "action,"

creating a thematic node of multiple implications bearing on the problematic relations of action and deception, of moral truth and aesthetic meaning.

Kate Croy is a character who acts in both senses. In her relations with Densher she takes the active part; he represents for her "all the high dim things she lumped together as of the mind," while to him she seems to exhibit a talent for "life," for action, a necessary complement to "his strength merely for thought" (I, 50–51). It is she who plans the act of deception upon Milly to which Densher passively accedes, effected by their acting as if she were not in love with him, as if he could therefore become involved with Milly. Densher, the man of thought and words, is left merely to name the act which Kate has planned: "Since she's to die I'm to marry her" (II, 225). Even the assignation which seals their bargain, forced upon her by Densher's single seizure of the initiative, is dependent on her act: she must "come to" him.

Kate's playacting is not just the result of her plot; it is the essence of her success in the whole social drama. Having chosen the world of Lancaster Gate, she must adopt the role assigned to her by Aunt Maud, leading Densher to see her as "a distinguished actress. As such a person was to dress the part, to walk, to look, to speak, in every way to express, the part, so all this was what Kate was to do for the character she had undertaken, under her aunt's roof, to represent" (II, 34). It is a situation in which Densher, again the passive member, finds himself "relegated to mere spectatorship" (35). As the man of thought Densher must be primarily defined by his perceptions, but Kate is defined and at last condemned by her acting and her acts. She is capable of what Densher genuinely regards as "an act of splendid generosity" in coming to him in Venice, but she vitiates it when, immediately after this tribute, she performs a paradigmatic act of waste and destruction, throwing Milly's letter into the fire (II, 386).

Densher *needs* to feel that he is passive, and therefore not responsible for deception. Long before Kate's full plan has emerged, in his first interview with Milly, he encounters the ambiguities of acting. Kate has misled her by pretending not to love him, by describing him as a disappointed suitor, and he now feels Milly acting on the deception. He tries to tell himself that the responsibility is only Kate's, "that he had himself as yet done nothing deceptive."

> It was Kate's description of him, his defeated state, it was none of his own; his responsibility would begin, as he might say, only with acting it out. The sharp point was, however, in the difference between acting and not acting: this difference in fact it was that made the case of conscience. He saw it with a certain alarm rise before him that everything was acting that was not speaking the particular word. (II, 76)

It is his failure to act, to remove the misconception, which results in his commitment, by the end of the scene, to acting a false part. In his need to feel morally "straight," he tries to minimize his responsibility. The avoidance of moral recognition implicit in the scene in the Piazza becomes explicit as he tells himself that "if [Milly] was upset it wasn't a bit his act" (II, 264), yet it remains true that, in contrast to Kate, "he had thought . . . much more than he had acted" (II, 294). It is his love for Kate which repeatedly leads him to allow the deception to continue. After she has left Venice he treasures to himself the memory of her coming to him: "No other act was possible to him than the renewed act, almost the hallucination of intimacy." He recasts his theatrical image so that this memory of her comes "in view as, when the curtain has risen the stage is in view, night after night, for the fiddlers. He remained thus, in his own theatre, in his single person, perpetual orchestra to the ordered drama." The movement from spectator to orchestra is toward a more active role, but he knows that Kate's act was meant to commit him to "that kind of fidelity of which the other name was careful action" (II, 236–38), that he must now "act absolutely in her sense" (242). Thus Densher, even in his passivity, is drawn into the ambiguity of acting.

In Milly these ambiguities become further complicated and ultimately transformed. For her the problem of acting is not that of engaging in deception, and consequently she does not, like Densher, try to withdraw from action into thought. Instead, as an intense and isolated consciousness, she tries to bridge the gap between them: she is consciousness seeking a mode of action. This is one meaning of her descent from her mountain elevation, where she appears as a static, symbolic figure, to the social world of London, where she interacts with other characters. Her problem is to find a way to act in that world and ultimately to act upon it, and her solution entails the acting of a role.

She first discovers the possibilities inherent in such acting when she unexpectedly encounters Kate and Densher in the National Gallery, an embarrassment for all three. They meet the situation with "their perfect manners," but she finds that her own manner is capable of considerable development.

> The finest part of Milly's own inspiration . . . was the quick perception that what would be of most service was, so to speak, her own native wood-note. She had long been conscious of her unused margin as an American girl. . . . She still had reserves of spontaneity.

133

> . . . She became as spontaneous as possible and as
> American as it might conveniently appeal to Mr.
> Densher, after his travels, to find her. (I, 295–96)

We see the success of her adopted role in its effect on
Densher, who is led to reflect "that American girls, when,
rare case, they had the attraction of Milly, were clearly the
easiest people in the world" (II, 72), and to ponder "the
phenomenon—typical, highly American, he would have
said—of Milly's extreme spontaneity" (II, 89). In time he
becomes aware that she is "able, by choice or by instinctive
affinity to keep down or display" the character of "the
American girl" (II, 215), but the discovery does not damage
its viability as a social mode. Instead, when Densher has
been left with her in Venice, he is able to maintain their
relationship only on the ground of "the national character," encouraging her to continue the role even as both
become thoroughly conscious of the situation. "They
really as it went on *saw* each other at the game; she knowing he tried to keep her in tune with his conception, and
he knowing she thus knew it. Add that he again knew she
knew, and yet that nothing was spoiled by it, and we get
a fair impression of the line they found most completely
workable" (II, 258). It is thus a kind of acting which is
free of deception and therefore closer to the realm of art.

Similar, and more significant, is the way Milly becomes
the dove by acting out a role. When Kate tells her "you're
a dove," she accepts the designation as "revealed truth."
"She studied . . . the dovelike. . . . She should have to be
clear as to how a dove *would* act," and her first trial of the
role with Aunt Maud shows her "the success she could
have as a dove" (I, 283–84). Her acting of such roles is not
only the creation of a successful manner, a mode of social
action, it is a way of giving meaning to herself and thereby,

if only briefly, to her social surroundings as well. In
Venice she creates an appropriate setting for her self-
dramatization, using her wealth to establish herself in the
Palazzo Leporelli "as a counter-move to fate" (II, 142). At
the party she gives "Milly, let loose among" what is only a
group of tourists, "in a wonderful white dress, brought
them somehow into relation with something that made
them more finely genial," so that it seems to Densher that
"the Veronese picture of which he had talked with Mrs.
Stringham" is almost, if "not quite constituted" (II, 213).
It is primarily to Densher that Milly becomes meaningful,
that the aesthetic quality she confers on her world is apparent. He recognizes that this effect is produced by the
"aesthetic instinct" (II, 299), an effect she creates chiefly
by acting as if she were not so ill as she really is, but even
this is done "with no consciousness of fraud" (I, 258) and
is thus free of much of the equivocal sense in which the
others must act.

Densher's development in the last two books consists
largely of his increasing awareness of Milly's meaning; we
have already seen how his divergence from Kate follows
the divergence between their interpretations of this meaning. In the final chapters, the relations of all three are
focused on Milly's letter and the different ways they make
it a symbol. Densher offers it to Kate "as a symbol of [his]
attitude" (II, 386), and her act of throwing it into the fire
damningly symbolizes her own. The thought of the destroyed letter comes to dominate Densher's mind, replacing his previously treasured memory of Kate's coming
to him. He ponders not "the intention announced in it"
but "the part of it missed for ever . . . the turn she would
have given her act. This turn had possibilities that somehow, by wondering about them, his imagination had
extraordinarily filled out and refined. It made of them a

135

revelation" (II, 396). Thus Milly's final act, her last use of her wealth "as a counter-move to fate" has succeeded in making her supremely meaningful to him.[52]

Although this symbolic meaning, like those of the scenes of perception and recognition we have considered, is developed by the response of an imaginative consciousness, it involves more than symbolic perception, for we have also seen it at least partially created by the acting out of a chosen role. James' concentrated vocabulary of "acting" thus carries implications concerning the relation of aesthetic creation and moral meaning as well as the involvement of action with deception. It seems to point to some resolution beyond the unresolved opposition of moral and aesthetic with which *The Ambassadors* concluded. But these are only suggestions as they appear in *The Wings of the Dove;* their development into a new basis for the creation of meaning takes place in James' next novel.

Just as *The Wings of the Dove* creates a greater concentration of meaning than *The Ambassadors,* so *The Golden Bowl* further extends this progression to an unprecedented degree of symbolic intensity. Here, as F. W. Dupee observes, ordinary social occasions and private experiences,

52. The symbolic meaning of the letter differs somewhat in kind from that of the symbolic scenes in that it results from sheer suggestion rather than interpretation. It is thus a striking example of the novel's frequently employed strategy of significant omission. An important instance in the dramatic action is the omission of the last scene between Densher and Milly, which figures only through its profound effect on him, through his feeling "that something had happened to him too beautiful and too sacred to describe. He had been . . . forgiven, dedicated, blessed" (II, 343). Both kinds of symbolism, however, have the same ground, the consciousness of the character who performs the interpretation or responds to the suggestion.

"the round of cards, the little dinner for six, the chance encounter on the terrace, the parley in the garden, are unbearably loaded with meaning."[53] Not only these events and the scenes in which they occur, but much of the novel's objects, events, words, and images are so laden, making it the most complex in English before *Ulysses*. Such complexity makes it necessary to select only a few aspects for consideration, but we should not allow the novel's dazzling concentrations of meaning to blind us to the way in which its complexity is not only a quality but a strategy.

The Golden Bowl combines a dense texture of meaning-fulness created by the suggestions of thickly interwoven motifs with situations in which the basic factual meaning, the true state of affairs, is obscure. An important example is the obscurity of Adam Verver's state of mind throughout the second volume. The question of his degree of consciousness, whether he is aware of the Prince's and Charlotte's adultery and of the intense struggle of wills going on around him, is of crucial importance to the other three major characters. Yet the question remains unanswered and Adam's consciousness inscrutable, his "unfathomable heart folded in the constant flawless freshness of the white waistcoat" (II, 305), like the white curtain of Poe's *Arthur Gordon Pym,* which represents to the Prince the impenetrability of the American mind (I, 22). There are several scenes which present Maggie and Adam in what she takes to be tacit but profound communion. The most important of these is their long talk in the garden at Fawns (II, 253–75), where Adam's words may signify all the knowledge which Maggie finds implied there or may contain nothing beyond their overt meaning. The reader has only Maggie's

53. *Henry James* (Garden City, N.Y., 1956), p. 232.

interpretations, with no way of either verifying them or establishing them as only the products of her imagination. There is thus a strong current of the sort of ambiguity noted earlier in *The Turn of the Screw* and *The Sacred Fount* as well as the ambiguity of rich multiple suggestions of meaning which are not clearly defined. Yet *The Golden Bowl* contains another factor which carries the Jamesian imagination beyond the unresolvable ambiguity of the earlier works. In Maggie Verver James creates a central consciousness capable of achieving essential knowledge even amid the welter of ambiguities and of finally creating her own meaning out of them.

The ambiguity and suggestiveness of *The Golden Bowl* require us to engage in interpretation of meaning before we can consider the way that meaning is created, but such a procedure is also made necessary by the degree to which the creation of meaning itself acquires thematic significance, making the two inseparable. This will be seen when we examine Maggie's role in the novel, but such an examination first requires a choice of the terms in which it is to be conducted. Again, the terms which I have found most appropriate for the aspects of the novel I shall be able to consider are those whose relevance to James we have already seen, particularly in the discussions of *The Portrait of a Lady* and *The Ambassadors,* and for which a great deal of James criticism has established the prefabricated categories of the moral and the aesthetic.

In the Prince the aesthetic sense is clearly predominant, necessarily so, since, as he confesses to Fanny Assingham at a point early in the novel, he lacks what the Americans would recognize as a moral sense. His own is like "the tortuous stone staircase—half-ruined into the bargain!— in some castle of our *quattrocento,*" as opposed to the Americans' steam-driven "lightning elevator." It is so "slow and steep and unlighted, with so many of the steps missing that . . . it's as short in almost any case to turn round and come down again" (I, 31). In its place he employs as supreme criterion the sense of style, "taste . . . as a touchstone" (II, 345). The first volume, narrated largely through the Prince's point of view, provides several examples of his consciousness operating on this basis, but the most important instances occur in the scenes at Matcham. Here his aesthetic sense arrives at its fullest recognition, its most intense response to the appeal of the sensuous and of style.

> Every voice in the great bright house was a call to the ingenuities and impunities of pleasure; every echo was a defiance of difficulty, doubt or danger; every aspect of the picture, a glowing plea for the immediate. . . . For a world so constituted was governed by a spell, that of the smile of the gods and the favour of the powers; the only handsome, the only gallant, in fact the only intelligent acceptance of which was a faith in its guarantees and a high spirit for its chances. (I, 332)

His recognition reveals to him "a higher and braver propriety" than that of the Ververs' "theory" that he and Charlotte may consort "in a state of childlike innocence" (334-35). The criterion of style, the touchstone of taste, thus requires their adultery, whose consummation is the direct outcome of the Matcham scenes.

Dorothea Krook has written at length and well on the allegiance of the Prince (and Charlotte) to the aesthetic, making it unnecessary for me to explore this element more fully. What seems to me more questionable is her interpretation of the countermovement which begins after the aesthetic has enjoyed its climactic recognitions at Matcham,

Maggie's painful emergence and ultimate triumph. Dr. Krook sees this development as the unequivocal ascendance of the moral over the aesthetic; Maggie's restoration of her marriage is seen as bringing the Prince (and presumably the reader) to the recognition of "the surpassing dignity, power and beauty of the moral by which it transcends the inferior dignity, power and beauty of the merely aesthetic."[54] Such an interpretation is not surprising in a book on James originally conceived as a supplement to a study of *Three Traditions of Moral Thought,* but it should give pause to the reader who recalls that James was not only a moral thinker but a highly self-conscious artist who argued in his criticism to an extent unprecedented among English novelists for the status of the novel as a work of art. It seems unlikely that he would devote his most ambitious work to demonstrating the inferiority of the aesthetic.

The difficulty in Dr. Krook's interpretation seems to me to be caused by too narrow a conception of the aesthetic, which appears in *The Golden Bowl* under not just one but two aspects. There is the aesthetic mode exemplified by the Prince, the passive appreciation of style, of surfaces and forms, highly susceptible to the "plea for the immediate" and judging life by the touchstone of taste. This is the sense in which the aesthetic is considered by Dr. Krook. But the aesthetic also involves the active process of artistic creation, and in this sense it is associated in several ways with the development of Maggie herself. In these terms, the redemptive process which takes place in the second volume consists of the redefinition of the aesthetic *and* of the moral so as to bring them into harmony. The result is thus not merely an allegory (Dr. Krook calls

54. *The Ordeal of Consciousness,* p. 272.

it "a great fable") of the redemption of Aesthetic Man by Moral Woman, for Maggie must "save" herself as well as her husband.

Maggie's development is another version of the expansion of consciousness, this time dependent, as Fanny predicts it must be, on the opening of her innocent sense "to Evil . . . for the first time in her life. To the discovery of it, to the knowledge of it, to the crude experience of it. . . . To the harsh bewildering brush, the daily chilling breath of it" (I, 385). It is such a recognition which Maggie confronts in the scene at Fawns that marks the full development of her consciousness in knowledge of herself and her situation, a recognition of "the horror of finding evil seated all at its ease where she had only dreamed of good; the horror of the thing hideously *behind,* behind so much trusted, so much pretended, nobleness, cleverness, tenderness" (II, 237). Maggie's consciousness grows not only in its capacity for content but in its imaginative capability, an aspect of personal development whose relation to the aesthetic we have already seen in Strether. James achieves a subtle presentation of this aspect by exploiting an inherent feature of his narrative mode, the intimate relation between the narrator and the character's consciousness.

The development of the imagination takes place in terms of a triangular relationship between these and several of the novel's most striking images. The drama of shifting emphasis in this relationship is particularly prominent in the first two chapters of the second volume, where Maggie's consciousness is first presented. The situation created by the interlocking marriages is imaged in the exotic figure of "some wonderful beautiful but outlandish pagoda" that has "reared itself" in "the garden of her life." It is "a structure plated with hard bright porcelain," whose "great decorated surface had remained consistently impenetrable and inscrutable," offering her no means of access (II, 3–4). The remarkable figure, elaborated for two pages, has often been taken to be the creation of Maggie's troubled imagination, her own "emblematic perception," but James makes it clear that this is not the case. Maggie's restless walking about the pagoda is her "circulation, as I have called it" (5); when the image shifts, it is with the narrator's parenthetical remark, "might I so far multiply my metaphors, I should compare her to . . . " (7), after which he elaborates "our new analogy," and a page later offers still further suggestions as to how she may "be figured for us" (8). Clearly, then, Maggie's consciousness does not produce these images; they are instead created by the narrator to "represent our young woman's consciousness" (4). These reminders of the narrator's presence are not gratuitous intrusions, "the mere muffled majesty of irresponsible 'authorship.' "[55] He must explicitly enter the narrative because at this point Maggie's own consciousness is too confused and incoherent to achieve the possession and definition of her situation implied in the ability to image it effectively. The organization of the images dramatizes this confusion; they pile up shifting unrelated vehicles in far-fetched comparisons, like that of Maggie with "a silken-coated spaniel who has scrambled out of a pond and who rattles the water from his ears" (6–7). The image of the pagoda has a dreamlike instability, metamorphosing from a "strange tall tower of ivory" and into "a Mahometan mosque," all creating a fantastic effect, the equivalent of Maggie's disturbed consciousness.

James' presentational strategy acquires added point when, in the next chapter, it reveals Maggie's consciousness making its first efforts to grasp the situation. In place

55. "Preface to The Golden Bowl," in The Art of the Novel, p. 328.

of the previous exotic imagery, the Ververs' situation is now compared to the "family coach," for which Charlotte has been brought in as the fourth wheel. James makes it clear that this figure is Maggie's creation; it is "her image," "her projected vision" (23), indicating that this is now more than just Maggie's confused consciousness of her situation as imaged and presented by the narrator; it is her first attempt to make that situation intelligible to herself. She develops the analogy, and now the "fantastic shape" it takes is her own creation, as she imagines that she and Adam, holding the Principino, are actually riding inside the coach, while Amerigo and Charlotte do all the work of pulling it. This is as yet but a tentative beginning of any full imaginative grasp of her situation, but once Maggie's imagination has begun to develop, it does not cease until her vision is complete. When she stands on the terrace at Fawns, reaching the full development of her imagination, its power is reflected in the facility with which she creates striking images. She sees the rejected possibility of venting her jealousy in a violent outburst as "a wild eastern caravan, looming into view with crude colours in the sun, fierce pipes in the air, high spears against the sky, all a thrill, a natural joy to mingle with, but turning off short before it reached her and plunging into other defiles" (II, 237). The exotic quality is deliberately chosen to express the foreignness of this option to her nature. Appropriately closer to home is her image for the discovery of unexpected evil: "It had met her like some bad-faced stranger surprised in one of the thick-carpeted corridors of a house of quiet on a Sunday afternoon" (237). Such imaginative, image-making power is associated with the artistic by the manner in which it is presented. The creation of these images is at first solely the function of the narrator, or "author's voice" and is then assumed by the character, so that Maggie, in this respect, becomes the analogue of "James" and her creation of images a kind of artistic creation.

Maggie's development requires much more of her, however, than the acts of consciousness involved in such imaginative perceptions. More than any of James' previous central consciousnesses, she must learn to act within her social situation. It seems particularly appropriate that James should have chosen to conclude his Preface to *The Golden Bowl* with his insistence on the artist's role as active, on art as "the religion of doing,"[56] suggesting the analogy between Maggie's active restoration of her marriage and the creation of a work of art. Her acting involves her in all the ambiguities of the word revealed in *The Wings of the Dove*. Milly Theale can engage in acting "with no consciousness of fraud," but this is not possible for Maggie, who must consciously lie and dissemble. In the opening pages of the novel the Prince raises the question of the ability of the moral to involve itself in action: "Goodness, I think, never brought anyone out. Goodness, when it's real, precisely, rather keeps people *in*" (I, 7). In Maggie the moral can become active, but only by adopting the aesthetic mode of conscious acting, reflected in the way she perceives herself as a performer in over a dozen theatrical images. Taking her first unsteady steps, she reminds herself

> of an actress who had been studying a part and rehearsing it, but who suddenly, on the stage before the footlights, had begun to improvise, to speak lines not in the text. It was this very sense of the stage and the footlights that kept her up, made her rise higher: just as it was the sense of action that logically involved

56. Ibid., p. 347.

some platform—action quite positively for the first time in her life. . . . She had all the while with it the inspiration of quite remarkably, of quite heroically improvising. Preparation and practice had come but a short way; her part opened out and she invented from moment to moment what to say and do. (II, 33)

Similarly, at various subsequent points, she sees herself as a circus bareback rider (71), as a young actress "engaged for a minor part in the play," who finds herself "suddenly promoted to leading lady" (208), as "some panting dancer of a difficult step" (222), and as an "overworked little trapezist girl" (302).

The element of invention is emphasized because Maggie is not simply recreating a preexistent role, but creating it herself as she goes along. She has "a part to play for which she knew exactly no inspiring precedent" (II, 307), creating a position which "would have been sought in vain in the most rudimentary map of the social relations as such. The only geography marking it would doubtless be that of the fundamental passions" (II, 324). Her acting, like Milly Theale's, is thus a way of giving herself meaning, especial-ly, she hopes, to the Prince. Her first deliberate action, charged "with an infinite sense of intention" (II, 9), is not to meet him at Eaton Square on his return from Matcham but to await him alone in their own home in Portland Place, hoping by this to give him his "first surprise." The situation she thus creates becomes in retrospect like a work of art, "a great picture hung on the wall of her daily life," or "a succession of moments" which are like "different things done during a scene on the stage" (11). In the end her performance has so captured her husband's attention that he sees "nothing but" her (II, 369).

Maggie's creation of meaning involves not only that

145

which she gives herself but also that given to the other actors in the drama; she is at times not just one of the performers but author of the play. Thus she begins to show "something of the glitter of consciously possessing the constructive, the creative hand" (II, 145) in manipulating others, especially Fanny. Looking in at the others from the terrace at Fawns, she sees them as "figures rehearsing some play of which she herself was the author," and passes on to consider another, unoccupied room, which appears "spacious and splendid, like a stage again awaiting a drama . . . a scene she might people . . . either with serenities and dignities and decencies, or with terrors and shames and ruins" (II, 235–36). In taking an active role James' heroine begins to show remarkable similarities to his earlier villainesses such as Madame Merle, deceiving and manipulating others to accomplish her ends. It might seem that the moral has been joined to the aesthetic only at the cost of losing its essentially moral quality. The crucial factor which differentiates Maggie, however, is her repeated willingness to bear all costs herself rather than exacting them from others. The redefinition and unification of the moral and aesthetic complicates both, but the resultant problematical quality does not subvert the essential value of either. In terms of Maggie's role as author, for example, she chooses, in the scene just cited, to reject the melodramatic, self-righteous alternative and to preserve the "decencies" at the cost of acute personal humiliation.

Just as the plot of *The Golden Bowl* requires of consciousness not only perception but action, so the creation of meaning becomes more active; the novel's crucial scenes often center on symbolic actions. The most melodramatically prominent of these is the scene in which Fanny smashes the golden bowl in an effort not to create but to

destroy meaning. Maggie has presented the bowl as providing her first true knowledge, knowledge of the Prince's
and Charlotte's previous intimacy. Fanny has committed
herself to the avoidance of knowledge ("We know nothing
on earth!" she asserts to her husband [I, 400]), and can
only consider the bowl as a threat. Significantly, without
ever learning just how it has conferred this knowledge,
she attacks its meaning. Learning that the bowl has a
crack, she declares to Maggie, "Then your whole idea has
a crack" (II, 178), and dashes it to the floor, hoping not
only to avoid knowledge herself but to destroy it in
Maggie: "Whatever you meant by it—and I don't want
to know *now*—has ceased to exist" (179).

She fails to shatter Maggie's conviction, however;
Maggie later tells herself that "though the bowl had been
broken, her reason hadn't" (184). Instead, she gives this
new development her own meaning, suggesting the course
of her future development:

> She felt within her the sudden split between con-
> viction and action. They had begun to cease on the
> spot, surprisingly, to be connected; conviction, that
> is, budged no inch, only planting its feet the more
> firmly in the soil—but action began to hover like
> some lighter and larger but easier form, excited by its
> very power to keep above ground. It would be free, it
> would be independent, it would go in—wouldn't it?
> —for some prodigious and superior adventure of its
> own. (186)

Rather than allow the conviction of her husband's in-
fidelity to limit her actions to the obvious response of outrage and denunciation, Maggie creates new, subtler alternatives of action and acting. She begins to act these out in
the latter part of this scene, where by revealing her new

knowledge to the Prince without directly accusing him, she creates "a basis not merely momentary on which he could meet her" (189).

Her fullest recognition of all that is implied by the course of action she has chosen does not come until the extraordinary scene which takes place largely on the terrace at Fawns. It begins as she sits, withdrawn from the others like "a tired actress who has the good fortune to be 'off' " (II, 231), watching the Prince, Charlotte, Adam, and Fanny at cards. She becomes intensely conscious "that if she were but different . . . all this high decorum would hang by a hair," that, "springing up under her wrong and making them all start, stare and turn pale, she might sound out their doom in a single sentence, a sentence easy to choose among several of the lurid" (233). The temptation assaults her violently, "as a beast might have leaped at her throat" (235), but she fends it off and moves out onto the terrace, imagining that each of the others is silently appealing to her to assume the burden of "the whole complexity of their peril . . . to charge herself with it as the scapegoat of old . . . had been charged with the sins of the people" (234). From the terrace, in a passage already noted, she conceives her possible courses of action as two opposed dramatic scenes she can create, and, as in the recognition scene of *The Ambassadors,* the metaphor of drama is joined by that of picture. She stops again before the sight of the others within, "as if the recognition had of itself arrested her," and sees, "as in a picture, with the temptation she had fled from quite extinct, why it was she had been able to give herself from the first so little to the vulgar heat of wrong" (236). She realizes "that to feel about them in any of the immediate, inevitable, assuaging ways, the ways usually open to innocence outraged and generosity betrayed, would have been to give

148

them up, and that giving them up was, marvellously, not to be thought of" (237).

This is Maggie's crucial moment of recognition, the recognition toward which she has been instinctively groping and from which her subsequent actions proceed, the realization of the full meaning of being condemned "to the responsibility of freedom" (II, 186). Unlike the crucial recognition of *The Ambassadors*, it does not involve the revelation of hidden factual truth. That recognition has already taken place through the agency of the golden bowl and, significantly, is never even dramatized. It is so far from being the emergence of reality through appearances that it absolutely entails the continued masking of reality by the appearances of "high decorum," now seen as "serenities and dignities and decencies." This is a more imaginatively advanced recognition, for it reveals how the consciousness which achieves it may become not the victim but the remaker of reality. Reality can be remade, can be given the desired meaning, but only by Maggie's submission to the most humiliating implications of the compromising false appearances she helps to perpetuate in a process of acting which is insistently associated with the aesthetic. Her suffering is thus both personally and symbolically the cost of joining the moral and the aesthetic. The problematic quality of their fusion is not one of detached irony but of anguish.

In the second half of this scene, picture merges into drama; Maggie's recognition is not embodied in the form of symbolic perception but of a symbolic action which follows as its consequence. In the room she has previously seen as a stage awaiting the drama of her choice, she receives Charlotte's challenge, which makes her feel "that the scene of life her imagination had made of it twenty minutes before was by this time sufficiently peopled," filled by Charlotte's "few straight words" and by "her consciousness of the part she was called on to play in it" (II, 246–47). Ironically, Charlotte's question, "Is there any wrong you consider I've done you?" offers her precisely the opportunity for the righteous outburst she has desired earlier, but she now knows she must abase herself and lie, accepting the moral-aesthetic paradox that "the right . . . took this extraordinary form of her humbugging . . . to the end. It was only a question of not by a hair's breadth deflecting into the truth" (250–51). The scene ends with the symbolic act of the kiss, its meaning grounded in Maggie's intense state of consciousness and enlarged by the entrance of the others as audience, the act by which Maggie becomes both betrayer and scapegoat.

This scene is linked with a later one, also acted by Maggie and Charlotte, which forms a parallel to it and expands its implications. As we have seen in previous instances, the parallelism is explicated by the character's consciousness; approaching Charlotte in the garden at Fawns, Maggie is aware of how their relation "hád turned itself round; Charlotte was seeing her come through patches of lingering noon as she had watched Charlotte menace her through the starless dark." Their encounter produces "a recognition not less soundless and to all appearance not less charged with strange meanings than that of the other occasion. The point however was that they had changed places" (II, 296). She sees Charlotte as fearing that she has come to take back her lie and make her accusation, but this is not the part Maggie has chosen, and she makes an effort to "look as little dangerous, look as abjectly mild, as possible" (310). She thus gives Charlotte her cue for the role she is to play, and soon she is "in possession of her part," the corresponding one to Maggie's, who has made it plain that she has "presented herself once more to (as they said) grovel; and that truly made the stage large" (313). The drama they act out is an ironic inversion of reality; Charlotte is allowed to play the part of the injured wife asserting her rights, while Maggie must be the defeated intruder, "admitting" that she has "worked against" Charlotte, tried to interfere in her marriage, and now has "failed."

With all the outward appearance of triumph, it is of course Charlotte who has failed; the only comfort allowed her is the preservation of her pride in pretending to choose the fate of banishment which is imposed on her. Just as in the earlier scene Maggie has literally hooded herself in her shawl "for humility" (II, 247), so now for Charlotte "pride . . . had become the mantle caught up for protection and perversity; she flung it round her as a denial of any loss of her freedom" (II, 312). It is ultimately her pride which encages her, while Maggie, abandoning all pride and seeking only some new "supreme abjection" (313), achieves the freedom not only to choose her own role but to impose one on Charlotte. There is a flavor of amoral manipulation about this, but also of moral charity; the moment when Maggie looks from her window, sees Charlotte going off to the garden, and resolves to go to her seems deliberately to recall the crucial scene of Dorothea's recognition of moral involvement and decision to go to Rosamond in *Middlemarch*. The coexistence of the two aspects reflects the complication which the moral undergoes in the process of redefinition. The genuinely moral quality of Maggie's actions has been sufficiently expounded by Dr. Krook and other commentators, but it must be further recognized that this action becomes possible only in an aesthetic mode. The suffering and shame Maggie is willing to bear "for love" (II, 116) give her freedom and an artist-like creative power. The new order which reigns at the close of the novel is therefore, like the stillness after Adam and Charlotte have departed, "not so much restored as created" (II, 366).

The meaning indicated by my interpretation of this theme involves a somewhat different kind of symbolization from that which I have emphasized in James. Here the creation of meaning by the central consciousness is itself symbolic of further meaning which lies beyond her range of awareness. Maggie, after all, is not consciously concerned with abstract categories of value but with saving her marriage. It is a difference between the perspectives established by the character's point of view and by the total structure of the novel. To take as an example one important symbolic element, the analogy between Maggie and the artist, partly created by her own images, is from her point of view a means for understanding her personal situation, but in the total context of the novel it also develops a thrust in the opposite direction, creating implications concerning art in general. Symbolic transposition and generalization are not performed by the character's interpretation but by the reader's, tracing the implications of imagery whose total structure cannot be grasped by Maggie's consciousness, even though she helps to create it.[57]

Symbolization through consciousness and beyond it

57. We should recognize, however, that the separation between these levels of meaning is exaggerated by analytical discrimination and by the tendency for interpretative categories to become hypostatized, converting the work into allegory. The moral and the aesthetic are not only abstract categories of value but modes of consciousness. They are thus as much a part of the dramatic action as are the objects of consciousness (the characters' conscious concerns), although they are revealed in a different perspective.

both contribute to the presentation of the golden bowl itself, and we can therefore gauge their relative importance by examining the sources of its significance. We should bear in mind, however, that the concentration of meaning in a central symbol like the golden bowl is a less frequent form of symbolization in James than that of those less portentously assertive images and events made meaningful by moments of consciousness in scenes such as those I have discussed. Because of its prominence, the golden bowl is too often taken as typical of James' symbolism and as an example of the "transcendent or magic symbol of the poetic novel."[58] Even it, however, gains much of its meaning through consciousness. Its significance may owe something to such extrinsic factors as allusions to the Bible or Blake, but it owes much more to the meanings it acquires at different moments for several of the characters.

As each of the characters encounters the bowl, he gives it his own meaning. Charlotte, wanting to give it as a present to the Prince, symbolizes her desire to give herself, and he, instinctively divining its flaw, refuses, showing the good faith with which he enters his marriage. He is not as scrupulous when, submitting at Matcham to the spell of appearances, he accepts her offer of herself and of "the day like a great gold cup that [they] must somehow drain together" (I, 359). We have already seen the accusing meaning the bowl holds for Fanny in the scene where Maggie reveals it to her: it acquires for her "a sturdy, a conscious perversity; as a 'document,' somehow, it was ugly, though it might have a decorative grace" (II, 165). This is the meaning she tries to destroy but which re-

58. Ursula Brumm, "Symbolism and the Novel," tr. Willard R. Trask, *Partisan Review*, 25 (1958), 337.

mains intact for Maggie, the breaking of the bowl coming to represent the disruption of her world. She thus tells Fanny that what she wants is "the golden bowl—as it *was* to have been. . . . The bowl with all our happiness in it. The bowl without the crack" (II, 216–17), and in the scene on the terrace at Fawns she thinks of the possible "terrors and shames and ruins" she could precipitate as "things as ugly as those formless fragments of her golden bowl she was trying so hard to pick up" (II, 236). The moment of fear and self-doubt she suffers there is also made to turn on opposed interpretations of the broken bowl. Guessing that Charlotte, now seeking her out and about to confront her, plans to undermine her position by complaining of her suspicions to Adam, Maggie is seized by the implications of such a possibility.

> If so much as this was still firm ground between the elder pair, if the beauty of apearances had been so consistently preserved, it was only the golden bowl as Maggie herself knew it that had been broken. The breakage stood not for any wrought discomposure among the triumphant three—it stood merely for the dire deformity of her attitude toward them. (II, 240)

The symbol of the bowl thus contains the same ambiguity we have seen arising from the question of Adam's knowledge, and Maggie can achieve her remaking of the bowl only by accepting this ambiguity and working within its terms. She must make of Charlotte's "confidence" and "operating insolence" a "new basis and . . . a new system" (240–41), the system of acting and abasement she then follows to its culmination in the kiss which concludes the scene.

But although much of the meaning attached to the bowl is created by different consciousnesses, its cumulative importance exceeds any single awareness. For each occasion on which it is present to a consciousness, either materially or in memory, there are numerous others when it is invoked only for the reader by James' suggestions, in allusions to cups overflowing or to things broken or the act of gathering up pieces, even in the frequent uses in many different contexts of the word "golden." The character's consciousness may therefore both partially apprehend and help to create its symbolism without totally comprehending it. An example is the symbolic meaning of Maggie's picking up the pieces of the shattered bowl, imaging her efforts to recreate the shattered order of her life. As we have seen, she herself uses this image for her efforts as she reaches the peak of her consciousness' development (II, 236), but this meaning is not present to her as she performs the act itself. It is the terms of James' presentation (and also the reader's knowledge of subsequent events) which makes the moment itself symbolic. Deliberately giving her husband time to collect himself, Maggie stoops to gather up the fragments: "Bedizened and jewelled, in her rustling finery, she paid, with humility of attitude, this prompt tribute to order—only to find however that she could carry but two of the fragments at once" (II, 182). The double import of the phrases: "humility of attitude," "tribute to order," creates symbolic overtones like those of the puns which express Milly Theale's recognition in Regent's Park. Here the overtones resound only in the consciousness of the narrator—and of the reader. Maggie's inability to hold more than two of the three pieces seems furthermore to prefigure the necessity of losing her father in order to rejoin herself to her husband, just as her act the next moment of holding the two pieces of the bowl together prefigures her efforts to accomplish this reunification.

This symbolic action seems to be again invoked when, at the conclusion of the scene with Charlotte in the garden, when she has at last "done all," Maggie takes up the two volumes of the novel (again two of three), "put them together and laid them down" (II, 318), symbolizing, though not consciously, the reunification she has now accomplished. Such correspondences between a realistic surface and an underlying symbolic level, with only the reader able to perceive their connections, are interesting in the light of subsequent developments in the novel, but are of relatively minor importance in James. Few readers have recognized the significance of Maggie's joining the two volumes, but the oversight has hardly mattered. In a novel by Joyce, it might be crucial. Here, whether or not we are aware that the symbolism of the golden bowl is being invoked, we know through Maggie's consciousness that she has indeed "done all."

The question of the kind of symbolism which is predominant in James leads to the further, and final, consideration of the degree of symbolism in his entire fictional mode. George Eliot's symbolism creates, in Barbara Hardy's words, "reinforcements of value rather than totally responsible vehicles."[59] Are James' symbols such totally responsible vehicles of meaning? Mrs. Hardy would seem to think so, considering them in terms of the whole pattern they create, the "figure in the carpet." She describes James' novels as creating structures of "total relevance" which incorporate every detail in their organizations of

59. *The Appropriate Form*, p. 199.

meaning: "James gives us a dramatically enclosed and self-contained world where everything has relevance to the main argument, where appearances, gestures, objects, conversation, all shoot out like sure arrows to the heart of the matter. His pattern is insistently centripetal, his relevance is total."[60] We have indeed seen the possible relevance of all such details on various occasions, but their *total* relevance is not only undemonstrable, it is positively disprovable. Even James' later fiction offers instances of details quite lacking in centripetal relevance. For example, in *The Wings of the Dove,* Kate's and Densher's first interview after his return from Venice can take place without fear of interruption because Aunt Maud is "engaged with an old servant, retired and pensioned, who had been paying her a visit and who was within the hour to depart again for the suburbs" (II, 316). The way in which these details "shoot out like sure arrows to the heart of the matter" is far from clear.

With some qualification, however, Mrs. Hardy's point is sound: James' novels, even the earlier ones such as *The Portrait of a Lady,* develop a higher degree of relevance than do George Eliot's and thus create a pervasive pressure of significance, of potential symbolism which plays a more extensive, more important role than that of her "reinforcements of value." Yet that potential is realized, as it is in George Eliot, in crucial scenes of recognition. James' structure of relevance is therefore not so much a figure in the carpet, a design hidden from the characters it embraces, as a system of implications which is revealed and organized by their own creative perceptions. The description of James' symbolism should center, accordingly, on those points where meaning is revealed, the

60. Ibid., p. 15.

focuses of his centripetal relevance. In general, these concentrations of meaning occur in and through moments of intense consciousness, creating scenes of symbolic perception and action. If we ask whether the symbolism of such scenes functions as reinforcements of value or totally responsible vehicles of meaning, we find the question inapplicable. It implies that only certain elements of the scene possess symbolic significance and either reinforce or assume responsibility from others. The distinction is applicable to George Eliot's recognition scenes, but in James the entire scenic complex is at once actual and symbolic, with no division or tension between the two aspects. The character's consciousness creates and inserts an image between itself and the world into which both are merged. The world and its meaning become one. For much of the symbolism not created by consciousness, however, the question is pointedly applicable. As we have seen in the symbolism of Maggie juxtaposing the two volumes, it is indeed only a reinforcement; our understanding of the scene is not dependent on it. The creations of consciousness constitute the essence of James' meaning; what lies beyond serves only to reinforce or extend that significance.

The creative vision of his central characters thus becomes not only the focus but the primary source of James' meaning, and in their struggle to grasp and finally to give meaning to their experience, they become not only the agents but the counterparts of the artist. "It is art," James wrote in a famous letter to H. G. Wells, "that *makes* life, makes interest, makes importance, for our consideration and application of these things, and I know of no substitute whatever for the force and beauty of its process."[61]

61. In *Discussions of Henry James*, p. 7.

In James' art, consciousness, borne in the vessels of his central figures, likewise makes life by making meaning. "Their being finely aware . . . *makes* absolutely the intensity of their adventure, gives the maximum of sense to what befalls them."[62]

62. "Preface to *The Princess Casamassima,*" in *The Art of the Novel,* p. 62.

JOSEPH CONRAD: Intrinsic Significance

Conrad's fiction presents a world which, even apart from the meaning it may be given by the interpretation of an individual consciousness, displays an inherently more symbolic quality than does James'. Objects, characters, and events, described in vivid, visual detail, also convey insistent suggestions of further significance. The opening chapter of *Nostromo* provides a striking example of this quality, since it presents the physical setting of the story for our undistracted attention before the characters take their places in the foreground. Of course, the symbolic significance of this landscape is more apparent in the context of the whole novel, but it is also conveyed by the initial presentation. The description stresses the isolation of Sulaco, cut off from the rest of Costaguana by "the towering and serrated wall of the Cordillera" (5)[1] and from the rest of the world by the great Golfo Placido, whose prevailing calms frustrate the approach of sailing ships. At night, the "black poncho" of cloud cuts off the heavens as well, and with them, seemingly, all relation to the transcendent: in such impenetrable darkness, say the seamen, "the eye of God Himself . . . could not find out what work a man's hand is doing in there" (7). The chap-

1. All page references are to the Uniform Edition of *The Works of Joseph Conrad* (London, J. M. Dent and Sons, 1923) and are incorporated in the text. Other Dent and American Doubleday editions follow the same pagination.

ter centers on the tale of the two "gringos" on the peninsula of Azuera, lost in an alien and totally unaccommodat-
ing setting.[2] The world presented in this opening description is one where, as Stein says in *Lord Jim,* man
"is not wanted, where there is no place for him" (208).

Conrad draws upon the significance of this symbolic
landscape when he later uses it as a setting for episodes
which relate the general theme of human isolation to the
fates of individual characters. It is a dark night on the
Gulf which isolates Nostromo and Decoud in the lighter.
The values men erect to shelter themselves from a humanly meaningless universe cannot withstand the annihila-
ting, isolating darkness. Decoud begins to lose faith in the
public causes and the private love to which he has tried
to commit himself, and Nostromo begins to lose faith in
the public esteem which has been his supreme value. Later,
it is in the unbroken silence of the Gulf that Decoud,
marooned on the Great Isabel, loses all sense of his identity into "the world of cloud and water, of natural forces
and forms of nature" (497); finally committing suicide, he
is both literally and symbolically "swallowed up in the
immense indifference of things" (501). Not only for the individual, but for the entire society, Conrad's vast symbolic
setting imposes a scale which reduces human actions to
meaninglessness. This is the perspective from which we
observe, with old Giorgio, the rioting on the plain before
the city:

> Knots of men ran headlong; others made a stand;
> and the irregular rattle of firearms came rippling to
> his ears in the fiery, still air. Single figures on foot
> raced desperately. Horsemen galloped towards each

2. Robert Penn Warren has noted this symbolism in his Introduction to the Modern Library edition (New York, 1951), p. xxxv.

other, wheeled round together, separated at speed.
Giorgio saw one fall, rider and horse disappearing as
if they had galloped into a chasm, and the movements
of the animated scene were like passages of a violent
game played upon the plain by dwarfs mounted and
on foot, yelling with tiny throats, under the mountain that seemed a colossal embodiment of silence.
(26–27)

Here, of course, it is not only the presentation of suggestive visual images which conveys significance; these are
glossed by the annotations of Conrad's rhetoric, of which
the last phrase of this passage is an example.[3] Yet even
without such commentary, the landscape of *Nostromo* is
insistently significant. Like much of the subject matter of
Conrad's fiction, it is exotic, thus claiming special attention, and it is relatively contrived, the arrangement of its
features controlled by an abstract meaning. The geography
of Sulaco enacts the theme of human isolation and of
cosmic indifference, a preexistent meaning which Conrad's narrator or characters discover rather than create.
This intrinsically significant quality of Conrad's fictional
world creates a situation in which, even in works where
individual consciousness plays a larger role than in *Nostromo,* it does not assume the crucial importance it has
in James. James' characters confront commonplace reality
and transform it into symbol; Conrad's confront an exotic
and already significant world whose meaning they may or
may not recognize. There is an important difference be-

3. The significance of the mountain appears to the narrator, not
Giorgio. We are specifically informed a few lines before the beginning
of the quoted passage that Giorgio "did not look up once at the white
dome of Higuerota, whose cool purity seemed to hold itself aloof from
a hot earth" (26).

tween the modes of symbolization exemplified by Milly Theale's experience in Regent's Park and by Marlow's in the Congo.

The relation between Conrad's symbolism and the consciousness of his characters will be more fully considered when we turn to those works where it plays a greater part, but the elements I have briefly noted in *Nostromo* already suggest another important difference between Conrad and James. Not only does Conrad's landscape hold a symbolic meaning independent of the meaning it may acquire for any character, but its symbolism is directed toward a more general level of significance than is James' symbolism. The suggestions it conveys are not primarily about the nature of individual characters or of society but about the nature of the universe. Conrad's works also deploy symbols on less metaphysical levels, but they repeatedly drive toward such a highly general meaning. Yet it is a meaning which, as several critical explorations have shown, does not share the stability of George Eliot's general concepts but displays an ambiguity, a problematic quality as great, though perhaps not as controlled, as that of James.[4]

4. As an example of critics who have recognized the problematic quality in Conrad's works produced by their unresolved tensions, we may take Dorothy Van Ghent *(The English Novel: Form and Function* [New York, 1961], p. 244), who concludes that in *Lord Jim* Conrad "put both the law and the self to question, and left them there." More common in Conrad criticism is the attribution, not unjustifiable, of such tensions to Conrad's own inner conflicts. Thus to Douglas Hewitt *("Lord Jim:* Conrad and the 'Few Simple Notions,'" in *Conrad: A Collection of Critical Essays,* ed. Marvin Mudrick [Englewood Cliffs, N.J., 1966], p. 60) the problematic quality of *Lord Jim* indicates, "very clearly, a conflict in Conrad's own mind." Albert J. Guerard sets out, in nine separate categories, a catalogue of "major inward conflicts" in Conrad *(Conrad the Novelist* [Cambridge, Mass., 1958], pp. 57–58). The most recent general investigation of such

Although the landscape of *Nostromo* is clearly, insistently symbolic, it is not as highly charged with significance
as that of *Heart of Darkness*. The progression from London to the "sepulchral city" of Brussels to Africa and then
on into the interior proceeds through an increasingly portentous landscape. Here, however, it is not presented
panoramically as in the opening chapter of *Nostromo,* but
as a succession of fragmentary impressions, charged images.
There is, for example, the French man-of-war: "In the
empty immensity of earth, sky, and water, there she was,
incomprehensible, firing into a continent" (61–62), an
image of the madness and futility of the imperial enterprise. The first Company station appears as a cluster of
images; there are the scattered "pieces of decaying machinery": "a boiler wallowing in the grass," "an under-
sized railway truck lying . . . on its back with its wheels in
the air," "a stack of rusty rails," the "wanton smash-up" of
drainage pipes tumbled into a ravine (63–66). These present the waste and incompetence which permeate the
Company's efforts; the enchained natives and those dying
in the grove, the pointless blasting at the cliff (like the
French ship firing into the continent) image their cruelty
and stupidity. Characters as well as objects are absorbed
into the imagistic stream. The fastidious accounting clerk,
for example, also appears as a cluster of images: "a high
starched collar, white cuffs, a light alpaca jacket, snowy
trousers, a clear necktie, and varnished boots. No hat. Hair
parted, brushed, oiled, under a green-lined parasol held in
a big white hand. He was amazing, and had a penholder

---

basic conflicts in Conrad has been made by Ian Watt, "Joseph Conrad:
Alienation and Commitment," in *The English Mind: Studies in the
English Moralists Presented to Basil Willey,* ed. Hugh Sykes Davies
and George Watson (Cambridge, 1964), pp. 257–78.

behind his ear" (67). Such detached images lend themselves to rearrangement for significant juxtaposition. Thus we find, joined in a single sentence, the clerk, "bent over his books . . . making correct entries of perfectly correct transactions" and, "fifty feet below the doorstep . . . the still treetops of the grove of death" (70), the contrast emphasizing the inhumanity of his "correctness." Beyond this, these images, with dozens of others, contribute to the cumulative effect of nightmarish unreality which surrounds this "sordid farce acted in front of a sinister backcloth." (61).

The sordid farce of imperialism is primarily presented in this imagistic manner, but as the narrative progresses, the center of attention shifts toward the sinister backcloth, "the silent wilderness . . . great and invincible, like evil or truth, waiting patiently for the passing away of this fantastic invasion" (76). With this shift in focus comes a change of method; the manner of presentation becomes less imagistic, more rhetorical, the locus of action less external, more within the consciousness of Marlow. *Heart of Darkness* is, of course, Marlow's tale almost from the beginning, and it is initially in the medium of his consciousness, in both his immediate response and subsequent reflection, that the images we have considered become significant. It is to him that the clerk appears "amazing"; it is his ironic perception which juxtaposes the "correct" bookkeeping with the grove of death. But as I have already suggested, consciousness in Marlow is not as centrally important as it is in James' protagonists. Like the narrator of *Nostromo*, he recognizes signficance but does not create it. His responses indicate meaningfulness, but even when they assign a particular meaning, it is often not in the form of full or adequate explication. An early example is the two women knitting black wool in the Company's offices. They are first presented without comment (55), an ominous image to which Marlow soon returns, finding them "uncanny and fateful" (57). Yet the suggestions of specific symbolic meaning in Marlow's adjectives ("fateful" = like Fates) are not as far-reaching as the general "eerie feeling" they inspire in him and therefore in the reader. His characteristic rhetorical meditation on these figures ("Often far away there I thought of these two, guarding the door of Darkness, knitting black wool as for a warm pall, one introducing, introducing continuously to the unknown, the other scrutinizing the cheery and foolish faces with unconcerned old eyes" [57]) is less important as an assignment of symbolic attributes than as a means of elaborating his affective state and his efforts to probe its meaning.

Marlow's consciousness therefore functions first as a focus of affect; it is furthermore engaged in interpretative efforts which do provide suggestions of specific meaning, but which ultimately serve to gesture beyond these toward an elusive yet threatening meaningfulness. Such gesturing may be rhetorical in substance, but it is dramatic in form, for it enacts the struggle of consciousness with mystery. This is Conrad's version of the drama of consciousness, a drama which increasingly dominates the latter part of *Heart of Darkness*. In the earlier sections the vivid, imagistic presentation admirably fulfills the famous statement of artistic intention in the Preface to *The Nigger of the Narcissus:* "to make you hear, to make you feel . . . before all, to make you see."[5] In the individual images we see the physical reality, and in their collective effect, lightly annotated by Marlow, we see the moral reality behind

5. *Joseph Conrad on Fiction,* ed. Walter F. Wright (Lincoln, Neb. 1964), p. 162.

them, "that glimpse of truth" which the Preface also promises. But as the tale progresses, another motive asserts itself: to make you suspect what cannot be seen. J. Hillis Miller has recently declared that the "key to [Conrad's] aesthetic theory" is to be found in this sentence from *Lord Jim:* "Only a meticulous precision of statement would bring out the true horror behind the appalling face of things" (30).[6] It is revealing to consider this sentence in its context. It presents Jim's thoughts as he testifies at the Inquiry, but we know that his precise statements there quite fail to "bring out the true horror" for most of his listeners. Only for Marlow (and perhaps Brierly) does something like this emerge, and the efforts of Marlow's consciousness to grapple with and express it require other strategies besides "meticulous precision of statement."

The latter parts of *Heart of Darkness* are filled with notably imprecise statements, such as, "It was the stillness of an implacable force brooding over an inscrutable intention" (93). To F. R. Leavis such language, the "adjectival insistence on inexpressible and incomprehensible mystery," the recurring phrases about "unspeakable rites," "unspeakable secrets," "monstrous passions," "inconceivable mystery," and so on, reveal Conrad's failure to achieve his effect by "the concrete presentment of incident, setting and image" which predominates in the tale's earlier sections. To Mr. Leavis, Conrad appears "intent on making a virtue out of not knowing what he means. The vague and unrealizable, he asserts with a strained impressiveness, is the profoundly and tremendously significant."[7] One may agree that Conrad's (or Marlow's) rhetoric does indeed

---

6. *Poets of Reality: Six Twentieth-Century Writers* (Cambridge, Mass., 1965), p. 38.

7. *The Great Tradition* (Garden City, N.Y., 1954), pp. 216–19.

become strained at times, but it does not follow that he should have continued to employ the imagistic method with which the earlier parts are presented. The change of focus from the corruption of imperialism to the wilderness and Kurtz requires a change of method. Marlow's journey changes in form from a voyage to a kind of quest, moving from the earlier "pilgrimage amongst hints for nightmares" (62) toward "the nightmare of [his] choice" (141). Marlow is detached from the sordid farce of imperialism, but the wilderness and Kurtz involve him more actively because of the unanticipated links he senses between them and himself, like his sense of "remote kinship" with the "wild and passionate uproar" of the savages, forcing him to realize that "the mind of man is capable of anything" (96), a suspicion borne out by Kurtz. Such intimations threaten the values of Marlow's world; Kurtz has "kicked the very earth to pieces" (144), and all the involutions of Marlow's rhetoric are the form taken by his efforts "to account to [himself] for . . . Mr. Kurtz" (117).

James, commenting on *Chance* in "The New Novel," naturally recognized the importance of consciousness in Conrad's last and most elaborate use of Marlow. He saw that Conrad's method resulted in a narrative with "the form not of such and such a number of images discharged and ordered, but that rather of a wandering, circling, yearning imaginative *faculty*."[8] It is such a form which the latter part of *Heart of Darkness* increasingly assumes, an appropriate form for the drama of Marlow's consciousness.[9] The content of Marlow's rhetoric is also appropri-

8. In *Selected Literary Criticism,* ed. Morris Shapira (New York, 1965), p. 38.
9. The "wandering, circling" movement to which James refers in *Chance* is, of course, primarily the product of its intricate shifts in time and narrative viewpoint, features largely absent from the pre-

ate, but not in the way one might expect. Its effect is not, as Mr. Leavis claims, to assert that the "vague and unrealizable . . . is the profoundly and tremendously significant," but rather to present consciousness assaulted by a sense of profound and tremendous significance which, despite all efforts to probe and express it, remains vague and unrealized. Such a "failure of the imagination" has recently been made the focus of a reinterpretation of *Heart of Darkness* by James Guetti.[10] As he points out, Marlow speaks of "reality" or "truth" in two distinct senses. On the one hand, there is the saving "surface-truth" of his work (97), in which a man may find his "own reality" (85), but on the other there is his sense of a reality lying below the surface and threatening it. From this perspective the "surface-truth" only shields consciousness by distracting it from the deeper reality: "When you have to attend to . . . the mere incidents of the surface, the reality . . . fades. The inner truth is hidden—luckily, luckily" (93). This primary reality is sensed both within the self, the darkness in every heart, and outside it, the heart of the

---

dominantly linear, first-person narrative of *Heart of Darkness*. Here such movement occurs mainly within Marlow's rhetorical meditations. But note how, at precisely the moment where Marlow begins to talk of Kurtz (115), chronological order is disrupted; he leaps forward in time, presenting a cluster of facts about Kurtz and reflections on them. The efforts of his consciousness "trying to account . . . for . . . Mr. Kurtz" (117) here produce a wandering, circling form.

This is perhaps a good place to emphasize that my distinction between the forms taken by the earlier and later parts is, for purposes of analysis, made sharper than it actually is in Conrad's tale, where the two manners of presentation overlap considerably. Visual imagery persists to the end, and rhetorical reflections appear from the beginning. The shift is one of proportion.

10. "*Heart of Darkness* and the Failure of the Imagination," *Sewanee Review*, 73 (1965), 488–504.

wilderness' darkness, which Marlow feels as "the amazing reality of its concealed life" (80). Although the action of the story and Marlow's own assertions present him as penetrating "deeper and deeper into the heart of darkness" (95), he is repeatedly forced to admit that the true nature of the reality he senses eludes him: "The essentials of this affair lay deep under the surface, beyond my reach, and beyond my powers of meddling" (100).

Marlow's consciousness cannot grasp the inner reality, but the very vagueness and unrealized quality of his rhetoric as he both tries to comprehend it and to protect himself from the threatening implications he senses in it still serve to gesture toward it, to dramatize as well as assert its ineffability, and thus to give it a kind of meaning. Thus *Heart of Darkness* creates two different kinds of symbolic meaning, which seem to correspond with Marlow's two kinds of reality. The sharp, visual images which anatomize imperialistic corruption and lunacy create a clear, definite moral meaning, perhaps analogous with the clear, definite moral values which Marlow preserves by adherence to the surface-truth of work. The portentous, rhetorically elaborated symbols of the wilderness and Kurtz create an obscure, indefinite metaphysical meaningfulness, not just analogous but identical with the dark inner reality. It is furthermore a metaphysical meaningfulness whose one established attribute is the threat it poses to all moral meaning. If Marlow could bridge the gap between them, the probable result would be annihilation, the fate of Kurtz, whose dying words present the most authoritative interpretation of the darkness. In the unresolved tension between the two realms lies the tale's problematic quality, fulfilling the expectations of the anonymous narrator, who anticipates "one of Marlow's inconclusive experiences" (51).

Together, the two kinds of symbolism produce a more symbolic mode than that of previous English fiction. In the shorter form and imagistic structure of *Heart of Darkness,* fiction approaches the poem. Action, the journey to the interior, and characters, the figures who become images, are readily transposed to a symbolic plane. Even in Marlow, the central character, realistic presentation may yield precedence to symbolism. This may be seen in Marlow's response to "the terrible frankness" of the savage drums, his sense of "an appeal . . . in this fiendish row" (96–97). Speaking from a realistic viewpoint, Albert J. Guerard is doubtless right to say that "we cannot quite believe the response of Marlow's heart to the beating of the tom-toms." But it is a misapprehension of fictional mode to attribute this "flaw" to "late Victorian" theories about reversion to savagery, "a currently accepted but false psychology."[11] What has instead happened is that symbolic motives have replaced psychological ones; Marlow's response accords not with any theory of human nature but with the symbolic patterns of the tale, to which its relevance is clear. With *Heart of Darkness* we have arrived at a point in the development of fictional modes where symbolism has clearly become a primary vehicle of meaning, where the human drama of character and action may even become reinforcements of the symbol. *Heart of Darkness* exemplifies Conrad's symbolic mode in a highly concentrated state; its qualities are necessarily modified in his longer works under the demands of other, more traditional novelistic concerns. Having now examined the symbolic quality of Conrad's fictional world and the way in which consciousness confronts it, let us see how these elements function in the structure of a full-length novel,

11. *Conrad the Novelist,* pp. 37–39.

ing as an example *Lord Jim*, written at the same time
Heart of Darkness and sharing many of its features and
concerns.

The most prominent of these shared features is the use
of Marlow, whose consciousness, whenever present, always plays an important part in Conrad's creation of
meaning. As the narrator of *Heart of Darkness* tells us,

> The yarns of seamen have a direct simplicity, the
> whole meaning of which lies within the shell of a
> cracked nut. But Marlow was not typical . . . and to
> him the meaning of an episode was not inside like
> a kernel but outside, enveloping the tale which
> brought it out only as a glow brings out a haze, in
> the likeness of one of these misty haloes that some-
> times are made visible by the spectral illumination of
> moonshine. (48)

This outside, enveloping meaning resides in Marlow's
consciousness, which, as he tells the story, literally encloses
the tale, and for which it "seemed to throw a kind of
light" (51). As we have seen, both kinds of Conrad's symbolism exist independent of Marlow's consciousness, but
they are presented through it, and in the case of the
second, more obscure kind, it is only through Marlow's
response, however inadequate, that significance can appear. *Lord Jim* gives greater scope to Marlow's "prolonged
hovering flight of the subjective over the outstretched
ground of the case exposed," and here it is more nearly
true that, as James wrote of *Chance*, "we make out this
ground but through the shadow cast by the flight."[12]

James again draws attention to the concern with consciousness which Conrad shares with him, yet the very

12. *Selected Literary Criticism*, p. 333.

terms of his metaphor imply another important difference between the two. Consciousness in Marlow is detached from the experience whose significance it ponders. In *Heart of Darkness* it is separated by time, in *Lord Jim* not only by time but also by the fact that the crucial experience is that of another person, Jim. Through rifts in the obscuring mists which always seem to surround him, Jim appears to Marlow "distinct of form and pregnant with vague appeal like a symbolic figure in a picture" (133). Marlow declares at one point, "I don't know why he should always have appeared to me symbolic" (265), but his many scattered remarks offer ample explanation of Jim's significance for him.

The ground of this significance is, as Marlow repeatedly insists, that Jim is "one of us," and it is precisely in his recognition and assertion of this bond that Marlow makes his greatest contribution to establishing Jim's significance. That Jim is "one of us" means, initially, that he is one of those men of the sea who are not content "to lounge safely through existence" (13), "an obscure body of men held together by a community of inglorious toil and by fidelity to a certain standard of conduct" (50). It is their cohesion which is crucial. In a world which, like that imaged in the opening chapter of *Nostromo,* lends no objective support to human values, men can preserve meaning only by their collective maintenance of such standards and by their mutual support of one another. It is for this reason that, to Marlow, "we exist only so far as we hang together" (223). In this perspective, Jim's failure becomes intensely significant. Although in itself it may be "obscure, insignificant . . . completely devoid of importance," to Marlow it seems to contain an "obscure truth . . . momentous enough to affect mankind's conception of itself" (93). Because he is "one of us," Jim's leap from the *Patna* ruptures "the solidarity of our lives" (224), and raises in Marlow's mind "the doubt of the sovereign power enthroned in a fixed standard of conduct" (50). Thus his prolonged brooding over Jim is, like his efforts to account to himself for Kurtz, an expression of the tension between conflicting meanings, an effort both to probe the enigma and to quell its threat. In Marlow's attempts to convey Jim's significance to his audience he greatly enlarges, and in a sense creates it for the reader, finally producing his own "amazing Jim-myth" (280), in which this unprepossessing young dreamer becomes a portentously symbolic figure.

Here consciousness is more adequate to its experience than in *Heart of Darkness*. Although Jim (or what he symbolizes) remains an enigma for Marlow, "Under a cloud, inscrutable at heart" (416), this aspect and the resultant "failure of imagination" are less emphasized. There is more scope for consciousness' ability to register, indicate, and enlarge significance. Jim does not initially possess the exotic, portentous quality of Kurtz or the Congo wilderness, and Marlow therefore plays a larger part in making him meaningful. Although Conrad does present Jim apart from his narrative, Marlow is essentially correct in claiming that "it is only through me that he exists for you" (224). With his greater capability comes a greater degree of participation in creating the form which the novel takes. Conrad makes significant selections, juxtapositions, and shifts in time, but these are also created by the movements of Marlow's consciousness as he remembers and associates incidents and characters. In the stream of his recollections, minor characters appear briefly and in isolation from any causally related plot sequence, like the servant in Stein's house, who admits Marlow and then "vanished in a mysterious way as though he had been a ghost only momentarily embodied for that particular

service" (204). Such characters, Brierly, the French Lieu-
tenant, Chester, litle Bob Stanton, and others, readily become symbolic figures whose significance proceeds from
their correspondence or contrast with aspects of Jim.

As with persons, so with places: the world of *Lord Jim*
is dotted with places which are located less in a physical
than a mental geography. The English parsonage from
which Jim comes is an early example, an abode of "piety
and peace," stable and insulated, where men can comfortably believe themselves possessed of "certain knowledge of the Unknowable" (5). When, much later, we see
Jim's last letter from home, it confirms this early ironic
view, leading Marlow to reflect on the family Jim left
behind in "that quiet corner of the world as free of danger
or strife as a tomb . . . breathing equably the air of undis-
turbed rectitude" (342). For all his failures, Jim has
achieved a truer confrontation with reality than these
"placid, colourless forms of men and women." Like his
place of origin, Jim's ultimate destination is presented in
terms of thematic qualities, not as neutral location. Patusan, place of "secular gloom," inhabited by "the old mankind" (265), is also isolated, but scarcely "free of danger or
strife." Here Jim, having failed the collective ideal, can
attempt to realize his own. Both character and place as
symbol are joined in the symbolic tableau which Marlow
makes of his last view of Jim: "For me that white figure in
the stillness of coast and sea seemed to stand at the heart
of a vast enigma." As Marlow sails off, leaving Jim on the
dark shore, he appears, "no bigger than a child—then only
a speck, a tiny white speck, that seemed to catch all the
light left in a darkened world" (336). Full commentary on
this passage would require consideration of the novel's
elaborate and extensive pattern of light and dark images,
of which this is a crucial instance. But even in isolation it

suggests the extension which has been given to the sense in which Jim is "one of us." The test Patusan offers his private dream also raises questions about the public values which are themselves ultimately a kind of dream. Not just Jim but all men appear as a speck of light against the darkness.

The novelistic structure of *Lord Jim* does exert more control on the direct incorporation of elements into a symbolic pattern than is felt in *Heart of Darkness*. Dorothy Van Ghent notes Conrad's ability "to make the circumstances of 'plot' the inevitable point of discharge of the potentiality of 'character.' "[13] Thus symbolic objects, characters, and events are sometimes drawn out of portentous isolation into the web of causal plot relations. The sunken wreck that strikes the *Patna* and Gentleman Brown not only symbolize hidden or unacknowledged aspects of Jim's character, they serve as catalysts for their emergence. Yet relatively few of the novel's symbols fit this description. Its overriding drive is toward the assimilation of fictional elements into patterns of significance centering on Jim, who himself becomes increasingly symbolic. The implications of this symbolism all point insistently toward higher and higher levels of generalization, toward the metaphysical level of meaning we have already noted as the objective of the symbolic landscape in *Nostromo*. Yet when we rise to this metaphysical level we find ourselves in an atmosphere not of superterrene clarity but of even greater obscurity. *Lord Jim* offers a paradigm of this aspect of Conrad in the famous oracles of Stein on "how to be," at once the most metaphysical and the most enigmatic pronouncements in the novel. Is "the destructive element" identical with or opposed to "the dream"? Critical interpretations

13. *The English Novel*, p. 234.

show no agreement on the question, yet it is crucial. The novel's conclusion is similarly problematic. Does Jim's death redeem his former failure or repeat it? Does it validate or condemn his dream, and do the same or opposite implications hold true for the collective dream? These questions have been argued both ways, but no matter which interpretation a critic upholds, the novel always presents insistent suggestions that the opposite is also true. I find no univocal reading satisfactory. The novel, like Jim, "passes away under a cloud," its tensions unresolved.

Stein's oracles provide an appropriate introduction to the general problem of revelation in Conrad, my final consideration. Although meaning, the meaning of certain experiences and their implications about general human meaning or values, are central concerns of both *Heart of Darkness* and *Lord Jim,* neither work is structured around central scenes in which meaning is revealed either to characters or reader. Instead there are brief, peripheral glimpses of a hidden central meaning, partial, enigmatic revelations around which consciousness winds the wandering, circling, yearning movement of its imaginative faculty. The content of these "hints for nightmares" is sensed as threatening to the registering consciousness and to its values. These fragmentary revelations need not come from events which are in themselves momentous. "There are often in men's affairs," says the narrator of "Falk," "unexpectedly—even irrationally—illuminating moments when an otherwise insignificant sound, perhaps only some perfectly commonplace gesture, suffices to reveal to us the unreason, all the fatuous unreason of our complacency" (169). It was such a trivial, devastating moment, Marlow believes, which lay behind Brierly's suicide: "The matter was no doubt of the gravest import, one of those trifles that awaken ideas—start into life some thought with which a man unused to such a companionship finds it impossible to live" (44).

These germs of destruction require an individual consciousness in which to grow; Marlow exemplifies a consciousness which can experience their impact and yet survive. He is therefore qualified to expound the relation of these momentary revelations and ordinary existence:

> It's extraordinary how we go through life with eyes half shut, with dull ears, with dormant thoughts. Perhaps it's just as well; and it may be that it is this very dulness that makes life to the incalculable majority so supportable and so welcome. Nevertheless, there can be but few of us who had never known one of these rare moments of awakening when we see, hear, understand ever so much—everything—in a flash—before we fall back again into our agreeable somnolence. (143)

His language here is strongly reminiscent of that used by George Eliot to describe the ordinary state, "well wadded with stupidity," and the threat which full awareness might hold, the possibility that "we should die of that roar which lies on the other side of silence." Yet there is a profound difference between the two. George Eliot's revelation is not of an exotic, inhuman heart of darkness but one which would result simply from "a keen vision of all ordinary human life"; the threat lies only in the inadequacy of our consciousness, not in the meaning itself.[14] In George Eliot's novels characters can become capable of

14. These phrases are from *Middlemarch*, ed. Gordon S. Haight (Boston, 1961), p. 144.

receiving revelation; its effect is not destructive, nor do they immediately relapse into "agreeable somnolence." Revelation, the character's recognition of meaning, exerts a positive, transforming effect on their lives. In Conrad this is impossible. The truth revealed is, as J. Hillis Miller says, "a truth which makes ordinary human life impossible."[15]

Here we see a close correlation between meaning and method. The destructive nature of Conrad's meaning does not allow for central, pivotal scenes of recognition such as we found in George Eliot and James. Even when consciousness in Marlow is intently searching for meaning he must also protect himself from it. It is the opposition between the two impulses which produces the wandering, circling movement. Without the possibility of central recognition, consciousness cannot be transformed, except by annihilation. Nor can it transform meaning, whose independence from consciousness we have already seen in Conrad's symbolism. There is a great difference between this situation and that found in James, where consciousness is capable of growth, and where both the self and the world may therefore be recreated. The difference in method has suggested a difference in world view to Dorothy Van Ghent, who finds in James "an open and fluid system, essentially creative; in Conrad, a closed and static system, incapable of origination though intensely dramatic in its revelations."[16]

Yet I believe we do find in Conrad the suggestion of a kind of change in consciousness which, though not dramatized, is felt to have taken place. This is one of the most important features of Marlow, and a reason for presenting

15. *Poets of Reality*, p. 33.
16. *The English Novel*, p. 234.

the narrative as part of his past. Marlow is subject to moments of devastating revelation but also has a capacity for recovery which distinguishes him from those who, like Brierly, are unused to the companionship of such thoughts. Jewel's account of her mother's death is such a moment for Marlow, revealing the illusoriness of human values and the humanly meaningless character of the world:

> It had the power to drive me out of my conception of existence, out of that shelter each of us makes for himself to creep under in moments of danger, as a tortoise withdraws within its shell. For a moment I had a view of a world that seemed to wear a vast and dismal aspect of disorder, while, in truth, thanks to our unwearied efforts, it is as sunny an arrangement of small conveniences as the mind of man can conceive. But still—it was only a moment: I went back into my shell directly. One *must*—don't you know?—though I seemed to have lost all my words in the chaos of dark thoughts I had contemplated for a second or two beyond the pale. These came back, too, very soon, for words also belong to the sheltering conception of light and order which is our refuge. (313)

Marlow's retreat is not simply a relapse into "agreeable somnolence"; the change in his state of consciousness is reflected in the irony with which he preserves self-awareness even as he reinstates the necessary illusions. To some extent, his ability to maintain this tension causes his values to appear as earned, not blindly accepted, personally if not universally valid. Consciousness in Marlow is thus able to embody, to dramatize, the unresolved tensions between incompatible meanings which run through Conrad's work, to participate in his unstable yet deeply resonant structures of significance.

D. H. LAWRENCE: The Revelation of
the Unconscious

In Conrad the character's consciousness, at least in Marlow, is prominent even when its ability to convey meaning
is sharply limited. In Lawrence's fiction consciousness
necessarily plays a more peripheral role. Lawrence too is
concerned with a heart of darkness located both within
the self and in the external world, a darkness which the
light of consciousness is unable to penetrate. Such a concern is expressed in his famous letter to Edward Garnett,
in which he attempts to describe his new concept of characterization: "I don't so much care about what the woman
feels—in the ordinary usage of the word. . . . I only care
about what the woman is—what she is—inhumanly, physi-
ologically, materially—according to the use of the word
. . . what she *is* as a phenomenon."[1] In creating a fictional
mode for presenting the realm of human experience which
lies below consciousness, Lawrence does not, like Conrad,
depend on the use of a character's consciousness to indicate a meaningfulness it cannot grasp. Instead, he also
develops methods for revealing the unconscious states
through which his characters pass. The need to develop
such a method results, in the progression from *Sons and
Lovers* to *The Rainbow* to *Women in Love,* in an increasingly symbolic mode. The basic impetus to symbolism
in Lawrence arises from the indirect presentation which
his essential subject requires.

1. *Selected Literary Criticism,* ed. Anthony Beal (London, 1956),
p. 18.

Lawrence's mode does not, however, depend entirely on symbolism in dealing with the unconscious. More than any of the novelists we have considered since George Eliot, he employs the convention of authorial omniscience. Lawrence's narrator has access to the unconscious as well as the conscious feelings of the characters and can expound them and their interrelation analytically. Thus, in *Sons and Lovers*, he informs us that Paul "was unconsciously jealous of his brother, and William was jealous of him. At the same time they were good friends" (69).[2] Lawrence's use of omniscience is not limited to the more realistic and traditional mode of *Sons and Lovers*. Throughout his next two novels, the characters' unconscious states are repeatedly expressed and interpreted by the narrator, though seldom in a way which makes his role as explicit as it is in the passage just quoted. Here, for example, is Gudrun's state near the end of *Women in Love:*

> What then, what next? Was it sheer blind force of passion that would satisfy her now? Not this, but the subtle thrills of extreme sensation in reduction. It was an unbroken will reacting against her unbroken will in a myriad subtle thrills of reduction, the last subtle activities of analysis and breaking down. (442–43)

The passage is typical in its unclear locus. We might suppose that it presents the contents of Gudrun's meditations as she turns from Gerald to Loerke, but in this instance Lawrence makes it clear that such is not the case: "All this Gudrun knew in her subconsciousness, not in her mind" (443). The omniscient narrator can thus give verbal

2. All page references are to *The Phoenix Edition of D. H. Lawrence* (London, Heinemann, 1954–64) and are incorporated in the text.

expression to subconscious states, but only in the form of discursive exposition. He can presumably tell us everything about these inner depths, but he can show us almost nothing. One alternative to this heavy reliance on the narrator's authority is to shift the emphasis from his objective vision to the characters' subjective lives, using them as a register of the forces which underlie the conscious mind. This is the method which has recently been described by Allan Friedman as the creation of "subjective correlatives," passages which "attempt to find phrases and analogies in the conscious life for the nonverbal and non-apprehensible and imprisoned unconscious."[3] It is in some respects a symbolic method, since it involves the use of analogies in which the tenor of the comparison remains unstated. As symbolism, however, it remains close to the kind developed by Conrad, that of rhetoric or images gesturing toward the darkness. What distinguishes Lawrence's method is that he also creates powerful symbolic scenes where hidden unconscious states are revealed in the form of dramatic presentation.

Lawrence's fiction contains several kinds of symbolism; the differences between them must be recognized if we are to understand his creation of meaning. F. R. Leavis claims that "significance in Lawrence's art is never a matter of a mere intended 'meaning' symbolized; it works from profounder levels and in more complex ways."[4] The claim is undoubtedly valid for some elements in Lawrence's novels, but for others the opposite is more nearly true. Lawrence's novels all contain elements whose significance might well be described as "intended 'meaning' symbolized," a single, unambiguous, conceptualizable meaning. Such elements

3. Alan Friedman, *The Turn of the Novel* (New York, 1966), p. 171.

4. *D. H. Lawrence: Novelist* (New York, 1956), p. 220.

correspond to Eliseo Vivas' conception of the "quasi-symbol" or "pseudo-symbol," for which the test is that its referent "can be grasped independently of the sign vehicle."[5] In some cases these devices draw on the significance of conventional emblems. Thus, in *Sons and Lovers,* the virginal Miriam is associated with white roses, whose "white, virgin scent" makes Paul feel "anxious and imprisoned" (160), while the more passionate Clara is given red carnations, which splatter their petals over her clothes and the ground when she and Paul first make love (311).

The relation between such conventional symbols and their traditional, iconological meaning actually becomes a focus for the conflict between Will and Anna in *The Rainbow.* To Will, the stained-glass image of a lamb is an object for rapt, mystical contemplation because he is concerned with its symbolic meaning, "the triumph of the Resurrection." Anna, however, resents his attitude and directs her ridicule at the discrepancy between the image's symbolic and actual aspects: " 'Whatever it may pretend to mean, what it *is* is a silly absurd toy-lamb with a Christmas-tree flag ledged on its paw' " (158). Lawrence's most characteristic symbolism seeks to prevent such a split between the image and its meaning. In his principal theoretical statement on the subject, Lawrence adopted the romantic opposition of symbol and allegory, in which allegory consists of images corresponding to an explicitly formulatable extrinsic meaning, while the significance of symbols is somehow intrinsic:

> You can't give a great symbol a "meaning," any more than you can give a cat a "meaning." Symbols are organic units of consciousness with a life of their own,

5. *D. H. Lawrence: The Failure and the Triumph of Art* (Bloomington, Ind., 1964), p. 275.

and you can never explain them away, because their value is dynamic, emotional, belonging to the sense-consciousness of the body and soul, and not simply mental. An allegorical image has a meaning. Mr. Facing-both-ways has a meaning. But I defy you to lay your finger on the full meaning of Janus, who is a symbol.[6]

Lawrence's assertion of the symbol's resistance to abstraction is clearly relevant to aspects of his own art, but, like the statement by Leavis quoted earlier, it tells us nothing about the source or nature of this resistance.

Lawrence does suggest one possible answer to this question when he describes the qualities of the Revelation of St. John which make the reader realize "that we are in the world of symbol as well as of allegory. Gradually we realize the book has no one meaning. It has meanings. Not meaning *within* meaning: but rather meaning against meaning." Such a tension of multiple meanings, with a richness that defies abstraction or paraphrase, an irreducibly problematic quality, this is the sort of significance we have seen created by the novels of James and Conrad, and shall see again in Joyce. In Lawrence's novels, however, the quality which is the primary source of resistance to abstraction is not this sort of complexity but rather a quality of intensity. If we consider Lawrence's mature fictional mode as exemplified in *Women in Love*, we do find an element of problematic complexity, exhibited most obviously in the running debate between Birkin and Ursula which is left still unresolved in the novel's final scene. But far more prominent are those scenes whose symbolic intensity has been remarked by so many critics: Gudrun and Gerald struggling with the rabbit, Birkin

6. *Selected Literary Criticism*, p. 157.

stoning the reflection of the moon, and several others. We can best understand the nature of the intensity which Lawrence creates in such scenes and its relation to the more conceptual aspects of his novels' meaning, such as that involved in the characters' debates, if we examine their development from the more realistic *Sons and Lovers*.

There we do not find the sort of symbolic scenes developed in the later two novels, but there is an intensity, comparable though of lesser degree, which appears in several natural descriptions. There is for example the scene which concludes the first chapter, in which Mrs. Morel, shut out of the house by her drunken husband, wanders through the garden.

> The moon was high and magnificent in the August night. Mrs. Morel, seared with passion, shivered to find herself out there in a great white light, that fell cold on her, and gave a shock to her inflamed soul. She stood for a few moments helplessly staring at the glistening great rhubarb leaves near the door. . . .
>
> She hurried out of the side garden to the front, where she could stand as if in an immense gulf of white light, the moon streaming high in face of her, the moonlight standing up from the hills in front, and filling the valley where the Bottoms crouched, almost blindingly. . . .
>
> She became aware of something about her. With an effort she roused herself to see what it was that penetrated her consciousness. The tall white lilies were reeling in the moonlight, and the air was charged with their perfume, as with a presence. Mrs. Morel gasped slightly in fear. She touched the big, pallid flowers on their petals, then shivered. They seemed to be stretching in the moonlight. She put her hand into

> one white bin: the gold scarcely showed on her fingers
> by moonlight. She bent down to look at the binful of
> yellow pollen; but it only appeared dusky. Then she
> drank a deep draught of the scent. It almost made her
> dizzy. (23–24)

It is a striking instance of Lawrence's capacity, noted by
E. M. Forster, for "irradiating nature from within,"[7] presenting it with unusual intensity.

The scene does not, of course, appear in the novel as a
wholly isolated descriptive passage; it is not without
thematic relevance. Dorothy Van Ghent notes the ap-
propriateness of the scene's juxtaposition of elements:
Mrs. Morel, pregnant with Paul, "is literally a vessel of
the life force that seems to thrust itself at her in nature
from all sides."[8] The passage might furthermore be seen
as part of a pattern of scenes involving flowers which runs
through the novel. Mark Spilka has attempted to explicate
one segment of this pattern as creating categories which
differentiate the characters on the basis of their attitudes
toward flowers.[9] Yet such explication seems relevant to
only a limited extent. Unlike the conventionally emblematic white roses and red carnations, these rhubarb
leaves and lilies have an intense concreteness of presence
to which the critic's abstraction of a "love ethic," or even
the abstraction implied in speaking of "the life force" is
not entirely appropriate.[10] The intensity of the passage

7. *Aspects of the Novel* (New York, 1927), p. 144.

8. *The English Novel: Form and Function* (New York, 1961), p. 248.

9. See "How to Pick Flowers," in *The Love Ethic of D. H. Lawrence* (Bloomington, Ind., 1955), pp. 39–59.

10. "Lawrence never called life a principle and disliked calling it a force." David J. Gordon, *D. H. Lawrence as a Literary Critic* (New Haven, Conn., 1966), p. 58.

does not reside in any power it may have to focus general thematic significance. (Because it occurs so early in the novel, nearly all such significance could only be retrospective, while its main force is clearly immediate.) Nor is it wholly in the intensity of Mrs. Morel's feelings after the violent clash with her husband. Although this is undoubtedly an important factor, the description emphasizes the qualities of the external objects more than their impact on her "inflamed soul." Lawrence presents these natural objects as mysteriously active presences. The moon is "streaming" and gives a shock; the lilies are "reeling," "stretching," and the air is "charged with their perfume, as with a presence." The natural world is intensely animated, but in a way which has nothing to do with the pathetic fallacy's projection of human emotion. Here, indeed, the opposite takes place, as the human is gradually assimilated to the natural. At the end Mrs. Morel loses consciousness of her present situation and has "herself melted out like scent into the shiny, pale air" (24).

Several other descriptive passages in the novel develop a similar intensity, though not always with this mysterious animated quality. It is an intensity which occurs "in those passages where [Lawrence's] urgency is to see *things* and to see them clearly and completely in their most individualizing traits, for the character of his vision is such that, in truly seeing them as they are, he sees through them to what they mean."[11] This is not so much a description of the method as of the effect of such passages, for the "meaning" of the objects they present is not to be found beyond them but in the sense of meaningfulness created by Lawrence's emphasis. His concentrated attention to these objects exceeds the apparent requirements of the narrative

11. Van Ghent, *The English Novel,* p. 251.

and thus lends them intensity, making them seem to mean more than they ordinarily would. Such intensity of presentation creates an aura around the object, "irradiating nature from within." This effect of heightened significance tends toward symbolism, but in the predominantly realistic *Sons and Lovers* it does not produce the symbolic revelations of the unconscious achieved by the later novels. Lawrence's capacity for such presentation is only one factor contributing to the fully symbolic creations of his mature art.

Another contributing factor, one of which all Lawrence's readers must be aware, is the intensity with which he is able to render the affective lives of his characters, a feature which is especially prominent in *The Rainbow*. Drawing on the poet's resources of rhythm, repetition, and imagery, he creates passages which attempt not only to describe but to give a verbal equivalent for the experiences they present. Here, for example, is Ursula's intense erotic passion as she comes together with Skrebensky:

> He kissed her, and she quivered as if she were being destroyed, shattered. The lighted vessel vibrated, and broke in her soul, the light fell, struggled, and went dark. She was all dark, will-less, having only the receptive will.
>
> He kissed her, with his soft, enveloping kisses, and she responded to them completely, her mind, her soul gone out. Darkness cleaving to darkness, she hung close to him, pressed herself into [the] soft flow of his kiss, pressed herself down, down to the source and core of his kiss, herself covered and enveloped in the warm, fecund flow of his kiss, that travelled over her, ffowed over her, covered her, flowed over the last fibre of her, so they were one stream, one dark fecun-

dity, and she clung at the core of him, with her lips holding open the very bottommost sources of him. (446–47)

Here, stripping away the accidental circumstances, not only of time and place, but even of person, Lawrence attempts to present that "other ego" of which he speaks in the letter to Edward Garnett, "according to whose action the individual is unrecognizable, and passes through, as it were, allotropic states which it needs a deeper sense than any we've been used to exercise, to discover are states of the same radically unchanged element."[12]

In passages of such intensity and immediacy, Lawrence attempts to present what Eliseo Vivas has called "the phenomenology of pure experience . . . to present in language the felt quality of experience . . . the ebb and flow of the affective life."[13] By presenting psychic states in such a "pure," impersonal form, Lawrence goes beyond "what the woman *feels*" to "what she IS." The "ebb and flow of the affective life" register the dark motive forces beneath. This affective intensity is on occasion joined with the kind of descriptive intensity we have already examined to produce some of the most striking scenes in *The Rainbow*, scenes which seem to generate their own symbolic energy instead of drawing it from their context. One of these is the scene of Will and Anna stacking sheaves. It also takes place in moonlight, as do several of Lawrence's symbolic scenes, and there are hints of the same mysterious activity in natural objects which we found in the passage from *Sons and Lovers*. Thus the sheaves are "riding hazily in shocks, like ships in the haze of moonlight" (116–17). The scene is too long to be adequately represented by quota-

12. *Selected Literary Criticism,* p. 18.
13. *D. H. Lawrence,* p. 203.

tions, but it is possible to indicate its most important features. Again, the description is heavy with incantatory rhythms and repetitions:

> She set the two sheaves sharply down, bringing them together with a faint, keen clash. Her two bulks stood leaning together. He was coming, walking shadowily with the gossamer dusk, carrying his two sheaves. She waited nearby. He set his sheaves with a keen, faint clash, next to her sheaves. They rode unsteadily. He tangled the tresses of corn. It hissed like a fountain. He looked up and laughed. (117)

Lawrence's rhythmic, alliterative prose provides the music to accompany the stately ritual dance which the lovers perform among the harvest emblems of fertility. Caught up in the rhythm of the work and immersed in the flood of moonlight, they seem to move at the instance of, again in the words of Lawrence's letter, "some greater, inhuman will."[14]

It is such a "low, deep-sounding will" which asserts itself in Will, which "vibrated to her, tried to set her in accord, tried to bring her gradually to him, to a meeting, till they should be together, till they should meet as the sheaves that swished together" (118). This impulse progressively quickens the pace of their dance as he works to overtake her.

> Till at last, they met at the shock, facing each other, sheaves in hand. And he was silvery with moonlight, with a moonlit, shadowy face that frightened her. She waited for him.
>
> "Put yours down," she said.

14. *Selected Literary Criticism*, p. 18.

D. H. LAWRENCE

"No, it's your turn." His voice was twanging and insistent.

She set her sheaves against the shock. He saw her hands glisten among the spray of grain. And he dropped his sheaves and he trembled as he took her in his arms. He had overtaken her, and it was his privilege to kiss her. She was sweet and fresh with the night air, and sweet with the scent of grain. And the whole rhythm of him beat into his kisses, and still he pursued her, in his kisses, and still she was not quite overcome. He wondered over the moonlight on her nose! All the moonlight upon her, all the darkness within her! All the night in his arms, darkness and shine, he possessed it all! All the night for him now, to unfold, to venture within, all the mystery to be entered, all the discovery to be made. (119)

Here Will's awareness of being on the threshold of a new, unknown realm is added to Lawrence's incantatory language and the imagery of the scene. The entire complex constitutes a symbolic scene because of the way its concrete action also involves large general themes, and it is characteristic of Lawrence's most successful symbolism in the extent to which general and concrete interpenetrate. The scene is not just a metaphor for the fruition of love; it also dramatizes the experience. The correspondence of the natural and the human does not appear as the contrivance of artistic stylization, as in Flaubert, or as the creation of a character's imaginative consciousness, as in James. Here the emphasis is not on creation but on discovery, and the correspondence appears as the revelation of an already existent underlying reality. Will and Anna's ritual dance brings them into accord not only with each other but with the natural forces whose rhythms they here enact. The scene thus fulfills Vivas' definition of "the constitutive

symbol," "a symbol whose referend cannot be fully exhausted by explication, because that to which it refers is
symbolized not only *through* it but *in* it."[15] Such inter-
penetration prevents the split between sign and meaning
exemplified by the stained-glass symbolic lamb.

It is by the symbolism of such scenes that Lawrence is
able to reveal in a dramatic presentation the profound
psychic states which underlie his characters' conscious
selves. When such revelation is achieved, there is an effect
of great depth (hence Vivas' assertion of the constitutive
symbol's resistance to paraphrase), a depth which results
in part from the intensity with which the natural world
and the characters' affective states are presented. Yet
despite the sense of depths opening far beneath the surface
of the conscious mind and visible world, much of the significance of such a scene is also quite openly manifest. We
do not find the tension or ironic disparity between realistic
surface and symbolic meaning which characterizes some of
Joyce's symbolism. The symbolic significance of the scene
is not so much *different* from its literal import as it is
greater. Analogical symbolism, whether in objective or
subjective correlatives, is less important than the symbolism of the universal within the particular. Because
such scenes both present and symbolize the experience
with which they are concerned, they create a strongly reflexive, centripetal concentration of meaning and as a
result tend to achieve a degree of independence from their
contexts. Yet Lawrence's novels also develop full, detailed

15. *D. H. Lawrence*, p. 208. One is also reminded of the interpene-
tration of tenor and vehicle in romantic nature imagery shown by
W. K. Wimsatt, where a "blurring of literal and figurative" is often
the result, as in the scene we have been examining, of both tenor and
vehicle being "wrought in a parallel process out of the same material"
(*The Verbal Icon: Studies in the Meaning of Poetry* [New York, 1958],
pp. 114, 109).

thematic contexts, created by patterns of imagery (such as, in this novel, the repeated image of the rainbow and the related images of arch and doorway), by the discursive exposition of the narrator, and by the statements of the characters themselves (especially prominent in *Women in Love*). Such elements must also be considered in any account of Lawrence's fictional mode.

Lawrence's contextual patterns implement a different tendency in his creation of meaning from that which leads to his symbolic scenes. As W. H. Auden has noted, "like Blake, Lawrence was interested not in 'individuals' but in 'states.' "[16] Such an artistic interest does not lead to a concern with a realistic human drama; it can, however, take two other possible forms of expression. The writer can create verbal structures which attempt to reveal such states in the form of dramatic presentation, of which the symbolic scene we have examined in *The Rainbow* is an example. Or he can create verbal structures which are instead *about* these states, which relate them to a scheme of concepts and values. The pursuit of the second alternative constitutes a tendency toward what I shall call allegory in Lawrence; we should now consider this aspect in more detail.[17]

In *The Rainbow* Lawrence's imagery of arches is related to both aspects of his creation of meaning. The two kinds of arches, Norman and Gothic, are used as emblems for

16. "Some Notes on D. H. Lawrence," *The Nation* (April 26, 1947), p. 482.

17. In introducing this term I do not, like Lawrence and his romantic predecessors, mean to distinguish allegory *from* symbolism; it is, in my terms, simply one *kind* of symbolism. Nor do I mean to imply the disparaging view of allegory inherent in the romantic distinction (and in its modern equivalent, Vivas' distinction between "pseudo-symbol" and "constitutive symbol"). My intent is to use these terms for purposes of analysis, rather than evaluation.

opposed spiritual attitudes. They appear as such to Will: "He had turned to the Gothic form, which always asserted the broken desire of mankind in its pointed arches, escaping the rolling, absolute beauty of the round arch" (234). This conceptual scheme and its formulation in these images is already present in *Sons and Lovers:*

> [Paul] talked to [Miriam] endlessly about his love of horizontals: how they, the great levels of sky and land in Lincolnshire, meant to him the eternality of the will, just as the bowed Norman arches of the church, repeating themselves, meant the dogged leaping forward of the persistent human soul, on and on, nobody knows where; in contradiction to the perpendicular lines and to the Gothic arch, which, he said, leapt up at heaven and touched the ecstasy and lost itself in the divine. Himself, he said, was Norman, Miriam was Gothic. (177)

Thus the two imaged concepts generate categories for organizing characters into thematic patterns. In *The Rainbow,* Anna is Norman, Will Gothic; their opposition breaks into conflict under the symbolic arches of the Gothic Lincoln Cathedral itself. Will desires ecstatic absorption into the cathedral's upward efforts at transcendence, but Anna resists this impulse, remembering that the cathedral is not, as Will wants it to be, an absolute, that "after all, there was the sky outside" (199), and she insists on "the many things that had been left out of the great concept of the church" (201). The rounded sky beyond the cathedral's pointed vault repeats the curve of the Norman arch, a curve which takes its final embodiment in the rainbow.

In this image, which the novel's title asserts to be its controlling symbol, the opposing impulses of vertical and horizontal, which the opening paragraph images in the church-tower at Ilkeston and the flat fields of the Marsh Farm, are placed in definitive relation by the rainbow's upward movement into the sky which yet returns to and embraces the earth. It recurs, like the onward-leading Norman arch, at the end of the sections concentrating on each generation (92 and 192–93), the symbol of values both achieved and sought, representing the wholeness of the completed self and of the true marriage, and finally, appearing to Ursula on the novel's last page, becoming the symbol of a future metamorphosis of the present sordid actuality:

> And the rainbow stood on the earth. She knew that the sordid people who crept hard-scaled and separate on the face of the world's corruption were living still, that the rainbow was arched in their blood and would quiver to life in their spirit, that they would cast off their horny covering of disintegration, that new, clean, naked bodies would issue to a new germination, to a new growth, rising to the light and the wind and the clean rain of heaven. She saw in the rainbow the earth's new architecture, the old, brittle corruption of houses and factories swept away, the world built up in a living fabric of Truth, fitting to the over-arching heaven. (495)

Thus Lawrence's pattern of imagery, both literal and figurative, elaborates his conceptual scheme and fulfills its programmatic intentions. It is therefore an expression of his urge toward allegory, the embodiment of an abstractable thematic formula in image and action which creates a meaning that is *about* certain states of being rather than consisting of them. The absence of supporting dramatic substance for this abstract meaning is particularly evident in the final symbolic rainbow, which functions only as a gesture of prophetic hope.[18]

But the account which I have given of this symbolic pattern is, as it stands, incomplete and one-sided. The actual relation between the different elements which contribute to Lawrence's creation of meaning is more complicated than the simple dichotomy of allegory and symbol (or "pseudo-symbol" and "constitutive symbol") would suggest. The meaning Lawrence attaches to the imagery of the arches receives a schematic, "allegorical" development, but it can also be presented with the intensity and immediacy which we have found in the symbolic scene with the sheaves. This is what happens in the cathedral scene, where Will is presented not only as allegorically assigned to the Gothic type but as actually experiencing the meaning it represents, where Lawrence's meaning is conveyed not only through the scene but in it. Here the dynamics of the Gothic spirit, which "leap[s] up to heaven and touche[s] the ecstasy" and also "assert[s] the broken desire of mankind," are enacted in Will's experience of the cathedral.

> Here the stone leapt up from the plain of earth, leapt up in a manifold, clustered desire each time, up, away from the horizontal earth, through twilight and dusk and the whole range of desire, through the swerving, the declination, ah, to the ecstasy, the touch,

18. This point is developed at greater length by Julian Moynahan, in *The Deed of Life: The Novels and Tales of D. H. Lawrence* (Princeton, N.J., 1963), pp. 53–56. Harry T. Moore cites passages from Lawrence's contemporary discursive writings that give a fixed conceptual significance to the rainbow, making it a symbol of the self which has "attained absolute being." See *"The Rainbow,"* in *The Achievement of D. H. Lawrence,* ed. Frederick J. Hoffman and Harry T. Moore (Norman, Okla., 1953), pp. 152–53.

> to the meeting, the clasp, the close embrace, the neutrality, the perfect, swooning consummation, the timeless ecstasy. There his soul remained, at the apex of the arch, clinched in the timeless ecstasy, consummated.
>
> And there was not time nor life nor death, but only this, this timeless consummation, where the thrust from earth met the thrust from earth and the arch was locked on the keystone of ecstasy. This was all, this was everything. Till he came to himself in the world below. Then again he gathered himself together, in transit, every jet of him strained and leaped, leaped clear into the darkness above, to the fecundity and the unique mystery, to the touch, the clasp, the consummation, the climax of eternity, the apex of the arch. (199)

Again Lawrence strives to render the affective intensity of the moment, revealing this state of being in a dramatic, symbolic scene. From our examination of this single complex of elements in *The Rainbow* we can now see the potentiality Lawrence's meaning contains both for schematic elaboration and for intensive symbolization. The relation between these two components of his fictional mode is not just one of simple opposition but includes numerous possible degrees of tension or mutual reinforcement. We can best examine some of these possibilities by turning now to *Women in Love*, at once Lawrence's most schematic and his most symbolic novel.

The novel's most extensive scheme elaborates its negative theme, the various paths of dissolution taken by both the individual and by the entire society, ranging between the extremes of the "African" and "Nordic" ways. It is the more exotic, African cluster of ideas and images which first clearly presents the theme of cultural dissolution in the pursuit of one extreme form of knowledge and being. Its emblems are the primitive sculptures in Halliday's rooms. One of these, a statue of a woman in labor, figures prominently in Chapter 7, "Totem," where Birkin declares it to be art because it "contains the whole truth" of the state it expresses, the product of "an awful pitch of culture . . . pure culture in sensation, culture in the physical consciousness, really ultimate *physical* consciousness, mindless, utterly sensual" (72). The significance of such a development in cultural history is pursued further in one of Birkin's meditations as he recalls another of the statues, West African, which represents an abandonment of all efforts at "pure integral being," turning to extreme refinements of sensual knowledge, "mystic knowledge in disintegration and dissolution" (245–46). Birkin then realizes that there is another possible way which travels to the opposite extreme from "the long, long African process of purely sensual understanding, knowledge in the mystery of dissolution." "It would be done differently by the white races. The white races, having the Arctic north behind them, the vast abstraction of ice and snow, would fulfill a mystery of ice-destructive knowledge, snow-abstract annihilation" (246).

Gerald Crich is the chief representative of this northern mode of disintegration, and from his first appearance he is presented in arctic imagery: "In his clear northern flesh and his fair hair was a glisten like sunshine refracted through crystals of ice" (9). When Birkin first conceives of the northern mode of dissolution he at once thinks of Gerald: "He was one of these strange white wonderful demons from the north, fulfilled in the destructive frost mystery. And was he fated to pass away in this knowledge, this one process of frost-knowledge, death by perfect cold?

Was he a messenger, an omen of the universal dissolution into whiteness and snow?" (246–47). The metaphors become literalized in the novel's concluding section, where, under Gerald's leadership, the central quartet of characters moves into the frozen white Alpine world. Here, in an inversion of pathetic fallacy, the symbolic landscape seems to project its meaning on the characters' minds: "The first days passed in an ecstasy of physical motion, sleighing, ski-ing, skating, moving in an intensity of speed and white light that surpassed life itself, and carried the souls of the human beings beyond into an inhuman abstraction of velocity and weight and eternal, frozen snow" (411). Birkin and Ursula, committed to "the old effort at serious living" (294), unwilling to "fall from the connection with life and hope," to cease the attempt at "pure integral being" (246), turn from this landscape of Nordic dissolution to the warm lands of the south, leaving the others to their chosen fates—Gerald's actual "death by perfect cold," and Gudrun's further pursuit of "ultimate reduction . . . disintegrating the vital organic body of life" (443).

I have sketched only the most prominent elements of this thematic pattern, whose pervasive ramifications include numerous other images and characters, scenes and statements. Water and mud and the water plants which grow out of them, the "flowers of dissolution—fleurs du mal" (164) with which Gudrun and Gerald are associated become part of the pattern, as do machines and industry, and debates about the role of the will. Lawrence's pattern underlies his schematic presentation of society; the country house world of Breadably or the bohemian one of the Pompadour Café, that "small, slow central whirlpool of disintegration and dissolution" (372), are two of the more carefully exhibited specimens of the process at work in the entire society, just as Hermione, hysterical advocate of the will, and Loerke, the artist in the service of the machine, "the wizard rat" swimming ahead in "the river of corruption" (418–19), provide further individual variants. All these elements and many more are controlled by the fundamental scheme which locates each instance of dissolution within the spectrum which extends from the African to the Nordic extreme.

Imagery alone might suffice to embody the theme of dissolution, but not to make the analytical discriminations between its various modes which Lawrence's scheme requires. Such discriminations are essentially conceptual, and to establish them Lawrence must introduce the concepts on which they are based, hence the large role played in the novel by debates between the characters, by individuals' meditations, and by the commentary and analysis of Lawrence's narrator. Here conceptual terms and ideas are introduced which provide a firm context for individual scenes. As we have seen in the case of George Eliot, such a well-established conceptual context creates a strong field of attraction, along whose lines of force images, characters, and events may be drawn. The effect is carried much further in *Women in Love,* creating a more pervasive symbolic quality, a greater potential for thematic significance in each detail than we have found in any of the novels previously examined. This aspect of Lawrence's symbolism is perfectly consonant with his schematism, and it is therefore the aspect with the strongest tendency toward allegory, toward placing action, image, and character entirely in the service of conceptual theme. We can see the predominance of such allegorization in Lawrence's presentation of Gerald as industrial magnate, which as Vivas notes is developed in "essentially . . . conceptual" terms, but we also find such schematism complicated in the presentation of Gerald as Birkin's friend or Gudrun's lover.[19] Yet, as I have already indicated, I believe that this sort of complexity is not the most important nonschematic factor in Lawrence's fictional mode, that this factor is to be found instead in certain of his symbolic scenes.

Some scenes of *Women in Love* owe their symbolic quality almost entirely to their place in its thematic patterns. An example is the brief scene at the beginning of Chapter 4 where Ursula and Gudrun watch Gerald swimming and Gudrun envies the masculine freedom his act represents (39–41). The chapter's title, "Diver," creates a significant emphasis, suggesting a meaningfulness in presenting Gerald in terms of this action, but our understanding of this meaning must be retrospective, taking his action in the context of subsequent events and thematic patterns. Gerald appears again as a diver in "Breadalby" and "Water-party," but the symbolic relevance does not emerge until much later, although in the latter scene, after futilely diving after his drowned sister, he utters reflections which hint at the doom which is coming not only for himself but for an entire civilization. "There's room under that water there for thousands . . . a whole universe under there; and as cold as hell, you're as helpless as if your head was cut off" (176). The significance of these words, however, is also dependent on contextual terms which have yet to be introduced, Birkin's conception of the northern fate. In the end, as helpless as if beheaded because his cardinal principles of mind and will have failed, Gerald takes his last dive, into the hollow basin of

19. *D. H. Lawrence*, pp. 242–43. Barbara Hardy also discusses this "truthfulness" in Lawrence's presentation of Gerald. See *The Appropriate Form: An Essay on the Novel* (London, 1964), pp. 149–54.

snow, where he meets his death by perfect cold. In the light of the novel's entire pattern, the earlier diving scenes become symbolic. In the first, despite the chapter's title, Gerald appears as swimmer more than as diver, and on the surface of the water he is magnificently capable, as much so as in his role of industrial magnate. But in retrospect we recognize the aptness of Lawrence's title: the impulse which will prevail is that toward the icy depths, the "quick jump downwards, in a sort of ecstasy" (419), contrasted to Gudrun's prolonged exploration of the "myriad subtle thrills of reduction" (443), both part of the northern mode of dissolution.

There are other symbolic scenes which seem to be just as fully in the service of the novel's thematic context yet whose significance is not so completely dependent on it. A striking example is the scene in which Gerald forces his horse to stand at the railroad crossing while a train passes (102–04). Vivas calls the scene a "quasi-symbol" because "its meaning is given us discursively in Chapter XII, 'Carpeting' and in XVII, 'The Industrial Magnate.'"[20] In the first of these two chapters, Gerald defends his brutal subjugation of the mare as necessary to make her useful to him. The other, of course, contains Lawrence's main exposition of Gerald as "the God of the machine," who has "conceived the pure instrumentality of mankind" (216). Here the general cultural significance of his industrial ethic is clearly expounded:

> It was the first great step in undoing, the first great phase of chaos, the substitution of the mechanical principle for the organic, the destruction of the organic purpose, the organic unity, and the subordination of every organic unit to the great mechanical

20. *D. H. Lawrence*, p. 242.

> purpose. It was pure organic disintegration and pure
> mechanical organization. This is the first and finest
> stage of chaos. (223)

As Vivas' statement implies, we might read the earlier
scene as a simple allegorization of these concepts: in sub-
duing the terrified horse Gerald demonstrates his will to
dominate and clearly subordinates the organic, the fine,
sensitive Arab mare, to the mechanical, the rumbling coal
train. Yet this meaning is clear in the scene; unlike the
diver scenes, it is not dependent on the later passages,
which re-express its significance discursively, generalize
it, and relate it to the novel's thematic patterns.

  The scene is symbolic in that it concentrates this general significance in a concrete, dramatic action, but it
also derives a symbolic quality, not dependent on later
thematic statements, from the great intensity it develops
in itself. The terror of the horse and the cold violence
with which Gerald asserts his will, their powerful effect
on Ursula, and especially on Gudrun, whose underlying
sadistic and masochistic nature responds to their impact
—the way in which the scene is indeed made almost as
great an ordeal for the reader—all contribute to its intensity, an intensity which has the effect of insisting on
its significance, on the depth of the psychic states in
Gerald and Gudrun which it partially reveals. Thus it
would be wrong to suggest that the scene creates only a
thin allegorical veneer over conceptual meanings. Even
though its central explicatable meaning is presented elsewhere, there is no split between the scene and its meaning.
Its intensity furthermore confers a degree of independence
on it which suggests the way in which other symbolic
scenes may have a still more complicated relation to their
context. It is, after all, not too great a step from this scene

to that of Gudrun, Gerald, and the rabbit, which Vivas calls a constitutive symbol. The absolute opposition of "pseudo-symbol" and "constitutive symbol" is easier to maintain in theory than in the close examination of artistic practice.

As the last car in the train passes, Gudrun imagines how the scene in which she has participated must look to the guard within, appearing "spectacularly, isolated, and momentary, like a vision isolated in eternity" (104). Many of the novel's scenes have such a spectacular quality and stand in formal isolation because of the narrative's discontinuity. They thus acquire a degree of significance, a portentous quality, even when their specific symbolic significance is not apparent, and when it is, as in the scene we have just considered, the emphasis created by their spectacular isolation increases its intensity. The narrative discontinuity of *Women in Love* is characteristic of the modern, symbolic mode. The arrangement of material is controlled by a structure of significance, replacing the traditional plot with its structure of causally related events. The formal isolation of components allows their significance to emerge more clearly; the pattern of meaning, of parallels or contrasts between scenes, is not obscured by the pattern of a plot which also relates them on another level. We can see the beginnings of such discontinuity in James' later novels, such as *The Wings of the Dove,* which contains several sharp breaks in the narrative and whose significant omission of certain crucial scenes is part of a general symbolic method. Conrad's fiction tends more clearly toward such an effect. His disruption of a linear temporal progression weakens the causal relations between events, allowing for significant rearrangement. In Joyce we shall find the fullest fictional development of symbolic structural principles, and the tendency is even more obvious in the contemporary poetry which takes extended forms. *The Waste Land* or Pound's *Cantos* provide outstanding examples of formal discontinuity and symbolic form. In the development of a symbolic mode, fiction moves in the direction of poetry.

But the nature of fiction always requires a higher degree of continuity than does comparably motivated poetry. Auden, in noting Lawrence's concern with states rather than individuals, also indicates the problems such motivation creates for the writer of narrative: "In writing about nature or strangers this does not matter, as these are only experienced as states of being, but it is a serious drawback in writing fiction which cannot avoid the individual and his relations to other individuals over a stretch of time."[21] In *The Rainbow* and *Women in Love* Lawrence tends to disregard much of the realistic, social level of his characters' relation to each other, attempting to reveal their relations on a deeper level, where they exist as elemental states. Scenes which reveal these states of being in isolated, spectacular moments are related by a pattern of thematic concepts *about* such states. As David Gordon observes, Lawrence thus solves his narrative problem "by submitting his material to a kind of allegorical scheme by means of which the parts relate to one another not so much causally or consecutively as analogically."[22] It is a strategy of poetry, even, as Mr. Gordon notes, of allegorical poetry: "roughly comparable to that in *The Faerie Queene.*"

The most intense and profound of Lawrence's symbolic scenes, however, seem to exceed the requirements of his allegorical scheme and thus to develop a kind of resistance

21. "Some Notes on D. H. Lawrence," p. 482.
22. *D. H. Lawrence as a Literary Critic,* p. 48.

to its gravitational attraction. One of the most successful of such scenes is the one which provides the title for Chapter 18, "Rabbit." Elements of its meaning both draw on and reinforce the novel's established themes. Again we see in Gerald the assertion of will, the subordination of the organic and vital, again symbolized in the subjection of an animal, in which Gudrun this time also participates. In this respect, the scene might appear even more fully controlled by Lawrence's conceptual presentation of Gerald than the one with the horse, since it follows immediately after the "Industrial Magnate" chapter. But here Lawrence places his central emphasis on the revelation of psychic states which are only presented peripherally in the earlier scene. The intensity of these states and Lawrence's ability to present them convincingly as deep, hidden, secret recesses within the characters establishes the scene's meaning on a different level.

The scene is mysterious, like the rabbit itself: " 'Bismarck is a mystery, Bismarck, c'est un mystère, der Bismarck, er ist ein Wunder,' said Gudrun in mocking incantation" (229), establishing the tone at the scene's beginning, just as it ends with the strange child Winifred crooning to the rabbit, "Let mother stroke its fur then, darling, because it is so mysterious—" (236). It is a mystery as an embodiment of vital energy, "magically strong," "demoniacal" in its resistance, "mad" in its swift changes of mood. In confronting it, Gerald and Gudrun participate in a mystery of another sort, an obscene rite of revelation and initiation, in which they become "implicated with each other in abhorrent mysteries" (234). The power of the scene results from the intensity with which Lawrence renders both mysteries, and the intensity and depth of the psychic revelations are increased here by their impact on the characters, who themselves participate in "the mutual hellish recognition" (234). Coming upon Gudrun struggling with the rabbit, Gerald sees, "with subtle recognition, her sullen passion of cruelty" (232). The "unearthly abhorrent scream" of the rabbit as Gerald strikes it seems "to have torn the veil of her consciousness," and "she knew she was revealed" (233). Gerald too is revealed, and the sense of viewing hidden inner depths is intensified by their juxtaposition with the outward surface, what these characters now know themselves to be with what they still pretend to be in their conventional words.

> "How many scratches have you?" he asked, showing his hard forearm white and hard and torn in red gashes.
> "How really vile!" she cried, flushing with a sinister vision. "Mine is nothing."
> She lifted her arm and showed a deep red score down the silken white flesh.
> "What a devil!" he exclaimed. But it was as if he had knowledge of her in the long red rent of her forearm so silken and soft. He did not want to touch her. He would have to make himself touch her, deliberately. The long, shallow red rip seemed torn across his own brain, tearing the surface of his ultimate consciousness, letting through the forever unconscious, unthinkable red ether of the beyond, the obscene beyond.
> "It doesn't hurt you very much, does it?" he asked, solicitous. (234–35)

Only at the end does either make any overt acknowledgment of the fact that they are both now "initiate."

> "God be praised we aren't rabbits," she said in a high shrill voice.

> The smile intensified a little on his face.
>
> "Not rabbits?" he said looking at her fixedly.
>
> Slowly her face relaxed into a smile of obscene recognition.
>
> "Ah, Gerald," she said in a strong, slow, almost man-like way. "—All that, and more." Her eyes looked up at him with shocking nonchalance.
>
> He felt again as if she had hit him across the face— or rather as if she had torn him across the breast, dully, finally. He turned aside. (235–36)

Her words complete the strange bond which has been established between them. Gerald's response recalls the earlier slap she has given him after dancing before the highland cattle and looks forward to the last blow she will give, foreshadowing the final form their tangle of sadistic and masochistic compulsions will take. The scene thus performs the structural function which Vivas ascribes to the constitutive symbol: "It is a complex situation or scene . . . which gathers the significance of events preceding it and illumines the scenes or situations that follow.[23] Yet it also develops a kind of self-contained intensity which gives it a stature almost like that of an independent poem, a powerful revelation.

This scene is as near as Lawrence comes in *Women in Love* to creating an actual scene of recognition, yet it is still far removed in function and import from the crucial scenes of recognition on which George Eliot's and James' novels so often turn. Recognition plays a lesser role in Lawrence because knowledge, especially conscious knowledge, is not as important a factor in his characters' development as the kind of relations they enter on a level which conscious knowledge can scarcely reach. Although

23. *D. H. Lawrence,* p. 281.

Gudrun and Gerald do experience a recognition which is a crucial element of the rabbit scene, it is not in itself a crucial element in their subsequent development. It consists of a kind of intense awareness which is not really conscious, not the possible subject of thought. (It is Birkin who must attempt to deal with these mysteries consciously, conceptually, precisely because he does not, like Gerald, have "direct and personal" knowledge of them within himself [196].) Thus it is a recognition which offers no possibility for change but rather confirms the characters in what they already are. In terms of their subsequent development, the scene's crucial function is to place them definitively in their essential relation, to which their recognition is ultimately only incidental.

Because it achieves this symbolic definition, it is appropriate that "Rabbit" is located at the center of the novel, as is the famous symbolic scene in the following chapter, "Moony," where the relation of the other two major characters is presented. Like the rabbit scene, the one in which Birkin, unknowingly watched by Ursula, tries to destroy the reflected moon bears a complex relation to the novel's schematic patterns. The two pages which describe the stoning of the moon are probably the best example in all of Lawrence's works of his ability to create symbolic depth by rendering affective intensity. The description is from Ursula's point of view, but the intensity seems to reside in the moon itself: as Birkin throws the first stone, "it seemed to shoot out arms of fire like a cuttlefish, like a luminous polyp, palpitating strongly before her." Not satisfied, Birkin throws more stones.

> Then again there was a burst of sound, and a burst of brilliant light, the moon had exploded on the water, and was flying asunder in flakes of white and

dangerous fire. Rapidly, like white birds, the fires all broken rose across the pond, fleeing in clamorous confusion, battling with the flock of dark waves that were forcing their way in. The furthest waves of light, fleeing out, seemed to be clamouring against the shore for escape, the waves of darkness came in heavily, running under towards the centre. But at the centre, the heart of all, was still a vivid, incandescent quivering of a white moon not quite destroyed, a white body of fire writhing and striving and not even now broken open, not yet violated. It seemed to be drawing itself together with strange, violent pangs, in blind effort. It was getting stronger, it was re-asserting itself, the inviolable moon. And the rays were hastening in in thin lines of light, to return to the strengthened moon, that shook upon the water in triumphant reassumption. (239)

The intense emotion, expressed in the medium of Lawrence's poetic prose, whose devices we have already examined (e.g. the assonance and alliteration of "the rays were hastening in in thin lines of light"), actually belongs to the two characters, Birkin's violent desperation and Ursula's shock, but it is contained in the image of the moon. Lawrence's ability to animate natural objects with an intense life of their own is again at work here, so that the tormented moon is at once a psychic correlative and an independent entity. The entire passage constitutes one of Lawrence's finest prose poems, even more detached from the narrative progression than the rabbit scene.

Yet its specific meaning is more dependent on context. Birkin prefaces his attack on the moon with the exclamation, "Cybele—curse her! The accursed Syria Dea!" (238), which refers us back to his earlier meditation on woman as the Great Mother, desiring to merge rather than maintain separation in love, to absorb and dominate the male: "He had a horror of the Magna Mater, she was detestable" (192). It is this aspect of Ursula which Birkin attacks in the archetypally female moon.[24] He thus deliberately acts on a symbolic level, creating his own ritual for the expression of his feelings. The scene might therefore have been a simple allegory, one contrived by the character as well as the author, were it not for the intense feeling it contains, making Birkin's behavior the acting out of psychic conflicts which exists on a deeper level than his (or Lawrence's) ideas about them. Again, the scene is not one of recognition, though a kind of recognition follows it in Birkin's meditation on the alternatives of disintegration and "pure integral being" and his determination to

24. It is discussed as such by Maud Bodkin, *Archetypal Patterns in Poetry: Psychological Studies of Imagination* (New York, 1958), pp. 281–84. Archetypal symbolism involves a larger frame of reference than that of the individual novel and thus lies beyond my primary area of concern. Such symbolism does play a part in Lawrence's fictional mode, as does the ritualistic form which the action of his symbolic scenes often takes, whether in the attempted exorcism of "Moony" or the obscene initiation of "Rabbit." Lawrence clearly invokes the familiar association of the primitive with the unconscious, each subsisting beneath the superstructure of civilization or consciousness, and he himself defined the symbol as archetype: "The images of myth are symbols," rooted in the unconscious, "the dynamic self, beyond comprehension" *(Selected Literary Criticism,* p. 158). Such archetypalism does not entail any specific external reference, however. Its purpose is rather to contribute an effect of increased depth or resonance to a meaning which is fully comprehensible in the novel's own terms. In "Moony" the significance of the moon is indicated by Birkin; no external reference is required. Vivas' attempt to explicate this scene by alluding to particular details of the cult of Cybele thus seems inappropriate and misleading. (See *D. H. Lawrence,* pp. 259–61.) Such allusions are sometimes a factor in Joyce's symbolism, but not in Lawrence's.

try to achieve the latter in marriage to Ursula. The symbolic scene itself, however, is concerned not with recognition but with revelation, creating an intense, isolated moment in which not only the specific orientation but the enormous energy of the unconscious is made manifest. Although the scene's explicable meaning depends on the context of Lawrence's allegorical scheme, it develops a centripetal symbolic concentration which resists assimilation to a purely thematic function. As David Gordon remarks, such moments in Lawrence's novels "have symbolic energy far out of proportion to the purpose of furthering the narrative; they absorb us in and of themselves as revelations of states."[25]

Despite the tensions which develop between the different components of Lawrence's mode, their collective effect is one not of incoherence but of increased richness and depth. His need to reveal unconscious states of being and to generalize their significance led him finally to create, in *Women in Love,* an original, highly symbolic fictional mode.

25. *D. H. Lawrence as a Literary Critic,* p. 49.

JAMES JOYCE: The Artifice
of Reality

In Joyce's work the progression from a realistic to a symbolic fictional mode is recapitulated on a level of consciousness where, to an unprecedented degree, the mode in which meaning is created becomes itself a crucial part of that meaning. We have observed similar tendencies in James' career and in Lawrence's development from *Sons and Lovers* to *Women in Love,* but neither displays such a dramatic and extensive shift in mode as that from the realistic stories of *Dubliners* to the almost totally symbolic *Finnegans Wake.* James' concern with the problematic relation between the moral and the aesthetic produces an increasing degree of modal reflexivity, where the creation of meaning by consciousness becomes not only a method but an important theme. But in Joyce the relation between symbolism and realism, as an aspect of the relation between art and reality, is, almost from the first, a central thematic concern. His work thus not only represents the culmination of the development toward a more symbolic mode but provides a perspective on the entire process.

In *Dubliners* this concern emerges unmistakably in a scene from "The Dead" which takes place as various guests are leaving the party.

> Gabriel had not gone to the door with the others. He was in a dark part of the hall gazing up the staircase. A woman was standing near the top of the first

flight, in the shadow also. He could not see the terra-cotta and salmon-pink panels of her skirt which the shadow made appear black and white. It was his wife. She was leaning on the banisters, listening to something. Gabriel was surprised at her stillness and strained his ear to listen also. But he could hear little save the noise of laughter and dispute on the front steps, a few chords struck on the piano and a few notes of a man's voice singing.

He stood still in the gloom of the hall, trying to catch the air that the voice was singing and gazing up at his wife. There was grace and mystery in her attitude as if she were a symbol of something. He asked himself what is a woman standing on the stairs in the shadow, listening to distant music, a symbol of. If he were a painter he would paint her in that attitude. Her blue felt hat would show off the bronze of her hair against the darkness and the dark panels of her skirt would show off the light ones. *Distant Music* he would call the picture if he were a painter. (227–28)[1]

By the end of the story this distanced, impersonal mode of contemplation has been destroyed. Gabriel is made to realize that his wife is not an aesthetic object, "a symbol of something," but an actual person whose individuality and otherness must be respected. The retrospective irony of the scene would thus seem to be directed entirely against the attempt to convert reality into symbol. The

1. Page references are to the following editions of Joyce's works: *Dubliners* and *A Portrait of the Artist as a Young Man* in *The Portable James Joyce*, ed. Harry Levin (New York, Viking Press, 1962); *Stephen Hero*, ed. Theodore Spencer (Norfolk, Conn., New Directions, 1963); *Ulysses*, Modern Library edition (New York, Random House, 1961).

situation is, however, far more complex, for the scene is indeed symbolic, though in a different sense from that which Gabriel intends. It gathers in a single dramatic image the crucial factors in the deficient relationship of the Conroys, juxtaposing Gabriel's self-regarding mild aestheticism with Gretta's abstracted thoughts of another. The distant music to which she is listening reminds her of the dead Michael Furey, and it is this past experience whose revelation exposes the shallowness of Gabriel's attitude, forcing him to recognize his wife as a person. From the entire complex of the scene, Joyce emerges as an artist who uses symbolic techniques to explore the relation of realism and symbolism.

The tension between modes which is symbolized in this scene pervades Joyce's fiction from *Dubliners* to *Ulysses,* though the relation between them is constantly shifting. The acute difficulty of interpreting his works is ultimately the result of this complex interaction of modes. Although the issue only emerges clearly in "The Dead," it is implicit in the earlier stories of *Dubliners* as well. Joyce's highly selective strategy of presentation studs these stories with isolated objects which protrude from their flat surfaces. These may be insistently symbolic, like the harp that appears briefly in "Two Gallants," which, "heedless that her coverings had fallen about her knees, seemed weary alike of the eyes of strangers and of her master's hands" (64). The dishonored harp is clearly an analogue for the servant girl, who appears only a few lines later, and a symbol as well of Ireland in her present degraded state, "The harp that once through Tara's halls The soul of music shed." Other objects, presented no less insistently, seem irreducibly actual, like the old papers or the "late tenant's rusty bicycle pump" mentioned at the beginning of "Araby" (39). In *Dubliners* symbolic and realistic images alternate; in *Ulysses* they are generally made to coincide. The earlier fiction does not, however, simply expend its energy in oscillating between the two modes. They define its limits, but its primary concern is with exploring the realm between realism and a fully determined symbolism. It is to this end that Joyce developed the scenic technique of the epiphany.

The concept of the epiphany has been of concern to Joyce's critics ever since his use of the term in *Stephen Hero* was brought to light. Both as an element of aesthetics and of fictional method, the term has usually been used simply in its etymological sense, "a showing forth," with whatever means and content of revelation the individual critic chooses to emphasize. Thus for one critic the epiphany is "in effect, the same device" as the selected realistic *"nuance,"*[2] while for another, "Stephen's epiphany . . . is what we call symbolism."[3] Such disparate critical emphases have been possible because, when realism and symbolism are conceived as opposed extremes, the epiphany tends to mediate between them. As may be seen from the following discussion, it falls within the broad conception of symbolism outlined in my Introduction, but the term enables us to make a useful distinction, differentiating the fully symbolic mode where the image becomes "a symbol of something," or where the symbolic aspect becomes primary, from the intermediate mode exemplified by the scene from "The Dead" discussed above. The root sense of the term is generally applicable to much of Joyce's early fiction, where meaning often appears as revelation, the dis-

2. Harry Levin, *James Joyce: A Critical Introduction* (Norfolk, Conn., 1960), p. 31.
3. William York Tindall, *A Reader's Guide to James Joyce* (New York, 1959), pp. 10–11.

closure of what has been hidden (we have seen similar impulses lead toward symbolism in Conrad and Lawrence), but the concept of the epiphany can lead to further understanding once we recognize the way it indicates not only the general intent of manifestation but a particular scenic method for achieving it.

To discover the term's specific bearing we need to consider both the theory and practice which center on it. In *Stephen Hero* the epiphany appears first as an experience, then as a theory:

> He was passing through Eccles' St one evening, one misty evening, with all these thoughts dancing the dance of unrest in his brain when a trivial incident set him composing some ardent verses which he entitled a "Vilanelle of the Temptress." A young lady was standing on the steps of one of those brown brick houses which seem the very incarnation of Irish paralysis. A young gentleman was leaning on the rusty railings of the area. Stephen as he passed on his quest heard the following fragment of colloquy out of which he received an impression keen enough to afflict his sensitiveness very severely.
>
> The Young Lady—(drawling discreetly) . . . O, yes . . . I was . . . at the . . . cha . . . pel . . .
>
> The Young Gentleman—(inaudibly) . . . I . . . (again inaudibly) . . . I . . .
>
> The Young Lady—(softly) . . . O . . . but you're . . . ve . . . ry . . . wick . . . ed . . .
>
> This triviality made him think of collecting many such moments together in a book of epiphanies. By an epiphany he meant a sudden spiritual manifestation, whether in the vulgarity of speech or of gesture or in a memorable phase of the mind itself. He be-

lieved that it was for the man of letters to record
these epiphanies with extreme care, seeing that they
themselves are the most delicate and evanescent of
moments. (210–11)

Later, as Stephen expounds his aesthetic theories to Cran-
ly, we learn more about what is shown forth in these moments. From Aquinas' three requisites for beauty, wholeness, symmetry, and radiance, Stephen derives a theory of
the stages of aesthetic apprehension. The epiphany is
associated with the third:

> Now for the third quality. For a long time I couldn't
> make out what Aquinas meant. He uses a figurative
> word (a very unusual thing for him) but I have solved
> it. *Claritas* is *quidditas*. After the analysis which dis-
> covers the second quality the mind makes the only
> logically possible synthesis and discovers the third
> quality. This is the moment which I call epiphany.
> First we recognize that the object is *one* integral
> thing, then we recognize that it is an organized com-
> posite structure, a *thing* in fact: finally, when the rela-
> tion of the parts is exquisite, when the parts are ad-
> justed to the special point, we recognize that it is *that*
> thing which it is. Its soul, its whatness, leaps to us
> from the vestment of its appearance. The soul of the
> commonest object, the structure of which is so ad-
> justed, seems to us radiant. The object achieves its
> epiphany. (213)

There are several problems in this exposition. The first
is the ambiguous locus of the epiphany: is it to be found in
the mind or in the object of contemplation? Making the
object the active element in "The object achieves its
epiphany" is confusing after the description of a mental

process. Again, even if mind should be considered the proper locus, what is its status? The second of the two quoted passages presents it in a process of active, systematic apprehension, but the first, where an actual epiphany is experienced, presents Stephen's mind as passive, receiving "an impression keen enough to afflict his sensitiveness very severely." We are shown no process of aesthetic apprehension here. Some of these are questions we can hardly expect Joyce to resolve. Concerning the problem of locus, for example, "the aesthetic of Stephen Dedalus may be thought of as epitomizing and holding unresolved a choice [between object and response] that has haunted not only aesthetics but general epistemology since early times."[4] It should further be recognized that this problem is more acute for literary theory than for literary practice. In a work of fiction epiphanic revelation will either be contained in a character's recognition (shifting the emphasis toward the perceiving mind) or be conveyed directly to the reader (placing more emphasis on the object). As is so often the case, what appears in theory as a clear-cut distinction appears in practice more as a matter of degree.

A more urgent question for both theory and practice, however, is that of the epiphany's content. Stephen's exposition here seems influenced by the religious use of the term: it is a "spiritual manifestation," in which "the soul of the . . . object" appears. Moreover, since it "leaps to us from the vestment of its appearance," this spiritual content is given a definitely Platonic tinge. The theoretical pronouncements of Joyce's later works firmly repudiate these otherworldly suggestions. In the *Portrait* Stephen

4. W. K. Wimsatt, Jr., and Cleanth Brooks, *Literary Criticism: A Short History* (New York, 1962), p. 134.

again describes his puzzlement over the meaning of Aquinas' *claritas:*

> It would lead you to believe that he had in mind symbolism or idealism, the supreme quality of beauty being a light from some other world, the idea of which it was but the symbol. I thought he might mean that *claritas* was the artistic discovery and representation of the divine purpose in anything or a force of generalization which would make the esthetic image a universal one, make it outshine its proper conditions. But that is literary talk. (479)

Similarly, when, in *Ulysses,* Stephen is confronted by the claims of A. E. that "Art has to reveal to us ideas, formless spiritual essences" (185), his thoughts reject this Celtic twilight mysticism: "Through spaces smaller than red globules of man's blood they creepycrawl after Blake's buttocks into eternity of which this vegetable world is but a shadow. Hold to the now, the here, through which all future plunges to the past" (186). Thus, in this respect, a definite clarification, or shift, takes place between *Stephen Hero* and the *Portrait,* where the theoretical emphasis is firmly on "the now, the here." It is true that the later version of the aesthetic theory no longer contains the term "epiphany." Although some commentators find this omission crucial, invalidating Stephen's later theory,[5] I believe it was probably motivated only by the desire to avoid giving any transcendental connotations to the moment in which *claritas* is apprehended. This revision is consistent with the *Portrait*'s emphasis on the concrete, individual essence

5. Thus Hugh Kenner: "The crucial principle of epiphanization has been withdrawn," *Dublin's Joyce* (Boston, 1962), p. 121. See also S. L. Goldberg, *The Classical Temper: A Study of James Joyce's Ulysses* (London, 1963), Chapters 2 and 3, especially pp. 63 and 71.

as the content of revelation.[6] For the critical analysis of Joyce's fiction, however, the term retains its usefulness precisely because it registers the tension between the (realistic) concrete and the (symbolic) universal.

In the theory of *Stephen Hero* such a tension exists between the romantic and the classical:

> The romantic temper . . . is an insecure, unsatisfied, impatient temper which sees no fit abode here for its ideals and chooses therefore to behold them under insensible figures. . . . The classical temper on the other hand, ever mindful of limitations, chooses rather to bend upon these present things and so to work upon them and fashion them that the quick intelligence may go beyond them to their meaning which is still unuttered. (78)

Stephen's account heavily favors the classical temper, but we should remember that when Joyce himself set forth this theory, in his essay on Mangan, he described both tempers as "constant states of mind,"[7] and Stephen himself conceives the artist as "mediator between the world of his experience and the world of his dreams" (*S.H.*, 77). Nevertheless, the thrust of the early theory (and, as I shall attempt to show, of the early fictional practice) is clearly toward the concrete "present things" upon which the classical temper chooses to bend. In both *Stephen Hero* and the *Portrait,* it is Stephen, not Joyce, who alternates between

6. William T. Noon, S.J., has pointed out that, in scholastic terms, this is actually a movement from the Aquinian *quidditas,* the Aristotelian specific universal, to the Scotist *haecceitas,* the individual essence, "thisness" rather than "whatness." See *Joyce and Aquinas* (New Haven, Conn., 1963), p. 72.

7. *The Critical Writings of James Joyce,* ed. Ellsworth Mason and Richard Ellmann (New York, 1964), p. 74.

the two poles. Thus, in the earlier work, Stephen reveals some definitely Blakean propensities:

> He toyed . . . with a theory of dualism which would symbolize the twin eternities of spirit and nature in the twin eternities of male and female and even thought of explaining the audacities of his verse as symbolical allusions. It was hard for him to compel his head to preserve the strict temperature of classicism. *(S.H.,* 210)

We should note that it is precisely these thoughts which are "dancing the dance of unrest in his brain" when he experiences the first epiphany, which thus appears as a returning impulse toward the here and now.

To move from the concept of the epiphany as an act of perception to its implications for artistic practice we need to discover the nature of the "unuttered" (i.e. implicit) meaning to which it directs "the quick intelligence" (i.e. of the reader). In the first place, we note that the epiphany is repeatedly directed at the traditional "low" matter of realism. Stephen assumes "the *vulgarity* of speech or of gesture" *(S.H.,* 211— my emphasis), and although this is in part a reflection of his attitude, it also gives an accurate indication. In *Stephen Hero* the Ballast Office clock is taken for an illustration, in the *Portrait* a basket. We should also recall Stephen's discussion with the President in which he maintains that Aquinas' definition of beauty "would apply to a Dutch painter's representation of a plate of onions" *(S.H.,* 95).[8] But if the epiphany selects the subjects of realism it also proposes "so to work upon them and fashion them" that they become more than

8. Cf. George Eliot's discussion of Dutch painting as a model for realism in Chapter 17 of *Adam Bede.*

JAMES JOYCE

simply realistic. To determine the procedures involved in this transformation we must consider not only Joyce's theories but the surviving Epiphanies which he collected, as Stephen says the man of letters should, and which became the materials of his fiction.

Like the snatch of conversation which Stephen hears in Eccles Street, many consist of a brief moment of speech or gesture, isolated fragments of experience, recorded without commentary. Robert Scholes has recently claimed that "it was the essence of epiphany in Joyce's youthful theory and practice that it had no context,"[9] but it seems to me that in themselves these fragments are not properly epiphanic. They manifest almost nothing, remaining merely small slices of life cut in an apparently arbitrary manner. Given the fact that they are supposed to be epiphanies, or simply the portentousness they acquire from their selection and isolation, we may find them vaguely significant, but we can discover specific meaning in them only by assuming as a context what we know of Joyce's sensibility, synthesizing the point of view to which these moments were significant.[10] Only when placed in the context of a fictional structure do these Epiphanies become capable of objective significance. According to Stephen, "the artist who could disentangle the subtle soul

9. "Joyce and the Epiphany: The Key to the Labyrinth?" *Sewanee Review*, 72 (1964), 75. Mr. Scholes proposes to limit the application of the term to "those little bits of prose which Joyce himself gave the name to," but since Joyce not only used the term theoretically but also used those little bits of prose and comparable passages in his fiction, a broader application seems justifiable.

10. This is in fact what has been attempted in the commentaries on each of the forty surviving Epiphanies in *The Workshop of Daedalus: James Joyce and the Raw Materials for A Portrait of the Artist as a Young Man*, ed. Robert Scholes and Richard M. Kain (Evanston, Ill., 1965), pp. 11–51.

of the image from its mesh of defining circumstances most exactly and re-embody it in artistic circumstances chosen as the most exact for it in its new office, he was the supreme artist" (*S.H.*, 78). This is what Joyce did in selecting his Epiphanies and then providing them with a fictional context.

In the various contexts which Joyce provided for these fragments, some receive a heightened significance, while others appear simply as bits of realistic detail. Even when an increased significance is apparent, it may not be fully or immediately epiphanic, especially when it is not registered by the consciousness of a dramatized perceiver. Here is an example whose use in the early pages of the *Portrait* will be remembered:

> [Bray: in the parlour of the house in Martello Terrace]
>
> Mr Vance—*(comes in with a stick)* . . . O, you know, he'll have to apologise, Mrs Joyce.
>
> Mrs Joyce—O yes . . . Do you hear that, Jim?
>
> Mr Vance—Or else—if he doesn't—the eagles'll come and pull out his eyes.
>
> Mrs Joyce—O, but I'm sure he will apologise.
>
> Joyce—*(under the table, to himself)*
>
> > —Pull out his eyes,
> > Apologise,
> > Apologise,
> > Pull out his eyes.
> > Apologise,
> > Pull out his eyes,
> > Pull out his eyes,
> > Apologise.[11]

11. *The Workshop of Daedalus,* p. 11.

By itself, this has very little of the significance it acquires
in the novel, where it is the first of a series of incidents
in which submission and conformity are urged upon the
growing Stephen. This effect is heightened by replacing
Mr. Vance with Dante, upholder of the Church's absolute
authority, and there may be significant foreshadowing in
having Stephen's response take the form of a poem. The
scene is also supported by the novel's patterns of imagery:
the eagles take their place in a series of images of birds
and flight which are linked with the theme of Stephen's
artistic vocation. To the illuminating effects of context
Joyce adds the emphasis of formal isolation. The brief
scene (even briefer in the novel) is immediately followed
by the first break in the novel's continuity (246). Yet in
spite of the scene's condensation of thematic significance,
its epiphanic or revelatory power is largely retrospective.
Other epiphanies are capable of a more immediate effect.

Even when a moment is designated as epiphanic for
an individual perceiver, it may not be so for the reader.
This seems to be the case with Stephen's original experience in Eccles Street: why is it an epiphany? what does it
reveal? Its significance is only partly accessible; the passage
seems to lie between the Epiphanies Joyce collected pri-
vately and those which were completely adapted for fictional purposes. Some contextual indication of the scene's
significance may be found in the narrator's remark that
it took place "on the steps of one of those brown brick
houses which seem the very incarnation of Irish paralysis."
The key word is, of course, "paralysis," which Joyce
claimed as his moral subject in *Dubliners*.[12] In the con-

12. "My intention was to write a chapter of the moral history of
my country and I chose Dublin for the scene because that city seemed
to me the centre of paralysis." *Letters of James Joyce*, II, ed. Richard
Ellmann (New York, 1966), p. 134. The word was introduced into the

versation itself, the exaggerated pauses of the young lady's speech might seem to suggest a kind of paralysis, while the man's words present him as concerned only with self ("I . . . I"). Together with the triviality and banality of the whole passage, these features may indicate some of its significance, but the scene is only partly realized.

Another passage from *Stephen Hero* which also consists only of overheard trivial conversation indicates the way in which an epiphany may be fully effective even without elaborate contextual support or registering its impact on an observer. It occurs as Stephen waits in the rain for his former schoolfellow, Wells, now a seminarist.

> A little band of students passed at the other side of the laurel bushes: they were talking among themselves:
>
> —But did you see Mrs Bergen?
>
> —O, I saw her . . . with a black and white boa.
>
> —And the two Miss Kennedys were there.
>
> —Where?
>
> —Right behind the Archbishop's Throne.
>
> —O, I saw her—one of them. Hadn't she a grey hat with a bird in it?
>
> —That was her! She's very lady-like, isn't she.
>
> The little band went down the path. In a few minutes another little band passed behind the bushes. One student was talking and others were listening.
>
> —Yes, and an astronomer too: that's why he had . . . that observatory built over there at the side of the palace. I heard a priest say once that the three greatest men in Europe were Gladstone, Bismarck

---

first paragraph of the first story, "The Sisters," in a similar indication of theme.

> (the great German statesman) and our own Arch-
> bishop—as all-round men. He knew him at Maynooth.
> He said that in Maynooth . . . (74)

The passage is not among the surviving forty Epiphanies,
but it is easily recognizable as the same sort of experience
the young Joyce recorded. Nor is it labeled as an epiphany
for Stephen; if it does afflict his sensitiveness we are not
told so. Instead the scene achieves its effect without additional commentary, epiphanizing the trivial and provin-
cial life of the seminary and thus generalizing what
Stephen sees in Wells.

Brief, isolated scenes which function almost as single
images are also capable of a much wider range of implication than that produced by the simple example just cited.
A series of three such scenes appears in the second chapter of the *Portrait,* juxtaposed without narrative transition
or commentary, each beginning with the words "He was
sitting . . ." (313–17). Earlier versions of the second two
are to be found in the surviving Epiphanies, but all three
work in the same way. The second is a good example:

> He was sitting in the narrow breakfast room high
> up in the old darkwindowed house. The firelight
> flickered on the wall and beyond the window a spec-
> tral dusk was gathering upon the river. Before the
> fire an old woman was busy making tea and, as she
> bustled at the task, she told in a low voice of what
> the priest and the doctor had said. She told too of
> certain changes they had seen in her of late and of
> her odd ways and sayings. He sat listening to the
> words and following the ways of adventure that lay
> open in the coals, arches and vaults and winding
> galleries and jagged caverns.
>
> Suddenly he became aware of something in the

doorway. A skull appeared suspended in the gloom of the doorway. A feeble creature like a monkey was there, drawn there by the sound of voices at the fire. A whining voice came from the door asking:

—Is that Josephine?

The old bustling woman answered cheerily from the fireplace:

—No, Ellen, it's Stephen.

—O . . . O, good evening, Stephen.

He answered the greeting and saw a silly smile break over the face in the doorway.

—Do you want anything, Ellen? asked the old woman at the fire.

But she did not answer the question and said:

—I thought it was Josephine. I thought you were Josephine, Stephen.

And, repeating this several times, she fell to laughing feebly. (314–15)

Joyce's discontinuous narrative texture isolates this scene and stresses its significance. Stephen's mind contributes only a few heightening touches: the skull, the monkey; but the epiphany is ours, not his. The scene crystallizes several of the novel's themes: Stephen's isolation and withdrawal into romantic dreams and the crucial question of his identity. Beyond this, the two old women, one briskly banal, the other senile, seem to reveal the nature of the world from which he withdraws, its paralysis or mental deadness. All this gains force precisely by not becoming explicit but by working through an eerie suggestiveness. The effect is partly achieved by the discrepancy between the apparent triviality of the moment and its implicit claim of unusual significance created by its selection and isolation. Its meaningfulness is thus the result

JAMES JOYCE

of its own form as well as of its relation to context. The scene and the figures in it are not fully symbolic, but in their power of suggestion they move in the direction of symbolism. Unlike the scene which centers on the insistently symbolic harp in "Two Gallants," the epiphany preserves contact with the realistic because it works in the terms of its concrete content. Its images are not absorbed into symbolic equations (harp = girl = Ireland) but are charged with greater meaning than they would carry in a purely realistic mode. The epiphany allows Joyce to operate in the realm between realism and symbolism, drawing on qualities of both.[13]

Most of the stories of *Dubliners* employ this intermediate, epiphanic mode, and they are distorted when, as has often happened, critics attempt to assimilate them to the more symbolic mode of *Ulysses*. William York Tindall, for example, offers symbolic readings of nearly every story in *Dubliners*. Noting that, in "An Encounter," the

13. Comparisons with contemporary poetry are suggestive. The writing, although not the publication, of most of the *Dubliners* stories and much of the *Portrait* precedes the promulgation of Imagism by Ezra Pound in 1913. Joyce's use of the scene as image, his juxtaposition of several without connections or commentary (cf. Pound's rejection of abstractions and his removal of connecting passages from *The Waste Land*), as well as his concern with epiphanic revelation (cf. T. E. Hulme's concern with the imagistic creation of insight) seem analogous. See Stanley K. Coffman, Jr., *Imagism* (Norman, Okla., 1951), and also A. Walton Litz' association of Imagism with the prose style of *Dubliners* in *James Joyce* (New York, 1966), pp. 50 and 113. We have noted such similarities in Lawrence, but in Joyce they are closer. His greater narrative discontinuity is one reason for this, but another is that Joyce's scenes, usually briefer, often fix their elements in a static, image-like configuration, while Lawrence's are usually kinetic, as in the ritual actions of the sheave-gathering scene or Anna's pregnant dance in *The Rainbow* and the rabbit or moon-shattering scenes in *Women in Love*.

two boys are on an expedition to the Pigeon House (the Dublin electric light and power station), he proceeds to interpret the story as a symbolic quest: "Light and power suggest God and the traditional icon of the Holy Ghost is the Pigeon. . . . The quest, therefore, can be taken as a search for the third member of the Trinity or, since Father, Son, and Holy Ghost are one, as that hunt for the father which was to become a theme of *Ulysses,*"[14] and so on, making only the most tangential contact with the actual story. A striking example of this sort of irrelevant symbolic interpretation is provided by Robert S. Ryf, who detects a crucial symbol in *Dubliners* somehow unnoticed by all previous commentators:

> Perhaps the most significant passage in "Two Gallants" is that in which Lenehan, an obvious captive of his lot, orders and eats a plate of peas while awaiting Corley's return from the assignation. This isolated incident is not particularly significant in itself, but in context with the *Portrait* it becomes richly meaningful. At the end of the *Portrait,* Stephen, about to depart, meets Emma Clery for the last time: "Talked rapidly of myself and my plans. In the midst of it unluckily I made a sudden gesture of a revolutionary nature. I must have looked like a fellow throwing a handful of peas up into the air." These two lots of peas now suggest pottage and birthrights. Stephen, leaving Ireland, pays his ransom by rejecting the symbol of bondage, and reclaims the birthright that Lenehan, remaining behind, trapped, sells daily.[15]

14. *A Reader's Guide to James Joyce,* p. 17.

15. *A New Approach to Joyce: The Portrait of the Artist as Guidebook* (Berkeley and Los Angeles, 1964), p. 67.

The exercise of such ingenuity proceeds in a critical vacuum, based on unexamined and highly improbable assumptions concerning Joyce's mode. While Mr. Ryf is minding his richly meaningful peas, he manages to miss the story's actual revelation, which comes in the last lines as Corley literally shows forth the coin he has cadged from the servant girl, epiphanizing the life led by these two gallants.

It is possible to describe this gold coin as a symbol, but we must recognize that its symbolism is of a sort which leads us directly back to the realistic human world of the story, not off to some realm of purely symbolic meaning dissociated from the actual objects presented. For all its modernity, *Dubliners* is like more traditional fiction in assigning an auxiliary role to its symbolic devices. This is not to deny that Joyce performed technical experiments in these stories which foreshadow his later methods. The rough Dantean parallel in "Grace," for example, looks forward to his use of Homer in *Ulysses* (itself originally conceived as a *Dubliners* story),[16] and the stories are linked with several motifs and repeated themes. But where these elements are artistically relevant, they do no more than generalize meaning (making individual cases representative of a general situation in Ireland); they do not transpose it into completely different terms. The realism of *Dubliners* is never a mere surface coyly masking deeper symbolic levels. Critical explications which fail to recognize this tend to be, in S. L. Goldberg's words, "either irrelevant or unconvincing."[17]

16. See Richard Ellmann, *James Joyce* (New York, 1959), pp. 238–39.
17. *James Joyce* (New York, 1962), p. 46. See also T. H. Gibbons, *"Dubliners* and the Critics," *Critical Quarterly, 9* (1967), 179–87, for a critique of systematic symbolic interpretations.

Like "Two Gallants," the stories of *Dubliners* nearly all end with a revelatory flourish which attempts to complete or crystallize their meaning, though not always in the sort of scene to which I have been applying the term epiphany. This feature of Joyce's method has been described by Irene Hendry as the "block" technique, in which the last moment, like a lettered block in a child's construction, fills the crucial gap and makes the whole design suddenly intelligible.[18] The ending of "The Sisters" performs this function in an epiphanic scene, providing information of the crucial incident in the dead priest's past, his breaking of the chalice and its effect on him, and, equally important, revealing the uncomprehending attitude of those around him.

> "And what do you think but there he was, sitting up by himself in the dark in his confession-box, wide-awake and laughing-like softly to himself?"
>
> She stopped suddenly as if to listen. I too listened; but there was no sound in the house: and I knew that the old priest was lying still in his coffin as we had seen him, solemn and truculent in death, an idle chalice on his breast.
>
> Eliza resumed:
>
> "Wide-awake and laughing-like to himself. . . . So then, of course, when they saw that, that made them think that there was something gone wrong with him. . . ." (28)

Again, there is an effect of eerie suggestiveness, hinting at the hidden sickness which pervades the world of the story, the "maleficent and sinful being" which the boy has sensed in "the word paralysis" at the beginning (19);

18. "Joyce's Epiphanies," *Sewanee Review*, *54* (1946), 451–52.

again, the effect is intensified by the tension between this vaguely sensed threat and the banal, awkward understatement through which it emerges. Joyce is able to terminate his story in an ostensibly arbitrary fashion, cutting it off in the midst of the old woman's speech, which yet completes its essential disclosure—an effect which is even more prominent in the conclusion to "Grace," which ends in the midst of Father Purdon's sermon, epiphanizing the banality of his secularized religion by giving formal emphasis to his commercial metaphor: " 'Well, I have looked into my accounts. I find this wrong and this wrong. But, with God's grace, I will rectify this and this. I will set right my accounts' " (190). The final blocks of these stories are moments of speech, just as "Two Gallants" concludes with a gesture. Revelation may also occur in "a memorable phase of the mind itself," but such moments tend to be closer to traditional recognition, such as that which comes at the end of "Araby." The young protagonist finds himself alone in the darkened bazaar, his romantic dreams deflated: "Gazing up into the darkness I saw myself as a creature driven and derided by vanity; and my eyes burned with anguish and anger" (46). Most of the characters of *Dubliners* are not capable of this degree of consciousness; their situations are instead rendered by Joyce in a manner which is apparently realistic and yet suggestive of further meaning.

It may be easier to recognize the intermediate, epiphanic mode in which most of *Dubliners* is written by comparison with "The Dead," written later than the other stories, which gradually moves out of it into a more symbolic mode. The first part of the story, that concerned with the party, is realistic, presenting several characters in their social relations, and filled with visual detail, as in the extended description of the dinner table (213–14). In the section dealing with the various departures the focus narrows; there is, as Kenneth Burke notes, "a symbolism emerging in the realism, when Gabriel tells the anecdote of the old horse that went round and round the monument."[19] I have discussed at the beginning of this chapter the thematic introduction of the complex relation of realism and symbolism at this point. The last section, bringing the relation of Gabrial and Gretta to a crisis and precipitating Gabriel's final recognition, gathers many of the story's images and motifs (snow, music, the west, generosity, the past) and fuses them in a symbolic complex. Gabriel has been made to realize, as his wife tells him of Michael Furey, the dead boy who loved her, how little he has actually known her and how much he has been absorbed in himself. Overcome with a sense of his own futility, he senses his very identity fading. The last paragraph renders his state of mind and final descent into sleep, but this more realistic aspect recedes as Joyce's words, crystallizing the story's meaning in a kind of prose poem, carry it onto a fully symbolic level.

> A few light taps upon the pane made him turn to the window. It had begun to snow again. He watched sleepily the flakes, silver and dark, falling obliquely against the lamplight. The time had come for him to set out on his journey westward. Yes, the newspapers were right: snow was general all over Ireland. It was falling on every part of the dark central plain, on the treeless hills, falling softly on the Bog of Allen and, farther westward, softly falling into the dark mutinous Shannon waves. It was falling, too, upon every part of the lonely churchyard on the hill where

19. "Three Definitions," in *Perspectives by Incongruity,* ed. Stanley Edgar Hyman (Bloomington, Ind., 1964), p. 147.

> Michael Furey lay buried. It lay thickly drifted on
> the crooked crosses and headstones, on the spears of
> the little gate, on the barren thorns. His soul swooned
> slowly as he heard the snow falling faintly through
> the universe and faintly falling, like the descent of
> their last end, upon all the living and the dead. (242)

The symbolism maintains a balanced ambiguity, one
whose underlying structure is the balance of judgment and
sympathy toward the world of *Dubliners*. The words, "The
time had come for him to set out on his journey west-
ward," for example, invoke the traditional association of
west and death, but also draw on the associations it is
given in the story. Gabriel's earlier rejection of the idea
of a vacation trip to the west has marked his alienation
from his country and his wife, who comes from western
Ireland. The phrase thus suggests a movement both toward
death and toward reconciliation. The snow, which has
also appeared realistically before, here becomes entirely
symbolic. It too suggests death, or frozen paralysis, but
also, as it joins all the parts of Ireland, living and dead,
past and present, suggests inclusive sympathy. Gabriel,
"his own identity . . . fading out into a grey impalpable
world" moves toward both annihilation and a kind of
transcendence of the self. We shall have occasion to consider the ambiguity of Joyce's symbolism again in the conclusion of *Ulysses*. Here the most important point is
simply the high degree of symbolism itself. The passage,
its last words repeating the story's title, extends its implications to the entire world of *Dubliners*, where living and
dead are joined in a kind of community and a kind of
living death, the meaning embodied in the words "snow
was general all over Ireland." The statement, like the
other motifs of the passage, has been introduced in a

realistic sense before (229); now it becomes symbolic. The epiphany must maintain a double focus: on the object and on the significance it acquires. Here the focus becomes single and purely symbolic; the object exists only for what it can signify. The symbol has become a primary vehicle of meaning.

Although in the conclusion of "The Dead" Joyce's fiction moves onto an entirely symbolic level, it is never dominated for long by any single mode. From *Dubliners* through *Ulysses* it reflects the tension between two opposed impulses. On the one hand it is moved by the powerful claims of the given: "so long as this place in nature is given us, it is right that art should do no violence to the gift."[20] Yet on the other is the urge toward its artistic transformation: "converting the bread of everyday life into something that has a permanent artistic life of its own."[21] Just as the relation of symbolism and realism becomes a thematic issue in "The Dead," so the process of transformation becomes a major theme of *A Portrait of the Artist*. As the epigraph from Ovid implies, it is a story of metamorphosis. The novel itself is the product of transformation; this becomes apparent in comparing it with the earlier *Stephen Hero*. As Father Noon observes, "the technique of Joyce in reworking the early manuscript version is precisely in the direction of symbolic transformation."[22] This process appears most obviously as one of distillation; the surviving portion of *Stephen Hero* is nearly five times as long as the corresponding section of the *Portrait*. As a

20. *Critical Writings*, p. 74. The sentence is included in Stephen's "Drama and Life" essay in *Stephen Hero*, p. 79.

21. Joyce's explanation of his intentions to his brother Stanislaus, quoted in Ellmann, *James Joyce*, p. 169.

22. *Joyce and Acquinas*, p. 65.

result the focus becomes concentrated more exclusively on Stephen's consciousness; characters who enjoy an independent existence in the earlier version become refined into images: Emma Clery becomes E—— C——. Action is likewise subjected to rigorous selection, reduced to a series of crucial experiences, often given the form of epiphanic scenes, whose arrangement is controlled by symbolic patterns. An important result is an increase in discontinuity: narrative transitions are suppressed, thematic connections left implicit. Whereas one chapter of *Stephen Hero* often resumes at the same point where the preceding one ended (e.g. pp. 98–99), the *Portrait* leaves extensive gaps between most of its chapters, and even within chapters (e.g. on p. 320, a hiatus of about two years). The effect is to emphasize the significance of the episodes selected for presentation.

The increased symbolism of the *Portrait* also appears in its complex interwoven patterns of motifs and imagery. As Hugh Kenner has pointed out, the first two pages constitute an overture in which many of these are introduced, presenting, among other things, an anticipation of Stephen's crucial experience of artistic vocation: "Dawning consciousness of his own identity ('He was baby tuckoo') leads to artistic performance ('He sang that song. That was his song.')."[23] We have already noted how the threatening eagles initiate a series of images, one which informs Stephen's vision at the end of Chapter 4 of the "hawklike man" and the wading girl, imaged as "seabird" and "dove" (429–32). Also introduced is the extensive pattern of water imagery: "When you wet the bed, first it is warm then it gets cold" (245). The pleasurable and unpleasant aspects create a structure which underlies the

23. *Dublin's Joyce*, pp. 114–16.

development of the first chapter, from the "cold slimy water" of the square ditch, into which Wells has shoved him (248) to the image of fulfillment which caps the triumph of his successful appeal to the rector: "In the soft grey silence he could hear the bump of the balls: and from here and from there through the quiet air the sound of the cricket bats: pick, pack, pock, puck: like drops of water in a fountain falling softly in the brimming bowl" (305). Imagery of water as both threat and fulfillment also plays an important part in Stephen's experience of revelation on the shore. Flowing water is associated with the life he ecstatically accepts; it joins him with the girl whose "mortal beauty" becomes an emblem of that life, and again provides a final image of peace and fulfillment: "the tide was flowing in fast to the land with a low whisper of her waves, islanding a few last figures in distant pools" (434). But the threat is there too, made clear by Joyce's Flaubertian juxtaposition. Stephen, identifying himself with the "hawklike man flying sunward above the sea," feels himself "soaring in an air beyond the world."

> An ecstasy of flight made radiant his eyes and wild his breath and tremulous and wild and radiant his wind-swept limbs.
> —One! Two!...Look out!
> —O, Cripes, I'm drownded! (429)

The sudden deflation suggests future downfall.

Here the imagery of water and flight is clearly controlled by a larger symbolic pattern, the myth of Daedalus.[24] The allusive dimension of Joyce's symbolism is reflected in his protagonist's name, combining St. Stephen,

24. For other instances of "images of flight and flow," see Eugene M. Waith, "The Calling of Stephen Dedalus," *College English, 18* (1957), 256–61. See also Litz, *James Joyce,* pp. 67–69.

cast out of his city and martyred for attempting to recount a vision, and Daedalus, "fabulous artificer," prototype of the artist. The passage just quoted suggests his possible correspondence with Icarus as well; the mythic analogue also contains both positive and negative potentials. The issue here is not the vexed question of evaluating Stephen but simply the way Joyce's elaborate patterns of imagery, motif, and correspondence result in a fiction highly charged with complex symbolic meaning. We should also note the degree to which this symbolism maintains meaning in its own terms (it is this which causes the difficulty of evaluative interpretation). The absence not only of an authoritative, commenting narrator, but even of a set of organizing conceptual terms prevents the abstraction of meaning from the terms in which it is presented. Conceptual terms are introduced, especially in Stephen's exposition of his aesthetic theory, but, unlike those established by the debates and meditations of *Women in Love,* they do not provide a stable framework for interpretation. This is not to say that the symbolism of the *Portrait* constitutes its primary level of meaning. It functions as context for Stephen's story, but it is an extraordinarily rich and irreducibly complex context, a stage in Joyce's development toward the point where symbolism may assume primacy.[25]

25. For a study which attempts to polarize the symbolic and realistic aspects of the *Portrait,* see Arnold Goldman, *The Joyce Paradox: Form and Freedom in His Fiction* (Evanston, Ill., 1966), pp. 22–73, who deliberately slights the "incarnational" aspect of the novel, in which we see symbolism "at its nearest approach to realism." The notion of incarnation is clearly similar to that of the intermediate fictional mode which I have been describing in terms of the epiphany. Such mediating terms as epiphany or transformation seem to me more important for understanding *Dubliners* and the *Portrait* than any modal dichotomy. Mr. Goldman's book, which appeared after

The revelation of his artistic vocation which Stephen experiences appears specifically in terms of transformation: "the artist forging anew in his workshop out of the sluggish matter of the earth a new soaring impalpable imperishable being" (429). Joyce's novel itself achieves such a symbolic transformation, but the success of its protagonist is less sure. Stephen tends to alternate between immersion in (and submission to) "the sluggish matter of the earth," the sordid reality which surrounds him, and withdrawal from it into the realm of dream, which is less a transformation than a denial of reality. We recall that in the earlier version Stephen conceived the artist as "mediator between the world of his experience and the world of his dreams" *(S.H.,* 77); here he appears as torn between them. The polarity is particularly evident in Chapter 2, which is largely concerned with his sexual development. His first vague stirrings of desire are directed toward the idealized figure of Mercedes from *The Count of Monte Cristo:* "as he brooded upon her image, a strange unrest crept into his blood" (310). He wanders alone, thinking he will find her: "He wanted to meet in the real world the unsubstantial image which his soul so constantly beheld," and believes that with that meeting "he would be transfigured. Weakness and timidity and inexperience would fall from him in that magic moment" (311). These romantic dreams coincide with his family's economic decline; they provide a refuge from the reality of "the change of fortune which was reshaping the world about him into a vision of

the first version of this study had been completed, is an important study of the relation between Joyce's realism and symbolism, which are considered not only as aesthetic but as ethical modes. Unlike his discussion of the *Portrait,* his view of the opposition of modes in *Ulysses* has much in common with mine.

squalor and insincerity" (313). By the end of the chapter, the increasing pressure of his desire has forced Stephen to the opposite pole. Instead of the ideal Mercedes, he encounters a prostitute. The episode is presented as an exact inversion of the earlier dream. Stephen again wanders through the streets, this time succeeds in meeting the image his imagination now constantly beholds, and is at last "transfigured": "In her arms he felt that he had suddenly become strong and fearless and sure of himself. . . . He closed his eyes, surrendering himself to her" (352). Joyce's ironic parallels stress the instability of Stephen's oscillation between extremes.

This demonstration of Stephen's inability to come to satisfactory terms with reality provides the setting for his first artistic effort, the poem to E. C. The process of composition appears as a withdrawal from the reality of the incident which has inspired the poem:

> During this process all those elements which he deemed common and insignificant fell out of the scene. There remained no trace of the tram itself nor of the trammen nor of the horses; nor did he and she appear vividly. The verses told only of the night and the balmy breeze and the maiden lustre of the moon. Some undefined sorrow was hidden in the hearts of the protagonists as they stood in silence beneath the leafless trees and when the moment of farewell had come the kiss, which had been withheld by one, was given by both. (317–18)

All the concrete details of the actual, which, as we have seen, Joyce made the basis of the epiphany, have evaporated. The scene becomes a vague, idealized reversal of reality: experience is transformed, not into art, but into wish fulfillment. Stephen's actions after completing the poem set the seal on his efforts: "he went into his mother's bedroom and gazed at his face for a long time in the mirror of her dressingtable" (318).

It would be wrong to deduce a final judgment on Stephen as artist from these early episodes, for he is capable of development. His surrender to the prostitute is followed by a returning swing of the pendulum to a forced and naïve religiosity, but as this yields, in his refusal of a priestly vocation, to the growing sense of his destiny as an artist, we see a new reconciliation with reality which does not merely repeat the mechanical pattern of oscillation. Now the commitment to earthly reality is consistent with the preservation of consciousness, permitting a crucial degree of detachment. This is evident in his capacity for amusement at the "trivial air" he hears in the street, tellingly contrasted with the "mirthless mask" of the priest (419), and in his pity for his brothers and sisters as he detects "the recurring note of weariness and pain" in their voices and joins their song (423). His acceptance of this world embraces both its corruption, imaged in "the faint sour stink of rotted cabbages" (421), and its "mortal beauty," imaged in the birdlike girl (432). It is revealing that in Joyce's earliest "Portrait of the Artist," the brief version of 1904 which preceded *Stephen Hero,* the artist-hero is presented at this crucial point in his development as becoming "conscious of the beauty of mortal conditions." Immediately following is the passage from St. Augustine which reappears in *Ulysses:* "It was manifested unto me that those things be good which yet are corrupted; which neither if they were supremely good, nor unless they were good could be corrupted."[26] It is precisely this middle, mortal state to which Joyce's technique of the epiphany is di-

26. *The Workshop of Daedalus,* p. 65. See *Ulysses,* p. 142.

rected, and Stephen's adoption of a similar orientation at this point seems a clear indication of his growth. This commitment to the here and now is elaborated in conceptual terms in his aesthetic theory, which, as we have seen, insists on the concrete individual essence as the source of aesthetic radiance.

Yet this development in Stephen, whether emotional or intellectual, is only one of attitude. As artist, it directs him firmly toward the reality of the world before him, but it does not guarantee his successful transformation of that reality into art. Stephen admits as much to Lynch: "When we come to the phenomena of artistic conception, artistic gestation, and artistic reproduction, I require a new terminology and a new personal experience" (475). Joyce's presentation of Stephen's attitudes must be taken in conjunction with that of his performance as artist, and from this conjunction arise new complications. Stephen's composition of the villanelle directly follows his theoretical exposition. The presentation stresses the process of creation, and Stephen's self-conception centers on the view of this process as transformation. He sees himself as "a priest of eternal imagination, transmuting the daily bread of experience into the radiant body of everliving life" (488). His terms are identical with those in which, as we have noted, the young Joyce declared his own artistic intentions. Here transformation is specifically directed at the erotic, both in the sublimation of the sexual urge into artistic creation ("conception . . . gestation, and . . . reproduction") and in the absorption of personal desire into the impersonal form of art.

Yet the actual process of composition appears more as erotic self-indulgence, once more taking the form of withdrawal into an unreal dream-world. There are pointed parallels with the composition of his earlier poem. Once more it is addressed to E. C. ("He had written verses for her again after ten years" [489].) Once more all concrete details of the actual girl disappear in the incantation of vague, suggestive images and adjectives. Finally, after completing the villanelle (whose ingrown form, constantly returning upon itself, suggests his own self-involvement), Stephen, by his actions, once more seems to set the seal on his efforts. He is aware that "all around him life was about to awaken in common noises, hoarse voices, sleepy prayers," but,

> shrinking from that life he turned towards the wall, making a cowl of the blanket and staring at the great overblown scarlet flowers of the tattered wallpaper. He tried to warm his perishing joy in their scarlet glow, imagining a roseway from where he lay upwards to heaven all strewn with scarlet flowers. (489)

Thus Stephen's artistic commitment to reality is firmer in theory than in practice; his poem represents only a partial transformation of experience and is partially a withdrawal from it. Joyce shows him turned in the right direction but still with far to go, and we know from *Ulysses* that "the reality of experience" which he goes to encounter so confidently at the close of the *Portrait* will impose new and crushing burdens on his imagination.

It has been necessary to engage in this much interpretation of the *Portrait* because of the unique degree of reflexivity between Joyce's meaning and his mode. Presenting the complex problems involved in the artistic transformation of reality, the novel itself appears as such a transformation. Again, this time under the aspect of the creative process, Joyce emerges as the symbolist of the relation between reality and symbol.

In *Ulysses* the relation of realism and symbolism becomes even more important and more problematic. Lecturing on English literature in Trieste in 1912, Joyce chose as his subject Realism and Idealism, taking Defoe and Blake as examples of these opposed tendencies.[27] The choice indicates his consciousness of the tension between realistic and symbolic modes and seems furthermore prophetic of his future development: *Ulysses* carries both realism and symbolism to new extremes. Its realism is apparent in the full presentation of character and action in a highly particularized social and material setting. It becomes extreme in the enormous quantity of detail, often trivial, which is included, such as the extensive information about Bloom catalogued in the penultimate chapter, "Ithaca."[28] Joyce's realism requires not only the verisimilitude of invented details but the verity of facts: *Ulysses* incorporates much of the sheer physical actuality of Dublin and historical actuality of June 16, 1904. Joyce's letters reveal his extraordinary concern with factual accuracy, requesting his relatives in Dublin to determine the answers to such questions as the following:

> Is it possible for an ordinary person to climb over the railings of no 7 Eccles street, either from the path or the steps, lower himself down from the lowest part of the railings till his feet are within 2 feet or 3 of the ground and drop unhurt. I saw it done myself but by a man of rather athletic build. I require this information in order to determine the wording of a paragraph.[29]

The reply must have been affirmative, for in *Ulysses* we find Bloom lowering himself "to within two feet ten inches

27. See Ellmann, *James Joyce*, pp. 329–30.

28. For the sake of convenience, I shall use the suppressed Homeric chapter titles.

29. *Letters of James Joyce*, I, ed. Stuart Gilbert (New York, 1966), p. 175.

of the area pavement" and dropping unhurt (668–69). Realism carried to such an extreme no longer serves any aesthetic purpose, but the realism of *Ulysses* as a whole performs, as we shall see, a crucial function in the creation of its total meaning.

Joyce's symbolism is developed with equal elaborateness in *Ulysses*. Its most famous element, the use of literary parallels, requires no demonstration by now. The analogies with the *Odyssey,* stressed by its title, as well as with *Hamlet,* the romantic opera *Martha,* and several other works, perform a function like that of more authoritative contextual elements in traditional fiction, providing a set of terms in which the significance of various major and minor elements may appear. Here, however, the situation is more complex; meaning may arise from either correspondence or disparity between immediate action and literary analogue; its import may validate or undermine either member of the analogy and with varying degrees of support or irony. In his voyeuristic affair with Gerty MacDowell, Bloom is the object of a strong irony produced by the contrast with Odysseus and Nausicaa; but appearing near the end of his day as "a competent keyless citizen" who has "proceeded energetically from the unknown to the known through the uncertitude of the void" (697), he more successfully withstands the Homeric comparison: getting through each day *is* the heroic voyage. Besides their potential for the mock-heroic and the redefinition of the heroic these analogies can, with parallel or contrast, create meaning by placing the novelistic action in sharp focus. In the comparison of Stephen with Telemachus, for example, we see clearly that, although his rightful place may have been usurped, he is in no sense searching for a father, attempting instead to conceive himself as the self-creating artist. These large-scale schemes of external correspondences are only one element in the symbolism of *Ulysses;* consideration of their relative importance must await our examination of other elements.

Ulysses also develops complex internal symbolic patterns by the repetition and interaction of numerous motifs. Most proliferate through the psychological associations of Stephen and Bloom and of these many function simply as indices to their recurring concerns. For example, the phrase *"Liliata rutilantium"* from the deathbed prayer appears five times in Stephen's thoughts as the signature of his mother's death, whose guilty memory he cannot escape.[30] Other motifs receive thematic significance in addition to their psychological basis. A prominent example is "metempsychosis," which appears a total of fifteen times. First introduced when Molly asks Bloom what it means (64), it becomes associated with her in his thoughts, then passes into the parodies of "The Oxen of the Sun" (408, 414) and the fantasies of "Circe" (473, 490), finally returning to Bloom's thoughts and at last to Molly's, where it began (754). Besides the personal associative meaning it has for Bloom, the motif suggests the general theme of rebirth (of which more anon), in particular the process by which, as it seems to Bloom, his dead son Rudy is reborn in Stephen. Furthermore, with the specific Greek associations it is given, the word reminds the reader of one aspect of the novel's method, the "reincarnation" of Homeric figures in Dublin of 1904.[31]

30. I have not thought it necessary to list the page number of each occurrence. Most may be found indexed in Richard M. Kain's Appendix D to *Fabulous Voyager: James Joyce's Ulysses* (New York, 1959), pp. 277–89, or in Miles L. Hanley, *A Word Index to James Joyce's Ulysses* (Madison, Wis., 1937).

31. Other motifs which create similar reflexive suggestions about Joyce's methods are "parallax" and "retrospective arrangement."

Individual motifs not only make their own voyages through *Ulysses,* they also converge in large thematic clusters. As an example I shall sketch one such cluster in which diverse elements are drawn into a symbolic pattern. The theme is introduced in abstract, speculative terms as Stephen, presiding over the morning history lesson, ponders unactualized historical possibilities.

> Had Pyrrhus not fallen by a beldam's hand in Argos or Julius Caesar not been knifed to death? They are not to be thought away. Time has branded them and fettered they are lodged in the room of the infinite possibilities they have ousted. But can those have been possible seeing that they never were? Or was that only possible that came to pass? (25)

Although he tries to dismiss the thought of alternative possibilities, it returns in the midst of his theoretical exposition in the library, this time apparently attributed to Shakespeare: "Here he ponders things that were not: what Caesar would have lived to do had he believed the soothsayer: what might have been: possibilities of the possible as possible" (193).

Containing implications concerning freedom and necessity, these terms also involve the theme of frustrated actualization (Pyrrhus yields pier, "a disappointed bridge" [25]), one which is most fully elaborated in the more concrete terms of procreation: the actualization or frustration of possibility become fertilization or sterilization, birth or abortion.[32] These themes are particularly prominent in the maternity hospital chapter, "The Oxen of the Sun," where Stephen makes clear their connection with his more abstract concerns: "But grammercy," he exclaims, "what

32. For a discussion which pursues these themes on a more abstract level, see Goldman, *The Joyce Paradox,* pp. 138–67.

of those Godpossibled souls that we nightly impossibilize?"
(389).[33] The medical students are particularly associated
with such frustration of possibility. When the thunder
interrupts their drunken merriment, the stern moral tones
of Bunyan point out "in that clap the voice of the god
Bringforth" (395), but the drinkers defy the biblical command, "for Preservative had given them a stout shield of
oxengut . . . that they might take no hurt neither from
Offspring that was that wicked devil by virtue of this
same shield which was named Killchild" (396). This context confers a new significance on several reappearing
motifs, such as the Childs murder case (410) and Stephen's
telegraphed quotation from Meredith: "The sentimental-
ist is he who would enjoy without incurring the immense
debtorship for a thing done" (412). Representing the opposite pole here is Mina Purefoy, who gives birth offstage
during the course of the chapter. The booming voice of
Carlyle praises the father: "By heaven, Theodore Purefoy,
thou hast done a doughty deed and no botch! . . . In her
lay a Godframed Godgiven preformed possibility which
thou has fructified!" and no less strenuously denounces
contraception: "Copulation without population! No, say
I! Herod's slaughter of the innocents were the truer name"
(423).

Other strands of the web spread out from this chapter.
Besides contraception and normal birth, the medical students dwell exhaustively on the varieties of "monstrous

33. Joyce apparently also intended to embody the theme allegorically. He wrote to Frank Budgen, "Am working hard at Oxen of the
Sun, the idea being the crime committed against fertility by steriliz-
ing the act of coition. . . . Bloom is the spermatozoon, the hospital
the womb, the nurse the ovum, Stephen the embryo" (Letters, I,
139–40). Although it is hardly realized in this form, the theme is made
fully evident in the chapter by more direct means.

births . . . which Aristotle has classified in his masterpiece" (411), a book which Bloom glances over at the bookstall (235) and which Molly disapprovingly recalls (772). It is "a misbirth with a trailing navelcord, hushed in ruddy wool" (37–38) which Stephen imagines the two "midwives" carrying in their bag. He associates them with the women who discovered Moses, now disposing of this unactualized possibility: "They have tucked it safe among the bulrushes" (45). Moses reappears frequently, a part of the analogy between Ireland and the Jews in Egypt which is made explicitly in the speech recited by Professor Mac-Hugh in "Aeolus" (142–43). The motif is usually associated with the two midwives (thus Stephen's "Parable of the Plums," in which they reappear, is also "A Pisgah Sight of Palestine"), symbolic of frustrated national potential. Similarly, the related motif of Agendath Netaim, the Zionist planter's company, becomes incorporated in the pattern. Bloom first thinks of it as a lush place of olive and orange groves when he reads the brochure advertising it, then decides that in reality it is "not like that. A barren land, bare waste. Vulcanic lake, the dead sea: no fish, weedless sunk deep in the earth" (61). It thus becomes an image of sterilized fertility, appearing as such in "The Oxen of the Sun": "All is gone. Agendath is a waste land, a home of screechowls and the sandblind upupa. Netaim, the golden, is no more" (414).

This complex pattern, of which many more components might be cited, involves several crucial elements of the narrative action. There is the unsuccessful attempt to actualize a new human possibility which resulted in the death of Bloom's infant son Rudy, and the consequent abandoning of normal sexual relations between him and Molly, a notable "limitation of fertility" (736). Other such limitations appear in Bloom's sterilized sexual relations with Gerty MacDowell and in Molly's assignation with Boylan which, contrary to the taunting prediction of Bello Cohen (541), does not result in her becoming pregnant. On a metaphoric level, there is Stephen's concern with artistic creativity (thus the link of Mina Purefoy with the hack author Philip Beaufoy), which accounts for much of his interest in Shakespeare ("After God Shakespeare has created most" [212]) and leads to his own artistic efforts, largely unproductive. By further extension, the pattern may suggest possibilities of spiritual rebirth (offered on one level by Dr. John Alexander Dowie), the actualization of new possibilities in the characters' lives which will improve their present unsatisfactory situations. Thus the internal symbolic structures of *Ulysses,* gathering the scattered strands of phrases, images, and events and weaving them into an ever-growing web of complex significance, finally direct their terms toward the problem of its ultimate interpretation. The weight given them in dealing with this problem will depend on how the mode of *Ulysses,* its way of creating meaning, is conceived, and such considerations must await the examination of other features of its symbolism.

Joyce's labyrinthine patterns are not, like his literary parallels, a new means of organization in the novel. We have observed patterns of thematic imagery in novelists from George Eliot onward. But in *Ulysses* they are elaborated to an unprecedented extreme of complexity, part of Joyce's general development of the symbol as artifice. This development is most evident in the novel's stylistic manipulations. Almost from the beginning of his career, Joyce adopts the strategies of stylistic indirection. Occasionally in *Dubliners* we find commentary which proceeds directly from an "authorial" source. Thus in "The Boarding House" we learn that Mrs. Mooney, the butcher's wife, "dealt with moral problems as a cleaver deals with meat" (74), but such traditional authoritative analysis soon yields to a style which is adapted to the point of view it reflects. Thus the simple, childlike style of "Clay" reflects the qualities of Maria's mind: "The matron had given her leave to go out as soon as the women's tea was over and Maria looked forward to her evening out. The kitchen was spick and span: the cook said you could see yourself in the big copper boilers" (110). Stylistically, the most important development in the transformation of *Stephen Hero* into the *Portrait* is the shift toward indirection, the reflection of Stephen's consciousness in narrative tone. Such indirection is clear in the opening presentation of his earliest childhood experiences ("His father told him that story: his father looked at him through a glass: he had a hairy face" [245]); it is less immediately clear in the fervid rhetoric which presents his visionary experience of artistic vocation: "His soul was soaring in an air beyond the world and the body he knew was purified in a breath and delivered of incertitude and made radiant and commingled with the element of the spirit" (429). Joyce's juxtaposition of these overheated tones with the vulgar cries of the swimmers does not, as we have already observed in another context, completely undercut Stephen, but it clearly reveals that this rhetoric proceeds from his present state, is conditioned by his limitations, and does not convey unqualified authorial support.

No style bears such authority in Joyce's fiction. Conrad's rhetoric of metaphysical immensities or Lawrence's rhetoric of affective intensity provide a solid ground of meaning, but all of Joyce's styles are conditional; meaning is based not on any one but on the interrelation of all. In *Ulysses* the passages where the normal novelistic elements of character, setting, and action occupy the foreground are presented in a style which blends the interior monologue's first-person expression of the character's consciousness with the indirect third-person notation of events, sometimes combined with dialogue. This style predominates in the first ten chapters, after which the musicalized style of "The Sirens" and the parodies of "The Cyclops," "Nausicaa," and "The Oxen of the Sun" insert increasingly obtrusive stylistic artifices between the reader and the novelistic level of character and event. This level is almost, though not completely, obscured by the fantastic drama of "Circe"; it reemerges somewhat in the no less artificial parody styles of "Eumaeus" and "Ithaca," after which all artifice is apparently dissolved in the stream of Molly's consciousness, unmixed with any third-person notations.

The development of increasing artifice creates an increasing distance between what is actually presented and what is, by novelistic hypothesis, "really" happening. This is another facet of the tension between symbolistic and realistic aspects in *Ulysses*. It first appears in the insertion of headlines into the narrative of "Aeolus" and is exploited for ironic effect in the contrast between the realistic first-person narrative of "The Cyclops" and its parody of heroic style and that between the parody of sentimental narrative and Bloom's interior monologue in "Nausicaa." Later chapters, especially "The Oxen of the Sun" and "Circe," increase the distance and tension much further. In "Circe" the great bulk of what is presented finds no direct correspondence on a hypothetical realistic level, operating in its own mode of expressionistic fantasy whose relation to either the actions or the minds of the individual characters is quite problematic.

A further aspect of the development in *Ulysses* of symbolism as artifice may be seen by comparison with the narrative method of the *Portrait*. There the move toward a more symbolic mode involved the highly selective presentation of a series of epiphanic scenes. In *Ulysses* Joyce's more strongly asserted symbolism develops by elaboration, the proliferation of multiple schemes of correspondence and patterns of motifs; instead of isolating an individual essence it now expands toward encyclopedic inclusiveness.[34] The individual scene, epiphanic or otherwise, is no longer the basic unit of action. Instead events are joined more loosely in the larger form of the episode or chapter, which becomes more sharply defined as an integral form, differentiated by style and, like the stories of *Dubliners* and the chapters of the *Portrait,* completed with a conclusive flourish. S. L. Goldberg has attempted to adopt the concept of the epiphany to the narrative method of *Ulysses,* applying it to articulated constructs developed within the characters' interior monologues. So redefined,

> epiphanies . . . are at one level acts of apprehension made by the characters—not rare and special moments of mysterious insight (such as Virginia Woolf's novels often turn upon), but common acts of understanding in everyday life. But they are also, at a higher power, as it were, the artist's apprehensions of the significance of these acts (their forms or "quiddities" perhaps). The characters perceive meanings in life; we are shown further meaning in their perceptions.[35]

34. A. Walton Litz has shown, in a study of *Ulysses* in process, how this shift takes place between the early and later years of composition and how the later development leads directly into *Finnegans Wake.* See *The Art of James Joyce: Method and Design in Ulysses and Finnegans Wake* (New York, 1964), especially pp. 35–36. It is precisely because the cosmic encyclopedicism of *Finnegans Wake* no longer exists in tension with the fictional particular that it lies outside the scope of any study which is, like this one, confined to the novel.

35. *The Classical Temper,* p. 253.

There is no doubt that the sort of component form described here plays an important part in structuring Joyce's interior monologues, replacing earlier scenic structure. In essence, however, such moments of dual perception are not greatly different from those we have analyzed in James. Furthermore, to designate them as epiphanies obscures the fact that *Ulysses* creates significance by means which, as I have indicated, differ markedly from those of Joyce's earlier, epiphanic fiction. Mr. Goldberg's choice of the term is affected by his wish to emphasize the more traditionally novelistic elements of *Ulysses* and to discount its more overtly, artificially symbolic ones. Once more, we are confronted with the question of the relation of symbolism and realism in *Ulysses,* their respective roles in its creation of meaning.

The earlier criticism of *Ulysses,* confronted by its un-precedented symbolic complexity, tended naturally to emphasize the intricacy of its artifice. The assumptions concerning its mode which underlie such an approach are explicitly set forth by Stuart Gilbert:

> The meaning of *Ulysses* . . . is not to be sought in any analysis of the acts of the protagonist or the mental make-up of the characters; it is, rather, implicit in the technique of the various episodes, in nuances of language, in the thousand and one correspondences and allusions with which the book is studded.[36]

Ulysses, in this view, is not in any traditional sense a novel. Its primary level of meaning is constituted by its symbolic artifice, to which character and action are strictly subordinated. More recent criticism has opposed itself to such a view. "It would be a grave mistake," A. Walton

36. *James Joyce's Ulysses* (New York, 1960), pp. 8–9. Gilbert's book originally appeared in 1930.

Litz writes, "to found any interpretation of *Ulysses* on Joyce's *schema,* rather than on the human actions of Stephen, Molly, and Mr. Leopold Bloom."[37] Similarly, S. L. Goldberg declares that *Ulysses* is essentially a novel, that it takes "the ordinary world of humanity as the primary object of its attention."[38] Robert M. Adams has attempted to resolve the question of mode by research into the background of *Ulysses* to determine whether various details are symbolic or realistic. He concludes that Joyce's artifice does not yield a "coherent symbolic message" and that

> readers who have sensed a mingled affection and contempt in the author's view of Bloom, a mingled admiration and irony in his view of Stephen, and a kind of sacramental vulgarity in Molly—who have sensed the novel's scope, relished its humour, and recognized a joyous brutal vitality behind the artifice—have not missed very much.[39]

Such a view will doubtless be comforting to many perplexed readers, but it completely avoids the problem of the meaning of *Ulysses,* novelistic or otherwise.

This problem is squarely confronted by Stanley Sultan, who is also intent on reading *Ulysses* as a novel and has attempted a comprehensive analysis of its meaning based on the narrative level of character and action, the "argument." In so doing, he makes explicit the assumption

37. *The Art of James Joyce,* p. 40.

38. *The Classical Temper,* p. 32. Concerning the mode of *Ulysses,* Mr. Goldberg asserts that "it is not 'Romance', not a joke, not a spiritual guide, not even an encyclopedia of social disintegration or a re-creation of Myth or a symbolist poem; it is a novel" (p. 30).

39. *Surface and Symbol: The Consistency of James Joyce's Ulysses* (New York, 1962), pp. 248–49.

which must underlie such an approach: all the complex
symbolism of *Ulysses* exists for only one purpose, "to
serve the story."[40] In other words, *Ulysses* is conceived as
using symbolism in essentially the same fashion as that of
traditional fiction, as an auxiliary rather than primary
vehicle of meaning, always subordinate to the realistic
level. The mode of traditional fiction, as we have seen in
George Eliot, depends on the use of an authoritative narrator to convey meaning directly, thus subordinating indirect, symbolic means; but Joyce's fiction, as we have
observed, contains no such authoritative voice. The difficulties created by this situation ultimately force Mr. Sultan into an extraordinary position. He finds the meaning
of the novel completely clear, without "any possibility of
ambiguity,"[41] but to arrive at this enviable state of cer-
tainty, he must, in effect, consider Joyce's symbolism as
constituting the equivalent of a thoroughly reliable narrator, completely identifying the work's artifice with its
author. Thus he declares that "in a pattern of symbols,
allusions and word-plays . . . Joyce has intimated the outcome of Bloom's story."[42] Here what began as a reading
on the realistic level has become a highly purposeful reading of the symbolism. The complexities of Joyce's inter-
acting modes, especially as they are developed in the
conclusion, seem calculated to frustrate any attempt to
place primary emphasis on either the realistic or symbolic
aspects.

It will hardly be possible here to determine the relation
of realism and symbolism in *Ulysses* on the basis of a detailed analysis of their respective functions, but by using

40. *The Argument of Ulysses* (Columbus, Ohio, 1964), p. 18.
41. Ibid., p. 447.
42. Ibid., pp. 414–15.

the framework of terms suggested by the existing criticism it should be possible to present a general outline supported by a few significant examples. In general, then, it would seem fairly clear that Joyce's symbolism does not operate exclusively as either primary or auxiliary vehicle of meaning, that its function ranges, in his own words, from the trivial to the quadrivial. Barbara Hardy has recently suggested that form and meaning in *Ulysses* may exist in three basic possible relations. Form may appear as "play," an arbitrary creation of significance which is not essential to the central meaning. A clear example may be seen in the incidental detail of the Homeric parallel, such as the analogy between Bloom's "knockmedown" cigar and the sharpened stake with which Odysseus blinds the Cyclops. Form may also assume its normal "appropriate" relation with meaning; presumably this would include all the traditionally novelistic aspects, where meaning is sufficiently evident in the narrative of character and action, and the aspect of symbolism as artifice is not obtruded. Finally there is "essential" form, which would yield symbolism operating as a primary vehicle of meaning, an aspect which becomes increasingly important as the work nears its conclusion.[43] An adequate description of the relation between symbolism and realism in *Ulysses* must take account of the way its center of gravity shifts between them.

One necessary approach to the problem is to observe the way it is, once again, given thematic expression; the relation between symbolism and realism in *Ulysses* is one aspect of the relation between Stephen and Bloom. Stephen begins his Protean meditations by thinking of the objects of sight as "signatures of all things I am here to read" (37),

43. See "Form as End and Means in *Ulysses*," *Orbis Litterarum, 19* (1964), 194–200. I have adapted Mrs. Hardy's terms to my own concerns.

converting visual perception into symbolic vision. Here, as in the crucial scene of the *Portrait,* Stephen stands on the shore and attempts to define his role as artist, now clearly in opposition to the natural flux of the sea, in which he avoids immersion. Having aspired to Daedalian artistry, soaring over the sea, he has, as he now recognizes, played a part closer to that of Icarus: "Fabulous artificer, the hawklike man. You flew. Whereto? Newhaven—Dieppe, steerage passenger. Paris and back, Lapwing. Icarus. *Pater, ait.* Seabedabbled, fallen, weltering. Lapwing you are. Lapwing he" (210). He thus appears as still subject to unstable oscillation, attempting as artist to forge a self-sufficient symbolic creation, yet threatened with possible collapse into the flux of history, his own and Ireland's, the chaos within him and that in the society around him.

Bloom, however, as competent Ulyssean voyager, willingly negotiates this sea, the natural flux of Dublin. Stephen goes through the day looking for symbolic signs in the natural world (thus, from the library steps, he looks for the birds in whose flight he had augured portents in the *Portrait* [217–18]), but Bloom is contentedly ignorant of even the most basic symbolic meanings. Idly observing the morning mass, he supposes that I.N.R.I. means "iron nails ran in" and I.H.S. "I have suffered" (81). His outlook is one of thorough realism, or, more specifically, naturalism. Stephen's thoughts surround his observations with a mesh of literary, historical, and theological allusions, while Bloom's, giving a much fuller reflection of the physical world around him, adduce the lore of popular science. He is recurrently troubled by the meaning of "parallax," the formula 'thirty-two feet per second per second," and the relation of black to heat: "conducts, reflects (refracts, is it?)" (57). While Stephen struggles to maintain himself in the role of artist, Bloom, student of "the modern art of advertising," also contemplates a literary effort, conceived in the vein of mechanical naturalistic reportage:

> Might manage a sketch. . . . Time I used to try jotting down on my cuff what she said dressing. . . . Biting her nether lip, hooking the placket of her skirt. Timing her. 9.15. Did Roberts pay you yet? 9.20. What had Gretta Conroy on? 9.23. What possessed me to buy this comb? 9.24. I'm swelled after that cabbage. A speck of dust on the patent leather of her boot. (69)

The different modes of *Ulysses* imply both points of view, both the abstracted reading of obscure symbolic signatures and immersion in natural flux. As with the two major characters, so with the two basic modes: neither is complete or sufficient in itself. They stand in a complex relation in which their respective qualities appear, perplexingly, as both complementary and incompatible.

The inability of either the symbolic or realistic modes of *Ulysses* to sustain a satisfactory reading may be seen at several crucial points. A prominent instance is the presentation of Bloom's estrangement from Molly, which is asserted with almost no realistic psychological support. Despite the wealth of realistic detail which is expended on less important aspects of Bloom's life, concerning this, the most important single factor in his situation, we are told only that it has somehow resulted from the death of his son: "something changed. Could never like it again after Rudy" (168). Similarly Molly reflects that "that disheartened me altogether . . . we were never the same since" (778). Although it might be possible to construct an adequate psychological theory to account for this situation, the point is that the actual terms of its presentation are not conducive to such an account. Rather, they leave what must appear in a realistic perspective as an area of nearly total obscurity at the heart of Bloom's life. In a symbolic perspective, however, Bloom's situation becomes abundantly meaningful. The sterility of his marriage accords perfectly with the complex of symbolism of sterility and fertility which we have already examined. Here it is fully supported by the elaborate variations on the theme developed by Joyce's multiple patterns of motifs. Thus this element provides an important example of the way the realistic mode of *Ulysses* fails to maintain consistent primacy.

Yet neither is the symbolism capable of providing terms for a complete account. If we attempt to read it as a coherent and consistent code to be deciphered, we discover curious internal oppositions. Stephen, for example, undertakes to help Mr. Deasy in his efforts against hoof and mouth disease, becoming "the bullockbefriending bard" (36). Since, as we have noted, the slaughter of the oxen of the sun is "the crime committed against fertility," he might thus appear aligned with the theme of fertility and opposed to that of sterility.[44] Yet Stephen also repeatedly appears as "hydrophobe, hating partial contact by immersion or total by submersion in cold water (his last bath having taken place in the month of October of the preceding year)" (673), and water also appears as an emblem of fertility. The symbolism poses and elaborates a question without resolving it. Again, to take another element of this complex, Bloom is also bullockbefriending, since one of his many schemes is the construction of a tramline for transporting cattle (58), but the suggestions of fertility symbolism here are vigorously opposed by the novelistic

44. Such an interpretation is in fact offered by William York Tindall, in *A Reader's Guide*, p. 142.

presentation of Bloom's sterile marriage and sterilized relations with Gerty MacDowell.[45]

Not only do we find different elements of the symbolism contradicting each other, and some symbolic suggestions firmly repudiated by narrative action, but we also find elements which seem designed specifically to frustrate the symbolism. We have already noted in *Dubliners* the way certain obtrusive objects resist symbolic explication. *Ulysses* likewise contains elements which, although made insistently suggestive, maintain strong resistance to assimilation into its symbolic patterns. An example is the mysterious man in the mackintosh, who appears eleven different times yet remains to the end a "selfinvolved enigma" (729). He becomes intensely suggestive, yet without ascertainable specific meaning, from a symbolic perspective an irreducible surd. Such elements are part of a strategy which denies full primacy to the symbolic level as well.

Even though neither the symbolism nor the realism of *Ulysses* is in itself sufficient, its meaning would not, of course, be problematic if the two modes were in general accord. Certainly there are several occasions where they are perfectly congruent. The three-masted schooner *Rosevean*, examined in my Introduction, exemplifies the harmonious coexistence of the realistic and symbolic aspects in a single image. Such congruence generally prevails in the earlier parts of *Ulysses*, but it is gradually disrupted and replaced by an increasing tension between the two aspects. S. L. Goldberg, expressing normal novelistic presuppositions, deplores any critical view of *Ulysses* which would create a "dichotomy of Naturalistic 'matter' and a Symbolist 'structure,' "[46] but it would seem that such

45. For other examples of inconsistency, see Adams, *Surface and Symbol*.

46. *The Classical Temper*, p. 247.

a dichotomy is actually developed and exploited within the work as it progresses. Artifice begins to clash directly with the realistic psychological presentation of character. Robert M. Adams has noted the insertion of a passage from Stephen's thoughts (202) into Bloom's meditations (280).[47] Whether, as Mr. Adams supposes, this is an instance of telepathic thought transference, or simply an arbitrary assertion of artifice, the effect is to undermine the realistic presentation of characters as autonomous persons. The firm boundaries of the individual *are* erased at several points in the action of "Circe." The elaborate fantasies developed there cannot be satisfactorily explained in realistic, or novelistic, terms, either as being actual hallucinations of the characters or as expressing the contents of their individual subconsciousnesses. Experiences of one character are transferred to another without regard for any possible novelistic rationale. Thus the phrase *"nebrakada feminum,"* which Stephen has read in a collection of charms from a book cart (242), appears spoken by Molly to Bloom (440). Here novelistic elements have been absorbed into the autonomous symbolic artifice. Yet *Ulysses* does not continue to the end in the mode of Circean fantasy. The level of character and action re-emerges sufficiently to pose a challenge to the artifice; neither alone can provide an adequate resolution.

47. *Surface and Symbol,* pp. 95–99. This is by no means the first instance of cross-referencing between Stephen and Bloom. Joyce correlates their morning activities by setting the fourth, fifth, and sixth chapters, which present Bloom's morning, at the same hours as the first three, which present Stephen's, and further links their minds by parallel thoughts, such as those of "Turko the terrible" (10 and 57), but such contrivances are not essentially unlike the parallels which a realistic novelist such as George Eliot establishes between characters. They produce a context of implicit comparisons between the two, not an obtrusive violation of probability and individuality.

The concluding chapters exacerbate the conflict of modes: the symbolism of *Ulysses* places an enormous weight of importance on the meeting of Stephen and Bloom and their subsequent actions, yet realistically very little seems to take place. In a symbolic perspective, this is the meeting of the father and the son, fulfilling the multiple elaborations of the thematic complex centering on paternity. It may be, in terms of the complex we have already examined, the means of actualizing important new possibilities. Stephen, knocked down by Private Carr, assumes the foetal position before being helped to his feet again by Bloom (608). Bloom likewise assumes this position before going to sleep, "the manchild in the womb" (737). The symbolism suggests rebirth for both. Acting on such suggestions, many critics have agreed with Edmund Wilson that "Bloom's encounter with Stephen is to affect both Stephen's life and the relation between the Blooms."[48] According to such a view, Stephen is "reconciled with the father," who represents a range of possibilities extending from the common man to God, and is thus at last enabled to become a true artist, while Bloom, also transformed, will now reassert himself and save his marriage (indicated by his request that Molly bring him breakfast next morning). Such readings must, of necessity, grant full authority to the symbolism, for the scant narrative action of "Eumaeus" and "Ithaca" offers them little support on a realistic level. Far from appearing reconciled

48. *Axel's Castle: A Study in the Imaginative Literature of 1870–1930* (New York, 1931), pp. 200–01. For a survey of several critical views of the conclusion, see William M. Schutte, *Joyce and Shakespeare: A Study in the Meaning of Ulysses* (New Haven, Conn., 1957), pp. 8–16. The latest critic to subscribe to the sort of positive interpretation set forth by Wilson is Stanley Sultan, in *The Argument of Ulysses.*

or regenerated, Stephen at first makes little response to Bloom's friendly, banal overtures, then attempts a few concessions to politeness, which are followed, however, by the gratuitous rudeness of his anti-semitic song. Finally, refusing the offer of a bed although he has nowhere to go, he departs, leaving Bloom to feel "the cold of interstellar space" (704).

Faced by such a disparity, the critic's interpretation of *Ulysses* will depend on his view of its mode. If he supposes that the symbolism is the primary constituent of meaning and must therefore reveal the true significance of the narrative's events, he will probably tend toward a positive version. If, however, he finds the disparity between modes ironic, the symbolism indicating a resolution which the novelistic action fails to achieve, a negative interpretation will follow. If we are willing to give sufficient weight to symbolic suggestion, the fact that the cocoa which Stephen and Bloom drink is described as a "massproduct" (677), i.e. mass-produced and produced for the masses, will indicate that, despite all realistic appearances of noncommunication, they are truly engaged in communion.[49] I see no way of proving that *Ulysses* does *not* work this way, but there is much in it which must qualify any such purely symbolic reading. For one thing, as we have seen in an earlier instance, its symbolism contains contradictory impulses. The motifs which elaborate the theme of possibility contain not only portents of rebirth but repeated threats of misbirth, the failure to actualize potentiality. Furthermore, regarding even the symbolism which seems to indicate a positive resolution, there is no more any way of proving its absolute authority than there is of disprov-

49. See Tindall, *A Reader's Guide*, p. 222, for one such reading. He also declares that, since cocoa is botanicaly *theobroma*, or god food, Stephen becomes through its agency the godlike creative artist.

ing it. The tension between Joyce's modes seems finally
to produce a stalemate.

The movement of "Ithaca," the last chapter to deal with
Bloom and Stephen, indeed arrives at such a stalemate. In
its impersonal catechism, the questioner persistently demands factual information, which the answerer generally
supplies in abundance. But as the chapter progresses, and
especially as it nears its conclusion, the answerer sometimes abandons his pseudoscientific replies for a more
fanciful, metaphoric style in his efforts to express the situation. The implacable questioner, however, continues to
insist on his naturalistic point of view, requiring objective reports ("How?" "When?" "Where?") and demanding clarification of the answerer's poeticisms ("Womb?
Weary?" [737]). The answerer is driven to further symbolic
extremes in reaction, reaching a climax in the mythic catalogue of variations on Sinbad the Sailor and in the following response, "Going to a dark bed there was a square
round Sinbad the sailor roc's auk's egg in the night of the
bed of all the auks of the rocs of Darkinbad the Bright-
dayler" (737), where the answerer seems to be inventing
the idiom of *Finnegans Wake*. Still unsatisfied, the questioner asks "Where?" to which the only reply is the em-
phatic silence of a large black dot. In this recapitulation
of the conflict of modes the dialectic is carried to the point
of exhaustion, then dropped, still unresolved. Resolution,
of a sort, comes only in the next and last chapter, achiev-
able only on the lower (because less complex) but also
more fundamental level of Molly's stream of consciousness. The juxtaposition of the last two chapters also epi-
tomizes the opposed tendencies toward artifice and toward
the natural.

The two modal perspectives yield very different final
images of *Ulysses*. The symbolic, with its schemes of cor-

respondences and patterns of motifs, constitutes the most "spatial" aspect of the book, that by which "the reader is forced to read *Ulysses* in exactly the same manner as he reads modern poetry, that is, by continually fitting fragments together and keeping allusions in mind until, by reflexive reference, he can link them to their complements."[50] This creates a perspective in which the three major characters finally appear as fixed, archetypal images, in whose total configuration the meaning of *Ulysses* is embodied. A possible interpretation of this meaning is suggested by R. P. Blackmur, when he describes Molly as "the basic building material" of any culture, "the problem that first *and* last must be controlled."[51] Considering Molly as primal matter seems to illuminate the famous identification of her with the earth more than does making her a fertility goddess.[52] She is, as passive female, all potentiality, but the active, male principle of actualization is divided against itself: Stephen and Bloom, father and son, artist and citizen, mind and heart, appear as complementary yet incompatible, fixed in their separate orbits above the spinning earth by the astronomical symbolism of "Ithaca." This is, of course, only one interpretation. If the reader chooses to see the final configuration of these three figures as united in a new version of the Trinity, the materials for such an interpretation are also provided by the text.

The novelistic perspective would not abstract the characters from the stream of time. Here they appear as having

50. Joseph Frank, "Spatial Form in Modern Literature," in *The Widening Gyre: Crisis and Mastery in Modern Literature* (New Brunswick, N.J., 1963), p. 18.

51. "The Jew in Search of a Son: Joyce's *Ulysses*," in *Eleven Essays in the European Novel* (New York, 1964), p. 45.

52. "MB = spinning Earth," Joyce wrote in his notes for "Penelope." See Litz, *The Art of James Joyce,* p. 46.

completed one day and about to begin the next, in which, again, they may seem either condemned to repeat the impotent circle of their unchanging existence or about to start a new day, in which their lives will be renewed, transformed. A reading which maintains the novelistic perspective must be more tentative in its interpretation, since the evidence which the conclusion offers on the realistic level is scant compared with its profuse symbolism. Nevertheless, the possibilities of opposed interpretations reveal that the two basic modes are locked in unresolved conflict not only with each other but with themselves.

Ulysses thus seems to conclude in complete ambiguity, producing a complex situation which, as Barbara Hardy observes, "like shot silk, can be seen in two ways, pessimistically or optimistically," forcing "the admission of paradox."[53] Mrs. Hardy's identification of Joyce's strategy with the way George Eliot complicates oversimple moral judgment in *Middlemarch* is, however, misleading. More than the complexity of a realistic human situation is involved here (though, of course, this constitutes an important element); Joyce's symbolism involves multiple levels of thematic generalization (cultural and philosophical) which are also left in a condition of stark paradox, as are its reflexive implications concerning the relation of art and reality.

We may see as an aspect of his encyclopedicism Joyce's inclusion of the entire range of ways in which fiction can create meaning. All the modal elements which we have examined in novels of the preceding half-century are reflected in *Ulysses*: the realistic drama to which symbolism is subordinated, the creation of meaning through the

53. "Form as Means and End in *Ulysses*," p. 199.

consciousness of a character, and the creation by authorial artifice of symbolic complexes which seek to achieve an independent existence. Yet the way these elements are combined moves *Ulysses* somewhat outside the tradition of the novel. Its meaning does not result from any resolution of modal conflict but in its perpetuation. Meaning finally resides in the relation itself, in a tension of polar opposites between which multiple possible meanings are held in suspension.[54] By locating its meaning in an area defined by the paradoxical relation between different possible sources of meaningfulness, *Ulysses* creates, on a level above that of artifice, a kind of symbolic significance which is different from that of the novel. When *Ulysses* first appeared over forty years ago, T. S. Eliot hailed it as having at last carried prose fiction beyond the novel: "The novel is a form which will no longer serve. . . . The novel ended with Flaubert and with James."[55] Recent criticism has rightly stressed the many novelistic qualities of *Ulysses*, but it is still true that, if we consider its multiple modes rearranged in a logical progression, there is indeed a point where Joyce does pass beyond the novel, as he actually did in *Finnegans Wake*. What distinguishes *Ulysses* from Joyce's later, wholly symbolic work (and makes it in a way

54. Arnold Goldman compares this strategy of radical openness with Kierkegaard's efforts to establish "the possibility of possibility." See *The Joyce Paradox*, p. 156.

55. "*Ulysses,* Order, and Myth" [originally in *The Dial*, 1923], in *The Modern Tradition: Backgrounds of Modern Literature*, ed. Richard Ellmann and Charles Feidelson, Jr. (New York, 1965), p. 681. In a note written in 1964 commenting on this essay, Eliot found himself "unfavourably impressed by the overconfidence in my own views and the intemperance with which I expressed them," and declared that "to say that the novel ended with Flaubert and James was possibly an echo of Ezra Pound and is certainly absurd." See *The Modern Tradition*, p. 681.

even more complex) is that its meaning as a whole depends on the novel's characteristic ways of creating meaning as a part of its unique multifaceted modality.

By his repeated thrusting at the limits of the novel, Joyce not only completes the historical progression from the realistic to the symbolic mode which this study has traced but offers a valuable perspective on it. In *A Portrait of the Artist as a Young Man* he impels the realistic toward the symbolic by means of a compressed centripetal form, of which an important feature is the suggestive epiphanic scene. In *Ulysses* symbolism becomes expansive, centrifugally moving away from the novelistic human drama, yet held in tension with it by a structure of ultimate ambiguity. In the shifting relations of his modal components, we see the extent to which the meaning of a work of fiction is not something which it represents but which it actively creates.

Bibliography

SECONDARY SOURCES USED IN THIS STUDY

Adams, Robert M., *Surface and Symbol: The Consistency of James Joyce's Ulysses*, New York, Oxford University Press, 1962.

Anderson, Quentin, "George Eliot in *Middlemarch*," in *From Dickens to Hardy*, ed. Boris Ford (Baltimore, Penguin Books, 1958), pp. 274–93.

Auden, W. H., *The Enchafed Flood, or The Romantic Iconography of the Sea*, New York, Random House, 1950.

———, "Some Notes on D. H. Lawrence," *The Nation* (April 26, 1947), pp. 482–84.

Auerbach, Erich, *Mimesis: The Representation of Reality in Western Literature*, tr. Willard R. Trask, Garden City, N.Y., Doubleday Anchor Books, 1957.

Axton, William, "*Dombey and Son*: From Stereotype to Archetype," *ELH, 31* (1964), 301–17.

Baudelaire, Charles, "*Madame Bovary*," in *Flaubert: A Collection of Critical Essays*, ed. Raymond Giraud (Englewood Cliffs, N.J., Prentice-Hall, 1964), pp. 88–96.

Beach, Joseph Warren, *The Method of Henry James*, Philadelphia, Albert Saifer, 1954.

———, *The Twentieth Century Novel: Studies in Technique*, New York, Appleton-Century-Crofts, 1932.

Bersani, Leo, "The Narrator as Center in *The Wings of the Dove*," *Modern Fiction Studies, 6* (1960), 131–44.

Blackmur, R. P., *Eleven Essays in the European Novel*, New York, Harcourt, Brace, and World, 1964.

Bodkin, Maud, *Archetypal Patterns in Poetry: Psychological*

Studies of Imagination, New York, Random House Vintage Books, 1958.

Booth, Wayne C., *The Rhetoric of Fiction,* Chicago, University of Chicago Press, 1961.

Brumm, Ursula, "Symbolism and the Novel," tr. Willard R. Trask, *Partisan Review,* 25 (1958), 329–42.

Budgen, Frank, *James Joyce and the Making of Ulysses,* Bloomington, Indiana University Press, 1960.

Burke, Kenneth, "Fact, Inference, and Proof in the Analysis of Literary Symbolism," in *Terms for Order,* ed. Stanley Edgar Hyman (Bloomington, Indiana University Press, 1964), pp. 145–72.

———, "Three Definitions," in *Perspectives by Incongruity,* ed. Stanley Edgar Hyman (Bloomington, Indiana University Press, 1964), pp. 142–51.

Coffman, Stanley K., Jr., *Imagism,* Norman, University of Oklahoma Press, 1951.

Conrad, Joseph, *Joseph Conrad on Fiction,* ed. Walter F. Wright, Lincoln, University of Nebraska Press, 1964.

Crews, Frederick C., *The Tragedy of Manners: Moral Drama in the Later Novels of Henry James,* New Haven, Conn., Yale University Press, 1957.

Dupee, F. W., *Henry James,* Garden City, N.Y., Doubleday Anchor Books, 1956.

Eliot, George, *The Essays of George Eliot,* ed. Thomas Pinney, New York, Columbia University Press, 1963.

———, *The George Eliot Letters,* ed. Gordon S. Haight, 7 vols., New Haven, Conn., Yale University Press, 1954–55.

Eliot, T. S., *"Ulysses,* Order, and Myth," in *The Modern Tradition: Backgrounds of Modern Literature,* ed. Richard Ellmann and Charles Feidelson, Jr., New York, Oxford University Press, 1965.

Ellmann, Richard, *James Joyce,* New York, Oxford University Press, 1959.

———, and Charles Feidelson, Jr., ed., *The Modern Tradition: Backgrounds of Modern Literature,* New York, Oxford University Press, 1965.

Fairlie, Alison, *Flaubert: Madame Bovary*, Great Neck, N.Y., Barron's Educational Series, 1962.

Flaubert, Gustave, *The Selected Letters of Gustave Flaubert*, tr. and ed. Francis Steegmuller, New York, Random House Vintage Books, 1957.

Forster, E. M., *Aspects of the Novel*, New York, Harcourt, Brace, 1927.

Frank, Joseph, "Spatial Form in Modern Literature," in *The Widening Gyre: Crisis and Mastery in Modern Literature* (New Brunswick, N.J., Rutgers University Press, 1963), pp. 3–62.

Friedman, Alan, *The Turn of the Novel*, New York, Oxford University Press, 1966.

Friedman, Norman, "Symbol," in *Encyclopedia of Poetry and Poetics* (Princeton, N.J., Princeton University Press, 1965), pp. 833–36.

Gibbons, T. H., "*Dubliners* and the Critics," *Critical Quarterly*, 9 (1967), 179–87.

Gilbert, Stuart, *James Joyce's Ulysses*, New York, Random House Vintage Books, 1960.

Goldberg, S. L., *The Classical Temper: A Study of James Joyce's Ulysses*, London, Chatto and Windus, 1963.

———, *James Joyce*, New York, Grove Press, 1962.

Goldman, Arnold, *The Joyce Paradox: Form and Freedom in his Fiction*, Evanston, Ill., Northwestern University Press, 1966.

Gordon, David J., *D. H. Lawrence as a Literary Critic*, New Haven, Conn., Yale University Press, 1966.

Guerard, Albert J., *Conrad the Novelist*, Cambridge, Mass., Harvard University Press, 1958.

Guetti, James, "*Heart of Darkness* and the Failure of the Imagination," *Sewanee Review*, 73 (1965), 488–504.

Hanley, Miles L., *A Word Index to James Joyce's Ulysses*, Madison, University of Wisconsin Press, 1937.

Hardy, Barbara, *The Appropriate Form: An Essay on the Novel*, London, Athlone Press, 1964.

———, "Form as End and Means in *Ulysses,*" *Orbis Litterarum, 19* (1964), 194–200.

———, *The Novels of George Eliot: A Study in Form,* London, Athlone Press, 1963.

Harvey, W. J., *The Art of George Eliot,* London, Chatto and Windus, 1961.

———, *Character and the Novel,* London, Chatto and Windus, 1965.

Hendry, Irene, "Joyce's Epiphanies," *Sewanee Review, 54* (1946), 449–67.

Hewitt, Douglas, "*Lord Jim:* Conrad and the 'Few Simple Notions,'" in *Conrad: A Collection of Critical Essays,* ed. Marvin Mudrick (Englewood Cliffs, N.J., Prentice-Hall, 1966), pp. 55–62.

Holland, Laurence Bedwell, *The Expense of Vision: Essays on the Craft of Henry James,* Princeton, N.J., Princeton University Press, 1964.

James, Henry, *The Art of the Novel,* ed. Richard P. Blackmur, New York, Charles Scribner's Sons, 1934.

———, *French Poets and Novelists,* New York, Grosset and Dunlap, 1964.

———, *The Future of the Novel,* ed. Leon Edel, New York, Random House Vintage Books, 1956.

———, "The Life of George Eliot," in *Discussions of George Eliot,* ed. Richard Stang (Boston, D. C. Heath, 1960), pp. 8–12.

———, *The Notebooks of Henry James,* ed. F. O. Matthiessen and Kenneth B. Murdock, New York, Oxford University Press, 1961.

———, "The Novels of George Eliot," in *A Century of George Eliot Criticism,* ed. Gordon S. Haight (Boston, Houghton Mifflin, 1965), pp. 43–54.

———, *Selected Literary Criticism,* ed. Morris Shapira, New York, McGraw-Hill, 1965.

Joyce, James, *Letters of James Joyce,* I, ed. Stuart Gilbert, II and III, ed. Richard Ellmann, New York, Viking Press, 1966.

———, *The Critical Writings of James Joyce,* ed. Ellsworth Mason and Richard Ellmann, New York, Viking Press, 1964.

Kain, Richard M., *Fabulous Voyager: James Joyce's Ulysses,* New York, Viking Press, 1959.

Kenner, Hugh, *Dublin's Joyce,* Boston, Beacon Press, 1962.

Killham, John, *"Pickwick:* Dickens and the Art of Fiction," in *Dickens and the Twentieth Century,* ed. John Gross and Gabriel Pearson (London, Routledge and Kegan Paul, 1962), pp. 35–47.

Kimble, Jean, "The Abyss and the Wings of the Dove: The Image as Revelation," *Nineteenth-Century Fiction, 10* (1956), 281–300.

Kitchel, Anna T., ed., *Quarry for Middlemarch,* Berkeley and Los Angeles, 1950; published as a supplement to *Nineteenth-Century Fiction, 4* (1950).

Krook, Dorothea, *The Ordeal of Consciousness in Henry James,* Cambridge, Cambridge University Press, 1962.

Lawrence, D. H., *Selected Literary Criticism,* ed. Anthony Beal, London, Heinemann, 1956.

Leavis, F. R., *D. H. Lawrence: Novelist,* New York, Alfred A. Knopf, 1956.

———, *The Great Tradition,* Garden City, N.Y., Doubleday Anchor Books, 1954.

Levin, Harry, *James Joyce: A Critical Introduction,* Norfolk, Conn., New Directions, 1960.

Lewis, C. S., "A Note on Jane Austen," *Essays in Criticism, 4* (1954), 359–71.

Liddell, Robert, *A Treatise on the Novel,* London, Jonathan Cape, 1965.

Litz, A. Walton, *The Art of James Joyce: Method and Design in Ulysses and Finnegans Wake,* New York, Oxford University Press, 1964.

———, *James Joyce,* New York, Twayne Publishers, 1966.

Lubbock, Percy, *The Craft of Fiction,* New York, Viking Press, 1957.

Mansell, Darrell, Jr., "Ruskin and George Eliot's 'Realism,'" *Criticism, 7* (1965), 203–16.

Matthiessen, F. O., *Henry James: The Major Phase.* New York, Oxford University Press, 1963.

———, "James and the Plastic Arts," in *Discussions of Henry James,* ed. Naomi Lebowitz (Boston, D. C. Heath, 1962), pp. 21–30.

Michael, Mary K., "Henry James's Use of the Word 'Wonderful' in *The Ambassadors," Modern Language Notes,* 75 (1960), 114–17.

Miller, J. Hillis, *Charles Dickens: The World of His Novels,* Cambridge, Mass., Harvard University Press, 1959.

———, *Poets of Reality: Six Twentieth-Century Writers,* Cambridge, Mass., Harvard University Press, 1965.

Moore, Harry T., *"The Rainbow,"* in *The Achievement of D. H. Lawrence,* ed. Frederick J. Hoffman and Harry T. Moore (Norman, University of Oklahoma Press, 1953), pp. 144–58.

Moynahan, Julian, *The Deed of Life: The Novels and Tales of D. H. Lawrence,* Princeton, N.J., Princeton University Press, 1963.

Murdoch, Iris, "The Sublime and the Beautiful Revisited," *Yale Review, 49* (1960), 247–71.

Noon, William T., S.J., *Joyce and Aquinas,* New Haven, Conn., Yale University Press, 1963.

Paris, Bernard J., *Experiments in Life: George Eliot's Quest for Values,* Detroit, Wayne State University Press, 1965.

Ruskin, John, "A Note on *Hard Times,"* in *The Dickens Critics,* ed. George H. Ford and Lauriat Lane, Jr. (Ithaca, N.Y., Cornell University Press, 1961), pp. 47–48.

Ryf, Robert S., *A New Approach to Joyce: The Portrait of the Artist as Guidebook,* Berkeley and Los Angeles, University of California Press, 1964.

Scholes, Robert, "Joyce and the Epiphany: The Key to the Labyrinth?" *Sewanee Review, 72* (1964), 65–77.

———, and Richard M. Kain, ed., *The Workshop of Daedalus: James Joyce and the Raw Materials for A Portrait of the Artist as a Young Man,* Evanston, Ill., Northwestern University Press, 1965.

Schorer, Mark, "Fiction and the 'Analogical Matrix,'" in *Critiques and Essays on Modern Fiction, 1920–1951,* ed. John W. Aldridge (New York, Ronald Press, 1952), pp. 83–98.

Schutte, William M., *Joyce and Shakespeare: A Study in the Meaning of Ulysses,* New Haven, Conn., Yale University Press, 1957.

Spilka, Mark, *The Love Ethic of D. H. Lawrence,* Bloomington, Indiana University Press, 1955.

Stang, Richard, *The Theory of the Novel in England, 1850–1870,* London, Routledge and Kegan Paul, 1959.

Steinhoff, W. R., "Intention and Fulfillment in the Ending of *The Mill on the Floss,*" in *The Image of the Work,* by B. H. Lehman and others (Berkeley, University of California Press, 1955), pp. 231–51.

Sultan, Stanley, *The Argument of Ulysses,* Columbus, Ohio State University Press, 1964.

Tilford, John E., Jr., "James the Old Intruder," *Modern Fiction Studies, 4* (1958), 157–64.

Tillotson, Kathleen, *Novels of the Eighteen-Forties,* Oxford, Oxford University Press, 1961.

Tindall, William York, *A Reader's Guide to James Joyce,* New York, Noonday Press, 1959.

Trilling, Lionel, "The Dickens of Our Day," in *A Gathering of Fugitives* (Boston, Beacon Press, 1956), pp. 41–48.

Turnell, Martin, *The Novel in France,* New York, Random House Vintage Books, 1958.

Van Ghent, Dorothy, "The Dickens World: A View from Todger's," in *The Dickens Critics,* ed. George H. Ford and Lauriat Lane, Jr. (Ithaca, N.Y., Cornell University Press, 1961), pp. 213–32.

———, *The English Novel: Form and Function,* New York, Harper and Row, 1961.

Vivas, Eliseo, *The Artistic Transaction and Essays on Theory of Literature,* Columbus, Ohio State University Press, 1963.

———, *D. H. Lawrence: The Failure and the Triumph of Art,* Bloomington, Indiana University Press, 1964.

Wain, John, *"Little Dorrit,"* in *Dickens and the Twentieth Century,* ed. John Gross and Gabriel Pearson (London, Routledge and Kegan Paul, 1962), pp. 175–86.

Waith, Eugene M., "The Calling of Stephen Dedalus," *College English, 18* (1957), 256–61.

Warren, Austin, "Henry James: Symbolic Imagery in the Later Novels," in *Rage for Order* (Ann Arbor, University of Michigan Press, 1959), pp. 142–61.

Warren, Robert Penn, "Introduction" to *Nostromo* (New York, Random House Modern Library, 1951), pp. vii–xxxix.

Watt, Ian, "The First Paragraph of *The Ambassadors:* An Explication," *Essays in Criticism, 10* (1960), 250–74.

———, "Joseph Conrad: Alienation and Commitment," in *The English Mind: Studies in the English Moralists Presented to Basil Willey,* ed. Hugh Sykes Davies and George Watson (Cambridge, Cambridge University Press, 1964), pp. 257–78.

Wilson, Edmund, *Axel's Castle: A Study of the Imaginative Literature of 1870–1930,* New York, Charles Scribner's Sons, 1931.

Wimsatt, W. K., Jr., "The Structure of Romantic Nature Imagery," in *The Verbal Icon: Studies in the Meaning of Poetry* (New York, Noonday Press, 1958), pp. 103–16.

———, and Cleanth Brooks, *Literary Criticism: A Short History,* New York, Alfred A. Knopf, 1962.

Index

W9-BHL-988

Whitetail Deer

Whitetail Deer

A YEAR'S CYCLE

Curtis K. Stadtfeld

Drawings by Lydia Rosier

The Dial Press
New York
1975

Library of Congress Cataloging in Publication Data

Stadtfeld, Curtis K   1935–
Whitetail deer: a year's cycle.

Bibliography: p.
1.   White-tailed deer.   I.   Title.
QL737.U55S74   599'.7357   74–14724
ISBN 0–8037–6101–5

For Peter Taft and Christopher Wallace
and Archie

Acknowledgments

In a work such as this, acknowledgments must be either endless or incomplete. Recognition must be given, though, to Dr. Ralph I. Blouch, supervisor of wildlife research in the Research and Development section of the Michigan Department of Natural Resources, who assisted in assembling material and also devoted considerable time to conversation and to reading, criticizing, and suggesting changes in the manuscript. His help not only expanded the author's scope of understanding, but avoided several minor errors. Others at the DNR helped too, including Dave Jenkins, John Byelich, Lyman Shippy, and John Nellist. Many librarians were of great help, including several at Eastern Michigan University and at the University of Michigan library, where the staff, unlike the guardians of the Edwin S. George Reserve, were most cooperative. Any remaining errors are those of the author.

—cks

Whitetail Deer

May

A whitetail doe pauses at the edge of the clearing, at the place where the shadowed security of the forest shades into the lighted openness of a field. For a moment, she stands on three feet, motion suspended, as though she had intended to take another step but had been interrupted by some taint in the air, some odd odor or strange sound. Her right front leg is bent, the hoof tucked back, the muscles tense. Now she lowers the foot and the hoof meets the ground as smoothly as a cat's paw might, bending down the grass without breaking it, leaving almost no track or trace, showing respect for the place she stood, as though she does not want to harm anything. She stands rigid and tense, altogether motionless, practically invisible in the sun-and-shadow dapple of the forest edge, nose up, ears out, testing the air for scent or sound of danger.

She is in a trance; a trance of caution learned through tens of thousands of years of successful survival in the midst of fierce and fleet predators; a trance in which every delicate sense vibrates in her body, a trance that tunes her—as a sensitive mechanism with a single purpose—to sort any danger from the sights and sounds and smells around her. She is taut as a violin string, and the tiniest threat will pluck the string and spin her bounding back to the shadows.

Her great soft ears are erect, and she turns them, scanning for strange sounds. The ears are nearly transparent in their early summer coat and the late afternoon sun shines through them. They tremble a little; half a mile away, a dog barks. She hears, but she does not react. It is a bark she has heard before, and the dog has never come nearer, has never threatened her, she has always been safe. She has learned, in any case, that she can outrun any lone dog. She can outrun any dog in the open, in the forest or field, that is; she has done it and she knows. She cannot outrun a dog in the deep snow of winter. But she does not know that; it is a lesson she will learn only once, if ever, and a lesson that can be learned only too late.

So she is safe, and she closes the dog from her consciousness and sifts the other sounds of the field and the swamp and the forest; sorts through birdsong, the scrubbing of leaf and branch, the sagging of limbs, scrape of the crickets, rustle of little creatures in the underbrush. Natural noises like those do not concern her. She listens only for threats. After perhaps a minute, she relaxes abruptly, the tension drained, the trance ended, and she puts her head down and strolls, browsing, nibbling the new growth at the tips of bushes. She strolls in the leisure of her tested safety out through the briars that ring the forest, out to where the last of the undergrowth ends and the field lays open before her.

Again she scans the scene, using her vague vision to supplement her much sharper sense of smell and sound. Her vision is no fine and precise thing; she sees only indistinct gray shapes. And motion; her eyes have evolved through the eons to see motion, any motion, the slightest twitch, so that for example if a great hungry cat crouches in a tree in stillness but moves the tip of its tail she will see the motion and flee; if a man stands hidden against a tree trunk and winks an eye she will see; if any of the quick flicks of motion that mean the possibility of danger to her occur on the field before her, she will see.

But the landscape is still. There is nothing. She is alone. She snorts, as though to clear her nose for any fresh scent that might come to her, or perhaps so that she can better test the quality of the grasses she samples, or perhaps for some odd and ancient reason that no man will ever know. And she grazes like a simple sheep for a little while, tearing off the tenderest tips of the fresh new grass.

She is lean, spare, bony, with an almost angular look, and she eats with the eager hunger of one who has known the edge of starvation. And so she has, in the long cold hostile months since fall. She had been plump then, fat even, with a sheen to her coat. There had been a thick layer of solid fat across her loins like a saddle, a reservoir of energy stored against emergency. There had been, too, little handfuls of fat in her body cavity and around the kidneys and there was a soft insulating sheet of fat beneath her hide.

All gone now, all the fat, burned away in the winter, in the cold, in the time when nature slips to sleep and the new green growth does not come, the stored fat all used up. She has come near starvation. Snow covered even the dead grass and the nuts and berries of fall had been lost to her beneath the ice and all that remained were the leafless twigs and the evergreens. Only the white cedar was left to nourish her. There were other shrubs that she would eat when her hunger drove her, though she might starve with a belly full of them.

In the fall, she had weighed 130 pounds. Now, she weighs just more than 100 and there is no gloss or glow about her, no fat, and she looks even a little scruffy where the winter coat has not yet been pushed away by the fair fine red hair of the summer coat. But though the fat reserves are gone, her round brown eyes are bright, her step is light, almost delicate, and she is alert and quick and strong and tough, as wild things are tough at the end of winter.

Her belly is stuffed with new little leaves, with the buds and shoots of trees and bushes and with the greenest, richest, choicest ends of the grasses. In winter, the cycle of nature had closed in on her, had squeezed and threatened her, had brushed her with death, but now in May, barely in time, it has turned and rescued her. When her reserves were nearly depleted, when even the marrow of her bones had turned soft and pink as the firm white fat was drained away, when her need for strength was greatest, the plants that form her food caught the sun and began to grow again and now, when she needs them most, they have their highest energy levels of the year. Food is rich and close and plentiful and her strength is surging back, flowing through her body as the sun soaks through her and warms her.

Her new red spring coat is nearly full. Only a few odd patches of the dead winter coat—the blue coat, hunters often call it—have not been pushed out yet. Once in a while, as though in irritation, she throws her head around and hikes up a haunch so she can reach the molting winter hair, scraping it loose with her rough tongue. She shakes her head and blows her nose again and eats, obliterating for the summer the terrible hunger of the winter yarding place, the death camp where she had huddled starving with the other deer, deep in the cedar swamp, waiting numbly for the sun of spring. Now it is over, the annual famine at an end, the season of plenty rich about her, and she is ready again for her place in nature, ready to play her role, to survive.

There is a restlessness about her that keeps her always on the move, quick steps, repeated throwing up of her head to look and listen, a restlessness that is redundant, unless to show that somehow she has a sense of the irrationality of her condition in nature, and that the problem irritates her. Perhaps not, perhaps the restless pacing reflects nothing more than the accumulated tension of thousands of years of surviving as a beast preyed upon. She has, after all, no very high order of intelligence that allows her to balance the problem and consider it; perhaps, no awareness of the problem at all.

For she is simply and complexly a wild deer; a creature of

nature with a place of her own on the invisible pyramid of life. But the pyramid is crumbling; it is the twentieth century, and a new animal dominates nature, that unprecedentedly clever and cunning animal called man, and much of nature is not natural any more. So suddenly, after eons of careful evolution in her specialty—the specialty of providing food for those animals which preyed on her while, at the same time, she avoided extinction as a species—the scheme of nature has been altered by man and her place on the pyramid is empty, she is unneeded, and thus she is alone in nature as she is alone on that lonely field.

In nature's plan, her place on the invisible pyramid was a high one. Below her were all the grasses and plants she fed on and the insects that contributed to plant life; below that the countless microbes that live in the soil, all the unknown legions of layers of life that raise up the greenery to clothe the land. Above her, at the peak of the pyramid, only the predators, the meat eaters; wolves, big cats, coyotes, creatures big and strong enough to catch and kill her and tear and eat her flesh.

She had evolved to be preyed upon, but the scheme has been twisted awry. Man the tinkerer has come, and he has killed all her natural predators or driven them away. He has put a bounty on the gaunt wolf and told terrible stories about him, stories handed down by the man's ancestors who had spent grim generations in the dark forests and had reason to fear the wolf. And so the wolf has been driven back into remote areas to bay in hungry outrage at the moon, and impatient man has violated even that. The big cats, too, have been killed for their quickness and their soft pelts and they no longer haunt the dark forests where the deer wait in fear. The coyotes have been trapped away to make the land safe for sheep and chickens.

So the only predator left is man, man with his clubs of steel and fire, and he no longer needs the deer.

Close as the deer is to man on the pyramid of life, she shares little with him. She has no part in his remorseless intelligence, makes or uses no tools, does not judge her place.

But she shares one ironic quality of nature with man; both are high enough on nature's pyramid of life that if they vanished, nature would not miss either of them. The natural trees and grass and bushes would green and bloom and thicken and flourish without either of them, and if both deer and man vanished from the scene, nature would clothe herself again in shrubbery and wait, green and patient, undismayed.

But man has not the patience of nature, he would make the world over today, and in making it over, he has made the deer a luxury. He has learned how to grow his meat in feed lots, and while his women once welcomed venison to their cooking pots, now they often turn up their noses at it and say it is "gamey" or "strong."

It is difficult to say how much the edges of swamp and forest need the deer; she prunes and clips, but her relationship to the flora about her is so complex that no one can say with assurance what needed functions she performs.

But if she is no longer a need for nourishment, she has become a symbol to man; a symbol of the hunt, a challenge from the vanished past. Man hunts her now artificially, only in certain ways, as his laws set forth. In many places in many years he does not hunt the doe at all, but only the buck, so the doe will be left to grow old and wear her teeth away and starve. Yet he tends the deer herd, lavishing public money and expensive professional study on it, keeping the deer alive for sport and pleasure, for the thrill of the hunt and the chase, and, unspokenly, alive as a hedge against his private fear of dark times after the disaster when he might have to hunt again from the shadows.

Now it is May, and the doe has nothing to fear from man. He might drive his machines on country roads or even walk clumsily through the forest simply to catch a glimpse of her, to thrill to her bounding flight. He carries no club of thunder in May. She knows none of this. As her instincts leave her with her fear of the wolf, a terror honed in her in all those centuries of evolution, she still flees from man the year around. There is no way for her to know that she is no longer a need in nature, but only a symbol for man. Of course there is no way for her to understand, for only man makes symbols; there are none in nature, they exist only in his mind.

So she feeds compulsively through the month in the field and the forest, and the year or the century make little difference in her behavior. She is as she has become, quick and curious, furtive and shy, surviving through caution.

A few miles away on a lake shore, birds lay eggs that have no life. Poisons from insecticides have made the birds sterile. Yet, as long as they live, they will lay their eggs on schedule and try to hatch them, dumb to reality, obedient to nature in her instructions to continue their role, carry out their purpose in the great web of life.

So too the whitetail plays out her role of caution and survival, not knowing that the watching hungry audience is gone.

She has evolved for a precise purpose, and that precision limits her. But the precision of her development leaves her also with impressive abilities that she has gathered through the eons.

There are things she will never do . . . she will never search the night for a missing mate . . . she will never have a mate at all, in fact, save for one breathless day each fall when she will allow a frantic buck to copulate with her, to impregnate her; and he will leave the next day when she refuses him, to search for another ovulating doe, and if they ever meet again there will be no recognition between them, no bond . . . she will never build a nest, defend a home, show sorrow or even interest at the death of an offspring, never call in darkness with that strange private anguish that a dog or a wolf shows sometimes.

As a creature of nature, she is its captive; delicate in step and graceful of movement not because these actions are beautiful and she has cultivated beauty, but because quick and quiet motions have helped her to survive. If men think that she is beautiful, it is of no concern to her; men define beauty for themselves, and she keeps no records.

She is soft of hide and tender of flesh not to add to the tone patterns of the dappled forest, but because her hide protects her through the changing seasons and the flesh was intended to be torn easily by toothy predators in need of sustenance.

And she is old; old in a way no man can be, though she has been on earth, this doe, barely two years. Men change, they adapt quickly, they learn, they write things down and remember them, they invent things and make new tools and change their ways of thinking and living. So they are new men and women, each generation gapped a bit from the one that went before, a little lonely in their newness, struggling for continuity, creatures and captives of change.

Not so the deer; continuity is her survival. She learns little more than responses to different dangers and limited reactions to different foods. Her instincts are ancient and controlling; her actions are determined almost entirely by those instincts, and she has the centuries-long continuity of survival. She is as she was when the Indians shared the land with her before the coming of the inventive white man. She is as she was before the Indians found the land. She is very, very old, and from the great void of those ages a voice speaks to her, sometimes quite faintly, sometimes in imperative command. It is a voice no man will ever hear; it is the voice of—well, perhaps of instinct . . .

The whitetail is a member of the oldest living family of mammals on the North American continent, and probably in the world. Biologists believe that she developed in the Miocene age, some fifteen to twenty million years ago. Survival has tuned her so well to the needs of the place that she has changed little, and she has survived.

The saber-toothed tiger came with its terror and then passed from history, and the deer survived. The mastodon came and vanished, and the deer survived. She has outlasted them all, all the hungry predators of history and prehistory which fed on her flesh. She has survived the coming of man, with his slow feet and his weak arrows. She fed and clothed him when he did not know or care about domesticating animals, when he found the whitetail a convenient prey.

And sometimes in the field when she feeds, if she turns and paces and shows her restless irritation, it is because she is geared for a more dangerous time, a more natural time, and her instincts key her so high that it is almost as though she remembers . . .

. . . As though she remembers when, thousands of years ago, the mound-building Indians in the central ranges of the continent made tools of the jaws and the bones of the deer after they had eaten the flesh and tanned the hides. The deer was part of the lore, the religion, and the life of countless vanished tribes and peoples.

And the deer was old already then, by many millions of years.

Just a little while ago, as nature and the deer reckon time, only a century ago in the Midwest, she followed the loggers and the fires north to new country, and she flourished and multiplied on the new food sources. She was food and clothing and sport for men, and they were armed with fine new weapons and hunted her casually to the brink of extinction. And we reckon time in such short spans, as though our thin little knowledge of nature and of our own history could control or define time, that we came to think, in the splendid arrogance of our species, that we knew all about the deer.

Of course we were wrong, for she is not many of the things men think her to be. She is not truly a forest animal, as many thought, for she must eat from ground-growing plants that are shaded out and die in mature forests. When the pines shaded the Midwest, there was no food for her among the needles and she did not occupy the land. When the trees were cut and the second growth came up, she found food. She prefers borders, edges of forest and swamp, places where there are sprouts and shrubs and grass and cover.

Nor is she primarily a browser, always preferring twigs and shoots. Rather, she is an eater of grass and leaves and acorns and nearly all the things men grow for truck crops. She adjusts her diet to what is available, and can live quite happily on crab apples, corn, and hay.

Once, in her restless search for a place to survive, she drifted into the new country as the forest was cleared, fattening on the new growth in the cut-over lands, and she has begun now to crowd south again as the northern forests have matured and her food supply has faded. She has pressed into the southern counties of the Midwestern states, to the farm lands, to the open country, to the swamps and fence rows where she can find food.

Always, she remains unchanged in basic instinct, looking much as she did a thousand or a million years ago, adjusting her behavior only slightly to avoid new threats or take advantage of new food. She lives the life of the chased and hunted, ready always to spring away to safety, always alert. She is a creature of escape, coiled for life on the fringe of flight.

It is as though she remembers, in her instinct, the great predators, and she has quickness for fleeing. With one strange exception, there seems to be no hostility in her. Nor is there possessiveness; she makes no claims on a mate, defends no territory, seeks no help in raising her fawns.

When threatened or frightened, she becomes the classic picture of beauty in flight, leaping and bounding with speed and strength and grace and with uncanny accuracy over barriers and through thickets. She can run as fast as 40 miles an hour and can cruise at 30 miles an hour for a few miles. No lone dog can bring her down, for she is too quick.

Yet despite this fleetness, despite the nervousness, she has moments of repose, moments when the breeze brings no hint of danger, when she is alone at peace or at rest with her fawns. In moments such as those, when the instincts of tension and terror are calm, she resembles nothing so much as a rather dull Jersey heifer, switching her 10-inch tail futilely against the flies, twitching her hide, blinking her brown eyes absently, chewing her cud.

She is a ruminant, her digestive system thirty million years in evolution, and it is a system that not only allows her to flourish on the green roughage but helps her to hide from her predators.

Such things as grass and twigs she converts to energy, to muscle and flesh and fat, through a complicated digestion process in the four parts of her stomach—the rumen, reticulum, omasum, and abomasum. Grazing or browsing, she tears food loose, chews it only briefly, breaks it up and moistens it, and gulps it into the rumen. There, bacteria and other microorganisms attack it, beginning the digestive process while the rumen kneads it gently. If food is plentiful, she will fill the rumen in an hour or so, and can go then to cover where she will lie hidden to ruminate.

Resting, she regurgitates little cuds of the partially digested material, chews the cuds for half a minute and swallows them again. Digestion is completed by the microflora in the rumen. The process will be complete and the waste discharged as feces within a day and a half of the time it is eaten.

As fugitive, this means she can slip out to her food supply at a time when safety suits her best, fill her rumen quickly, and complete the process of digestion under cover. She has no need to drag a body back to a tree as a lion or leopard might, nor to return to the scene of a kill.

One might almost say that she carries inside her belly a yeasty fermentation vat which she may stuff full and then it will draw the strength from the rough stuff she eats.

The reticulum portion of the stomach serves to help churn the roughage for digestion. It may also screen out foreign particles; in the deer's domesticated cousins, the reticulum may fill with nails and stones and bits of glass, which might otherwise reach the more tender parts of the stomach and tear holes in them. The wild deer encounters such man-made particles infrequently.

This elaborate digestive system allows the deer to select an incredibly varied diet, which she adjusts to the region where she finds herself. It is a region larger than most think; deer are found from Canada to mid-South America, and from coast to coast in the United States. Far down on the Florida Keys, where deer thrive as a species much smaller than the Midwestern whitetail, they live largely on water-related plants, have less marked seasonal coat changes, and spend much more time in the water. There are places in Ohio and Pennsylvania where deer may live largely on crab apples and the corn left by farmers; they have become gleaners. And in the Southwest, they depend on the same dry range grass and coarse shrubs that the half-wild cattle scrabble from the arid land.

Our doe is a whitetail, and she lives in central Michigan in the border country where the northern Coniferous Forest merges with the hardwoods. There are deciduous trees and evergreens, farms and small cities. She has learned to hide well, and she multiplies, nourished on the native flora and on the things man left behind.

We have developed a pattern of tolerant co-existence, we and the deer. They will live quite close to us, with only a little space and the night between us. There are usually more deer closer than men realize in the Midwest. They keep to their edges; edges of swamps and woodland, edges of fields and rivers, fence rows and farms, the edges of day and night. They hide.

There is plenty of amusement in these patterns of tolerance. One day in early summer, I had mowed down rank June clover and gone on to other tasks. Returning on the tractor, I drove out from a field of tall wheat and surprised two deer, poaching the clover. They were caught in the act, all right, great green wads of sweet hay hanging out their mouths. They have little fear of the tractor; its noise does not seem dangerous to them, and its smell must overpower mine, for they allow me to drive within 75 or 100 feet of them. It was high noon, and they were not afraid; they gave me the stare that they would give any interloper; stared me down and drove me off, irritated that I should invade their domain.

We both pay taxes on that land; I in cash, they in the end with their lives. We share the place, and they are welcome to the clover, though I hope they stay away from the wheat.

We begin our journey through the year of the deer in May, we begin it in mid-America, and we begin it with a doe for simple enough reasons.

The seasons never end, the cycle never stops, so we must begin at an arbitrary place and May is a time of beginning, of new strength, a prelude to birth and summer.

We put our imaginary deer in mid-America because that is where I live, it is where I share a farm with deer and other wildlife, it is the place I know best. It is the place where I can tell the story to completion. We will talk about the way deer live elsewhere, but this doe will be as universal as I can make her.

And we center our tale on a doe because she is more central to the story of the species than the buck. He is a lonely, selfish fellow, with no role in the family, no permanence of mating, no duties as provider. He is the symbol of the hunt, and we will talk about that, but the doe is the center of the biological family. Our particular doe will be called Alpha, to differentiate her from does in general.

First, a broader look at the species.

In the Americas, there are some thirty subspecies of white-tails, and they range from southern Canada to Venezuela and Columbia. Our particular deer is *Odocoileus virginianus borealis,* or, more commonly, the Northern Woodland White-tailed Deer. This is the largest of the subspecies, the most numer-ous and it has the widest range. They thrive from Nova Scotia and southern Maryland on the east, all across the continent north of the Ohio River and west to the Missis-sippi River. The biggest mature buck will weigh more than 200 pounds in good flesh, the does somewhat less.

In the wild, they look bigger than they are, perhaps be-cause they are so erect and active, perhaps because of the electric excitement of seeing them. They stand no higher at the shoulder than a tabletop. Visitors to game farms often ask if the place has no adult deer.

The state with the most whitetails is Texas, where there are perhaps three million. The Michigan breeding herd is perhaps 400,000. The Department of Natural Resources, which has legal responsibility for the herd, has promised to increase its size and there is talk of "a million by 1980." Three-quarters of a million hunters stalk the deer each fall in Michigan, and they kill 60,000 to 100,000.

In Western states, the primary deer is the mule deer, so called because of its large, mule-like ears. The black-tailed deer, a mule deer subspecies, dominates the Pacific Coast from California to Alaska.

There may have been forty million deer in the continental United States four or five centuries ago, perhaps as few as half a million at the turn of the century when laws were established to prevent extinction. The best guess is that there are between nine and ten million in the United States today.

The whitetail is perhaps the most American of species. It has little to do with the deer of Europe; the North American Elk is more closely related to the Red deer of the European continent. Ancestors of the whitetail and the mule deer may have crossed from Asia on the last land bridge millions of years ago, and they have evolved in isolation.

Deer have been successful in their evolution in part because their ruminative digestive system enables them to take nourishment from at least six hundred species of plants. Whitetails pick and choose with considerable ability to find the ones most nourishing. They change their diet with the season, adjusting to the best food available. Only when near starvation will the judgment falter; starving deer will stuff their bellies with useless fodder and die of starvation, but only when nothing better is available.

Deer will eat mushrooms, avoiding those which might be poisonous. They probably ingest algae from the pond where each drinks a couple of quarts of water each day, and may sample a few species of broad-leafed aquatic plants. A few mosses appeal to them at certain times of the year; they are known to eat thirteen different types of ferns. More than five hundred different grasses and seed plants are taken by the whitetail.

Now, in May, in the spring, the sprout growth of trees and shrubs bulks large in the diet. They are surprisingly nourishing, with fat content comparing favorably with corn and wheat. Adult deer require 5 to 7 pounds of first-rate food each day. They must get it a nibble at a time, tearing and cutting the twig ends. They have no incisors, or cutting teeth, on their upper jaw. Small twigs can be cut by pressing them between the lower incisors and the pad of flesh above them on the upper part of the jaw. Larger shoots must be torn off by holding them firmly in the mouth and jerking them loose with a toss of the head.

Cheek teeth are efficient grinders, easily macerating leaves, grass, twigs, acorns, or even cherry pits to the pulpy mass that the rumen requires. This is done at some expense, however, for as the teeth grind and wear away, the deer's ability to feed itself diminishes.

Earlier this May, the whitetail doe Alpha still was part of her family. She was nearly two years old and had no fawns of her own as yet, although some does breed their first fall, and she could have borne a fawn when she was a yearling. It is not common for a yearling doe to fawn in the wild, however, because she must be nourished exceptionally well. If she does give birth as a yearling, she will invariably have a single fawn; as she matures, twins are usual and triplets as common as single births. Last year's feed was not so plentiful that Alpha had been bred as a yearling, so she stayed with her family.

Whitetail families are strictly matriarchal. The fawn or fawns stay with the mother until near their second birthday. A common family in fall or spring will include the mother doe as the head, one or two yearlings, and the fawn or fawns from the previous spring.

Hunters often see a buck or two traveling with a doe in the fall and mistakenly assume that they are together as mates. More commonly, the buck with the doe will be her male fawn in his second fall, sporting his first antlers, still a little diffident about seeking his first breeding partner.

The ties of the family are loosened in the winter yard, when the strongest deer make first claim on the food and the youngest and weakest take last choice. In the spring, when they drift from the yard to their summer ranges, the family may re-establish itself. Sometimes the young bucks will leave the family and strike out to new territory but the does usually remain with their mother. Alpha was still with her "family."

Her yearling brother was with them; Alpha's mother had borne twins the spring before but one did not survive the winter. The young buck was growing his antlers and, early in May, the first swellings appeared on the pedicles of bone at the top of his skull. These small swellings, the first antler growth, are present on most male fawns from the age of six months on, and hunters sometimes call the young bucks "button bucks." If he is well nourished, the antlers will be more than 2 inches long, and at the end of the month, the first fork will be obvious, the antlers growing a quarter inch a day.

Antlers are the most distinguishing feature of the white-tail. They make the buck a trophy and are displayed with pride by the successful hunter. Yet they are among the least understood of all the natural functions of the deer.

Only bucks grow them regularly, although now and then a doe will be found with some abortive antler growth. This leads conservation officers to use the term "antlered deer" rather than "buck," because a few does have some antlers.

Why do bucks grow them? Perhaps as weapons, although when bucks fight they push each other with their heads, rather than slashing or fencing with the antlers. Only in captivity or under conditions of extreme stress will the buck use his antlers as lethal weapons.

Nor do they seem to be of much value in fights with enemies. They are a function of the breeding season, an extension of the male sex organs, and there is much about them no one knows.

The cycle of their growth is controlled primarily by the hormone testosterone, the primary hormone secreted by the testicles. Probably one or two other hormones secreted by the pituitary influence the growth. The hormones are secreted early in the spring, and the result is the growth of the antler.

If a doe is injected with testosterone, she may well begin to grow antlers. If the buck is castrated after the velvet-like antler covering is shed, the antlers will drop off in a matter of days.

Only when the growth is complete, and the antlers are polished on trees and shrubs, does the testosterone hormone begin to urge the buck to copulate. He will seek a doe in the fall, with a quite mad passion persist until she accepts him, then quickly leave her to seek another and another until the breeding season, or "rut," ends. Then, when the breeding is done for a year, his testicles will shrink to half the size they are when he is sexually active, his antlers will fall off, and he will become for all intents and purposes a sexless animal until the hormone secretion is signaled by the lengthening days of spring and begins again.

Although we know that, we do not really know much, have not done a great deal more than to begin to describe what happens as the result of countless years of evolution under conditions we understand only generally. When the question of the function of the antlers is pressed, the answers are evasive.

In breeding farms, the antlers are routinely sawed off as soon as they are mature and before the bucks are allowed to join the does in the breeding pens. This is done because in the pressures of captivity, the bucks may fight with each other in their sexual madness. Or they may attack a doe that refuses them. In the wild, fights are almost never fatal; the doe will flee to safety. But in the pen, she may be cornered and killed by a frantic buck. So the pen managers cut the antlers off at their base with a meat saw. The buck, briefly tranquilized for the operation, does not mind. He may still butt heads with the other bucks but they cannot hurt each other. He will breed as eagerly with any available doe, and she accepts him when ready without regard to the presence or absence of antlers. So while it is agreed that the antlers are functions of the sexual system, their precise function is not known.

Further evidence that they are not needed for weapons can be seen when the deer is forced to fight: it usually uses its front feet with the sharp quick hooves. In the stress of a winter yard, if a fight erupts, the deer rear up on their hind legs and strike out with their forefeet. Does are often the best fighters and dominate the herd or family when short rations drive them to a show of strength.

Or if a doe is forced to fight, if she is threatened with a predator she cannot escape or if she chooses to defend fawns threatened by, say, a coyote, she will use her forefeet and is often successful in her defense against small predators.

The bony growths are called antlers, by the way, rather than horns, because horns are permanent extensions of the bony structure of the skull while the antlers are grown new each year.

Yet, in our ignorance, we cannot dismiss the antlers as useless, or as simply illustrations of the buck's symbolic strength. Nature does nothing idly, she has no symbols, everything has an explicit function, and in particular, she does not evolve such a complex thing as antler growth without purpose. So we must say that if we do not know exactly what purpose they serve, it must be an important one.

Antlers are grown completely new each year, the growth consuming nearly as much energy as would growing a major part of the skeleton. And the system that has evolved for providing the nourishment for their growth is uniquely complex.

Antlers rise from a thin plate of bone grown on the top of the skull, sandwich-like on the pedicles at the front of the skull. Three complete sets of arteries are required to provide the rapidly growing antlers with sufficient nourishment.

One set of arteries grows on the inside of the antler, carrying blood to the interior of the growing bone. A second set is on the outside of the growth. When the antlers mature and harden, the second set is visible as a series of ridges on the outside of the base, larger toward the bottom of the rack. A third arterial system is in the "velvet," the soft skinlike material—almost a placenta—that covers the antlers during their growth, when they are soft.

As the antlers mature, and as the flow of testosterone diminishes late in the summer and the breeding season nears, the three arterial systems die.

The arteries on the inside of the antlers die from the extremities to the pedicle, and the antlers ossify. The arteries on the outside harden in the same manner, and form the ridges mentioned earlier. The soft and bloody velvet dies too, and the buck rubs it away on trees and bushes, polishing his antlers in the process until they are a fine brown-to-yellowish color, hard and sharp, pointed, but, as far as we know, pointless.

But these things are all to come, this is still May, and the doe, aside from her restless roaming, is quite patient; she is well fed for the first time in months, and her small range provides her with a fine supply of food.

She is not very eager to roam, and moves generally only from cover to feeding place, down to a swamp where she could find water. Most whitetails, if the home range is complete with these things, will spend their life in an area no larger than a few acres.

Their restlessness, or perhaps some more complex instinct, keeps them moving while they feed. They do not stand in a place and feed all around themselves, as a cow or a sheep might. They sample and move on, as though they were programmed not to destroy, but to sample each plant lightly so it will not be harmed and will grow again so they may feed from it all summer and again the next year.

When they occasionally kill a plant it is almost always because their range is overstocked, or by accident they will whip a small plant to death in the process of cleaning the antlers.

In their search for varied food, they seek a few delicacies. A favorite is apples, and they smell them from considerable distances and seek them out. The apples have a good deal of nourishment, but they are a favored food even beyond their nutritious value and must be considered a treat for a white-tail.

Later, in the fall, they search out acorns and can put on their winter fat in a few days if they have a good supply of nuts.

In lake country, they will stand in the water and eat the plants growing up from the bottom of the pond. They are more adapted to water than is generally realized, and can swim for great distances. They have been observed swimming far out in lakes, even in the oceans along the coasts, and some insist that they have clocked the deer at swimming speeds of up to 15 miles an hour.

There are stories of deer hiding in streams, standing on the bottom in places so deep that only their noses stick out as they seek to evade a predator. The stories are doubted, and it is difficult to know if they are fact or myth.

Alpha gains strength rapidly in May. Sometimes she comes out to eat in the daytime, though she keeps largely to a nocturnal schedule. We do not know for sure how natural is this preference for night. Perhaps she has learned that she is safer in the dark, safer from man. There is some evidence that deer were less nocturnal in their habits before man pressed them, and that the more threatened they feel, the more nocturnal they become.

Of course darkness matters little to them in the problem of navigation. Their world is one of odors and sounds more than one of sights. They see poorly in the day, and probably only a little less well in the dark, so it does not matter much. They react largely to movement.

May is about to end; the days are long and warm and the nights pleasant. There was rain, but it does not bother Alpha. The foliage is full and tasty. Then one day, she separates herself, irritated, from the "family" she had been close to for so long. Something she does not understand is happening and she paws and stamps her foot. But instinct is welling up, she is unable to defy it, and she responds.

For Alpha is a captive of the ultimate parasite, the fetus.

Slowly at first, more quickly as the two-hundred-day gestation proceeded, quite rapidly as birth nears now, it has drawn strength from her body, borrowed her nourishment, claimed its own life from hers.

She has forgotten, of course, that mad mid-November day when a buck came to her and they mated and she conceived.

And she does not know that at the beginning of May, the fawn in her womb is fully clothed in its spotted coat and is in appearance ready to be born. It is perhaps 12 inches long, and will grow one-fourth larger by the end of the month.

She knows only what her instincts tell her, and they do not tell her that one morning soon she will leave the others to make her own family. She has survived, and she will be alone with her instincts, to give birth.

June

June is the month of change. The doe Alpha will be struck by nature as Saul was struck by God on the road to Damascus, and the change will be just as dramatic, as total, as abrupt. No longer will she be a lonely passive survivor, with no function but to be an indifferent occupant of an empty place on an invisible pyramid. She will give birth, she will be a mother, and, like any of us, she will have a hostage to fortune.

She is not aware of her pregnancy. She is host to the fetus in her womb as she is host to the worms in her lungs. They are claims placed on her body; she nourishes both parasites, but she does not notice them, does not identify one as promise and the other as threat. She does not anticipate the birth, has no premonition of it, save perhaps for an uneasiness a day or so immediately before, a strange stirring that may lead her to separate herself a little from the others. She seeks no special place for birth.

One morning, after she is finished feeding, and as she drifts back to the cover of the forest, she begins to circle quickly, as though irritated or alarmed. She strains as if to defecate, again and again, and two tiny forehooves appear through her vulva. She is panting. She lies down briefly, struggles clumsily—a strange thing for her, this animal of such grace—and rises and paces again. About an hour from the time the little hooves were first visible, she lies down again and seems to rest. Then she struggles as if to rise and a buck fawn lies on the ground behind her, the birth quicker, easier than for a human mother.

. . . And a voice calls to her; quickly, now, quickly, there is little time . . .

She twists her head to reach the little deer with her tongue and spends ten minutes cleaning him, perhaps imprinting him with her scent, drawing in for her own guidance the bloody scent of herself on him, stimulating him to life as a physician spanks a baby to life, licking him so vigorously that sometimes he is lifted partially off the ground. He falls back with a tiny thud and his heart beats faster. She tongues away the remnants of birth and dries the Little Buck. He lifts his head and blinks, stimulated by the vigorous action of the cleaning.

. . . Quickly now, finish it up, there is no time . . .

She twists her head around and begins pulling the placenta from her body, tearing it out with her teeth and lips, swallowing it. No part of it touches the ground. No odor will mark the site. She finishes in about fifteen minutes.

. . . Good good, the roaming wolves will never know . . .

The umbilical cord was broken when the fawn was expelled from her body. She licks at the stub, then bites it off close to the body. For several days, she will lick at it often, cleaning it, protecting it against infection. If she did not, he would be likely to be infected and die.

. . . Hurry now, feed him . . .

She nuzzles close to the Little Buck, and he pokes at her, finds a nipple, and nurses. The rich warm milk floods into him; nourishment, life, and with it the information that this is Mother, this is the Source, this is the link with the ages.

There is an almost desperate urgency to feed the Little Buck quickly, so that he will be fed, and so that he will know.

. . . Hide hide, Little Buck . . .

He is not naked, and for a little while, although he is helpless, he is rich in protection. He lies absolutely still on the ground, nose tucked beside his body, ears flat against his head. He is so close to the ground that a man would have to stumble on him to find him.

But what if the wolf should smell him out?

The Little Buck has no odor. For a few days, he simply emits no smell. A dog could jump over him and never scent him. He will have no scent until he can walk a little, begin to learn the business of flight.

. . . He is safe now; he is cleaned and fed and stilled; protect him . . .

And the mother gives some gentle soft signal, learned a million years ago, when she was young, and he knows, and she leaves him, goes a little way away to rest. For she is scented, and if the big cats come, she will know, and she will run, and they will not find the Little Buck.

. . . Yes, rest now, he is safe, the first step is over . . .

Not every doe eats her placenta. The act is common among deer, though, as it is among many mammals. Occasionally the ingested placenta will upset the mother's digestive system and she will be ill and probably a few die.

Secrecy is a main reason for this act, but it is not the only one. There may be special nutrients in the placenta that stimulate lactation so that the doe's milk flow is strong. This is a complex system, and we are only beginning to understand. After all, her nature is older than our knowledge.

The placenta that nourished the unborn fawn is high in nutrition, and the doe recognized the need for special nourishment while nursing. Perhaps that is part of the reason she eats it. She may seek out other special nourishment too; some think that she will eat fish or bloodsuckers to supplement her diet while milk production draws so heavily on her.

As there are no symbols in nature, there is no romance. She

sought no shady forest glade for the birth, but dropped the buck where she was when the cycle came complete. If there are flies—and it seems that for the whitetail there are always flies—he will have to learn to live with them and he may as well begin now. If there is too much sun, or if the ground is damp, it is a quality of nature, and she is a part of nature, has no instinct to protect him from it.

No romance, ever, for the whitetail; no love at conception, no expectation in pregnancy, no joy in birth. Duties, relentlessly ascribed by nature and insisted upon, the price of survival extracted without leniency. No joy.

But there is something else; a flooding of instinct perhaps not so different from the floods of emotion and instinct, hardly separated, that human beings feel for their own children. Alpha does not love the Little Buck as we say we love our children, but she is bound to him as we are bound, and her ties, her bonds, are very old.

In the morning, she had been a survivor. Now she is a mother.

She is freed of her parasite, the fetus has become the Little Buck, and she is captive now of the new demands nature has put upon her. She must nurture and teach him, clean him and hide him, and even protect him against enemies she cannot lure away. She must teach him the rules of survival.

The Little Buck's role is simple at first. He must only show enough strength to nurse. If he can manage that, his mother will provide.

The doe has given birth to an animal men believe to be one of the most beautiful in nature. It is a mistake, though, to say she is proud. Pride is a thing defined by the Greeks and debated by philosophers with a leisure she will never have. Pride has no place in the life of the whitetail. As is the case with most animals, she has no sentiment toward her young. She is bound to him by all the old laws. She does not dote on him, but she will preserve him. He is her new assignment.

The Little Buck is a single birth. In later years, if the doe survives, she will normally drop twins, and perhaps an occasional set of triplets. If she has a multiple birth, the fawns will be dropped about an hour apart. If a twin birth produces one fawn of each sex, both will mature normally sexually. The female twin will not be sterile, a "free-martin," as is the case with some animals. In the wild, nature wastes nothing.

The Little Buck weighs about 6 pounds. A doe fawn would have been about a pound lighter. The ratio between the mother's weight and his is about 16.5 to 1. Approximately 51 per cent of all fawns born are males. Male fawns require higher protein food for maximum growth than do doe fawns.

The early nursing identified mother for him. Should they become separated, he will seek her out by smelling other deer's udders, or her nose, where she licked and cleaned him.

After that first urgent nursing lying down, she will not make much effort to be accommodating. If the winter had been especially severe for her, and she were terribly weak, she might have given birth to a fawn so feeble it could not rise to reach her udder. If that happened, she would simply allow it to die, would free herself from the need to produce milk, easing the strain on her body, surviving.

She has four nipples, so in theory she could nurse four fawns. In the wild, she would probably not be able to provide adequate milk for that many. Quadruplets are rare, and the doe, even a well-fed mature doe, would likely have difficulty in adequately nourishing three, let alone four.

One spring, on a breeding farm run for scientific purposes, I watched a pathetic and silent little drama played out. A doe with new fawns died and left orphan twins. Game managers decided to see if they could get other does to adopt the orphans. This is always a tricky business; some will be adopted, some not, and there is no way of predicting.

One doe was given one of the orphans along with her own newborn. She never allowed the strange fawn to nurse. It died in a few hours.

The second doe was more generous; she allowed the new fawn to nurse, and it appeared healthy for a day or two. Without any milk, it would have died quickly, and it did not, so the men were sure it was nursing and they began quietly to congratulate themselves.

Then the doe refused it, and the fawn died some twenty-four hours later.

Why did she turn the fawn away, after accepting it once? Did she somehow determine that she would not have milk enough for the third fawn and make a conscious decision to save the milk for her own? Such a decision would indicate incredible precocity of instinct.

Perhaps some other factor, like the odor of the third fawn, was the reason for the rejection.

She took no interest in the dying fawn, nor did the two healthy fawns. After bleating a little, it lay down quietly, away from the others. Its eyes were bright and its head was high until about an hour before it died. None of the other deer took any notice when the keeper removed the body.

The doe's milk is rich. It has more than twice the proportion of solids present in the milk of a Jersey cow, which is in turn richer than the milk normally available in supermarkets. Fat levels are nearly three times higher, as is the protein. It is much like the milk of reindeer, or caribou.

The fawn's instinct to hide is made more important because of the special pattern of his coat. At birth, the fawn's coat is dappled with some three hundred pure white spots, each about one-quarter to one-half inch in diameter, showing in a background of bright red or bay. A man could easily sit on a log with the fawn at his feet and never see it. Or another predator, its eyes keyed to find motion, might do the same while the fawn lay still, motionless, scentless.

When the Little Buck lies hidden, his mother does not lie beside him. She will lie perhaps 50 feet away, sometimes on a little elevation, so that she can see the spot where the newborn waits, but so that she can also distract invaders.

Each spring, conservation officers and humane societies all across the country are presented with fawns that have been found "abandoned" and "saved" by well-meaning persons who stumbled across them. But unless the doe has been killed, as for example by a car, she will not abandon the fawn. She will watch from cover, usually afraid to come out into the open, while the fawn is "saved." She will be agitated, but her fear of man is so strong that she will not normally expose herself to protect the fawn. The baby has been stolen, not saved.

If a small predator, for example a coyote, which singly would not threaten the adult deer, should find the fawn, she will try to lead the intruder away. If she cannot, she may defend the infant, rising on her rear legs and striking with strong front legs and sharp hooves. At the very least, she is likely to raise the price of the attempted kill so high that the would-be predator will abandon his attack.

When he is hungry, the Little Buck will call to his mother with soft little bleats similar to those of a lamb or a calf. Deer are far from voiceless, although most of their sounds are subtle as befits their retiring nature.

If he calls, she will react as she thinks proper, going to him or ignoring him, or perhaps telling him with a gesture or a grunt to drop to the ground and be still.

There will be times when she is uneasy, and she passes the tension to him as she passed life to him through the umbilical cord before birth. In the air there will be something; an odd smell, or faint sound, something more felt than known, and it will set her pacing. She will mutter then, almost constantly, a series of low nervous grunts and snorts. She will pace in circles, test the air with her nose raised, sniff suspiciously at her udder as though there was an intruder there, twist her ears to listen.

If she confronts a danger, she will raise that one front foot again and stamp, stamp, hoping to frighten the intruder away, hoping to smooth threat from her life. The Little Buck will be as intent on her as possible, for his one good sense tells him that he is new to nature and does not know the rules. But she will teach him; she is mother, and she nourishes and nurtures and she will teach him of the tigers, warn him of the wolves, though all are gone for decades. He listens, for he knows she is nature to him, and survival; she represents the only time in his life when he will have any teacher save trial and error, the vital link with the past million years.

She is like a human parent in that much of what she will teach her offspring will be wrong. The reason for the error will be different, however; the human being errs because of ignorance, or superstition, or emotional problems. The deer errs because of her great age, and because of what man has done to it.

Nature has taught her to survive; she has learned well, learned from her own mother and the others in the herd. But more important, she has inherited those millions of years of carefully nurtured instincts that have allowed her to survive. Many of the instincts and thus much of the teaching will have little to do with her real world, the world where men have taken away the natural predators and substituted hunting seasons and powerful rifles.

If she teaches the Little Buck too much about the wolves that shaped her fear, she will at least teach him to be cautious and alert, to retreat rather than to make a stand. So perhaps she is also a bit like human parents in that; she may teach too much of one thing, too little of another. But if he survives, the balance will be even in the end.

The Little Buck is intent on her, drawn to her along that taut string of parental dependence. As soon as he is able, he will follow her if she paces and grumbles, and when he sees the thing that frightens her, he will know that thing as danger.

If she tells him to wait, he will be patient, lying still, pressed to the earth, moving only to blink or to twitch against the flies. If hunger or fear become too strong for him to bear in silence, he will call to her, first with a feeble little bleat, finally imploring with loud lamblike baas.

The doe, too, has many voices, and if she is so excited that she is moved to flight, she can make a screamlike whistling sound, shrill and piercing, audible at some distance, especially to a waiting deer.

I had thought the deer were largely silent animals until I sat one evening alone in the middle of a breeding farm. The place lay well back on a dirt road off a two-lane road miles from any highway, and there was no traffic, no sound of man as I sat still and listened.

Dozens of does with new fawns were nervous under the strain of captivity, and of my alien presence, and they were especially tense with the new responsibilities of motherhood. Nature urged them to take their fawns away from the danger of man, and the woods were visible not far away. But the fences were too high, and they grumbled and paced. The sound struck me as that of a group of soldiers muttering cautiously to each other in the dark on the eve of battle. Occasional sneezes were heard, and once in a while, a doe driven near panic would scream and run to the far corner of her pen and the others would tense and listen and wait, alarmed, while the fawns watched and wondered.

One especially high-strung doe showed her tension with an almost crippled-looking run. She wished she could leap and leave, but there were those fences, and her gait became almost a caricature of flight. As each pair of legs reached the top of their swing, she would stop, pause for the faintest fraction of a second, then continue, disjointedly, her fraying nerves making them jerk raggedly. Her panic finally drove me away in pity.

The Little Buck is grasping life. It is all he knows yet, this clinging to each breath, each taste of warm good milk. He is learning that the world is a hostile place, filled with hazard, but he is well served with many things that will give him a good chance of growing to maturity.

His scentless time is short. When the Little Buck begins to walk around, to follow his mother, she teaches him to urinate on the tarsal glands on the inside of the rear legs. This may be to increase the level of the individual scent that the deer trails behind it. As it grows up, the white hairs that cover the tarsal glands are stained with the deer's own urine. The doe makes a concerted effort to teach the fawn this habit, encouraging him each time he puts his feet together, licking his tarsal glands to show him the importance of accenting his own scent. There are interdigital glands between the points of the hooves, and as he grows, they will leave scent wherever he walks. One result is that the doe can track the fawn to his bed. There may be other reasons for the habit, but like the function of the metatarsal gland on the outside of the back legs, they are unknown.

Some of the Little Buck's senses are acute soon after birth. The slightest sound may make him nestle closer to the earth. When he can walk, he has enough sense of smell that he will identify adult deer by their odor. If the family group forms again, the little fawn will sniff at another deer, seeking its mother. He cannot see very well, and may sniff at a buck, searching for a familiar udder. He will probably earn a sharp kick for his effort.

For the first day or so, a fawn has little fear of man. His mother may teach him the fear. As an adult, he can learn it.

In breeding pens, does are inclined to keep their distance. Fawns will approach to within a few feet of man in their curiosity, but will not willingly allow themselves to be touched.

For most of June, the Little Buck remains still and hidden much of the time. He begins to follow his mother late in the month, and in July, he will trot alongside her. It may be that the harder he is pressed, by fear of man or of other predators, the more quickly he will become active.

At first he is nourished only by his mother's milk. She is anxious to teach him about other food, anxious to relieve herself of the burden of nursing. He is not a ruminant at birth, could not digest grass or forbs even if he should ingest them. He must have bacteria in his rumen to start its digestive action, and he picks them up from his mother's mouth, when she licks him around the face, or from her body as he nurses, or perhaps from the ground or from touching plants that his mother has sampled. In one way or another, or perhaps in several, he is inoculated. When he is a little more than a week old, he samples a dandelion. In July, he will be able to digest seedy fruits or berries, or perhaps even acorns or corn. When he is six weeks old, he will drink water, ingesting more bacteria in the process. By the end of July, he will be a ruminant, but still unable to survive without milk. He will not be weaned completely until he is three or four months old, although he could probably survive if he lost his mother any time after he is three months old. If his mother is indulgent, he may nurse until the breeding season begins in November.

His birth weight will be doubled by the middle of June, and quadrupled by the time he is a month old. By the end of June, he will weigh nearly 25 pounds, and he will be one-fourth as heavy as his mother, who gains little weight while nursing.

The doe spends the month in the most intensely domestic time of her life. Aside from her own bodily needs, she gives much attention to her fawn, cleaning, teaching, imprinting her scent and behavior patterns on him. If there is no pressure from predators and if the range is good, she may form again some of the relationships with the family she left when the Little Buck was born. The herd will stay fairly close together, and half a dozen does may feed as a group.

If it is a calm time, if the pressures from predators are low and the range is healthy, the Little Buck is likely to grow up more tame, less infused with fear. The reactions of the older deer affect him deeply, and they react from patterns learned through time. In an area where they have never been hunted, if they see a man, they will run a little way and wait, keeping safe distance from him, but not plunging headlong into a cover. But if they have heard the guns and have seen other deer killed or perhaps more importantly heard the shrill whistle of fear, they will run farther, stay hidden longer. They never completely lose their fear of man in the wild, but they can become quite tolerant of him.

Deer are among the most successful reproducers among wild animals. Conception rates in the wild approximate to 99 per cent; hunters who claim that the woods are populated with barren does because of an absence of bucks are almost always incorrect. There are rarely serious problems in giving birth, and the survival rate of fawns among well-nourished deer in the wild ranges around 90 per cent.

The biotic potential which has permitted the deer to survive its major historic predators is a problem now, as much as a strength. Left alone, with the predators removed, deer quickly multiply beyond the carrying capacity of their range. The result is mass starvation until the herd and the food are again in balance. At that point, the deer again multiply and the cycle is repeated. The result, in this unnatural world, can easily be tragedy.

In 1928, two adult male and four adult female whitetails were transported from Grand Island in Lake Superior to a 1,200-acre enclosure in southern Michigan. The area was fenced so that no wild deer could enter nor could any escape from inside the fence. Five years later, the herd was counted, and there were at least 160 deer in the preserve.

If the carrying capacity of the range is sufficient, and predators are rare or absent, as is the case in most of the Midwest, a deer herd will double in size each year.

The fecundity of deer—potentially tragic because of the artificial imbalances in nature—can be illustrated again in the case of South Fox Island, a little more than 3,000 acres, about 5 square miles, some 17 miles from the northern Michigan mainland into Lake Michigan. Deer long ago had reached the island somehow, either across the ice or by swimming. A few homesteads were established there, but by the middle of the twentieth century the island was used mainly as a source of timber, and was essentially unoccupied. The deer herd had been extinguished, perhaps by keepers of the lighthouse and by early settlers. There were no deer on the wooded island in 1962. Much of the cut-over area was ideal deer range, however.

Owners of the timberland who were logging on the island at that time convinced game officers to plant deer on the island. In September 1962, the Michigan Department of Conservation, now the Department of Natural Resources, released six bucks and eleven does. At least two died that winter, so no more than fifteen deer were alive on the island to begin its repopulation.

For a few years, no one thought much more about the deer there. Owners of property began shooting trophy bucks with large racks.

In 1969, seven years after the first deer were planted on the island, the herd numbered at least five hundred. At least forty more deer had been taken by hunters.

A special hunting season was established, as the DNR decided that the herd was too large for the available food. Hunters killed 188 deer that fall. Conservation officers believed the herd was still too large.

In the fall of 1970, an even more intense effort was made to harvest deer from the island so that the herd would again be in balance with food supplies. The DNR issued licenses to 612 persons, who killed 382 deer, including bucks, does, and fawns. In the spring of 1971, a check showed that the island had 194 deer; a population that fall of 400 was expected.

In eight years, the original 15 deer had produced a herd from which at least 620 deer had been killed and the herd still numbered 15 times larger than the number put there in the first place.

If continued intense hunting is not practiced, the herd will double each fall. The island once could provide food for approximately eight hundred deer. Its carrying capacity has now dropped to possibly four hundred.

The equation is unavoidable. Unless hunted, the deer will determinedly breed themselves out of house and home. The weaker will then starve until a new, but always temporary, balance is obtained.

Examples are not confined to Michigan, nor to the whitetail. In 1906, President Theodore Roosevelt created the Grand Canyon National Game Preserve. A million acres were set aside from regular development. The area was home for some three thousand Rocky Mountain mule deer, so isolated on the Kaibab North Plateau in northwestern Arizona that they were virtually a subspecies, big and strong, the bucks growing magnificent antlers. The deer stirred the hearts of conservationists, and they determined to protect them.

It was a lovely land, with pine, fir, and aspen, flowered

meadows, fresh streams, deep canyons, and open desert.

Once, it had been home to buffalo, elk, moose, and antelope. But unrestricted hunting had all but eliminated those animals. So the Forest Service was given the task of preserving the herd of mule deer. Energetic but ignorant, the service made two decisions.

They banned hunting. And they declared war on the predators—the coyotes, mountain lions, bobcats, and gray wolves, which preyed on the mule deer.

The Navajos had not hunted the coyotes, holding them as sacred, and they did not threaten the lions or wolves. Government hunters entered the preserve with poison, snares, guns, and traps. In the next twenty-five years, they killed 4,889 coyotes, 781 lions, 554 bobcats, and 20 wolves. Many others were killed by hunters hired by the stockmen who wanted the land safe for commercial grazing.

The deer herd expanded, and conservationists cheered. By 1918, the herd had grown to an estimated 15,000. In fact it was almost certainly larger than that.

But the range was failing. Cattle were forced from grass to woody plants, in more direct competition with the deer for food; the foliage was thinning, gullies were appearing on the newly bare slopes. The winter food was overbrowsed.

By 1923, there were at least 30,000 deer in the preserve, and may have been 100,000. A third were on the verge of starvation. The remainder were ghosts of their recent ancestors; no longer proud trophies, they were thin and hungry, ribs often more prominent than antlers.

The Forest Service began to reduce grazing permits, and trapped the deer, offering them for sale at $35 a head. Few were trapped, fewer still sold. In desperation, the service offered bargain hunting licenses; for $5, the hunter could take any three deer. The result was a kill of 675 deer, approximately one-tenth the number born that spring.

Reluctant to order mass killing by government-hired hunters, the Forest Service tried to drive the deer from the area and failed.

Controversy raged. On one hand, well-intentioned citizens were determined to protect the herd from slaughter. They resisted efforts to reduce the herd artificially. Thousands of deer starved and froze each winter.

Finally, any-deer seasons were introduced, and the hunters and nature reduced the herd to approximately 20,000 by 1931. The range began to recover. So authorities restored the buck-only program in 1945. Quickly the herd doubled and the range began to suffer again. By 1955, the herd numbered only 12,000, fewer than in any year since 1916.

Nature does not simply abhor a vacuum, she is unable to allow it. If the natural predators are taken away, man must substitute himself. If he does not do so, nature introduces starvation. But unless the deer are completely eliminated, that solution is only temporary. For when the herd decreases again and the food supplies recover, the population explosion recurs.

The deer is out of kilter with modern civilization. Its natural biotic potential is no longer synchronized with need. Man has touched the controls of nature, has introduced his will, and he must take the responsibility for his work or the deer will starve each time the cycle reaches the point of high population.

Meanwhile, the whitetail doe Alpha has a final lesson to teach the Little Buck in June. As they walk one afternoon, she suddenly becomes rigid with alarm. The fawn takes his cue and freezes, watching. The doe's tail is stiff and upright, the white hair on her flanks erect. She walks in a tiny circle, then suddenly springs into the air and comes down with her feet nearly together. Again and again she jumps. Stopping finally, she watches the ground until satisfied, then walks stiff-legged away. The fawn, curious, inspects. A snake still writhes slightly, though slashed to tatters by the sharp hooves. It is the only natural inhabitant of the whitetail's range that she attacks without provocation. She has nothing to fear from snakes. But they are her only target of aggression. The Little Buck watches. He will remember.

July

They walk in the languid warmth of summer nights; Alpha always a little ahead, the Little Buck following, stopping when she stops, listening when she listens, going fast or slow with her, turning, circling, watching her and the things she watches, learning, absorbing her habit patterns into his own evolving personality, becoming like her, like a deer, like nature.

The long soft days are for resting, the Little Buck curled sleeping in the sun, the doe a thicket away, watching over him, ruminating, patient for the shadows of evening, when they will begin again, go out to feed, to search the fields for food and to stir in the misty animal memories of a million years for places and events that flicker faintly at the fringes of instinctive consciousness. When there is an alarm, a clean decision to be made, her instinct is precise and she will run from danger. But much of the time she moves in patterns without reason, at random, old instincts stirring from the Stone Age, for reasons that are relics of the time of the ice, the old ways roiling up; she is listening for sounds no one has heard for a hundred thousand years, a creature of the ages, old, old, old . . .

She knows the night is coming, and an hour or so before the sun finally fades away, she lurches to her feet, sniffs the air to be sure the way is safe, and the Little Buck follows; they wander together to the fields, their journey as quiet and gentle as drifting milkweed down.

She knows, or senses, that man has fled the threat of the forest darkness, has taken his tractor and noise and left the fields. He will huddle in his house or barn for the night, reassured with his electric fires, safe, his instincts duller than hers but still keeping him away from the dangers of the dark, the dangers she remembers so sharply.

The traffic sounds of the day die away. The breeze is going down with the sun. For a little while, in the hours of the night, man's intervention is over, the animals come out and the land is natural again.

There are new shapes, new profiles among them. The young are growing quickly, the yearling bucks already showing antlers as long as a man's hand. These soft first antlers are covered with the placenta-like velvet, and they are tender so the bucks are careful not to brush them against shrub or tree. The bucks are cautious and shy.

They are recruits in the army nature raises up each year to defend herself against the obliterations of time, and like recruits in any army, they vary in size and temper.

Most adult does weigh little more than 100 pounds. A few of the biggest bucks weigh more than twice that. None of them is as heavy now as in the fall. Then, the doe will be freed from the demands of nursing and there will be a few quick weeks to put on the fat for winter. The buck will finish with the demands of antler growth, and he will put on fat, first for the rigors of the rut, then against the cold. Those thin bleak days are far from the deer now, and if they stir in their consciousness at all, it is only in that irritating vagueness that pushes them along.

Nature is not quite fair with the deer; they are not permitted much memory, not allowed to recall with any clarity the bleak agonies of winter. Perhaps it is so that they will not run south, where life would be easier. Nature wants them where they are, tied to a small home range, not easily driven away, not given to wandering very much. So she does not permit them to remember how hard life can be, how difficult things will get in a few months. Perhaps it is selfishness, perhaps compassion, the compassion of design that helps human beings forget the pain of childbirth and remember the joy so that they will conceive again in love and forget the hurt.

Now and then, the sleeping instincts crowd close to consciousness. The doe Alpha turns one morning while they are feeding and butts the Little Buck, hooking him hard with her head so that he has to stumble a step to the side to catch his balance. She butts him in the belly, just back of his front legs, and he looks at her numbly, wondering why she has struck him, brown eyes focused on her, alert, intent, but dumbfounded as any child whose parent has given him an aimless cuff without warning.

She gives him her hard stare, the stare of challenge, the stare reserved for an intruder or a potential enemy. He does not know what she meant; the stylized gesture of challenge has not yet been learned. And even if he had known, he would not have understood.

Nor does she; there is just suddenly in her for a moment a vague angry frustration, a stirring, when memories of the hunger and helplessness of winter stirred in her, nudged at the edges of awareness, and she very nearly remembered and was angry, angry at nature for giving her such a difficult life. But before she could quite grasp the feeling, give it shape, it slipped from her, and she drops her stare and looks away from the Little Buck. She begins to eat again and he forgets too and tosses his head and follows her.

If she had known what she was protesting, she might have called it nature's habit of not being over-generous to her creatures. No deer in the wild ever reaches its greatest potential size. Captive deer, fed controlled and balanced rations, will be 20 or 30 per cent larger than wild deer, which can only cope as best they can with the offerings before them. Fully nourished deer will continue to grow until they reach their full size at four or five years. Man has learned to provide for himself, to change nature, to win his battles with her, and each generation of men is a little larger in the richer countries than the generation before. The deer lacks man's cunning and must simply do the best it can, always losing a little in the contest with a stingy nature.

There are long-bodied deer and stocky deer; their coat tones vary and the white markings of legs, throat, and belly differ in size. Men who work with them give them names like "Red" or "Ranger," acknowledging these differences. As for the deer, they make their distinctions largely by odor.

The Little Buck had eight incisor teeth when born, and they quickly became sharp and hard enough to hurt his mother's nipples. She was patient, and let him bite her once or twice hard enough to hurt, but then she gave him a kick and he is more gentle now. Twelve premolars join the incisors during the first two months of life; he is assembling, while living largely on her milk, the cutting and grinding mechanism that will sustain him through his adult life.

He passed through kindergarten in the first few days of life, learning how to lie still and keep safe. The elementary grades are nearly finished by midsummer; he knows how to look and listen and take some foods. He is getting ready for junior high school, learning, pressured because the clear voice comes from the cold ages to him, warning, reminding him that he must be quick for there is not much time.

He learns to read the rich symphony of the swamp and the forest; to listen for the changing chirps of the crickets which tell him things about the weather and the time of day and things that may be passing through their area; to endure the continual buzz of the flies that will plague him all his life, to listen for the call of robin or jay. To listen especially for the caw of the crow, for the crow joins the whitetail in its wariness of man, and often, it is the alarmed call of the sentry crow from treetop or fencepost that first alerts the deer to man's presence.

He would be ready for a similar assignment a little later in the summer. One day he would lick up a tasty snail from the ground and get, along with his snack, lungworms. The deer lungworm, *Leptostrongylus alpenae,* may infect half the whitetails in the herd. The worms hatch in the lungs, migrate up the bronchial passages to the trachea and to the throat. The deer swallows them and they are passed out of the body with the feces. They find their way from there to the bodies of little snails and the process continues.

Snails also enter the cycle of the deer in the process in which many deer acquire parasitic liver flukes. Deer pick up the flukes, in the larval stage, from lily pads or other marshy vegetation, or from snails. The flukes are worms; hunters often call them liver-rotting bloodsuckers; their biological name is *Fasciolides magna.* Whether ingested via snails or aquatic plants, they find their way to the liver, mature, and produce eggs that pass from the deer in the feces. If the eggs are dropped in wet places, they hatch into microscopic forms that attach themselves to plants or snails and the cycle begins again. The adults often found in deer are large flat brownish worms and they give the liver a scarred and mottled appearance. A hunter, looking forward to enjoying the taste of venison liver, is often disgusted by them. Yet they probably do the deer little harm, for the liver is an organ of excess capacity and the flukes are rarely fatal.

In fact, neither these parasites nor others play much role in the survival pattern of the whitetail. Only when weakened by hunger is the deer likely to succumb to any of the common diseases. It bears them at least as casually as men bear the common cold.

Now that the Little Buck is growing a little, looking around, becoming more mobile, he has found that he lives with a sizable herd of other deer. Perhaps thirty adult does share a range of a square mile or so, and each doe has a fawn or two, so that along the trails they use between cover and food and water, the population is fairly dense.

The Little Buck has seen other fawns, and they have explored each other's company. They touch noses, even lick at each other, and sometimes they frolic, running about together.

It would be nice to say they play. The storytellers have long populated sunny forest glades with little fawns at play while mothers beam and fathers watch proudly. The truth is somewhat different, perhaps less romantic but surely more natural.

If we may define play as a pattern of activity that is intentionally repeated solely for the pleasure it gives, with no special purpose of learning or security, it may be proposed that the deer does nothing that fits this definition. It is practical, a learning process, rather than an aimless pursuit of pleasure.

Fawns will jump and run together, and may even seem to playfully chase each other. But they are growing rapidly, and the new surges of strength that flow into their muscles make random activity as compelling as the morning stretch of a growing young person whose muscles need to be lengthened to their new size after the night's idleness.

Deer seem to practice some of the activities they will carry out more intentionally as adults, including the mating chase or domination fights. They may even leap over each other, but it can be argued that they may as well be leaping over any imaginary barrier and are learning to jump, a skill that they will develop to a high level. They may be led by a doe on a swim that is apparently aimless, but it can be said that the doe is teaching them not to fear the water, and how to find food in it.

The cartoonists have led us to believe in pretty places where the fawns play and the parents watch. And it would be pretty thinking to believe it was so, but I do not. I simply think that they are creatures of instinct, without the kind of brain development needed to make them creatures of play.

Early one July long ago, I went with my father to mow the hay in a field near the woods. We had seen deer there all our lives, and noted frequently places where the long grass was pressed down when the deer had made a bed. We went early one morning, and surprised several does and fawns feeding at a swamp edge. They fled the field for the cover of the woods, even the little ones by this time easily leaping a sagging fence. We watched in admiration, perhaps even a little in awe.

"They are the most graceful things in the world," said my father, a man not much given to poetry. I agreed.

Neither of us had ever seen a deer stumble over a snag, but they do. Some have scars on their bellies, proof of times when they scraped what they meant to leap.

One hunter found a snag in the belly of a deer he killed and butchered. A fir branch more than a foot long and half an inch thick had entered the body between the fourth and fifth ribs on the right side, had missed the lung, pierced the tip of the diaphragm and the point of the liver, and come to rest under the backbone. It had almost surely been forced there when the deer jumped or fell against it. No vital organ had been seriously damaged, and the animal was fat and healthy when killed. The body had healed itself around the snag. There was a tiny scar where the stick had been forced through the hide years before. It was a hardy deer, but a clumsy one.

It may seem odd to speak of a learned deer. But they live in the library-laboratory of nature, their students are their fawns, the course of study is survival, and only those that learn the curriculum live to see July. Of course they learn.

Precisely how much is an issue. Several articles in the scientific journals discuss the problem, try to measure the learning. One reporter measuring the distances and speed of retreat among deer on hunted land as compared to deer on protected land. The hunted deer ran quicker and farther. So we can assume that they learn some fear, and that the learning has been documented. I was not surprised; like millions of other boys raised on a farm or ranch in the wide range of the whitetail, I have watched them with fascination all my life and I saw a fawn learn something very special a long time ago.

Our back fields border forest and swamp, ideal deer range. Deer have always been there, they have never learned to fear the tractor much, and in July, as the grasses begin to dry and the heat lies heavy in the fields, they seem bolder, less flighty.

We were working a field near the woods one day in early July, and the deer would not have paid much attention, but the dog chose to come along to check things out, and the wise old doe with squatter's rights on a particular swamp edge became frightened, and fled.

She was wise to run; dogs are, in most of the Midwest, the most serious predator left. Here and there, bands of wild dogs, who were abandoned by their owners or vice versa, prey on the deer. They are most effective in winter, when the deer sink in the snow, but they can threaten in summer as well. Sometimes they are not wild dogs at all, but just an ad hoc pack of two or three or more teaming up for what they find fun—the chasing of the deer. Sometimes too their old instincts get the better of them, and they will kill, as though simply for sport, or fulfilling that ancient instinct.

Our dog was no wild dog, only a pet, and, as pets tend to be in farm families with numerous children, he was exceedingly domesticated, friendly, and playful. Also, he was well fed, and had no need to hunt for food.

But dogs love to chase things that flee from them, and now and then he had pursued, in his happy way, a bounding deer. It was a game for him, if not for them. One day in early July, he went back with us, and the doe fled, and he followed only a little way, not caring that much about chasing her. But she had left her fawn, and he stumbled on it, and it was still quite small and did not run from him.

The dog was interested, not malicious, and they nuzzled each other a little, filling their noses. They stayed together, not playing perhaps, but something stirring in each, something of those ancient instincts we know so little about, and they were together an hour or so, until we left on the tractor for the house and the dog trotted along. I imagine the doe was terrified when she reclaimed her fawn.

The dog had time on his paws and the scent in his nose, and he came back in a day or two and the small range of the deer presented no major search problem for him. He found the fawn, and again they explored each other, that strange bond between them.

We did not work the field for a while, and we forgot the incident, saw no more of this strange wild friendship.

And then in the fall we went to work the field again and the dog wagged along. I remember that it was afternoon, and the doe and fawn were startled from their feeding and ran. But then the fawn lagged behind, almost waited, and the dog ran up to it. They pushed their noses together, and walked odd little circles around each other. Then the fawn trotted away, and the dog went about his domestic business.

Individual deer learn many things for themselves, including fear. Or, in this case, some halfway state where curiosity reached a little way toward trust and perhaps even friendship.

Very early in July, a doe on the same range gave birth to triplets. She was unusual in that she had not been bred in her November day of heat. She came in heat again in mid-December, was bred, and dropped the three late fawns.

Two were healthy and strong, getting up quickly to nurse. The third struggled, but could not rise. She did not happen to lie down closely enough to it so it could get that first thrilling surge of milk. She was busy with the others, did not really notice, and the third fawn never touched her nipple, never tasted her milk, there was never any bond between them.

In only a few hours, the fawn's eyes glazed over very quickly and it died. The doe sniffed it once; there was nothing much for her to smell, no way for her to know it was a part of her; she paid no more attention.

Flies found the little body, laid eggs on it. The eggs quickly became a larvae called maggots, and in a few days only bits of hair were left. There is so little to a fawn, save that precious spark of life.

Late one July night, as a herd sorts through a swamp for browse, the deer reach the edge of a road. They have never quite mastered roads; they will pause at the edge of one, examine it closely, and then leap in front of a car often as not. The technology of highways and automobiles is simply too much for these creatures of such ancient instinct.

Some of the deer cross quickly to the other side, continuing their reconnaissance. One doe stands in the middle of the road, licking salt from the surface.

She is startled by the sound of a car and looks up, looks into the devil glare of headlights. She flashes the light back, for her eyes are provided with a reflector behind the retina to aid her in night vision. The reflector makes her several hundred times more sensitive to light when she is in darkness than when in daylight. The reflector gives her a second chance, in a sense, for night vision. But when she is hit with a light, she is flooded, her senses are overloaded, her instinctive network of responses is short-circuited.

"Look, a deer!" the girl in the car calls to the boy driving.

"Yes, and there's another alongside the road—see?" He moves his foot from accelerator to brake and slows the car but the deer, caught in its trance, moves away too late. The car is moving perhaps 30 miles an hour when it strikes the doe on her left shoulder. The girl screams and the doe tumbles into the ditch at the side of the road.

The car skids to a halt, the boy gets out to look at the fender. He finds blood and hair in the new creases. He goes back to look for the doe, but cannot find her. He swears to himself, and grumbles to the girl. He will have to pay for the damage to the car, and doesn't even have the venison from the deer to compensate him.

The doe struggles away from the road, her fear driving her to flight even as she dies. After 100 yards, she can go no farther and lies panting, bleeding. Her fawns come bleating after her but the body is cooling when they find her. She does not get up when they nuzzle at her udder. They draw out the last of her milk and wait.

The rest of the deer go on about their feeding, returning to cover by day, showing no interest in the dead doe. All the next day, the fawns bleat and become increasingly frantic. Another doe comes by once, and they run to nurse, and she kicks them away without paying much attention.

The doe fawn, a little smaller and weaker than the buck, dies on the third day. Her brother dies the next afternoon. Both are still near the mother's body.

In the town, men sympathize with the boy who had hit the deer. He makes arrangements to repair the fender.

One of the deer's most important enemies, the automobile, has accounted for three more unreported deer kills. No deer will ever identify the automobile as enemy, but in Michigan alone in 1969, 8,890 deer were reported killed by cars. Many others were struck and died undetected.

Eleven persons died in those collisions.

One such deer killed recently by an automobile and found was taken to a laboratory for dissection. The veterinary pathologist found a "madstone" in the rumen, and he cleaned it up and put it among his trophies.

Technically called a bezoar, or calculus, the "madstone" is found occasionally in the digestive tracts of deer and some other animals. In the deer, it is usually found in the frontal section of the stomach, rather than in the abomasum.

This one was typical; egg-shaped, slightly less than 2 inches long, weighing about 4 ounces. The nucleus can be any hard material—a tiny stone, a piece of nut shell. In this case, if the pathologist had cut to the center, he would have found a .22 caliber slug which someone had fired at the deer years earlier. The animal had not been fatally wounded and the slug had lodged in the stomach where the calculus built up around it. Minerals formed around the nucleus in alternating light and dark brownish layers, growing like the layers of wood in a tree, resembling a sedimentary rock. The surface became smooth and hard.

These objects have been known for centuries, and are called madstones because they were once thought to have magical properties. They could cure rabies, men believed, or neutralize poisons. But most of all, they could cure madness, and among ancient monarchs, who seemed always in special need of such cures, the madstones, covered with precious jewels, were prized gifts.

We are much more sophisticated and knowledgeable today, of course, and we no longer attribute any magic to the madstone. But we are not yet so sophisticated and knowledgeable that any scientist can give a reasonable explanation of why those intricate, delicately layered stones are formed.

But then, the whitetail has always been the object of strange beliefs. Long ago, the Apache Indians of Arizona poisoned their arrows by rolling the shaft in the liver of a deer which had been killed by rattlesnakes. There is no evidence, no reason to believe that this in fact put any poison on the arrows. No animal, and no man shot with them, showed any effects other than those of the arrows themselves.

Perhaps, though, before we make light of the Apaches, we should explain about the madstones. And we simply cannot.

At the end of July, the Little Buck is nearly two months old. He weighs just under 40 pounds, is nearly able to survive alone. He could easily escape a man who tried to capture him on foot. He could probably outrun a dog if he had to.

He follows his mother all the time now, keeping pace with her as they trot the trails between cover, swamp, and field.

But he is not fully grown up yet. The responsibilities still pulse strongly in her, and they sleep and rest apart. He is obedient, a good baby, and he sleeps soundly while, upwind, she stays alert and keeps watch for the vanished wolf.

August

The omens of August are hidden from man. Our senses are shallow and react best to the presence of immediate reality. An evening chill, a morning frost will remind us of impending winter. But the more subtle things, like the summer solstice, the longest day, pass without note. There is no observation, no holiday, no celebration of the threat of winter as there is, later, of the promise of spring. We know, if asked; we know that the earth is tipping away from the sun's rays; the rays are like the beam of a dipping searchlight that brightens, warms, and passes. We know the sun will soon swing away, and that when it dims, the planet will be left in the wreath of winter. But we do not think much about this. We live in the present, in the moment, our intellectual knowledge less moving than an instinct would be.

Not so the deer. They have no knowledge, and do not know, in any human sense of knowing, that winter is coming. But they have instinct, and it rules, that internal clock that ticks deeper inside them than can any knowledge, any consciousness. The instinct is ancient, their sense of survival has paced the rhythms of the year, memorized the turns of the seasons. For they are subject to the seasons, must prepare for winter, must change or die. The omens are felt, signals carried to the deer through endless space from ageless time, signals that have become part of the deer through millions of years, messages that nature sends to natural things.

. . . Begin, comes the faint whisper from the empty past. There is still no need to hurry, but there are things that must be done, done now, while there is still time. Begin . . .

So the winter of the deer begins in August, and it begins not in the meadows where the grasshoppers clatter in the brittle stalks of drying grass, nor in the steam of the swamps where the fireflies flicker in the night, but deep in the glands of the deer, triggered by the shortening of days that wither as the sun retreats. Their senses are deeper than ours, the message is an old one, and they know of the coming of winter and begin to make the changes needed for survival. They know what is needed, and they begin.

The coat must be changed. The fine hair of summer, which opened the skin of the deer to cooling breezes, must be replaced with a warmer, heavier, insulating coat. Ovaries which have lain idle for months must be activated so that young can be conceived; testicles that have been shrunken and dry must be roused for the frenzy of the breeding season. The body metabolism must be altered so that it can slow in the cold, to conserve energy.

But most immediately, most obviously, most gloriously, the symbol must be tended, the trophy polished; those great pointing racks of bone, the antlers, those Taj Mahals that the bucks grow up for the rut must be hardened, the velvet must be scraped away, the points brushed to a gleam, necks strengthened to carry them with style and flourish. And fat must be stored, to be spent soon in passion and in fury, then to be stored again for a winter reserve.

The deer cannot read our telegraph, nor can we read theirs.

So we understand only generally the messages they receive and the exceedingly complex reactions they make. Physicians and veterinarians and biologists and endocrinologists are working together to learn more about the process, and they have only begun to unravel the mystery. But even before their studies are complete, we can say that glandular secretions cause various biological changes in the deer. Many of the glandular reactions are interdependent, and the precise triggering mechanisms of the change are sometimes obscure.

Some of the things that happen are obvious, like the process of growing and shedding antlers. Other changes are becoming known through research, through the work of quiet, careful men and women who have the patience to begin the search back through time, to seek the answers to those ancient questions.

Up they spring, those incredible antlers, nourished by the lush growth of the early summer range, needed for mysterious purposes in the mating season.

Bucks a year or more old have been growing their antlers since May, and the growth will be complete now, sometime in mid-August. Deer farther north will finish a little earlier; farther south, a little later. But here in mid-Michigan, half-way between the north pole and the equator, growth will be complete about a third of the way from the summer to the winter solstice.

It takes time and energy for a big buck to grow a big rack of antlers.

Young bucks usually have the smallest antlers, though antler size is not a very precise measurement of a buck's age. Hunters are familiar with the "spikehorn": a buck with antlers that are simply single tines, rather than the larger racks with several forks, and points, on each antler. Such deer are usually found on poor ranges; the young "spikehorn" buck has had a difficult time making it through his first winter, and his body still needs to grow to reach full maturity. So the needs of growth will come before the energy is shared with antlers, and only spikes will appear.

It seems that if he survives that first winter, the summer

range will fill him out and in other years, he will find the nourishment to grow bigger antlers. The "trophy" racks, of eight or nine or ten points, are usually found on old bucks where the hunting pressure is light and they have had years to learn the fine points of survival and, as a result, have what might almost be called the leisure to grow great racks.

The diameter of antlers is a good indication of age in bucks; it may double by the time the buck is six or seven. Teeth are the real indicators of age, and the state of their wear is the best way to tell how old a deer really is.

And there are the legends; the legend of the "swamp buck," gray-black from his years in the dank swamp, clever and crafty, with an enormous rack—an animal that fits this description may be old or young, but certainly he is from a good range, for he needs much energy to grow the antlers, and his darker color is inherited, as is hair color among human beings.

The size potential, too, is inherited, as are long bodies or legs. There are different markings, within the variations of the species, and a hunter or gamekeeper can identify different deer as easily as a first-grade teacher identifies her pupils. Some biologists suspect that even specific patterns of antler growth are inherited.

But whatever the size and shape of the deer and the antlers, the messages from the sun control antler growth, which is completed in August. The "velvet," that soft placenta-like covering of skin that carried nourishment to the growing antlers through its maze of blood vessels, has completed its work. It begins to dry and die, and will fall free from the antlers or be rubbed away, clinging to a shrub and finally falling to the ground where it enters the cycle of nature again. It dies first at the tips, gradually down to the base in a matter of days late in August, and if the buck is not patient enough to let it fall he will rub it away. Perhaps it itches.

It is his irritated activity in brushing away the dead velvet, in rubbing hard the dying arteries on the outside of the antlers, and in polishing the tips of the antlers that give the buck the reputation of "shadowboxing" or of practicing to fight. In his passion to get the antlers clean, he may scrape the bark off dozens of trees. Unfortunately for some farmers, he may be feeding now in the waning days of summer in fruit orchards, and he may choose to rub against the bark of small trees. He may tear off so much of the bark that the tree dies; there have been reports of entire small orchards wiped out in a night by bucks with no regard for man's husbandry or for their own future food needs.

The velvet will be shed by the end of the month or shortly after; the polishing will be finished, and the man who sees the buck then will be impressed and delighted at the sight, and will report that the buck holds the antlers high and displays them with pride. It is probably more tension than pride, for the muscles are wiser than the brain in the wild; the big racks weigh several pounds and are cantilevered far out at the end of a long neck to make no small burden. The neck is strengthening to carry the load.

Testosterone, the primary sex hormone, is one of the key stimulants to antler growth. When the velvet is gone and the pedicles are solid and the rack secure, the hormone will be free from that task and ready to signal the enlargement of the testicles for the rut. There will begin the restlessness in the buck's loins, the faint early stirring of the lust that will drive him mad a little later.

Less glorious, perhaps, but more important in winter survival, is the August change in coat. All the whitetails begin to lose their summer pelage. The short fine hairs that helped to camouflage them in the leaves and light of summer have done their work. The summer coat was worn for three months, and it is time already to begin changing it for one better adapted to winter.

Hairs of the winter pelage grow from the same follicles that grow the hair of summer. The growth is regulated by hormonal changes, as is the growth of the antlers and the flow of the doe's milk. The summer hairs are crowded out, one by one, by the new hair and they fall away. In the spring, the winter coat fell quickly, loosening in patches and often licked away in a hurry. But the change for fall takes place more slowly. The new coat can be seen in changing colors through the old, the "blue" of winter replacing the "red" of summer, first on the neck and shoulders, finally on the belly and rump.

The winter hairs are short and fine at first, but they will grow to meet the coldness, becoming longer and expanding in diameter until midwinter. They are new now in late August, and lie flat and slick. But as the days and nights grow colder, they grow larger and crowd together until they stand upright and make the deer look smooth and sleek and fat into the later winter, even when fat and flesh are dropping away in hunger.

The hairs are hollow and, as they enlarge, the hollow centers fill with a pithy substance and insulate the deer so well that in winter, snow or frost may cover the animal without melting; the body heat is held close in a superbly efficient thermal blanket. By January, the hair that now, in August, is beginning to grow will be 2 inches long, crowded into a thick mat, and there will probably be a light growth of small, furry hair close to the skin, curling around the coarse hairs and completing the protection.

The Little Buck now makes his first change toward adulthood. He loses the fawn spots. He will never be spotted again. They were his protection, or part of it, in the spring of his life, when he was ungainly and slow; but he is quick now, nearly as fast as he will ever be, though not yet half his mature weight, and he has learned about danger by watching the other deer. So he graduates, one might say, to long pants.

Nature permits a little slippage in this matter; here and there, a deer or two may show a few spots as an adult. The chromosomal control will be slightly out of focus. But for the most part, the pattern will be the same, the coat of solid color, black fringes on face and legs, white tail, belly, and throat.

The hollow hairs of winter will float. Early observers of the whitetail noted that a deer shot in the water might sink in the summer but would float in the winter. They attributed this to the buoyancy of the coat, but it is probably due more to the fat in the body.

A few deer will have white patches; perhaps one in ten thousand will be all white. True albinos, complete with pink eyes that indicate absence of pigment, are rare, although there was once a herd on Grand Island north of the Michigan coast into Lake Superior in which the deer were largely white. But these are artificial conditions, created by man, who controls the predation levels. Nature is less tolerant of difference, unless it has specific survival value.

All these changes—the growth of new coat, the maturing of the antlers, and the beginnings of hormonal shifts—occur in a peaceful time. The restlessness that precedes the rut has not begun in August. As the demands on their bodies for nursing and for antler growth have lessened, the adults have begun to regain some of their winter weight loss. The doe has gained back some 10 pounds of the nearly 30 she lost in the winter. The Little Buck weighs more than 50 pounds; in another month it will be difficult to tell the spring fawns from the mature deer from any distance.

And it is at a distance that they are seen in August, for the most part; man is content to leave them alone, to catch a glimpse of them from time to time, to wait the more than two months until the season of the hunt begins in mid-November.

It was not always so for the whitetail. Natural predators take no season, nor did man when he and his weapons were more primitive, before the balance of nature came more under his control.

Some thousands of years ago, the mound-building Indians of North America killed the deer when they could. They ate the flesh for sustenance and the marrow of the bone as a delicacy. It was an animal central to their lives; they carved the leg bones into tools and made the shoulder bones into hoes fastened to the ends of wooden handles. They tanned the hides for moccasins and clothing. And the deer was more, even, than source of food and clothing and utensils; it became part of their legends and religions. They wore the antler racks as a ceremonial headgear and made the shapes of those graceful growths symbolic in their religions, as did many of the later Indian tribes across North America.

Farther south, the Aztecs did these things too, and they learned over the years ways of preserving the hides that were so effective that the few records of their civilization the Spaniards were not able to find and destroy are kept on buckskins tanned with that process, a process lost and not equaled since. The bits of hide with the odd marking on them survive today, as does the whitetail itself, always older than man's history, an air of mystery still holding.

In many areas of North America, the deer was more important to the Indian than was the Bison. The natives wrapped themselves against the winter in deer hides, learned how to make elaborate and decorative clothing from them. They sewed them together to make dwellings and respected the fact that the deer shared nature with them. So the Indians shared the land with them, hunting them in need with neither malice nor mercy.

The whitetail is known scientifically as *Odocoileus virginianus* because it was first seen in Old Virginia. Early explorers had noted them, smaller than the European deer and more curious, edging around the little outposts and available for meat and skins.

The first attempt the English made at a permanent colony in the New World was on Roanoke Island. Settlers were left with a year's supplies, and built their fort. But when the ship returned the next year, the people had vanished without a hint of where they went or why. Their buildings were left, there were no notes, no signs of massacre or struggle, no indication that they had been killed or driven off by Indians, no sign that they had been under attack. It was as though they had simply walked off one day, and whether they were driven away by fear or hunger, or lured by some promise, we will never know. The bewildered Englishmen who pondered the problem before they established another, more successful, settlement at Jamestown, wrote of what they found at the abandoned Roanoke settlement: "We found the fort razed down, but all the houses standing unhurt, saving that the nether rooms of them, and also of the fort, were overgrown with melons of divers sorts, and deer within them feeding on those melons. . . ."

It was the whitetail, specialist in bounding flight, that helped the frontiersman learn how to shoot with speed and accuracy.

The American pioneers were quick to expand the uses of the animal. They used deer tallow for making soap and candles, tanned the hides for clothing. Members of the Lewis and Clark expedition wore deerskin moccasins until they found them inadequate protection from thorns and learned then to make footgear from the tougher Buffalo hide.

Strips of buckskin were used for the netting in snowshoes and to patch telegraph lines. Antler racks were used as hat hangers, and as chandeliers. The bone was carved up for knife and pistol handles, and when all the usable pieces were gone for implements, the early Americans used the rest to make sizing for clothing and for the manufacture of ammonia. They stuffed their furniture with the hair.

When, a few years after the Revolution, Americans tried to establish the sovereign State of Franklin in eastern Tennessee, the governor's annual salary was set at one thousand deerskins. The Chief Justice was to be paid five hundred skins a year. By law, the citizens of Franklin set the value of a deerskin at 6 shillings, the same as the best beaver and otter skins.

Traders working among the Indians of the Mississippi Valley in frontier days swapped a quart of bad brandy for two skins.

As the population spread over the country, the settlers decided that they must control hunting if the deer were to survive. Rhode Island established the first season in 1646, and Connecticut and Massachusetts followed suit in a few years.

Across the new country, hides formed an important part of early American trade. Between 1775 and 1778, an estimated 2,601,152 pounds of deer skin, the hides of some

600,000 animals, were shipped from the port of Savannah to England.

As small cities grew, so grew the need for meat, and none was more prized than venison. From St. Paul, Minnesota, nearly 7,500 saddles of venison were shipped in November and December 1877. The meat sold for 8 to 10 cents a pound, and a hunter could shoot two to four thousand deer a year.

A trader near Waco, Texas, baled and shipped 75,000 skins between 1844 and 1853; such trade founded his and other Texas fortunes long before oil was important.

Wealthy colonists established deer parks, largely as scenic attractions. George Washington had such a park on his estate along the Potomac; he imported fallow deer from England and kept them along with the native whitetail.

As recently as the Second World War, venison and buck-skin were important to the economy of the United States. In 1942, an estimated 54 million pounds of dressed game, much of it deer meat, was taken from the forests. In 1943–44, patriotic hunters donated 238,262 buckskins to the military for use in clothing.

Today, the economy has changed, as has the country, and it is the hunting itself, the sport, that makes the deer of economic importance. In Michigan alone, deer hunters— tourists of a sort—spend at least $7–10 million each fall on travel, lodging, equipment and supplies. Similar amounts are spent in many other Eastern and Northern states, and in the West, where the mule deer is hunted. In many Northern towns, the hunting season is an economic boom time, a warm-up for skiing time.

Now and again, resourceful men have tried to domesticate the whitetail. All such efforts have failed. There is too lengthy a legacy of instinctive fear behind the whitetail. Wild deer struggle so desperately against men when cap-tured that they must be tranquilized to be shipped or stud-ied. They often kill themselves trying to escape nets or traps.

Even if they are raised from birth as pets, and have no fear of man, they may attack without warning. A doe defending fawns, a buck cornered in the breeding season, is unexpectedly quick and strong, and they have injured trusting keepers or others who have kept them as pets. They can be raised in captivity, and may appear tame as dogs, but must never be trusted, for they may turn on man without warning at any time. They are wild and will remain so; their tolerance of man may be high, but it is never complete; we are newcomers here, and they believe the place is theirs.

In late August, the Little Buck is less dependent on his mother. He wanders from her sometimes, exploring for himself, though never very far, for he returns to nurse. He is curious, and this may explain an action for which no other answer seems available.

Deer enjoy various fungus growths, including mushrooms. At times, mushrooms may even form an important part of their diet. Yet among all the dozens of species is one they will not take. It is *Amanita verna,* the "destroying angel," a mushroom so poisonous to man that it is almost always fatal.

But why do deer avoid it? It is probably not really very dangerous to them. The whitetail's digestive system is so different from that of man that perhaps the mushroom poison would not affect it, or at least it would be much less toxic. We do not really know how dangerous it is to deer, but we know they avoid it scrupulously.

Have they *learned* to pass it by? How to teach such a subtle thing, this one species to be avoided among all those dozens? And *why?*

Is it instinctive? If so, how can such an intricate discrimination be inherited? So many of the eating habits of the deer are learned, and they vary so from region to region and time to time, that it is difficult to comprehend how such a delicate piece of information might be transmitted through heredity.

Can it be the shape of the mushroom that enables the deer to discriminate against it? Or perhaps the smell? If so, how could this fear of a particular shape, a particular smell, so slightly different from so many other shapes and smells, be transmitted through generations? The deer, after all, will sample several hundred species of plants and dozens of different fungus.

We can speculate: Adult deer become quite conservative, taking food they are accustomed to, following old trails, wandering their ranges like an old man seeking always the same sunny park bench, knowing that there is warmth there if anywhere. They are so conservative that they may not eat corn even if they are starving, unless they have been introduced to it before. If one of the deer recognizes corn as food and eats, then the others will imitate, but there is need either for education or for one especially adventurous deer.

But fawns are less conservative, less learned, more willing to experiment and explore and test. A fawn may nuzzle a dog, may even become calm in the presence of man.

So can it be that does have seen their fawns sample that poisonous mushroom and die? Remember that the fawn's stomach is not yet a functioning rumen, is much more like the digestive system of a human, and so the mushroom would probably be more toxic. Perhaps the doe associates the death of a fawn with the taking of a particular mushroom, and avoids it herself.

This is highly speculative theory, but these are wild creatures, there are many mysteries about them, and this remains one.

So August ends. The dramas are internal, the days are serene, the food ample, and the deer stay as sedentary as possible, confining their range to the minimum size possible for the provision of their daily needs, content to extend their vacation from hunger.

. . . Rest, the silent voice might tell them. There is drama ahead, and violence aplenty. Build your strength . . .

September

It is September now, and fall is not far away, though the crystal chill of frost has not yet glazed the meadows and left them brown. In the swamp, night mists are colder and cling later in the mornings, but the coolness is hardly a noticeable discomfort to the sleek deer. Grasses that the doe sought in the spring for their succulence are sere now. The yellow dandelion that the Little Buck sampled as he was learning to eat is dormant. Chlorophyll is leaching from the leaves of the giant hardwoods, leaving behind the pigments and sugars that flash in brilliant colors briefly in the fall sun. The colors are a splendor that men will drive miles to see, and the doe walks beneath them daily, not knowing, for she is color-blind.

Her winter coat is pushing in rapidly now, as is that of the Little Buck. There are stirrings in her body, indistinct messages that she barely notes—not yet the stirrings of the breeding season, but the changes of other glands, early changes, like that of the thyroid that has begun to prepare itself to slow the body's metabolic rate in winter. And all the changes that began in August continue, though slowly.

The deer forage quite boldly, a little less cautious, often in open fields until midday, as though they sense those subtle omens and know that winter crowds near. They graze less, browse on seed plants more, and slip up in the night to taste the windfall apples in the orchards, find late berries and crab apples in the wild fence row, perhaps grain if there is any, nuts if any are around.

One morning, as the doe feeds, the breeze shifts a little and she lifts her head. Odors flood her nose and she is confused for a bit, because there are so many of them. But there is no threat in any of the smells, she hears nothing, and after a minute or two the wind changes, no longer brings the scent to her, and she returns to her feeding. The Little Buck smells all that too, and watches her, but when she does not bolt, he decides that the scents are not hostile.

The deer have smelled a plowed field. Three-quarters of a mile away, upwind, a farmer has turned down an old sod so he can work the ground for wheat. The plowing has broken a million stems, turned up trillions of bacteria, exposed fungus to the air, shattered the serenity of the soil, sent nature scurrying in a frenzy to react to the trauma of the plow. If the plowman had stood among the fresh furrows he would have smelled the outpouring of odors from the scattered spores and bacteria. Even high on his tractor, he was vaguely aware of it. But he washed it out of his consciousness as the doe screens out sounds and sights and smells not connected with danger. The odor of his plowing is not associated with his economic profit, and he pays no attention to it. But the doe survives with her nose, and all smells must be considered.

To say that the doe has a keen sense of smell is to say that the Rockies are rugged; it is true, but it is not enough. We must say that the deer is assaulted with smells; they slap her like a hand across her face, they flood her senses, electrify her brain, and the cataloguing of them is a primary duty of her intelligence. Odors can drive her to frantic flight or lure her half a mile to the delicacies of apples. They can irritate her, alert her, anger her, terrify her. Her sense of smell is like a tender nerve drawn across the world around her, and it tingles always in a million odors we will never know.

Olfaction is the sense of smell, a function of the olfactory epithelium, a tissue that lines the cavities of the nasal passages. It works because all living things constantly give off tiny odorous particles which are separating from the substance's essential oils. These particles drift in the air like blowing thistledown, invisible, molecular. They enter the nostrils and reach the moist olfactory tissues, the mucous membranes. The particles dissolve there in the moisture, and the chemical action of their dissolving is interpreted by the brain. The larger the quantity of epithelium, the greater the sense of smell.

A dog's sense of smell has been measured, and the result is simply not to be understood by men, although we can measure it. The dog has a hundred times as much epithelium in proportion to his body surface as has man. If the amount of tissue in his nose was stretched out in a single unit over the dog's body, it would be equal to one-eightieth of his skin. In man, the ratio of epithelium to surface skin is one to eight thousand.

The result in keenness of sense of smell is even more startling. Fatty acids are useful in testing, for they give off an odor that is easily identifiable. It is the primary odor of sweat. When a man works and perspires, he is pungent with the odor given off by the fatty acids in the sweat. If an animal runs and sweats, the odor is carried in the air and a pursuer is aided in the chase if he has a keen sense of smell.

To test the acuteness of a dog's sense of smell, men in a laboratory put a fatty acid in dilution. They diluted the mixture until they could no longer detect the presence of the fatty acid. At that point, the dog could still find it easily. They continued the dilution, trying to see how long it would be until the dog could no longer identify the smell. When the solution had been diluted ten million times below the level where men could no longer find the odor, the dog could still identify it. Thus the dog's behavior must be considered in the framework of a sense of smell so much more keen than ours that it is really impossible for us to comprehend.

So what of the doe? Her olfactory epithelium is much larger, proportionately, than man's. She can surely smell much better than we, but can she smell as well as a dog? We know a deer can catch the sharp scent of man at several hundred yards, can find an apple orchard perhaps half a mile away, and the buck can scent the doe in heat far away through the forest. They give great attention to the staining of their tarsal glands by urinating on them, and this must have some function.

One day, I sat near a doe who feared me but could not escape. I sat motionless, or as nearly so as possible, and was as silent as I could be. There was no breeze, as far as I could tell. She was curious about me, although she could hardly see me because of some wirework between us that confused her already diffuse vision. But she could smell me, and it was a smell of danger, but it was not identified, not catalogued, so she could not resist approaching, her nose stuck out at me, sniffing. She would come slowly nearer, and when she got perhaps 60 feet away, she would jump as though her nose had hit an electric wire, and she would whirl and run to the farthest corner of the enclosure. Then she would look back, peering intently, listening, waiting. From 75 feet away, she could hear me swallow and would react by turning away as though to flee. After a few minutes, her curiosity would overcome her and she would approach again, slowly, nose out, until the limits of my scent touched her and she would jerk away again.

I talked of this to a pathologist who had spent much of his lifetime in the study of deer. I asked him, "Precisely how well can the deer smell?"

He was indulgent enough with me, if amused. "Pretty well, I think."

I was exasperated and pressed the question. Finally, he was

able to make it clear to me. We can train the dog, who indulges us in his domesticity, and we can take him to the laboratory and conduct an experiment and write it down in the textbook that under controlled conditions, the dog can detect the odor of a fatty acid in solution ten million times more dilute than can man. But how to conduct such an experiment with a deer? We cannot harness its behavior to the rigors of the laboratory. We can dissect and describe its eyes, the auditory organs, the quantity of olfactory epithelium, and we can make highly educated guesses from such examination. But we cannot really test with precision.

How well can the whitetail see? Not very well, only vague and fuzzy shapes, as though the world was gray and out of focus, although it is excellent at detecting motion. It can hear quite well. It has a pretty good sense of smell. There is considerable privacy in wildness.

Because men like to hunt the whitetail, or merely to look at it, and because we have a long history of tampering with nature, trying to turn her to our increased advantage, we take great pains in managing the deer herd. Hunters want more deer, always more deer, and to that end many states have extensive establishments to study the deer and to find ways of preserving existing herds and increasing populations so the hunter, even the clumsy hunter, can bring home a trophy. Our efforts to invade the privacy of the wild animals on the land are steady and effective. Slowly, laboriously, expensively, and usually patiently, we replace the "common knowledge" and "folk wisdom" with scientific fact. It is difficult, and it is slow, though not so slow as the acceptance of new information by the sportsman who "knows" all about deer and is not about to have his knowledge cluttered up with changing information.

The difficulty of learning about deer, and the growing appreciation of what a complex animal it is, both biologically and in behavior, have generated a great respect from the biologist. It is a respect at least as large as that of the hunter, who must develop a deep appreciation of the cleverness of the whitetail. There are arguments between the hunter and biologist, but they share a realization that there are secrets that will long resist investigation.

A few years ago, professional biologists working with the questions of deer herd management met at a conference. They presented scientific papers, admitting sometimes as much ignorance as information, and then they fell to talking, to interpreting the nature of their problem.

One of the respected and senior members of the fraternity paid an impressively irritated tribute to the whitetail.

"It's almost predictable," he said, "that when researchers and deer managers get together, the deer managers will say we need some research to indicate to us what will happen if we treat a piece of land in a certain way. Have either the researchers or the managers ever sat down and tried to work out the various combinations—the astronomical number of combinations of factors that are working on a piece of land that determine what happens if you do this or that? They say, now, if you take a swamp edge, and cut it over *this* way, *this* will happen. In a pig's ear it will! It might happen sometime, but it isn't going to happen that way all the time. We'll be lucky if it responds that way ten per cent of the time.

"I wonder if the time will ever come when we can develop a good way to measure habitat. Sure, we can do it at the research level, but how do we do it statewide? How do you turn it over to all the district men and have them all working on the range measurements? They'd never do anything else. When could they do the prairie chicken dancing surveys and other things they have to do that are absolutely important? So we come up with ways to do this. Perhaps we can put a computer and then have it feed back the answers as to what the range conditions are. You know what the computer is— a deer. He takes all the data—all the known range factors and snow depth and everything else—and he puts them through his computer and he comes up with a certain physiological condition. Now we have to learn to measure those factors. Once we can learn to measure the deer and get the information out of him, we might be able to come to the point where we are carrying just enough deer or we are carrying too few deer. It is very difficult to measure range conditions—and do it on a practical basis so you can do it in the spring of the year before you set your hunting regulations. That's the practical end of the thing."

A colleague agreed: " . . . part of our problem, at least in the far north, is that we don't really understand what motivates this animal—what he's responding to . . ."

And another: "I agree about the difficulties here and it's sort of the Harvard law of animal behavior—under carefully controlled conditions, deer behave as they damned well please . . ."

It is the end of September now, and the Little Buck has a nearly complete set of teeth. There are eight incisiforms, twelve premolars, and four molars. He will grow, if he lives, eight more molars. But he will grow no more teeth until spring. The focus of life is shifting for him. There will be no more major demands on his body for a while. He can put on some fat now, store it against the coming winter. The good months are ending. The vacation is nearly at an end. He does not know it, but famine lurks in the chill of the night mist.

. . . And the voice that calls to him from that mist is cooler now, faintly ominous, but the message has no focus and is too faint to be heard . . .

October

For the big bucks, it is beginning. They polish in apparent aimlessness antlers that already gleam. They have wandered over their home range through the summer together, generally ignoring the does and fawns, displaying their indifferent companionship with each other. But now, every so often, one will turn to another, to a companion with which he has spent the summer in peaceful harmony, and lower his head, give the stare that is the first sign of the formalized, ritualized belligerence of the rut. But there is little of that, and nothing more; no crash of fighting, none of the driven maddening lust of November.

Now and then, an old buck lifts his head and sniffs, testing, waiting, searching for a forgotten scent. It will come to him soon, wafted thick across the field, a wild perfume that will lure him pounding in heedless hurry loud through the fallen leaves and dry underbrush. He waits for the maddening aroma of a doe in heat. It has been promised to him, promised by that prehistoric voice that stirs just beneath his consciousness.

But it does not come, and he forgets, and goes back to his feeding, waiting. It is beginning, but it is not yet.

October simply passes. It is a month of little drama; no major new activity begins. The whitetail is not a migratory animal, and its only major annual journey, the flight to the protection of the winter yard, is still to come.

Days shorten. Hormones continue their preparations for winter. The doe is fattening, as is the Little Buck. They gather seeds and berries and nuts and the late fruits of fall for treat and strength.

But the human activity that concerns the deer is never-ending, and we can safely leave the animals for a moment to take a little calm reflection while they enjoy the last calm days of their year . . .

We have said that the whitetail occupies an empty place on the invisible pyramid of nature, and that nature no longer needs the whitetail. But, as it was not enough to say the deer has a keen sense of smell, to dismiss it as futile in nature is to say too much.

Surely man does not need the whitetail; a few steers fattening in feed lots would replace the missed venison, and the alchemists in the factories would be happy to produce a synthetic substitute for the hide. If we did not hunt, perhaps nothing else would happen except that we might be driven a little closer to the violence of football, the current substitute for the gladiatorial games of Rome.

Still, we are children in the study of nature. So much remains unknown. There may be vital seeds that the deer carries from place to place, their work in controlling the growth of shrubs may be more important than we know. There are stitches in the fabric of nature that have purposes we do not understand, and we unravel them at our peril.

Even as we come to know more, we find new things that

we cannot explain. It is true in nature, as in all things, that as the island of knowledge rises higher, the shoreline that measures our ignorance becomes longer.

We have admitted our ignorance of the ultimate function of the antlers; let us do the same for the metatarsal glands, marked by tufts of white hair on the outside of the rear legs, at the joint that was once the ankle. We know that they must have a fairly important function, for the markings are one of the things that differentiate the various species of deer. But no biologist yet knows that function with any precision. Search the scientific literature, and you will find articles by pathologists who have dissected the gland and who describe it in minute detail. There are tentative guesses about its function. It touches the ground when the deer lies down, and may have some purpose in regulating body temperature in the lower half of the animal. The purpose may be more than that, or different. The secret persists.

Dilemmas remain, too, about many patterns of behavior. The deer fear man. This is partly through instinct, partly because they are taught this fear in the early days of imprinting when the mother teaches them to fear all things that she fears. Individual deer, exposed to hunters, learn this fear. Yet they are compellingly curious about us. We have talked about the penned doe so frightened she became spastic. Yet she screws up her courage again and again to inspect the danger as closely as she can. It is as though she needs to touch the danger, test it as a man tests the edge of a knife blade with his thumb. Why not simply look at the blade to see if it is sharp? Why wiggle a loose tooth? Why not hide at the far corner of the pen until danger passes? It is part of our nature, we say blandly, to wiggle the tooth and test the blade. Equally so, to hide patiently in the presence of an undefined danger is not in the deer's character.

Her character. Do not make her into a semi- or subhuman; she has those ancient instincts and survival patterns of her own, and is her own species. She does not have character in the sense that we speak of a respected friend as having character. But she has it, if we use the word in defining behavior among species and individual members of the species.

Deer form loose groupings. Some like large groups, some small ones, a few seem to like to be alone. Groups have similarities among their members; each group has a character. Some are more nervous, some more exploratory and wide-ranging, some more sedentary, some quite bold. Individual leadership is not much of a factor here. Dominance emerges largely in stress, as we shall see in the cases of the winter yard and to some extent in the rut. It tends then to be an expression of the animal's need to survive, either in the competition for food or for a mate. But it remains largely individual. Bucks take no harems, individually dominant deer collect no followings, groups have no apparent regular leaders, no family or group takes privileges to itself as a group. In starvation situations, if a doe can dominate a bale of hay or other bit of food, she does not include her offspring, much less a group, in her protection. The second-strongest individual takes second choice. There is no dominant group.

If they are individuals, they are not solitary, however. Nearly all prefer groupings. It does not seem to be common for individuals to strike out to new areas on their own. They have in fact a tremendous instinct for place.

We talked earlier about the overpopulation of the Kaibab in Arizona. When it became generally agreed that the population was too great, and yet the public shrank from mass slaughter, a plan was proposed by the famous Western novelist Zane Gray. He suggested that experienced cowboys simply round up the deer in the Kaibab and drive them out to new areas where the deer population was below range capacity.

It was an exciting idea, one that suited both the conservationists and those with a fondness for the romantic image of the cowboy. So the drive was organized, and whooping riders drove the deer in great herds down the long canyon to the opening where they would fan out into new areas.

But a strange thing happened. As the herd neared the edge of their known range, the deer began to resist the drive in increasing proportions. A few began to force their way back through the ranks of the cowboys. And when the herders reached the range border, not a single deer was driven before them. Every animal fought back through the line and stayed on the home range, to die if necessary, but to die in a place it knew. It was the most spectacularly unsuccessful drive in the history of the American West.

Yet, they do move into new territory; as has been mentioned, the numbers in southern sections of Midwestern states have increased dramatically in recent years. Farmers, less hospitable than hunters to large deer populations, are not totally enthusiastic about the change. They have accused the Department of Natural Resources of smuggling deer south in unmarked vans in the dark of night. The conservation officers can only plead innocence; and their ignorance of the way the deer move into new ranges.

The deer's instinct to group in winter, their ability to find things they need, are admitted as impressive if they are not understood.

When I was a boy of twelve or so on a farm in mid-Michigan, the snows came early one winter and a small patch of corn—five acres or so—was left in the field, standing in shocks in snow so deep we could not drive tractor and wagon out to bring them in. We were not especially concerned; the corn would freeze and winter there in the shocks as well as in the crib, and we would go and get it in the spring, husk it out and grind the grain for summer feed. The field was open on all sides, some three-fourths of the way up from the woods to the road and only 100 yards from the barn.

Deer have shared the place with us as long as anyone remembers. We see them in pairs and in small groups. Once, when I was a child, we even found a fawn, and took a picture of the spindly two of us wrapped around each other. Last summer, I spent considerable time watching a fine buck through binoculars, charting his moves, trying to think myself into his head while I contemplated the writing of this book. So it could not come as a surprise to us that there were deer in the area.

We were not prepared for what happened, though. That winter of the deep and early snow, we saw more deer than we had ever seen before. Somehow, they found the corn. We do not know how; if a faint scent drifted on the cold wind and they traced it from miles away, or if some wandering deer found it and somehow shared the information with the others. Either explanation seems improbable. But find it they did, and they spread the word up and down the swamps for miles around, and I know because I went up one afternoon in full daylight on some errand and I saw a hundred deer there, almost under my feet, picking at the shocks of corn, tearing away the husks, eating the corn from the cobs and eating parts of the husks, and stalks, too.

It was our corn, and we needed it for next summer's pigs, and we were furious. A shotgun fired in the air sent the herd flying, white tails up like a regatta of sailboats heeling in Long Island Sound, and they ran back to the woods.

They were back the next day, and the shotgun blast sent them only partway to cover. They waited, and a few minutes after I went back to the house, they trotted back to the corn. By the end of the week, the shotgun would cause them only to raise their heads to look curiously at the visitor. To separate them from the corn, we had to go out and chase them away by hand. Even then, they would run just beyond stone's throw, and be back in one end of the field by the time I reached the other. They stopped running from the dog, so he stopped chasing them.

We sought assistance from the conservation office, and were told quite clearly that the deer were wards of the state, that they were under their protection, that we could not shoot any under penalty of law, and that we must see to our corn ourselves.

We grudgingly admitted the beauty of the scene. Only on private hunting preserves in the North have I seen so many deer at one time. And somewhere, beneath the irritation of seeing our crop looted, there was the admission of our duty to share with our neighbors.

The situation raises more questions that it can possibly

answer. How did they find the corn, and how did so many find it? And where did they all come from? In that country, that many deer must have represented the total population for miles around. How did they all come there?

One has the impression of one deer finding the corn, telling the others in the group, and they in turn spreading the word by whitetail telegraph to the others starving in swamps around the county.

When we finally gathered the shocks in the spring, they were picked pretty clean. They had stolen two or three hundred bushels of corn from us. And we never saw such a herd again. While I would not have wanted the task of convincing my father of it at the time, it was probably a useful lesson in the long run. I remember it better than many a circus.

For everything we can confidently state about the deer, it seems we must make some exception. I suppose we should not be surprised about that; we have been studying them seriously for only a hundred years or so, while they have been around for millions of years, and we should be prepared to wait a while for all the answers. It is useful to have respect for our elders.

On occasion, as a boy on my way to get the cattle, I would find that there would be twenty heifers where there should be a dozen. The others were deer; they would choose the company of the cattle and graze together, almost a group, neither seeming to mind the presence of the other, the deer having chosen not to be alone.

I was always tremendously excited when that happened; there was an instinct in me to be thrilled to see a deer. I am still thrilled by them today. Perhaps if I knew why, I would have traced an instinct in myself as a hunter that has long been lost. If I could draw it out, perhaps on a psychiatrist's couch where I would find too the reason why snakes vibrate my nerve endings, then I would know something more about the history of my own species. And I might know how they found that corn and told each other about it.

In October, we are not far from the hunting season. The

leaves are falling, there are wisps of snow now and then, and heavy frosts in mid-Michigan. In a few weeks, we will take our rifles and we and the deer will stalk each other at the fringes of the woods.

My own first hunt was as a teenager. I had listened to tales told by city men, and I knew we had deer at the back of our place, so I bought a box of slugs for the 20-gauge shotgun and got up long before daylight of opening day, dressed and hid at the edge of the woods, shivering on a stump.

There was soon a crashing, snorting, and no more than 50 feet—it seemed like 10 feet—away a magnificent buck stopped to look at me. I held the shotgun in my hands, and we stood still for what seemed like a long time. Then, as though he had faced me down, he snorted, pawed a little, and went on about his business. When he was out of sight, I broke the gun, unloaded it, and went back up to the house to do the chores. I never told anyone about it, because I was afraid they would think me a sissy. But it seemed simply that I had no right to him, because I did not need him. It was as though there was an agreement between us. The place was big enough for both of us.

For many years, I did not hunt. Lately, I have taken it up again. I am very purposeful about it now, and quite successful.

We have gone to the north woods in the hunting season every fall for several years, a good friend and I, and our efforts have been rewarded every year. This may strike you as a much higher than average success; in Michigan, one of six or eight hunters brings home a deer. Perhaps we do better because we know something you do not know, so I will tell you about our hunts.

We have gone to the same place each year, a bit of woods in northeastern lower Michigan. It is quite open, with mixed hardwoods, some aspen and birch. There are open fields nearby, farms, swamps, and roads. For the last couple of years, we have begun the opening day at the same spots, he about two-thirds of the way up a hill behind a blind we have built, I against a tree nearly a quarter-mile away. We both command good views of places where deer feed or pass on their way from one feeding place to another.

He usually makes a fire. The odor of the woodsmoke kills his own, and he doesn't mind keeping warm and having something to do while he waits. I have made a fire in the past, but find it so interesting that I forget to watch for the deer, so I have given it up. I simply sit.

Sometimes, the deer wander past us. Other days, we seek them out, stir them up, perhaps taking turns, hoping that the other will have a good chance at one.

We get into the woods before daylight, and last fall, two deer drifted in front of me so close that even I, no marksman, could hardly have missed. But the ground haze was too thick, the early light too thin, and I could see no antlers. I did not shoot. In a little while, they drifted down the old logging road again, out of sight. They never made a sound that I could hear.

After a while, I sometimes get bored and I go over and talk with my friend, or perhaps make a circle. We know there are deer around, and sooner or later, they will come out.

Last year, while I was wandering over to the other blind, a big buck jumped up a few yards before me and ran. I had no decent shot, so I made as much noise as possible and ran after him; he seemed to be heading for the spot where Archie sat. I plunged along, and up to the blind, and asked him if he had seen the buck. He had seen or heard nothing. So I tracked the buck, and he had made a quick left turn, circled back to the place where I had startled him, and was apparently still in the trees on the hillside. The tree cover is quite open, and you can see through it, and I looked at it hard for a while. While Archie kept watch, I circled the area, and convinced myself that the buck was still in there, in the grove of trees on the knoll, in an area perhaps 200 yards square. I tramped it back and forth, and nothing showed.

In the course of our search, Archie had sat on a stump on a runway, while I circled the spot where the buck hid. I made the circle slowly, carefully, probably making no more noise than a foraging bear. When I reached a point where I thought

I could see everything that Archie could not, I sat down and decided to try waiting the old buck out. In a little while, I heard him move behind me; a sharp snap of a twig or branch, too loud to be made by a small animal. I waited, to be sure, and when another branch near the same spot broke loudly, I turned, slowly, watching carefully. Some 50 feet away, two birds sat near each other on a dry branch. The sound of their landing was the noise I heard. It had seemed so loud because my ears were opening up. The months of urban living, when the sounds of the city are screened out as the smell of the plowed field is screened out by the farmer, were slipping away, and I could hear again.

I had moved, broken my vigil, so I got up and continued the circle back to the stump where Archie waited. When I saw him, I was amused at his artistry in concealing himself. He had sat down behind a large bush, and only the vivid red of his coat revealed him to me. No color-blind buck would spot him. I walked up and just before I spoke, realized that the only thing there was a bush, not a man in a vivid red coat. As I looked at it, I saw that the bush was a faint tinge of rust, only slightly more red than the general tone of the fallen leaves. Yet my eyes had softened so to the subtleties of color that it struck me as vivid.

As I walked on to the place where he really waited, I thought about escalation. Escalation of sounds, so that the students in my classrooms enjoy music only at a volume that may threaten their hearing over a period of time. Escalation of colors, so that not even the psychedelic flashes of the brightest posters are enough any more, but must be enhanced by black lights and other artificial devices. No sounds have been sharper to me in a long time than the sound of those birds landing on that twig, no color brighter than that of the pale-rust bush. For a while, I thought it would be nice to share this, and then I realized how quick and vivid the world is today, and that not many of us have the patience for such subtleties.

We gave up that day's search for the old buck. The next morning I found the tracks where he had stood, waiting, a few yards from one place I walked. He walked out after I had tired of the search, not hurrying, passing a few feet from my original stand. I hope he was amused by our futile efforts to run him down, but I am afraid he was more likely disdainful.

I have not fired at a deer for several years now, though Archie bagged a fine one last fall. In perfect honesty, I am not sure I could kill a buck. I have no criticism of those who do, and realize the necessity of the harvest for the survival of the herd. I know too that the odds are much more in favor of the deer than I once thought. Their instincts do well against our rifles, their abilities to hide far exceed our ability to stalk. But though I know of the need to hunt and harvest, we keep to our more passive role, sharing the woods with the deer, and we do not measure our success in the antlers and venison brought home. For a day or so, after we come back, my ears are offended by sirens and such, and then they close up again, and I hear less. My eyes and ears become urban. Maybe next fall I will hear a bird again, find that bush, and we will have had a successful hunt once more.

But in our calendar, October is ending. For the deer, it is finally to begin, that swirl through the whirlwind. The quiet voice of instinct will scream and shout.

November

It is November now and all the barriers are broken, all the rules suspended, there is no caution, the rhythm of the year is shattered, for the maddening odor of the rut is in the air and all the laws are forgotten save one—the law of reproduction, the need to mate, to breed, to continue the species so that again next year, no matter what toll the winter takes, there will be survivors.

The mating of the whitetail deer takes no time for the tenderness that many animals share. There is no permanence of pairing, as is so common among male and female in the wild; no affection, no joy. There will be only the maddened drive to implant the seed, to impregnate, each buck seeking as many does as will accept him, each doe standing for any buck to mount her in her brief day of heat, the buck plunging over the range without caution until the season has passed and the rage is spent.

Family units dissolve; bucks in their second year may have maintained a loose association with their mother, but they are ready to breed and they separate from their family and begin the lonely driven life of the whitetail buck. Does the same age will be in heat, attracting the bucks, and at least for a time they will separate from the familiar group. Mature does will confuse their spring fawns by their odd behavior, though the fawns may rejoin her after she is bred.

One of the first to know is a gamey old buck. He is the father of the Little Buck, but neither knows nor cares. In the indifferent, unattached loneliness of the wild deer, there are no fathers and sons, only old bucks and young ones.

He is tough and strong, in his prime at five or six, on the prod, on the muscle, testing the air in impatience for that hot scent of the breeding season, anxious to begin—for he remembers, or nearly so. Real memory, on the level of the human brain, is beyond him. He cannot store in his mind an impression or an image and call it up at will. He can learn successful reactions to experience, and when similar experiences confront him again, he can behave in the ways he has found that work. What he has of memory lies somewhere in a gray unmeasured distance between simple animal instinct and human memory; somewhere between the dark silence of ignorant confusion and the clarity of that mysterious voice that sometimes whispers instructions to him. But he knows, somehow, that there are messages to come. Now, in November, at the beginning of drama, he is much closer to the light of memory than to the dark of blind instinct.

His testicles are ready now, pulsing with life, strong after the long dormancy of winter and the summer antler growth, and they flood his body with the hormones of desire, dominate his behavior as he drives to find a receptive doe. He has been through it before, this fellow, he is ready, and he is impatient for it to begin.

Restless, he finds a spot of soft earth near a swamp edge. Repeatedly, determinedly, he urinates in it, paws and stamps until the churned mud reeks, and then he rolls in it, covering himself with the filthy mess in a bold advertisement of himself, a stinking testimony that he is virile and eager, and he roams his range smelling to high heaven. Or at least, he hopes, as high as the nearest ovulating doe.

It is unusual these days for whitetails to build this "soiling pit." It is more common for the Red deer of Europe to do so; some biologists have never seen such a pit among whitetails, doubt reports of such behavior. But the old literature, the reports of observers who watched the whitetail before the pressures of human population had the impact on their behavior that it does today, reported the activity as though it were common. It may be that this is another of the habits that the deer had when their range was more distant from men, when their behavior was, like ours, less corrupted. We do not really know, after all, how much change there has been, what behavior patterns have altered. Penned deer behave differently from totally wild deer; our heavy intrusive presence has perhaps put the shadow of a pen around all the deer.

For most of the year, adult bucks associate in a kind of cool tolerance of each other, without any displays of affection but apparently preferring this cautious companionship to solitude. Now they are likely to be hostile, suspicious of each other, and while in the rut they form a little territory around themselves, a little space in which they assert the primary right to a doe, and they may fight if they think that they are threatened. It is not a static territory, rather a little distance around them, wherever they happen to be, breathing room, or perhaps sniffing room.

As the doe became more than a passive survivor when she gave birth, the buck now ends his time as passive eater of browse and grower of antlers and takes an active role, the role of breeder.

He has been hunted, this old buck, and he escaped from the rifle fire unhurt and hid until the men left. He will react cautiously to the hunter, as he reacts in caution to any potential predator. But his primary instinct now is to breed, and there is little in him of caution.

Ready to breed for weeks, frustrated by the absence of a willing doe, he has become more and more irritable. His major test of strength came the week before, from a buck he had wandered with much of the past year. He suddenly decided that the other buck, younger but about his size, was a threat and he moved to eliminate the challenge.

The two deer stared at each other, a long fixed glare while they stood stiff-legged, ears flat against their necks, heads extended and lowered a little, a rare and rigid pose, the first stage in challenge between two bucks. Usually it is enough; one buck will yield and turn away, and that will be the end of it. But that day the stares continued until the old buck jacked the challenge up a notch.

He began to sidle toward the younger deer, turning about 30 degrees to one side, holding his head high now and tucking in his chin. He erected the hair along his back and rear legs and took several stiff steps toward the other buck.

Still the younger buck did not yield, and the old one put his head down, thrusting his antlers forward.

The pattern was not new so far; in several places and in years past, the old buck had gone through this ritual and at the antler threat the other buck had wheeled and abandoned the challenge. Not this day, however; the dominance of the older buck would have to be established by force. The younger one thrust his antlers forward.

As though at a signal, both charged, their antlers crashed together, and they were joined in combat, pushing with their heads.

Antlers are not weapons in such a fight; the prongs keep them from touching each other's heads.

Both the bucks were as strong as they would ever be. The summer range had been a healthy one, and since their antlers had matured they had fleshed out and put on some fat. The effort of carrying the antlers and the exercise of scrubbing off the velvet had strengthened their necks, which were half again as big now as at other times in the year. Their necks had swelled, too, from hormonal action which expanded them in an action similar to that which causes males of some species to grow crests.

Blowing and snorting, the two bucks shoved at each other, pawing up the earth like angry bulls, turning slowly in great circles, neither able to force the other to give ground. They pushed and shoved for nearly an hour, strong in muscle and will, not separating after the first contact was made. They drew no gallery; other deer wandered by or watched with at most marginal interest. Their tongues hung out as they gasped and panted with the effort and then suddenly the young buck slipped and lost a step backward, then another, and a third. He freed himself from the struggle by leaping quickly away; he turned and fled, and the old buck pursued only a token step or two, tossed his head in relief, and looked about him. No other buck challenged him. It was over. He had proven himself, he had won, and he was alone again.

There are great woodsmen's tales of bucks fighting to the death, of locking their antlers together so that they cannot separate and starving as a result. They are fine tales to tell around hunters' fires and they should be told, for there are traces of truth in them. Now and then, bucks do become locked in combat and do starve. But such a thing is so rare that few have ever found evidence of it. The appeal of the tale is in its rarity.

Bucks never deliberately fight to the death; the only fights that end in death are a result of some accident such as antler locking. And the antlers are not used as weapons; the fights are shoving contests. Nature is usually too selfish to allow members of a species to kill one another.

In captivity, the end may not be so clean. A buck at the peak of his lust would kill a doe if she refused to stand for him. In the wild, she would simply run away. Bucks in breeding farms will injure each other if their antlers are not removed; it is because there is no room to escape, no place to go. The instinct is to protect a space, not to destroy, and deaths are accidental or a product of an unnatural condition.

Even such fights as the one the old buck won are rare; usually, posturing will do, and the assertion of dominance is more a test of nerve than of strength.

For several days, the old buck rushed to sniff at the vulva of every doe he saw. None was quite in heat, and they would not stand for him but ran away.

Then one morning the scent came, and he went for the doe in a great almost clumsy rush and found her to be only a day from estrus and he postured and the other bucks left him and he stayed with her, eager, following when she fled, oblivious of food, attentive, almost kind to her as he waited.

She was ready in the morning, and he mounted her and drove himself in, copulating for perhaps thirty seconds, nearly knocking her to her knees as he thrust himself to ejaculation and then stood beside her with his madness spent for a moment, and for a few brief hours of her heat, there was something nearly like fondness between them.

They mated three or four times that day, and the doe stood for any other buck that would mount her. The bolder ones, deferential to the old buck but with their need too, would service her when he was too spent to interfere.

By the next morning, it was over for the doe, she no longer accepted the buck, and he followed her for a few hours to be sure that it was finished and left her, seeking over the range for another mate.

Before November ended the old buck mated with half a dozen does, seeking them out, staying with them in their day of heat, leaving each to find another. Nearly all does are bred in their first heat; only a few have a second estrus. Now and then, a doe will conceive late in the winter, but by then the peak of the passion will be behind them and the late-fawning doe is a rarity, as is the barren one. So her sex life is little more than a moment, one desperate day each year, while his is a matter of madness, and he is driven by it; as long as the odors are in the air he is heedless of distance or danger, he goes without eating, a creature possessed by perhaps the most central need of nature.

A doe may be pursued when she is not ready for mating;

she becomes wise in the ways of escape. In a forest where deer were sometimes trapped for study, an enclosure was built with one fence on a steep slope so that a deer could easily jump into it but once inside could not get back out. A doe learned to elude an ardent suitor by running full for the fence, turning just before reaching it, and the careless buck would often as not jump inside. Every morning in the breeding season, the keepers would open the gates and set loose a buck or two who had been tricked by the wily old doe.

There is a covering of snow some mornings, the first the Little Buck has seen, but the adults have no attention to give to it, and the Little Buck, watching, learns that this drift of snow is not a matter of importance. He is curious, and sniffs the snow, and tastes it, and finds that it becomes water, and he can live without drinking if there is snow to eat.

Now into this confusion comes man, driven, like the buck, by a need he understands only dimly, driven into the woods to hunt the deer, and he brings with him many things.

He brings food, in cans and boxes and bags, for even if he is successful in his hunt, the deer is to be taken home as a symbol of success, served to family and shared with friends, food too important to be entirely consumed in camp. It is more important as a symbol than as nourishment.

He carries clothes of vivid orange or bright red, to show his colors in the cover and distinguish him from the deer so that no armed hunter will shoot him. They are not clothes to be worn for their warmth at other times of the year, but clothing to be set aside, laid away, a special uniform for a special event.

He brings knives and axes and lengths of rope to serve his briefly bloody purposes if he is successful in bringing down a deer.

He brings firearms; weapons to hurl a lead slug weighing about a third of an ounce nearly half a mile in a second with great accuracy; firearms machined and honed. And rifles; firearms with sharp scents of oil and care; firearms with clattering mechanisms of levers and slides, warm wood stocks to touch his cheek at the moment of action, firearms with triggers and actions and curves that draw their owners with a force of affection far beyond the simple usefulness of weaponry.

You will see no plastic stocks on these weapons, you will find none without some ornamentation; and if you are in a hunters' camp at night, you will find the hunters testing the working parts, handling the weapons, talking about them, fondling them absently as you might scratch the ears of a faithful dog, not checking them out as a soldier would on the evening of battle, but something more than that, more personal, for the firearms are part of the reason for being there, they are almost as important as the deer.

Some men hunt in the camps of their habit, going back year after year to the same places with the same friends, sitting in the same blinds or on the same stumps, watching the same shrubbery and runways, at home in familiar places, and they have not checked reports of deer populations and moved their camps accordingly, for they know better than the experts, they know why they are here, and the reason is more than the deer alone.

Many men support deer preserves, and they devote time and money for years to provide a lodge and ensure the presence of a deer herd. They may be members of large organizations and the families may come to the lodge in summer to enjoy the woods and the quiet, but the hunt is what supports the place.

Some stay in motels, and venture out in the morning nourished by the Hunter's Special at the Holiday Inn. Some stay in wretched hovels of shacks, quarters they would scorn in the city, happy with rude meals that they would reject at home, praising a friend for cooking that they would send back to the kitchen at their favorite restaurant. For that is part of the adventure too, the pleasure of roughing it, a contact with the old ways, keeping in touch with the lingering instincts of the hardships of the hunt as it was practiced in the cold dark days of the cave and the hut.

It is easy enough to describe the deer hunter statistically. Detailed studies have been done in most states; the Michigan results are used here, and they do not vary much from state to state.

One out of four of all men living in Michigan who are between the ages of twenty-five and forty-four hunt deer regularly. Only 7 per cent of all hunters are women. Hunters represent an almost exact cross section of population in that they have about median education, are of median age and median income. The proportion of blue-collar workers to white-collar workers is about the same as the proportion of blue-collar hunters to white-collar hunters.

The average hunting group is five, and they hunt for slightly more than eight days a season, or the amount of time available in a week's vacation. About 70 per cent of deer hunters in Michigan hunt small game also. The hunter who lives in the north has killed an average of twelve deer over his lifetime, while the hunter who lives in the southern part of the state has killed three deer. Northern Michigan hunters seek the deer near home, southern Michigan hunters fan out across the state. Only 18 per cent hunt in their home counties.

Few have made much apparent effort to expand their knowledge about deer through the facilities of the Department of Natural Resources; nearly 90 per cent have never attended a meeting, hearing, or demonstration sponsored by that agency, which is responsible for deer herd management in Michigan.

They cling to their "common knowledge" about deer; nearly half say they can tell the difference between the tracks of does and bucks, while professional biologists admit that they cannot—they can tell only which deer are larger, and guess from that.

Hunters have an aversion to killing does, resistance to killing the female of the species, and the reasons can only be guessed at; there is the desire for the rack of antlers as a trophy, some vague feeling that it is not "sportsmanlike" to kill a doe, a desire to preserve the herd, an expressed aversion to taking the life of a female who is possibly, in the hunting season, pregnant.

Some statistics are not readily available—how many go simply for a vacation, or for the companionship of old friends in an all-male atmosphere (the classic "stag party," after all), or a love of the out-of-doors or the challenge of the hunt or a simple mute need to touch the past, to pay homage to a time that flickers in memories so dim that they are aroused only by wood fires in dark places, memories of a time when the successful hunter was the good provider, the simple moment of the man who fulfilled his duty when he brought a carcass home from the forest and put it before his family.

For tens of thousands of years, we lived as food gatherers and hunters. In those times, we learned things as the deer learns them; slowly, over long stretches of time and through long immersion in repeated experience. Such instincts do not vanish without a trace simply because a man lives in the age of factories and plastic, and has signed on to work by the hour or the year in a plant or an office. Some things are learned quite readily in a matter of a few years; the programming of a computer, say, or, less easily, the nasty and lonely business of constructing a readable sentence in the recalcitrant English language. But the skill of the successful hunter comes with more difficulty, and it came to man over countless generations, hard-won knowledge nurtured with care and passed on with concern from father to son, a skill prized beyond treasure because it enabled survival, and we institutionalized it and added ritual and it was part of our lives, not so long ago, when the women and children tended the fires in the caves and waited patiently. These instincts are set loose by the snap of a twig or the flash of the white deer tail. Or perhaps by some distant voice of our own, that warns of the coming winter, that takes note of the shortening days, that makes some change in our own glands. We have such voices, as do the deer, and part of their authority is in instinct and part of it is in something else.

So we will hunt, and we will not be entirely rational about

it, for there are reasons tucked away in lost corners of our brains, and if we do not understand it all and cannot explain it all, do not press us for complete answers. For we are men, and there is much we do not know about ourselves, and in that there is privacy along with the fear, and, sometimes, there is unexplained joy.

They do not remember about the annual hunt, the deer; their biological clocks are automatic, controlled by other means for other purposes, and they do not post a warning that the hunting season is near, for men's laws are new and the instincts of the deer are very, very old. There have been seasons for hunting in Michigan, for example, for not quite 120 years—the first was in 1859—and longer in the East. That is not long to the deer, who is still worried about the wolf or even the tiger of a dozen thousand years ago.

So they are surprised, even the old buck, searching for the scent of a ready doe, to find there the scent of man, an odor uncommon in the range, but one to trigger fear. He is surprised, too, when he hears the first gunshots, and they do not matter much to him, for there is no connection for him between sharp sounds and danger. What alarms him are strange things; strange scents, strange actions, strange shapes.

Late in the month, he was tracking a doe by scent one morning. There was only a little light about him, nothing else that he paid attention to. He had left the last of his several mates two days ago, had not found a new one, and the pressure was building up, the need was sharp in his loins. There were hints of smells in the air that would usually alert him to special caution, but this is not the season for caution, for the survival needs are in conflict with each other.

He crashed along his way, stopping now and then to rub the air against his senses, and he was within 20 feet of the seated hunter before he knew. Then there was the motion as the man leaped to his feet, a scream of action as the rifle was raised, the hot blow that struck the buck in his chest. He sprang straight past the hunter, up a slope, and the two shots that followed him were wide, for his hair was all up, the white splash of the flanks looked wide as a racing sail, his tail was up and flying like the windsock at an airport. He looked double his real size and although the excited hunter fired twice more, neither of the later shots came very near him. The buck gained the top of the hill and was out of the sight of the hunter.

But he was dead; it had been a good shot, the 170-grain slug from the .30–.30 had entered his chest at 2,250 feet per second, expanded quickly as it tore through hide and tissue, was distorted and flattened and nearly twice its original size by the time it reached the heart and tore it apart and passed on out the other side of the body. It still had force then to fly against a tree and scar the bark and stick there, the mark of man in the forest.

The buck had been walking at about 4 miles an hour when he was hit. He reached a bounding speed of nearly 30 up the slope as the last motions of his exploded heart sprayed the blood inside him, and he made more than 100 yards before his strength dissolved. His front legs collapsed and he fell nose first into the dry leaves. His hind quarters pushed a stroke or two and he twitched a few more times while his eyes lost their light and then it was over. He was still by the time the running hunter reached him.

The noise of the shot carried through the deer range, and across a swamp and up a hill a quarter of a mile away, where the doe Alpha and the Little Buck were feeding, and they heard. But the sound made no impression on them.

The Little Buck had noted the foreign, intruding smells and was watching his mother carefully. He watched her lift her head at the odors and turn her ears toward the sharp sounds, but the threat kept its distance and the range was good, so they fed. Her body was urging her to store fat, and she paid little attention. The Little Buck was not very alarmed.

Then suddenly there was a hunter before them, too; a whirlwind of sharp scents and quick motions and strange clicking sounds. They spun in a single motion and ran, tails up, all white flag to the hunter, who had seen no antlers and knew that his hand was stayed by law. So the Little Buck was not too concerned over the threat, it had been easy to escape, and he kept his curiosity. If death were to come to him from man, it would be quick and without lesson for him, but he did not know this and he was happy to stay with his mother, who had calmed again after that strange day with the old buck, and he felt safe.

There was a mature buck in another place on the range and he knew more. He had been near a hunter in dusk a year ago and the tongue of fire had passed across his chest and gone away to be spent in the forest, but pain was imprinted on his mind now and when he found the trace of gun oil and sweat in the air he knew.

He did not run, for he was able to judge how far the hunter was and he wanted to find the threat and fix it in place like he might fix an oak tree, keeping clear of one and returning to the other for the treat of the acorn.

The buck found the hunter and watched him, decided that this was a manageable threat and slipped away to go about his business with the special care that seemed called for in these strange days.

The hunter concluded that there were no deer in that part of the forest; he had sharp eyes, after all, and was well armed, and knew the ways of the whitetail, and that what was needed was better management to fill the woods with deer so that his adventure would be complete for telling around the bar in winter.

Of all the myths men nourish to bolster their self-confidence, perhaps none is more exaggerated than the belief in the ability to find and kill deer at will. Hunters complain about the game biologists, insist that the herds are depleted and that the woods are empty of game and the does are barren. They refuse to believe that deer starve by the thousands because of overpopulation—after all, they spent several days in those woods and saw no deer. They refuse to shoot does, out of some sense of gallantry, perhaps, not willing to accept the notion that overpopulation means fewer deer, not more.

Perhaps one of the most striking evidences of the ability of deer to evade hunters is established by the case of South Fox Island. This was mentioned earlier; officials planted fifteen deer on a 5-square-mile island and the population exploded to perhaps six hundred in seven years. Game officers established a special hunt designed to reduce the population and bring it in balance with the carrying capacity of the range.

In 1970, the Michigan Department of Natural Resources issued 612 hunting permits. The hunters were allowed to take any deer they saw, and to take two or three. The importance of the allowance for taking more than one is that many hunters, seeking a trophy of a big rack of antlers, will often pass by a doe or a small buck, even if it would be legal to kill them, because they want to hold out for a trophy. In this case, they could shoot any deer, knowing that there would still be a chance for a trophy.

There were more than one hundred deer per square mile on the island, or more than one for every 6 acres. There were an equal number of hunters, operating without restraints, and they had as long as nine weeks to hunt.

Incredibly, more than half the hunters—54 per cent—never bagged a deer. Thirty-one per cent of all the hunters shot a single deer; 14 per cent shot two, and only 1 per cent of all the hunters—six persons—shot three deer, as they were permitted to do.

The hunters shot 108 adult bucks, 134 adult does, and 140 fawns, for a total of 382 deer. Despite the intensity of the hunt, after nine weeks of hunting, nearly half of the original deer were alive, in roughly the same balance of age groups and sexes as before the hunt; unless the special season were repeated annually, it seemed likely that the herd would exceed its peak population again within two years.

The statistics illustrate the explosive biotic potential of the deer, and the experience demonstrates the ability of the deer to escape the hunter.

And so, with the deer rather more relaxed and unconcerned than the more tender observer might expect, with the balance of the contest between hunter and deer rather more even than one would anticipate, the season ends. The hunter had prepared himself with all the power of his technology, and the deer had responded with their tens of thousands of years of instincts and their superb senses, and battle had been a rather fair one after all. The hunt was not such a thing of horror—the real horror lay ahead, in the deep snow and bitter nights of winter.

The hunt question must be posed cleanly and answered personally.

Is it unmanly, inhuman, to hunt, to kill?

It would be difficult to say that it is not manlike to hunt and kill, for thus we survived for eons, taking plants or animals from nature, only recently domesticating both. We have hunted longer than we have farmed, and we remember. Nor can we say very convincingly that it is inhuman to hunt deer but human to enjoy a prize fight between boxers or wrestlers, to savor football. Even the most gentle of us may take quiet pleasure in winning a game of bridge or chess, or at least in the spirit of the competition.

But is it not unkind to take the life of a deer violently, with a firearm, letting the lifeblood out on the land? It is a choice we must make, for we are, artificially, the major surviving predator. We have driven the others away, and with our instincts to preserve the life of the deer, we feed and protect and care for them and they multiply. It is a simple choice then to kill them as quickly and as cleanly as possible, more neatly than the wolves and mountain lions do sometimes, perhaps with less terror in pursuit and anguish in dying, or to let them grow old and die when their teeth are worn away or to suffer from their own tendency to overpopulate and starve slowly in the cold.

It is not a choice that can be avoided; inaction leads to overpopulation and starving, the cycle is inexorable.

How difficult is the death in the barren winter? Listen; a few deer on our range will soon know.

. . . And the voice from the instinct of space has no lilt any more, and no promise, but only a chilling urgency that calls the deer to icy death. The doe hears, and she is nearly angry again, for the cold touches her and she would seek refuge, would have the chalice pass from her. But it is not to be—the role is set—the director beckons . . .

December

Now the winter solstice draws near. It is the dark time, when there is less light and more night than in any other season, the nadir of the year, the season when our barbaric ancestors dragged an evergreen tree indoors and made desperate celebration, begging the gods to turn the sun back toward them and return the promise of spring. It is time for the deer to end the orgy of the rut, to settle back to sanity and caution, and, as with a man who was the loud life of the party a few moments ago and now drowses in the back seat on the way home, the madness departs the deer and the careful ways of the fugitive return. The edge of winter is upon them.

The winter preparations that began in August are nearly complete. Antlers have fulfilled their ambiguous mission and begin to loosen. The union of bone that welded them to the skull begins to die and weaken. It may be that the death is caused by new life; the very early beginning of the growth of a new base for next year's antlers may bring about the rotting of the foundation for the old. In any case, in a month or so the antlers will fall off, to be eaten by other animals, recycled, to vanish.

Many secrets persist in the antler-shedding process, as they do in the process of growth, and especially in the reason for growth of antlers. It was once assumed that strong animals kept their antlers longer, and the weaker ones lost theirs first. Then the researchers demonstrated that the healthiest bucks were the first to lose their antlers, and it was assumed that the shedding process was a deliberate one, an active sloughing off of something no longer needed or wanted, as is the sloughing off of a snake's skin.

But a biologist friend wrote to me recently about a curious thing that happened on a large breeding farm in Michigan. The deer there had been supporting themselves for years on the natural range, and the managers decided to convert some to artificial feeding for research purposes. The result was healthier, stronger deer. And in the spring, the bucks still had their antlers. The experts, my friend among them, simply throw up their hands in bafflement. One learns a great deal of respect for the private ways of wild things.

Alpha's milk production is finished. The Little Buck is on his own now in the matter of nourishment. His mother will abide his company, show him the winter refuge, allow him to tag along. But she is more guardian now than mother, something of an older companion with experience in the wild, rich in the knowledge of the range, tuned to the changing sources of food and practiced in the elemental art of survival. The breeding season cut the instinctive umbilical cord that bound them together; the flood of instincts that caused her to care for him is ended, the voice speaks to her of other things now.

Their thoughts are on survival again, the selfish thoughts of simple things, inward thoughts. The broader cares that come with parenthood or the breeding season have narrowed down again to the narrowest thought of all; to stay alive. It is a thought that will glow warmer as the days grow colder, and in a short time will be a single tiny hot spark of determination that will be very nearly all that stands between the deer and death.

They are done with glamour now, all of them, the buck past his magnificent madness and preparing to shuck his antlers, the doe finished with her attention to the fawn, the Little Buck heavier and quicker and able to go it alone now, his spots gone, scented, alert, grown old enough to be a fugitive in his own right. With the drama behind them, they are as they always are at center—survivors.

Quickly, the location of the home range is terribly important, more than just a matter of eating crab apples and loblolly pine rather than acorns and cedar. There is the matter of snowfall, and its effect on the mobility of the whitetail. In the middle and southern part of its range—in much of Pennsylvania, in Ohio and Indiana, in southern Michigan, for example—there will be cold, enough to make a hardship, to make a doe and fawn curl in the lee side of a shelter, hiding from the chill. But in the North, the snow settles on the land in blankets and in the cold, it stays, does not melt away. Winter winds pile it into great drifts, too high for the deer to see over or plunge through, and the herds will be forced to seek shelter at the expense of food, for they are immobilized by the snow. The long and merciless race to the release of spring begins.

Alpha and Little Buck are at the border of these ranges; December brings enough snow—5 or 10 inches—to be a bother, but usually not enough to be a threat. Farther north, in upper Michigan, in the upper peninsula, and in upstate New York and New England and Minnesota and the Dakotas, it may be two or three times as deep. But not here. Not yet. So there is time for them to finish with the things of fall and to eat a little.

The doe is something more useful than wise; she is practiced. She knows her range and she roams it now, quickly, impatiently. A hundred generations ago, she might have migrated. There was a great herd of whitetails that moved north in Michigan in the summer, slipped south again to Wisconsin to avoid the worst of winter. Elsewhere, similar migrations were recorded; up and down the mountain ranges, around to the south slopes in the fall, down in the valleys in the winter, shepherded to safety by nature. These instincts are still there, but they are tempered with caution, for there is man to be avoided, the roar and clatter of civilization to be balanced off against the food supply, and the deer migrate no more.

But they roam; the doe to cornfields where she has been led to grain in years past by older deer, the year-and-a-half-old bucks often farther, 20 miles or 30 or 40, no protective instinct keeping them in their home range, and this is one of the times that the herds establish themselves in new ranges.

The Little Buck may learn of corn; he is less adventurous now as he matures, less experimental, and if no older deer taught him to eat grain he might scorn it though starving. But he watches and eats and lays on fat quickly. The spots of his fawn coat are gone forever. No mother's milk will warm his stomach again. The vacation of youth is past.

There is no new growth of shrubs in the Michigan winter, only nuts and evergreens, the twigs and branch tips of several species of dogwoods, viburnums, sumac, blackberries, oak, red maple, and depending on the availability of various plants on the range, many more. And acorns, always acorns.

They came to an oak tree one day, and cleaned the acorns from the ground beneath it. The doe saw, somehow, that the squirrels rattling around in the branches above would sometimes shake down an acorn and she waited and picked them up when they fell and the Little Buck watched and imitated her.

They found a corner of a field where the harvesters had been careless and had left a few dozen hills of potatoes, and Alpha had learned from another deer how to dig them. The Little Buck watched her and learned, too. They ate for a little while, then fixed the spot in their minds and wandered on, restless as always, moving on, but remembering now, and they came back another day and returned until the potatoes were all gone. The last few, they dug from beneath the snow.

Most groupings of deer in mid-Michigan and similar ranges at this time of the year are fairly small. There will be a doe and her fawns of the spring, or at most a couple of generations, rarely more than half a dozen deer in a group. Perhaps this is because of the pressure of the times; the groupings may have been larger once.

In the idyllic days of the whitetail, when men had cut over the great forests, there had been food in riotous abundance. Every tree that lost its trunk to the sawmills left behind a top for winter feed; leaves and twigs. And the roots shot up shoots in a frenzy of restoration and the range flourished. There were not many men around, and the wolves and wildcats had been cleared from the forest, taken for their pelts or killed in an unreasoned rage as though the hunters remembered vaguely, in the dim memories of their own vague voice calling from the past, that they had once been forced to hide from the wolves. So now the men had new weapons, and they wanted to exterminate the wolves so they would never be threatened again. Thus the deer were left unmolested, not torn by the wolves or hunted the year around by men, and they enjoyed that tremendous explosion in population that is only partly legend, and has much basis in fact.

The oldtimers—men now in their sixties and seventies—remember seeing long strings of deer, forty or fifty in a group, an old doe at the head with her descendants trailing along, three or four generations with their offspring, almost a caravan, browsing along from hill to swamp. Now they move in smaller groups, three or four or half a dozen, forming larger groups only in the depths of winter.

They outgrew the range and the range outgrew them; both sides of the equation pressed in on them at once. The more deer there were, the harder they pressed on the food supply. As the forest matured again, the higher trees stretched up too far for the deer to reach the greens in the winter and the tall trees shaded the ground and there were fewer shoots and less new growth in the summer.

They starved by the tens of thousands, always the weaker, the more timid, the less experimental first, the strong struggling through to spring, the does giving birth to single fawns and the weakest of those dying quickly. It was a time of terrible selection, and the survivors were tough and edgy, as they are today.

The more adventuresome found new ranges, and some now crowd in toward the cities. Every county in Michigan, including populous Wayne County (Detroit), now has a native herd of whitetails.

People are often surprised to find deer; they expect them in the primitive backlands of the Upper Peninsula, but they are surprised to see them in the suburban areas. In Michigan, the highest highway deer kill is recorded each year on a section of Interstate Highway south of Lansing, the state capital, two-thirds of the way down the lower peninsula. The herds are there, and individual deer wander sometimes into shopping centers in the cities. Their visits are reported in the newspapers and people wonder where these wild things come from. They come up from the stream beds and the woodlots and the fence rows where they have taken up residence, they come in search of food, but mostly they come in terrible confusion, concrete under their feet and glass before their eyes as alien to them as though a man were thrust without warning in the midst of a strange science-fiction civilization on a distant planet. So the suddenly urbanized deer is without perspective or focal point, and will plunge through glass and bleed and die.

Deep hunger has not yet come, though, to Alpha and the Little Buck. They have fattened, their hides are strong and thick and soft, a pliant layer of fat between hide and body, winter hair thickening, insulating.

When the Little Buck was four to six months old, the marrow in his leg bones was red and soft. But now, he has matured and put on fat, and the marrow has become solid and is a rich, creamy white.

The Little Buck is nearly as large as the doe; 70 or 75 pounds to her 110. The small difference between them could be critical when the snow fall is thick. His breast is 18 inches from the ground, hers is 21. In one of nature's more dispassionately grisly equations, this means simply that she has a little more clearance to move through the snow, can manage 21-inch drifts with reasonable ease, while he will become bogged down in anything deeper than 18 inches. It is one of the factors in the survival equation; her chances of seeing spring are a little better than his, if the snow is deep.

Rarely, in mid-Michigan, does the snow accumulation exceed 12 or 15 inches and so this small difference is not often a factor. But farther north, February accumulations of 40 inches are not uncommon and the deer has only limited and hazardous choices.

When the snow is deep, the deer can plunge through the drifts for short distances to reach food. But they must be short trips, and they must be successful, for it is a time when the energy reserves are low. If the wintering place, or "yard," is heavily populated, the deer will maintain paths, and move about with ease. Or often, the alternate thawing-freezing will put a crust on the snow, a crust the deer can walk on, and their release will be immediate and quite effective.

But if the paths fill and the snow is soft, they must wait, without options, hoping only for the rescue of spring. And at such times, the inner voice has no message for them.

So the solstice comes, late in the month, and the stakes go up. In the homes of humans, it is time for holiday, for defiant celebration of the winter we have conquered and no longer fear. For the deer, there has been no such victory, and it is no holiday at all, but a signal of the end of the holiday from hunger.

January

"As the days begin to lengthen, the cold begins to strengthen." It is an old adage from the back country, coined by people who measure the length of the winter still to go by the length of the woodpile still to be burned. It is one of the sayings people use to help talk each other through the winter. Only humans really know that spring will come, that the sun will turn and the seasons will succeed each other, that the earth will be warm again. Yet we find it comforting to finger the calendar and to look ahead to the bright pictures of spring, reassuring to remind each other that the land will bloom again. It is easy to believe, in January, that the world will end in snow and ice.

And the deer know nothing; they do not know, for instance, that the year has been divided into months, and that this is the first month of one of man's new years. They do not know that they will ever be warm again. Nature leaves them in empty ignorance, without reassurance, without hope or promise, and they know only that as the ice thickens in the swamp and the snow comforts the earth, they must find food and cover, must grasp another moment of life from the hostile range, just one more moment, led on by the bleak voice that is carried to them now on the chill wind that drifts the snow . . .

. . . The voice comes now from the ice bank, and it speaks a single word: Survive . . .

It is a simple message, but the oldest of all, and it comes with force of authority gained in a million years of successful survival. It focuses all the animal's instincts on the simple matter of life and death, of browse or starvation, of cover or chill. Today is to be endured; there is no tomorrow. And the will to live burns ever warmer and brighter in the cold dark days of January.

Some things nature does for the deer without mention; she gears the glands to slow the body's rhythms so that in the days of famine, energy needs will be reduced and the chances for survival will improve.

One of the keys to winter survival is the heat equation. Warm-blooded animals, like man and the whitetail deer, must maintain a minimum body temperature to sustain life. Human beings can tolerate only a fairly narrow range of temperature variation; as air temperatures in summer approach or exceed our body temperatures, we drip sweat or seek an artificial environment of water or air conditioning. In winter's cold, we retreat quickly to heated buildings or pile on layers of clothing. Or we exercise; stamp our feet or flail our arms.

The laws are the same for the deer. They have fewer options; there are no heated buildings in winter, only a fresh breeze in summer. But their heat tolerance is very, very specialized.

In summer, the deer is in balance with the natural temperatures throughout its range. Day-night variations are dealt with quite easily by the insulation of the coat, by curling to sleep at night, by exercise to warm the muscles in the morning.

Winter is less generous. A break-even point for the deer is a temperature of about 40 degrees Fahrenheit. If it is colder, the deer begins to suffer and, in almost all cases, to lose weight as it burns up fat reserves to generate heat.

And will the fat have fuel enough to last until spring? Men can ask, and nature knows, but the deer simply endures.

The most obvious preparation for winter is the growth of the insulating coat. It protects so well that on cold mornings frost will lie unmelted on the animal's back, and it can sleep on the snow without melting the surface beneath its body. It is heavy where the summer coat was light, tight against the air as the summer coat was open to it.

But there is another adjustment at least as important as the coat, a reserve system that provides the animal with an internal refuge against the worst. As the days begin to lengthen in January, the endocrinal system marks the change, preparing the glands. The thyroid begins to shrink rapidly, slowing the metabolic rate, slowing too the growth of the fetus in the pregnant doe. In late January and in February, the thyroid will be about 40 per cent less active than in the summer, when the body's work load is high, when there are fawns to nurse and antlers to grow and mates to be sought. Now there are no such demands, there is only the waiting, and the animal slows inside, nature giving it a slower pace, a waiting pace, to conserve energy.

There is a catch in this, one of nature's harsh little "Catch 22s," and it has to do with the suddenness of the onset of violent weather. The drop from normal metabolism to fasting metabolism takes several days, and it is triggered by temperature changes. The glands are ready to make the change, and they will make it in response to severe weather by dropping the rate of activity in the deer's body. But if the cold comes too quickly, before the animal is ready, if it comes in a sudden plummeting of temperatures that stay low, the deer may succumb to weather that it could endure once it had become adjusted. Ideally, there should be a steady drop in temperature over a period of several days, and the deer's reaction will be something bordering on a hibernation activity; it will simply turn in on itself, and wait. It is the sudden fall of temperature in a matter of a few hours that can shock the animal to death.

This metabolic adjustment is a specialty of the whitetail; the Red deer of Europe or the Elk of North America do not seem to have the ability to slow their body functions in winter. Nor do domestic animals of North America; cattle and sheep must be sheltered and fed. I suspect that the American Bison have the same ability, though I know of no research to demonstrate it.

And of course the adjustment is not perfect for the deer; it is no final solution to the threats of the cold. The whitetail does not curl in a hibernating sleep, impervious to the weather. After no more than a short time—perhaps a few days—of idleness, it must move about and take on moisture either by drinking water or eating snow. And it must eat. The need for nourishment is lessened, not suspended. So nature's solution is a compromise, not a conquest, and the increased stress of winter will eliminate the old and the weak from the deer herd. Perhaps in another few million years of evolution, the system will be better. But for the moment, it is a help, not a salvation.

Some of those that die will starve. Their teeth do not renew themselves, and they are not good forever. Molars and incisors begin to erode as soon as they mature in the animal's third year. They wear away with use, from the constant grinding of twigs and branches and other forage, and by the time the deer is six or eight years old, its ability to obtain and chew browse is significantly reduced. Past that age, the struggle to eat becomes always harder.

Few bucks in hunting states lose their teeth and die in the swamp. A majority are killed when they are a year and a half old, in that first fall that they have antlers, when they are still inexperienced in eluding the hunters and are in the grip of the passion of their first rut.

But for does not taken in the hunt, the end is inevitable. In the days of the wolf and the bobcat, all the deer that survive to maturity grow slow eventually and fall to the predator, which prunes the herd, taking those that are easiest, less able to resist. Where wolves still control the size of the herd, as in parts of Canada, they take older animals than do hunters. Their selection is based on the ease of capture, after all, not on the size of the trophy.

But those predators are gone now, and though a few wild dogs prey on herds of deer in the United States, the loss to them and to other predators is minor. And if men do not wish to accept their role as predator, and refuse to kill the doe, she will run out her string in nature, she will grow old and hungry and she will die, probably in the winter.

A few of the older deer will feel the effects of perennial illness for the first time. Nearly all deer have liver flukes or lungworms or bot flies or some other infestation, or all of them. But when the animals are strong and vigorous, they do not notice the parasites. It is when they weaken in old age that the added burden will become too much, and they may die of disease, as an old person dies of a disease he fought off easily a few years earlier.

And some deer will simply starve. The snow and the cold will be too much for them; their food supply will be inadequate, they will become weak and unable to find food, or they will eat the available food in their yarding place and not understand how to seek out more. The effort will simply be too much for them, and one day they will lie down and their life will leave them and nature will take back her protein and recycle it.

Not this month, though, not in January. Their instincts and their learned responses will carry them through, will send them to shelter, slow their heartbeats, nudge them to find the spots where they are protected, where they are safe for a little while yet from the final price we all pay for our time of quick life.

The antlers go. There is a deterioration of the bone that holds them fast to the skull, and probably a stirring of new growth of next year's antlers which pushes the old beams off their pedicles. The two beams may fall at the same time, or a few days apart; now and then, in late January, a buck is spotted with a single antler. If so, he will lose it shortly. Their heads will smell faintly of decay when the antlers break loose and fall, and the base of the fallen antler will have this same smell. But that is a smell offensive only to man, and the small animals of the range will seek the antlers out and chew them for their protein and calcium. It is rare to find discarded antlers in the wild.

The shedding process makes the lately aggressive buck a little shy; his head is tender for several days, and he seeks solitude while his hangover passes. Then he resumes his life among the others.

He becomes more submissive to the does in the herd, following, as though he were returning to a habit of his youth.

Days are short now. At the depth of the winter solstice, the sun rose in central Michigan more than two hours later and set two and a half hours earlier than on the longest day in summer. The result is a day with four and a half hours less sunshine.

It is cold. Average temperatures have fallen by about 50 degrees from their summer levels, and average only about 17 degrees Fahrenheit, some 23 degrees below the point where the deer begins to lose weight.

Farther north, the days are even shorter and the cold more intense.

Nothing grows. The cedars bow under the snow. Nature is in suspension.

In central Michigan, 10 or 15 inches of snow and sleet will fall this month. Some thaws, so there will be no accumulation sufficient to immobilize the whitetail; they move about freely.

Farther north, the story will become grim sooner than here; it is common in Michigan's upper peninsula, as it is in upper Maine and New York and Minnesota, for 30 or 40 inches of snow to fall in January and for all of it to remain, unmelted on the ground.

Here, though, Alpha and the Little Buck are inconvenienced but are not threatened.

But if she is only inconvenienced, she is alert to the problem, her instincts control, and she seeks out the protected yarding place where she found shelter last winter. The Little Buck follows her there and it is imprinted on him; it becomes his place, too, fixed forever in his habits, and he will return there each year as long as he lives, as will the doe. They might eat away the available food supply. There might be a better wintering spot just over the hill, a mile or less away, but they will not find it. They are simple creatures, and have these wonderfully strong old instincts that they have learned through the ages to trust. When they have survived a winter or two in a good place, in a good yard, they do not try to "trade up." They repeat, and if there are too many of them, their instinct for place may kill them. The good white cedar will be gone, and they still stay, stuffing their stomachs with useless fodder, and they will die of an overdose of balsam fir and habit. But they will die at home, home in their range; simply, habitually, instinctively, hopelessly home.

Their need for shelter, for protection from hostile temperatures, dominates them now. Their bodies can survive days of fasting; their rhythm is lower and their needs are less and there are reserves of fat to be consumed. But the cold must be escaped, so they drift to the least windy places of the swamp, where a high cover shields them from the wind and the insulating snow lies thick on the cedar. It may be 10 or even 20 degrees warmer there where they rest than in the open fields.

These snug yards are rarely placed where food is abundant, so they move back and forth, from feeding place to bower, moving more when it is coldest, not just to keep warm with exercise but to balance their lives between shelter and feeding range. If it does not snow much for a few days, their trails will be well worn so that even in snow build-ups of several feet they will have a good path. Such paths serve them well as they pass between cedar browse or unharvested corn and shelter. But if the snows accumulate, the paths become trenches, and deer, like men, sometimes die horribly in trenches.

The whitetail is not, after all, an animal of the north, and its adaptation to the snow is as marginal as it is marvelous. Such things as automatically lowering metabolisms and sheltering instincts are beautiful and delicate and are in fact parts of an exceedingly complex protective mechanism that we only partly understand. But they are compromises; this is a four-legged animal and it must walk on hooves.

If you look closely sometime at the hoof of a whitetail, you will find that it is a lovely thing, dark brown or even black, hard and shiny and delicate as the finest carving of jade. But it is small, hardly larger than a crutch tip. And, like the crutch tip, it thrusts all the animal's weight on a small surface; the result is that on any but the most solid surface, the deer will sink in, will make a print, a print that is deeper in softer things. Like snow.

Look then, at the fleshy pad of the foot of a dog, or a cat, and think how that pad will spread and buoy up the animal, carry the predator over the top of soft snow where the deer will sink to its breast.

Then you will know why the wolves and the mountain lions found it easy to corner the deer in the paths in the snow, to make the deep-cut paths into trenches, to trap the deer and kill it quickly and thus survive the winter. You will know, too, why wild dogs, killing perhaps as much for sport as for food, can wreak such serious destruction in a deer herd in winter.

Still, there are positive values to the hooves, even in winter. The deer can use them to break through ice when ponds are frozen and there is no snow. They can smash through to the water they need to survive. Or they can dig through the frozen ground to find roots, like the potatoes Alpha and the Little Buck found. And they can kick apart the frozen crusted snow to find acorns or crab apples not eaten earlier.

Finally, of course, the sharp little hooves are excellent weapons, and the deer do not hesitate to use them.

But the hoof is part of what makes the whitetail an animal of range and swamp and forest openings and upland clearings. Their rangeland is frozen now under a blanket of snow, their twigs and roots are dead and dry and without nourishment. It is quiet now in the swamp, and they are calm, but it is still, in January, the calm quiet of peace. The stillness of death is close, though.

Toward the end of the month, the last of the apples are gone. The deer have either eaten the acorns or lost them under the snow. They are skilled at choosing the best foods, and they take them in an order of preference that begins with the most nourishing.

White cedar is the favorite, and the best, but even it will not carry the deer through the winter without a weight loss. The deer will eat only about two-thirds enough cedar to maintain weight.

The larger deer have their advantage here, as they have in the deep snow. They can reach higher, and in an area where the foraging pressure is heavy and the food supplies grow short, they can rear up on their hind legs to pull down trees from as high as 6 feet.

Once in a while, a deer will use its feet to bend down a branch low enough so that it can reach to tear away some food. This simple action is probably as close as the whitetail ever comes to using a tool.

In an over-browsed area, it is as though they are slowly drowning; the height of the food recedes above them, and if they can no longer reach high enough to get at it, it is of no good to them.

As cedar becomes less available, they eat less desirable foods, like aspen and jack pine. Twigs and leaves of maples are taken. Sumac is sought out. They eat ash and basswood, yellow and black birch, but white birch is a low choice, eaten only in desperation. Grass is of little value in winter.

The choice is complicated by availability. A snow drift may cut them off from one feeding place, and they will seek out other browse.

Swamps, with their variety of food and shelter, are favorite places in winter. Mature hardwood forests, where there is little low growth and protection from the elements, are more hostile to deer now than at any other time.

If the deer are less adapted to snow than their predators, they are better equipped for winter feeding than some smaller game, and in some places have been able to practically force rabbits, hares, ruffed grouse, wild turkeys, and gray squirrels from an area.

Alpha and the Little Buck lose weight quickly in January, as do the other deer on the range. By the end of the month, they are 10 or 15 per cent lighter than at the beginning of it. Most of the loss is in fat, and none of it would be apparent to an observer. They are sleek-looking, partly because their winter coat is at its fullest. The thick coat gives them a rounded appearance separate from the condition of their flesh.

They are lean, though, despite appearances, and tuned to the struggle of survival. They are bright of eye and quick of foot, alert and eager, quick. Their paths are open, and they feed easily. They are in control, in command.

. . . And that cold old neutral voice gives them no warning of February . . .

February

It came gently at first, the snow, sifting down to settle on earth and evergreen. It came gently, it came in beauty, and it came in peace. The deer blinked at it, trampled it, did not really notice. It was nothing to them; not food, not cover, not survival, not threat. So in the simpleness of their attention to survival, they did not absorb it into their warm and tiny little circle of awareness.

But the February snows of Michigan are the pollen of cold. In the fall, the snowflakes touched the ground and vanished, the warm earth taking them into her yeasty bosom and storing them as life-giving water. Now Mother Earth has fallen asleep, has gone rigid with cold, and she is indifferent to the things above her. The plants are dead and brittle, the pools of water are covered with ice; what life there is to be on her surface for the rest of winter is life left over from summer. Even the clouds wheel and tumble as though in a vacuum;

they lurch across the sky above an impassive earth that pays them no heed in the dead of winter. Where she was fruitful and generous a few weeks ago, earth is frigid and barren now, and the warm-blooded creatures on her surface must live for a little while on stored provender or on lean leavings.

The deer store nothing, save for the reserves of fat inside their bodies. There are no caches of nuts or hoards of corn. They are like astronauts on the surface of a hostile moon. Spacemen have their fine insulating suits, the deer those fine insulating winter coats. But the moonmen have smuggled food from earth, and the deer, less skilled, are at the mercy of the frozen landscape.

And soon the snow was gentle no longer. It came in a howling fury, dumped from those rejected clouds, spilled to earth like unwanted waste from the heavens. The cold air of the north clashed with the warm air of the south, and the tension of the meeting sent gales across the north to whip the snow into great dune-sized drifts that coiled around the forest edges and camouflaged the swamps.

The cold kept the flakes intact. In warmer days, they were soft and delicate. Now they were little missiles of ice, and the reeling winds fired them with stinging force against every living creature that moved on the winter-crusted earth.

So the deer Alpha and the Little Buck do not move, not out in the open where the storm rages. They wait, quiet in the swamp, in stillness there while their body rhythm slows, huddled beneath the cedar boughs, curled nose to belly, ears tight against their heads, dozing. The winds do not bother them in the lee of the swamp. Even the snow is a comfort there; branches and boughs catch it, accumulate it, let it pile into roofs, and the deer lie beneath those roofs so that any body heat that might escape them is reflected back.

Yet theirs is the safety of the refugee, who waits in an unnoticed cellar while the battle rages above. Both must come out, the deer and the human refugee, when the holocaust moves by them, for both must eat.

The storm is a fierce one. It continues with only slight

breaks for two nights and a day. Now and then the wind lulls, and the deer lift their heads. But they are not deceived, and each time they tuck themselves in again, and do not move until the wildness of the winds is finally spent.

While they rest, safe in the protective covering where the wind-chill influence is as much as two hundred times less than in the open, the balance of their environment shifts harshly against them. They will emerge from the swamp when the snows stop to find their frigid world entombed, and the rules changed, their life made harder.

The relentless series of pruning pressures has begun. And each of the pressures feeds on the one before it.

First, there is the cold. As soon as the temperature drops below 40 degrees, the deer loses weight as stored reserves of fat are burned to generate heat.

Then there is the dwindling food supply. The last acorns are gone, and the only natural food left is the evergreen. So, slowly, the deer must begin to eat its way through a natural cupboard that will not be replenished until spring.

Now there is the snow, which will make it difficult to reach food supplies. At the very least, the struggle through the drifts will be harder, even where it is still possible.

The more cold, the more snow, the more feed is needed if the deer is to maintain its energy and survive. And the more cold and the more snow, the less food is available.

. . . And the voice gives no encouragement, whispers no promises. It is nothing more now than a faint warm breath to keep aglow the burning desire to survive for another moment . . .

The glands have made their adjustment, have turned down the metabolic burner, conserved the energy. Those plans that were begun unnoticed in August, begun by nature without consulting or informing the deer, come to maturity now. The deer reach what biologists call their "fasting metabolism," and during the time they are in this cold-induced doze, they expend little more than half the energy they would in normal times.

Note should be made again of how unusual this is. The normal action of the thyroid in warm-blooded animals is to speed up as temperatures fall, so that the body will have a higher metabolic rate and keep warm. That is the normal action in domestic animals, in laboratory animals, and in you and me.

Those millions of years have not been in vain, and the whitetail adjusts in its very special way.

Last February, having burrowed my way through the books and the journals so that I knew all these things, I decided to make a spot check and so I walked back across the fields of my own farm to see if the deer were behaving as the books predicted. What I found was a scene of very special beauty.

In a low place near a willow swamp, a neighbor had been unable to harvest a corner of a corn field because of the fall wetness and the deer had found the ripe corn. (There it is again, that mysterious telegraph of theirs. How had the first deer found it, and how had the message been communicated to the others?) The tracks gave evidence that a dozen, perhaps as many as one hundred deer were feeding on the corn. It seemed that there were three different groups. One came from a swampy creekbed only 200 or 300 yards to the west. A second group came from its yarding place a little farther away to the north. And a third group made a longer trip, more than a quarter-mile across the open fields from another swamp.

I visited them, uninvited, invaded their range on a day after a snowfall of several inches, in the middle of a bright cold day when all their tracks were fresh on new snow that had fallen the day before.

The back of the farm looked like a school playground, the paths wide and beaten, as though the deer were playing a great game of fox-and-geese between corn and cover. I made an inventory of the corn, and found that by mid-February, the deer had taken between 10 and 20 per cent of it. They eat very carefully, conservatively, beginning at the outer end of the ear and eating down toward the stalk, only rarely dropping a single kernel in the snow.

Curious and impolite, I pressed my intrusion, tracking them along those wide and insolent paths to their swamp and found the places where they spent the night. Old trees have fallen there, tipped over in high winds. The mucky foothold of the roots is not strong enough to withstand the force of high winds on tall trees, and the biggest trees simply tip over in the end, eased down through the tangle of smaller ones, and rest at an angle, sometimes greening on a few boughs for several years of death throes. The tipped-up root systems make walls as high as 8 or 10 feet, and as children, we sometimes played around them, using them as forts. Naturally, I assumed the deer would use the imaginary forts of my childhood as winter covers.

They are wiser than I, though, or perhaps it is just that those old voices are clearer to them than my books are to me. At any rate, they do not need that kind of cover, for there is no wind in the deep swamp. They seek spots where the fronds of the evergreens droop low and they sleep beneath them, in places where what body heat escapes is reflected back against them. The snow in the beds where they slept was packed, but not melted, and I was impressed by the insulating quality of their winter coats.

Of course they heard my blundering along and they fled. But I was too few for them, there were too many of them for all to avoid me, and eventually, I was able to stand on a busy run as a group came toward me. I stood still as a stump, there in the icy quiet—the temperature that day was a little below zero at noon—to watch them and test some theories.

A doe led the group; I could tell it was a doe because I could see her head quite clearly through the glasses, and there were no pedicles, no bumps of any kind. She could not see me through the thicket, for when I was very still, the shape of my body merged with a million tangled shapes around me. When she was still, I could barely see her, though my color-sighted eyes were aided by seven-power binoculars.

She knew I was there, though, and she stopped, irritated, perhaps 50 yards away. She turned her ears and moved her head around, probably a trace of scent in her nose despite the absence of wind. Possibly I had made an alien sound. I could not hear myself breathe, but perhaps she could.

If she did not know precisely what had come to disturb her and the family that trailed along behind her, she knew it was *something,* and she stamped at me, first one front foot and then, when I did not flee, the other. She glared, gave me that hard stare. She moved her head up and down, thrusting it out in challenge, peering at me. And slowly, the rich old caution and the compelling young curiosity warring in her, she edged closer, quarter-step by quarter-step, trying to sort out just what I was.

As I watched her through the glasses, she was little more than an arm's length away. The closeness did not help my vision much, though; her color and shape and stillness made her nearly invisible against the background, and I gained a new respect for the relative uselessness of vision in the swamp.

In a little while, the cold crept up my toes and fingers and I had to move for warmth. The deer were gone instantly, the three or four of them wheeling and ducking out of sight.

I followed, hoping they would go to an opening where I could tell for certain just what kind of family group they represented. But they circled, moving just far enough so that I could not see them, and then they waited, always in the cover of the swamp. Again and again, I saw her waiting, watching, wondering, almost not afraid there in her own protective element. But in the end, she was too cautious to let me get a very good look.

Finally, I gave up and left them alone. The next morning, I checked their tracks again and could see that they went out to the corn field again in the night, gleaning strength from it kernel by kernel.

I hope we miss a little corn each fall, either my neighbor or I, for the deer are in fine condition, their droppings firm and frequent as is normal in well-fed deer. Sometimes, I think I hear a voice that tells me that it is only fair to share a little with them.

The storm that had imprisoned Alpha and the Little Buck ends, the weather breaks, the winds die, the clouds churn away, and the cold flat sun of winter throws sculptured shadows over the undulating, newly lunar landscape.

They lift their heads, and hear that the wheeze of wind is gone. There is some change that they know, that tells them the storm is ended, and they shake free from the snow and walk, in the afternoon, out to search for food in the dull dusk.

They need the food badly. The doe Alpha has lost, abruptly, in the fasting time, nearly 5 per cent of her body weight. Winter-slim, she is adjusted, alert, and very hungry. She seems little the worse for the ordeal of the fast through the storm. The Little Buck is more shaken. His glandular adjustment is still incomplete, this is the first time he has reached back for the mechanics of the fasting metabolism, and the effect is imperfect. He has felt the shock more. He fretted under the pressure of the storm, once jumped up when he thought the winds were gone, circled the cedars as though anxious to go out and hunt for food. The doe ignored him. And although he no longer felt under her strict orders, when none of the others seemed inclined to move about, he settled down again to wait.

Now though, they all come out, and with the doe in the lead and the Little Buck close behind, they move, half a dozen of them, out through the soft unbroken snow of the forest to the harder packs of the open drifts.

The skills that the doe remembers from another winter are useful now. They watch her, and learn quickly. They make a new path to a corn field, where a few stalks remain. The new trail lies along the edges of the drifts. Usually, deep paths in the open are quite straight between objectives. Now, though, they take the lines of least resistance, not plunging through the drifts, calculating, somehow, the balance of the need to hurry against the energy savings of taking the easiest way.

They finish the corn in a day or two. The spot is small, and the deer take every kernel off every cob, then paw through the snow until they are sure it is all gone.

The doe stops pawing suddenly, as though the futility of the search has struck her at last. She lifts her head, turns into the breeze. Her eyes seemed to dim a little as she concentrates, all the fire of her determination to live burning in her desire to find something in the breeze; a scent of food, a favorable sound, a memory, or even, even, the voice she sometimes seems to hear . . .

. . . There is no scent, no sound, no voice, only the emptiness of the ages.

She tosses her head, turns, and they drift back toward cover.

About 2 feet of snow has fallen. The drifts are too much for them, but easily avoidable. It is difficult going in some places, but not impossible, and after a trip or two between some cedar they like and their hiding places, a path is made, and then another, and life is little worse than it has been.

The equation is pressing harder. The cold clings, the snow does not go away, everything is a little more effort than it has been before the storm. Even as the paths wear smooth, travel is a little more difficult for the doe Alpha and the Little Buck and the others. And even when they are tucked in their cedar cover, fasting, the weight loss continues—slowly, almost unnoticeably, but inexorably, reserves being steadily claimed by a patient nature.

Their food supply is diminishing. The corn is gone. The acorns are lost. Only the cedar remains.

They begin special little forays in search of food. Four or five days after the storm ends, the doe spots a patch of browse outside the path and climbs toward it, gingerly, testing the snow. The sun has melted the top of the snow, the night chill has frozen it, and there is a crust. The deer are suddenly completely liberated again, for the crust will bear them up as easily as ice on a lake, and they can move with virtually complete freedom again over their entire range.

The crust gains them several days, by opening again some food supplies that had lain behind drifts.

And they can reach higher browse while standing on the crusted snow, reach higher than when standing on the ground, and they find food they had not been able to reach before. It is as though they walk on stilts given by a thoughtful nature.

The doe is reaching for a cedar bow nearly 8 feet above the ground. She can just reach it, standing on more than 2 feet of crusted snow. It is barely within her reach, but she is hungry and extending herself to the utmost. She rears on her hind legs, waving the now nearly useless front hooves in the air, almost dancing, nose up, lips skinned back from her teeth, reaching, stretching, when the crust breaks under her and she plunges through, hindquarters sinking into the snow. She crashes down, her flailing front feet break through too, and she has a moment of panic, as though she is being buried alive in the snow.

Lunging, desperate, she fights through the snow back to the safety of the trail. The crust has softened in warm days and will no longer hold her. Her struggles complicate the journey. But there is no coolness in her to help reason her to calmness; she struggles, plunges, desperately fighting back to the trail, and there she finally stands on the packed snow, winded. She stands for a moment panting, tongue out, gasping for breath, front legs apart, knees bleeding from the scraping on the crust.

It will be some time before she finds the courage to explore a snow crust again.

The blood dries, the small wounds heal quickly. The frenzied expenditure of energy has saved her.

But another source of food vanishes. Her reserves are lessened. The room for survival grows smaller.

Farther north, the snow comes earlier and stays longer and lies deeper. We have studied the survival behavior of deer quite carefully there, in a place where we can watch them in a winter yard.

The place is in the Upper Pensinsula of Michigan, and as is the case in much of the northern range of the whitetail all across the continent, deer crowd into protective yards for a hundred days of the year.

We watched the herd there, all of us, the "outdoorsmen," the biologists, the conservationists, the curious. We watched while they yarded in the same place every year. They tore away all the available browse, ate it up faster than it could grow again, and they starved. They reproduced desperately, and overgrew the range, and they starved.

We had introduced ourselves into the natural equation, had eliminated the wolves and the other natural predators that would have held the herd in balance. Yet we hesitated to take the role of those we had driven off; we hesitated to kill, to prey.

Finally, though, several years ago, we had had enough and we began to cut, each winter, in the Cusino area of the upper peninsula of Michigan, about 5 or 10 acres of evergreen swamp and feed the cutting to the deer. They learned quickly; they hear the power saws now and come to stand just out of reach. When the men leave at the end of the day, they hurry in, a herd of two hundred or more, and they eat the cut cedar.

They are prisoners of the yard, the snow, the winter. They do not know that the cutting is done under guard by other prisoners—inmates of a state penal institution. The deer do not know that inmates of one prison are helping them to escape from theirs.

Evening after evening, from February to late April of 1970, the biologists sat in elevated blinds and watched the deer through binoculars. They learned to identify most of them quite easily. Some of the deer had been trapped and tagged earlier, and could be identified easily by a code number. The bucks were identifiable by antler scars on their pedicles. Fawns were noticeably smaller. So the biologists watched, and made notes.

The herd has become dependent on the cuttings. They surrender their independence at least as readily as you and I surrender forty hours a week for food, clothing, shelter, and companionship. They drift off to cover in the daytime, though rarely farther than half a mile from their handout; perhaps they want to stay within easy earshot of the sound of the power saws that bring the cedar down within their reach.

Sometimes, in the day, the hungry little ones will join the men at work and eat among them. Now and then, a doe will join them. But the bucks stay away until the men have gone.

They keep in tight little groups, the most common of those being that of a doe and her fawn or fawns of the previous spring. The larger group, the herd, is an expression of geography as much as anything else. This is the area, the place of their traditional winter yard, a sense of landholding passed down from doe to fawn to form a behavior pattern that persists through generations. The habit of using this particular yarding place is the tie that binds. There are no blood lines, no generational groupings beyond that simple doe-fawn link. If one family group should drift away from one herd to another, the new fraternity would be as indifferent as the old.

The whitetail seems to be, by disposition, the most solitary of the large, hoofed animals—the cervids. Though most whitetails live in groups, those groups serve no apparent purpose other than to give warning in time of danger. The group has no activity, there is no pairing, no bond. It is as though such grouping expresses nothing more than a chance matching of mutual interests. Thus they sometimes form groups, but they are like the crowds of people outside a movie house waiting to get in, individuals with no lasting relationships beyond those of the moment.

Increased stress seems to concentrate the deer; as their range of choices in the survival struggle decreases, they come together in apparently common pursuit of the few remaining options.

In quiet days, when the range is generous, the doe-fawn

family may persist through several generations. But this family bond is weak, shatters quickly in stress. When the whitetail struggles for survival, it struggles alone, a competitor with any other deer.

The buck, with no family tie at all, probably wanders most, in his restless search for an unchallenged fall mating.

But in the end, each of them, young fawn, old doe, mature buck, each deer dies alone, untended, unmourned, unnoted.

In that special study, some leader-follower relationships were apparent. As the biologists watched, they found that two does attached themselves regularly to a particularly aggressive buck, presumably because their proximity to him gave them a slight advantage in the competition for food. He made no gesture to acknowledge or encourage their company, and made no particular effort to be of assistance to them.

No persistent male-dominance pattern was observed, however, as a young buck might attach himself to an aggressive doe several years older than he. After all, they are without sex now. Their primary characteristic, the one most needed for survival, is aggressiveness in the competitive search for food. Any attachments are practical and temporary, formed for the purpose of improving their immediate condition.

There is no memory of past attachments, no thought of any in the future. There is no family tie that influences behavior. Nor is there any extension of protection; if a doe dominates a food supply, she passes none of the benefits of her domination to her fawns. They take their own place in the order of favorites, and gain no value from her dominance unless they benefit from simply being close.

The deer form a herd, a mob, not a community.

This winter yard is the whitetail's death camp, their Auschwitz or Treblinka, the situation of ultimate stress. Competition for survival is the rule.

In that yard, watched by the specialists, the deer fought each other for the food. They began with the classic whitetail confrontations, as described earlier; the ear drop, hard look, rush, strike, sidle, flail. When we talked about the conflict between bucks, there was no flailing, no striking out with the forefeet. Bucks make their final step the interlocking of antlers and shoving. Flailing is the more common ultimate step in conflict situations between animals without antlers, in the sexless time, as in the yard.

Most of the confrontations followed the standard sequence, and an ear drop or hard look resolved more than one-fourth of all conflicts. But in many cases, in this crowded and threatened situation, the deer struck at each other, sometimes with one front hoof, sometimes flailing with both.

Sometimes, they struck at another deer from the rear or from the blind side, without warning, and there were cuts in the hide or patches of hair missing on some animals, presumably from such attacks. One fawn died of a broken back, probably as a result of a blow from another deer.

The biologists observed 417 contests. The most frequent —ninety-eight of the encounters—were between does. Two-thirds of those encounters reached the stage of striking or rushing at the other animal.

Does challenged fawns eighty-five times, and those challenges reached the strike or rush stage nearly three-fourths of the time.

Bucks challenged does eighty-four times and rushed or struck the does on more than half of those occasions. Bucks challenged fawns fifty-nine times and struck or rushed them more than half the time. Bucks challenged other bucks thirty-nine times and, again, struck or rushed slightly more than half the time.

Fawns challenged other fawns twenty-eight times and struck or rushed on more than three-fourths of those occasions.

Finally, fawns challenged does four times. But of those four times, they struck out three times and reached the final stage of conflict, flailing at the adversary with both front feet, once. It was the act of a desperate little deer, trying to avoid taking his place in the icy final bier of the northern snow.

Relatively few of the encounters reached the final stage of flailing at each other. In only 4 per cent of the cases was that level of fighting recorded, and most of those conflicts were between buck and buck. Only rarely was that stage reached between buck and doe or doe and doe, and never in the case of buck over fawn or doe over fawn.

As the winter drew along and the tensions built, the fear mounted, and the frequency of conflict increased but the intensity fell.

Bucks dominated all fawns and 80 per cent of the does they challenged. The most dominant animals were bucks three years old.

Observers ranked thirty-four deer in a social hierarchy. The three most dominant were bucks; eight of the first ten were bucks. The most submissive were yearlings, with very old deer also ranking low in the hierarchy. The most dominant buck won eighteen conflicts with other deer, and lost none. Among the most dominant ten deer, there were ninety-nine victorious confrontations and only ten times did deer ranking lower on the scale get the best of such a confrontation. Of the eight most dominant deer, the first four were defeated in no contests. The others lost one each.

Among the group was an old buck, perhaps thirteen years old, past his prime, past his aggressiveness, perhaps past even lust in season. His teeth were nearly gone. He was old, and he was patient, and he waited.

In the competition for the cuttings, he waited his turn like a two-year-old, took what he could get, took the leavings.

It was extraordinary that he had lived for so long. Many bucks are killed the first season that they sport antlers. Few survive more than two or three seasons. Few of either sex live in the wild more than six or eight years. But he was an exception; wily, quick, experienced, learned, even nearly wise in his years.

His cheek teeth were worn to the roots, so that the jaws fitted close together and he had the look of a toothless grandfather, his mouth sagging in on itself. Perhaps age had dulled the edges of his behavior, but the human observer would have had difficulty noticing; his coat seemed good, his gait no more than a trace slow.

And if grayness was to be used as an indication of age, it would have misled; he was brown and white, and other deer many years his junior showed more gray than he.

If his antlers had been measured the fall before, there might have been a slight decrease in diameter from that of his best days.

There were observers watching, however, with senses sharper than those of men. Coyotes, patient predators, saw things about the old buck that we would not. They knew. And they waited.

And he knew, and he waited. There was no sense of fear, no sense of foreboding, no panic. The old buck waited with no more notion of his end than a leaf on a tree has of its falling.

Then one afternoon in late winter, as the herd drifted toward the cuttings, the old buck felt especially weary and fell behind the others. The coyotes knew. Their wait was over. They surrounded him. No other deer paused to help, or even noticed.

He lowered his head in the formal challenge. It was ritual, and both deer and coyote knew it. They went through the ceremony and then struck him, slashing, first at the rear, then at the throat, and the snow streamed red. He was probably in shock after the first serious wound was inflicted; nature is quite direct about feeding one species with another, but she is not cruel about it.

It was all over in a matter of a few moments. He had lived far longer than most deer, had survived many seasons, fathered many fawns.

He had been as much a miracle as you or I, that old buck: He had been conceived in a female womb, had grown in a profuse and precise explosion of cells to become a little buck fawn. He had learned the secrets of his ancient nature, had been infused with the instincts handed along the invisible line and spoken by that silent voice. For a few seasons, he had trimmed the edges of the forest, paced and fretted, blustered and courted, fathered young and endured the agony of the bitter hungry winters.

He had given pleasure to dozens of people who saw him in his glory, full in his antlers, and he had given sport to hunters who tried to bring him down and failed.

He had been touched by the glory of being alive. Nature had assembled those millions of cells, manufactured a creature from them, and cast the creature up to prance upon the earth. He had eyes to see, a sense of smell, hearing, fear, irritation, a heart that beat. He had animation, some choice of action, some random motions, and he had done many unpredictable things. He had known that incredible inexplicable spark that is life.

Now nature called in the loan owed to her by all things that live—the loan of life. The coyotes were her impersonal agent; they took what they wanted, and left the odds and ends to rejoin the cycle as fertilizer.

As always, the final question in nature is not "What?" but "When?", and for one creature, the answer had been given.

For the others, the question still hung heavy in the cold air. Most of their fat was gone by the end of the month. First, the fat between hide and flesh had been absorbed. One reserve had gone after another, the fat around the heart perhaps the last to go. Now the deer were down to their last reserve, the fat in the marrow of their bones.

In November, when the deer are at their strongest, the marrow is white and solid, loaded with fat. By the end of February, the animal has absorbed as much as 10 per cent of that fat from the upper leg bones. Some of the marrow has a slightly pinkish tinge; most of it is yellow. This change in color of bone marrow from white to yellow and finally to pink is the most reliable index of starvation.

All the deer are lighter now, weighing 20 to 30 per cent

less than in the fall. They are still strong and quick, though, the instincts intact, their reactions keen. They are hungry at the end of February, but they are not starved.

The reserves are very low, however, and the voice of instinct is very faint.

March

March is the cruelest month, for it hints of rescue while it threatens death.

Rescue smiles in warmth; average temperatures all across the northern range of the whitetail are 5 or 10 degrees higher in March than in February. And rescue beckons in the promise of safe release from the confining snow; only rarely will there be added snow this month, and that still on the ground is settling away.

But even the melting snow bares only death; there is little room for life in the narrow, shrinking space remaining between the need for energy and the nearly vanished food supply.

For all but the most fortunate deer, the food is nearly gone. All the cedar they could easily reach is gone; they have stretched and struggled and pruned it as high as they can and it waves a little in the breeze, just beyond their best reach, tickling their noses, tantalizing them. If they were intelligent enough to know frustration, it might drive them mad.

And finally now, at the bitter end of a bitter winter, their body reserves are nearly exhausted.

Yet the need to sustain life continues, the spark still glows, the drive persists.

Nowhere is there new food. Nothing grows, nothing falls from heaven but cold rain and March sleet.

Even the most fortunate deer, those with a good supply of white cedar, have lost 20 to 30 per cent of their body weight. They can afford to lose no more.

Many of the less fortunate have been forced to eat "stuffing foods." These are the shrubs and twigs and fronds of plants with little nourishment. They may satisfy the pain in the groaning stomachs, but they will not satisfy the needs of a living body. The deer know better, really; they have a precise affinity for those foods which are most nourishing. But even their fine senses will finally break down, and like a man dying of thirst who will knowingly kill himself by drinking salt water, the deer will in the end tear at the balsam and tag elder and spruce, stuff their bellies full, and lie down in false contentment and die.

Some, in fact, are already ghosts. The spark of life has burned too low. It may glow still, but it is the glow of a dying ember that is below the critical mass needed for survival. No breath on earth will ever make it flicker again.

A human observer, even a trained one, might not notice this ghostly quality. Like many wild things, deer appear to be strong and quick right to the end. These doomed ones walk about and feed on whatever comes to their reach. Their eyes are quite bright and their step seems quick enough. One day soon, though, they will collapse and die.

The problem is that the balance of microorganisms in their rumen has reached the point where the digestion of food—any food—is beyond the animal's capability. The deer are beyond help.

The rumen, that yeasty fermentation vat in the deer's belly, digests by bacterial action. Different foods are digested by different bacteria, or combinations of bacteria. When the deer were small, for example, when the Little Buck was a baby, he needed an inoculation of bacteria so that his rumen would begin to develop. He received the inoculation from an older animal and the ability to ruminate slowly developed.

Until the development was complete, the fawn lived on milk. As an adult, with a fully functioning rumen, he makes use of woody foods like twigs and evergreens because the bacteria are able to convert them to energy.

As the animal starves, the amount of high-quality food in the rumen decreases. And as it decreases, the ability of the bacteria to digest food decreases.

There is a day when the border is crossed, and the rumen no longer functions adequately. Even if food is made available then, the deer cannot make use of it. The animal may walk about for days, go through the motions of eating. It may stagger about for weeks, but the lifeline is broken and the deer is doomed.

This process is not widely understood, and is the basis for many false beliefs. One of these is that deer will not eat alfalfa hay, or that it is of no value to them. This error is based on observations of starving deer which were given alfalfa hay. Some would not eat the hay; others did and died anyway. So men assumed that the hay was not good for the deer. The fact is that in such cases, the bacterial activity in the rumen was simply so low by the time the alfalfa was made available that no hay or cedar or anything else would save the deer.

Alfalfa is good deer feed, in reality, as are the other legumes commonly grown for hay, like clover. If the deer have a sufficient supply of such hay, it will help see them through the winter.

But they must have it in time. Even a dry log will not catch if thrown on a fire that has burned too low.

The doe Alpha was very near this point. Her behavior was becoming a little vague, her reactions a little slow. She was dull and passive, almost docile. There were times when she simply stood, head down, and did not listen.

She had forgotten time, and one day near noon she stood on a trail, her fear submerged by the need to find food to live. She had been moving slower and slower, and she stopped as though she could not complete the stride.

The brown hide on her gaunt right shoulder twitched for no apparent reason. It was as though a fly had landed there and she wanted to twitch it away. But it would be weeks before any flies would come to the range; it was an aimless, useless motion, unconsciously triggered.

Then the shoulder began to tremble, the muscles shaking, quivering. The shivering spasm of collapse curled across her breast and back along the belly muscles to her hindquarters. The muscles vibrated aimlessly, and her hind legs began to lose their strength. One leg nearly buckled under her; she almost fell.

For ten or fifteen seconds, she stood that way, swaying first to one side and then to the other. The sagging rear leg straightened, but then the other faltered. The right front leg jerked convulsively and she nearly fell, again.

Her head remained parallel to the ground, nose out, but it settled slowly down toward the trail as her neck weakened.

And somehow then the ember in her fogging brain flared a little, and she threw her head high as if in defiance. She struck the rigid pose that she always held when seeking the source of danger. The trembling stopped.

She focused her senses to find the threat. And she found that she was alone, was not threatened by any predator, that all the danger came from within.

So she threw them off, those signals of death, fired her last determined resolve through her nervous system, charged her muscles to attention, tuned herself again to the task of another moment's survival.

She saw a woody twig that she had missed before. She snapped it off briskly with her teeth, chewed it briefly, mashing it into a coarse wad soaked with the juices in her mouth, and swallowed it. Her rumen began to knead it gently, to digest it. Her system absorbed those signals of life, and she stepped quickly along the trail again.

In the loosely knit herd that included the doe and the Little Buck, the first animal to die of starvation fell early in March. It was a fawn, and it missed reaching its first birthday by three months.

The problem is simple enough to describe. The supply of cedar was limited. The herd of deer ate it away in a predictable pattern; the easiest-to-reach first, then the higher branches, the less convenient ones, reaching, stretching for the pieces farther from the ground. For the fawn, the supply receded beyond reach. The little animal then packed its rumen with useless stuffing food, the microorganisms starved, and the digestive system ceased to function. The marrow in the fawn's bones changed from the hard white of fall to a watery pinkish substance with less than 5 per cent fat content.

Death by starving comes quietly. The fawn became weaker and weaker, and was unable at the end to get up. Its system collapsed all at once like a house of cards. One day it seemed fairly strong, and the next it simply lay down in the snow and died.

The Little Buck sniffed once or twice at the dead fawn. They had eaten from some of the same brushes for months. But there was no real fraternity between them; they were simple and solitary animals that shared the same range and the same time. He was just a fraction bigger, could reach just an inch higher, and survival at this point was just a matter of that tiny distance.

And a matter of time; even a few moments mattered.

The dead fawn went scentless in the cold, as she had been scentless in those first few hours after birth. No life sense came from her. The Little Buck paid no more attention.

. . . And the doe was listening again, and the voice spoke again with a single word, and the word was "Now" . . .

Of course the agony is in survival, rather than in succumbing.

It is not so bad to starve and freeze and die in the cold, once we or the deer become reconciled to it. A numbness creeps through the body, anesthetizes it, and the end is probably not much different from settling into a deep sleep.

Starvation is more painful in its middle stages than in its later ones. The cramping pain goes in the end, and along with it the energy to fight for survival. Even the will to care slips away.

So the struggle is for survival, and some wage it harder than others. The doe had touched death and turned from it.

There is no way to measure the will to life among men, much less among deer. Some give in quite easily and go gently into that good night. Others explore and roam and dig and find bits and ends of food, and extend their lives moment by moment.

After the smallest and the weakest have died, the old go. Their teeth are worn from the years of browsing. They have not been able to chew and grind their food very well, and so their reserves were lower in the fall. Their strength wanes and they succumb to the cold, or to pneumonia, or to parasites that did not bother them when they were in better health.

Or, occasionally, as with the old buck, they fall to predators. In northern ranges, where there are few humans, there are still a few natural predators; not only the coyotes, but mountain lions in the west, bobcats in the east, even a few wolves yet in the far northern forests. It has been a hard winter for them, too, and they need the deer for their lives.

Over most of the range, however, such natural enemies have been beaten back by man so the old does and any bucks that survive the hunting seasons die of natural causes. They are likely to die in March. And they die unmourned, untended, unnoted.

The deer herd in Michigan, and generally throughout the northern ranges, reaches its lowest population figures at this time of the year. The research biologists have drawn a model of the population changes throughout the cycle of the year. Although we use the figures for Michigan, the proportions are probably quite similar elsewhere.

In Michigan, in a typical recent year, the herd numbered approximately 400,000 in April. In May and June, 400,000 fawns were born, so the herd doubled in size to more than three-quarters of a million deer.

By November, two out of every five fawns—160,000—had died. Some were born too weak to survive. Some succumbed to disease, and perhaps a few ate poison mushrooms. Some were killed by cars or lost their mothers in accidents. In any case, some 240,000 fawns—the strongest and the luckiest, presumably—survived to November.

In that same period, May to November, 80,000 adult deer died. Some were hit by cars, some met with natural accidents or enemies, and undoubtedly many were taken by poachers. No very precise accounting is available for these months.

In the hunting season, some 90,000 were taken legally—perhaps 50,000 antlered deer, 40,000 does.

Many were killed illegally; no one knows for sure how many.

The herd numbers about 400,000 again in March. That means that 70,000 starved or died of old age in the winter, nearly as many as are taken in a normal hunting season.

Major causes of death for the deer, then, are these:

—Legal hunting, some 90,000 in a normal year in a herd of 400,000.

—Infant mortality, nearly twice as many.

—Old age and starvation, nearly as many as by hunting, 70,000.

The winds of March are softer, less biting, than those of February. So too are the sounds of the forest; there is less ice to creak in the bending limbs or crack on a folding cedar bough.

There are only vague stirrings.

Two such are in the womb of the doe Alpha. They are the

embryos impregnated there in November. At the end of the month, they have grown—patiently, slowly, undemandingly —to nearly half the size they will reach by birth. Together, they weigh about 5 pounds. Their skin is beginning to show the white spots, hinting at the dappled coat of the fawn to be. Their noses are already dark, the hooves are beginning to darken. Each fetus is about 9 inches long, the ears are folded over their heads, and there are little dark swirls of hair already on the top of the head where the buck will grow his antlers. The doe has the potential for them, too, but if her glandular balance is normal, they will not develop. The growth of the embryos is still slow, the demands gentle, and they stir only occasionally.

The Little Buck's changes are confined to the growth of two teeth, his second molars. He will grow four more in the summer to come, and then his supply of teeth will be complete.

The pedicles at the top of his head are hardening; preparing for his first antlers. But the changes are slight, almost unnoticeable.

Nothing at all seems to stir the plant life.

The frenzies of fall are long past, the memories slumbering below consciousness, to rise again when needed. The hurried eagerness of the early winter food seeking has faded to a rather listless progression of dull days. The deer take what food they can find, and they take it almost calmly. It is as though they know that there is little more that they can do, as though they realize that rescue must come from other than themselves, other than the false promise of warming sun and melting snow. They have done what they can, and again they wait.

While they struggled, the margins of survival grew steadily narrower. Cold and snow pressed from both sides, lack of food from all directions.

It is always the quality of the winter range that determines the size of the deer herd. There is nearly always plenty to eat in summer; the amount of food available in winter is the deciding factor in range-carrying capacity.

The deer in March are like a duck in fall that is swimming in a pond that freezes in from all shores. Their fate will be determined by whether the ice freezes them and catches them, or whether the process will be reversed.

The young and the old die, those with less determination give in. The others wait, conserving their energy, sluggish, working no harder than necessary, watching, waiting, listening . . .

The deer do not wonder about spring. For them, there is not even a tomorrow, only this moment at hand.

Then one day at the end of the month, the doe stops suddenly, as she had earlier when she had made her decision against death. She freezes mid-stride in her almost dazed stroll. Something, some *thing* is there. She listens, looks, twitches her nostrils to clear them so she can catch the scent.

It is beyond her, on the other side of understanding, outside her grasp. But she stops often from that moment on, searching. Something has happened. Something has changed.

April

The sun . . . that great nuclear furnace. Earth tips toward it again, draws warmth. Real, enduring, sustained warmth that soaks into the dormant plants like a warm rain on an arid desert. Plants turn their buds to it, tasting life with the eagerness that a child knows when he turns his hot tongue to a cold ice cream cone.

Together, the sun and the plants work a miracle. They convert the nuclear energy of the sun into protein. Into food.

. . . The doe Alpha and the Little Buck turn their faces to the sun. Something in it touches them, something more than just the warmth. He listens, waits. He is a yearling, nearly, more independent, older. The instincts that are the voice are stronger in him, and he waits on his own for the whisper, not watching the doe, as she waits too. Both turn to listen . . .

. . . There is a sound, but it is still too faint to grasp, and on the first day of April, they cannot quite make out the message.

So they search, though they are in ignorance of the miracle around them. They see the sun as light and warmth, without inkling that it is a great hydrogen bomb, ultimate source of all the energy on earth. They do not know that they and their environment are being bombarded with rays that would be lethal were it not for the distance and for the filtering of that moist atmosphere of innocent blue sky and white fluffed clouds. Odd appearance for a filter, after all.

But the rays are filtered with precision, and the plants are keen to them, and when the temperature reaches a certain point, the plants begin to convert the light energy into chemical energy. It is a process that has fascinated many of the best minds of science for generations. Cells multiply. Plants green and grow.

Man's name for the miracle is photosynthesis. We have much knowledge about it. Books explain it in great detail. Then we learn something new and must write new books, with new explanations. So it is with miracles.

The deer are more patient in their ignorance; they know only that the days are warmer, that the snow is melting, soaking into the earth even down deep in the sheltered swamp where the sun is filtered again by fallen boughs and broken trunks. They wander about, lured by that elusive voice, urged on, searching for the message, seeking the miracle.

Perhaps the doe thinks she has found it when one morning, as she kicks along the swamp edge, she notices a strange rising in the dead leaves at her feet. It looks rather like a deer track, as though the leaves have been tamped down by a dainty hoof and then popped up when the pressure was lifted. But it is not a track. The leaves of fall had lain frozen through the winter, had not yet rotted much, and still mat the ground. And now they are pushed up from beneath by the first new growth of spring.

They do not amount to much, these first plants; the tender brief growth of the skunk cabbage, a few flowers, thin things, unsubstantial, so fine they do little more than tease the yawning stomach. They are hints, promises, and she presses harder along the trail, encouraged to seek the miracle.

She is thin, and looks thinner. The ends of the hairs on her winter coat are brittle, and have begun to die. The need for their insulating warmth is nearly past. Some break off as she brushes against branches.

They are beginning to molt already, the doe and the Little Buck, the growth of fine red summer hair crowding out the thick round brown insulating hair of winter, pushing it out as the adult teeth of a human being push out the baby teeth.

Because of this combination of thinness and the coarse and dying winter coat, she looks almost haggard. In winter, when the coat was thick, she looked sleek even after her fat was gone. Now, in early spring, she looks in even worse condition than she really is.

If the voice has not yet reached her, in her precarious place high on the pyramid of life, it has reached up as far as the plants, and they understand and respond. On trees and shrubs, buds begin to bulge. Deep in the earth, signals have been received, sap begins to flow, strength rising from deep in the rich forest soil to hurry the summer's green. Carefully, Alpha and the Little Buck pick these new growths when they can reach them, stretching, smoothing their lips over them, plucking them with their teeth, hungry, greedy.

As they range the edge of the forest, they find here and there a bit of seed or grain or fruit that had been covered in the fall by snow and is emerging now from its winter refrigeration. They eat quickly, and, their memories stirred, they paw the rotting snow for more.

A need for new strength is screaming in her womb. In April, the embryo will increase nearly one-third in size. Growing quickly now, having held back its demands on the mother host through the worst of the winter, it is calling on her now for quick energy, and she needs nourishment to respond to the call.

The Little Buck, too, is experiencing something new. His head is suddenly tender. Once, he brushes in irritation, finds that it hurts. He becomes cautious, careful. By the end of the month little nubs will appear at the top of his pedicles, and he will be a "button buck," growing his first antlers. In two months, the growth will be well along, the antlers quite noticeable.

His glands are ordering themselves, too, preparing for the secretions that will swell his testicles in fall for his first rut. But that is months away, and he knows nothing of it. He knows only that his head hurts if he brushes it, and he becomes careful and a little shy.

It will not be so very long before he is no longer a little buck.

Now the forests and fields and swamp come to life quickly, tiny leaves and shoots of grass growing, glowing in the new warmth, and the deer eat quickly if sparsely. Birdsong rises about them again, all the life of the forest that had slept through the winter begins to move again, to chirp and wriggle and clitter.

They do not inquire of the deer about the cold season, these lower things that sleep away the winter. Coldness does not exist for them, any more than America existed for ancient Europeans. They had no awareness of it, and so the summer plants and creatures have no notion that the deer have lived through something quite beyond their existence.

The Little Buck watches his mother, as the sounds come back to their range, watches to see which noises will frighten her. His learning of the previous summer and fall is reinforced, and he learns again to be concerned only with those sounds that alarm her.

It is his first spring, and he finds new things to eat. He finds mushrooms, and buds and leaves he has never tasted, and he samples with the hunger of any adolescent with an eternal gnawing in his belly. He tries some of the things his mother has ignored, finds some bitter, others good, and there is a sense of purpose about him that helps him to select the most nourishing items.

The Little Buck watches his mother carefully, glad for her leadership, alert to her alertness, as though he knows that his apprenticeship is nearly over. The ties between them are thin, she is more tolerant than demanding. He could make a life on his own now, and very soon she will change again and he will be ignored, driven away, first by her attention to new fawns, then by his own expanding interests as an adult buck. But still they are together, not yet as equals; there are still things for him to learn.

Then sometime late in the month, they hear the voice, and they understand.

For the doe, it has happened before, and she is able to orchestrate all the odors flooding in from all around her; the smell of earth and decaying leaves, the changing forest bed, the living swamp, the freshening field. The smells of growing things, of green spring and forest mold, of all the new life that the sun draws up from the earth. It has happened before, she is ready, and when the voice comes, she knows.

One morning she stands near the edge of a clearing, at the place where the shadowed security of the forest shades into the lighted openness of a lonely field. For a moment, she stands on three legs, motion suspended, and she hears . . .

. . . You are now in the cycle of spring. You are safe. The hunger is behind you. You are home. You will survive . . .

Bibliography

This bibliography does not include all material on the white-tail deer examined or used in this study, but only the more important or unusual books and articles as they relate to various categories. This is intended to assist the general reader wishing to pursue a point and the specialist who may take issue with any contention and seek authority.

A few major books, in order of importance

TAYLOR, WALTER P. (ed.), *The Deer of North America.* Harrisburg, Pa.; Stackpole Co., and the Wildlife Management Institute, 1956.

    The most comprehensive single volume on *Odocoileus*, this work includes sections on the whitetail, mule, and blacktail deer.

DASSMAN, WILLIAM, *If Deer Are to Survive.* Harrisburg, Pennsylvania;

Stackpole Co., and the Wildlife Management Institute, 1971.
This work concentrates on deer herd management.

GREGORY, TAPPAN, *Deer at Night in the North Woods.* Springfield, Illinois; Charles C. Thomas, 1930.
An account of photographing deer in Michigan's Upper Peninsula.

CATON, JOHN D., *The Antelope and Deer of America.* Forest and Stream Publishing Co., 1877.
A classic early account.

SETON, ERNEST THOMPSON, *Life Histories of Northern Animals.* New York; Charles Scribner's Sons, 1909.
Another of the early works by a careful observer.

Articles, alphabetically by topic

ANTLERS

FRENCH, C. E., et al., "Nutritional Requirements of White-tailed Deer for Growth and Antler Development," The Pennsylvania State University College of Agriculture, Agricultural Experiment Station, University Park, Pennsylvania, *Bulletin 600P,* July, 1955.

GRAHAM, EVARTS A., M.D., et al., "Biochemical Investigations on Deer Antler Growth, Alterations of Deer Blood Chemistry Resulting from Antlerogenesis," *The Journal of Bone and Joint Surgery,* vol. 44–a, no. 3, pp. 482–88, April, 1962.

KUHLMAN, ROBERT E., et al., "Biochemical Investigations of Deer Antler Growth (Part II: Quantitative Microchemical Changes Associated with Antler Bone Formation)," *The Journal of Bone and Joint Surgery,* vol. 45–a, no. 2, pp. 345–50, March, 1963.

MAGRUDER, N.D., et al., "Nutritional Requirements of White-tailed Deer for Growth and Antler Development II," The Pennsylvania State University College of Agriculture, Agricultural Experiment

Station, University Park, Pennsylvania, *Bulletin 628,* December, 1957.

MOLELLO, J.A., D.V.M., et al., "Histochemistry of the Deer Antler," *The American Journal of Veterinary Research,* vol. 24, no. 100, pp. 573–79, May, 1963.

WISLOCKI, GEORGE B., "A Possible Antler Rudiment on the Narsal Bones of a White-tailed Deer," *Journal of Mammalogy,* February, 1952.

BEHAVIOR

BEHRENS, DONALD F., et al., "Summer Flight Behavior of White-tailed Deer," *Journal of Wildlife Management,* vol. 34, no. 2, pp. 431–38, April, 1970.

DOWNING AND MCGINNES, "Capturing and Marking White-tailed Fawns," *Journal of Wildlife Management,* vol. 33, no. 2, pp. 711–13, July, 1969.

GRAF, WILLIAM, "Territorialism in Deer," *Journal of Mammalogy,* vol. 46, no. 2, pp. 314–27, May, 1965.

HAWKINS, R.E., "A Preliminary Study of the Social Organization of the White-tailed Deer," *Journal of Wildlife Management,* vol. 34, no. 2, pp. 407–19, April, 1970.

————— "Movements of Translocated Deer, as Determined by Telemetry," *Journal of Mammalogy,* vol. 33, no. 1, pp. 196–203, January, 1969.

OZAGA, JOHN J., "Aggressive Behavior of White-tailed Deer at Winter Cuttings," Michigan Department of Natural Resources *Research and Development Report* No. 232, February, 1971.

————— et al., "Winter Feeding Patterns of Penned White-tailed Deer," *Journal of Wildlife Management,* vol. 34, pp. 431–38, April, 1970.

THOMAS, JACK WARD, et al., "Social Behavior in a White-tailed Deer Herd Including Hyogonadal Males," *Journal of Mammalogy,* vol. 46, no. 2, pp. 314–27, May, 1965.

TREFETHEN, JAMES B., "The Terrible Lesson of the Kaibab," *National Wildlife,* June–July, 1967.

RONGSTAD, ORRIN J., et al., "Movements and Habitat Use of White-tailed Deer in Minnesota," *Journal of Wildlife Management,* vol. 33, no. 2, pp. 366–379, April, 1969.

GLANDS

QUAY, W.B., "Microscopic Structure and Variation in the Cutaneous Glands of the Deer," *Journal of Mammalogy,* vol. 40, no. 1, pp. 114–27, February, 1959.

———— "Geographic Variation in the Metatarsal Gland of the White-tailed Deer," *Journal of Wildlife Management,* vol. 52, no. 1, pp. 1–11, February, 1971.

ROBINSON, PAUL F., "Organ-body Weight Relationships in the White-tailed Deer," *Chesapeake Science,* December, 1966.

HUNTING AND POPULATIONS

ANON., *Deer in 1970,* Michigan Department of Natural Resources, Lansing, Michigan.

ARNOLD, DAVID, *Stalking Highway Deer,* Michigan Department of Natural Resources, Lansing, Michigan. (Undated.)

BENNETT, C.L., JR., "A History of Michigan Deer Hunting," *Research and Development Report* No. 85, Michigan Department of Natural Resources, Lansing, Michigan.

BYELICH, JOHN, *Deer Business,* Michigan Department of Natural Resources, January–February, 1970.

CLARKE, C. H. D., "Autumn Thoughts of a Hunter," *The Journal of Wildlife Management,* vol. 22, no. 4, pp. 420–26, October, 1958.

HARGER, ELSWORTH M., "South Fox Island, 1970," *Research and Development Report* No. 249, Michigan Department of Natural Resources, Lansing, Michigan.

HEUSER, KEN, "What's Happening to Our Deer?," *Field and Stream,* October, 1971.

PETOSKY, MERRILL L., *Hunting Deer at Home,* Michigan Department of Natural Resources, Lansing, Michigan. (Undated.)

———— *1,000,000 by 1980,* Michigan Department of Natural Resources, Lansing, Michigan.

RYEL, L.A., "Deer Hunters' Opinion Survey, 1970," *Research and Development Report* No. 255, Michigan Department of Natural Resources, Lansing, Michigan.

VAN ETTERN, ROBERT C., et al., "Controlled Deer Hunting in a Square-mile Enclosure," *Journal of Wildlife Management,* vol. 29, no. 1, pp. 59–78, January, 1965.

MISC.

MCCULLOUGH, DALE R., et al., "Progress in Large Animal Census by Thermal Mapping," reprinted from Jordan, Phillip, ed., *Remote Sensing in Ecology,* University of Georgia Press, Athens, Georgia, 1969.

MOSBY, HENRY, "Deer 'Madstones' or Bezoars," *Journal of Wildlife Management,* vol. 32, no. 3, pp. 434–37, July, 1969.

OZAGA, JOHN J., et al., "Response of White-tailed Deer to Winter Weather," *Journal of Wildlife Management,* vol. 36, no. 3, pp. 892–96, July, 1972.

————"Some Longevity Records for Female White-tailed Deer in Northern Michigan," *Journal of Wildlife Management,* vol. 33, no. 4, pp. 1027–28, October, 1969.

SILVER, HELENETTE, et al., "Effect of Falling Temperatures on Heat Production in Fasting White-tailed Deer," *Journal of Wildlife Management,* vol. 35, no. 1, pp. 37–46, January, 1971.

VERME, LOUIS JR., "An Automatic Tagging Device for Deer," *Journal of Wildlife Management,* vol. 26, no. 4, pp. 380–92, October, 1962.

———— "An Index of Winter Weather Severity for Northern Deer," *Journal of Wildlife Management,* vol. 32, no. 3, pp. 566–73, July, 1968.

The biologists' comments quoted in the September chapter, pages 69–70, are from the proceedings of a symposium, "White-tailed Deer in the Midwest," presented at the thirtieth Midwest Fish and Wildlife Conference, Columbus, Ohio, 1968, reprinted in the United States Department of Agriculture Forest Research Paper NC–39, 1970. The first speaker is Dr. David Jenkins, Michigan Department of Natural Resources; the second, Louis Verme, also of the Michigan DNR; the third, Dr. Dale McCollough, University of Michigan.